Media Relations in Sport
Fifth Edition

Titles in the Sport Management Library

Case Studies in Sport Diplomacy

Case Studies in Sport Marketing, 2nd Edition

Developing Successful Social Media Plans in Sport Organizations

Developing Successful Sport Marketing Plans, 5th Edition

Developing Successful Sport Sponsorship Plans, 5th Edition

Economics of Sport, 2nd Edition

Foundations of Sport Management, 3rd Edition

Fundamentals of Sport Marketing, 4th Edition

Law in Sport: Concepts and Cases, 4th Edition

Media Relations in Sport, 5th Edition

Sponsorship for Sport Managers

Sport Facility Management: Organizing Events and Mitigating Risks, 3rd Edition

Sport Governance in the Global Community

Ticket Operations and Sales Management in Sport

PUBLISHING

For a current list of Sport Management Library titles visit
www.fitpublishing.com

Media Relations in Sport

Fifth Edition

Craig Esherick,
Philip H. Caskey, and
Brad Schultz

FiT Publishing
A Division of the International Center for Performance Excellence
375 Birch Street, WVU-CPASS
PO Box 6116
Morgantown, WV 26506-6116
www.fitpublishing.com

Library of Congress Card Catalog Number: 2019951659

ISBN Print: 9781940067360
ISBN eBook: 9781940067391

Cover Design: Wendy Lazzell
Front cover image: shutterstock.com I By: Cooler8 I ID: 1007080735
Back cover image: shutterstock.com I By: Maxim Tarasyugin I ID: 619218677
Editor: Eileen Harvey

10 9 8 7 6 5 4 3 2 1

PUBLISHING
A Division of the International Center for Performance Excellence
West Virginia University
375 Birch Street, WVU-CPASS
PO Box 6116
Morgantown, WV 26506-6116
800.477.4348 (toll free)
304.293.6888 (phone)
304.293.6658 (fax)
Email: fitcustomerservice@mail.wvu.edu
Website: www.fitpublishing.com

Table of Contents

List of Exhibits and Photos

Foreword

Despite myriad developments that have changed the landscape of media relations in sport, there has been nothing but an increase in the demand for more: more events, more athletes, more media outlets, more analysts, more analysis, more specialty coverage, more technical innovations, graphics, and video, more data, more insider connections, more cross-branding, and more components of an audience demanding more input and interaction.

Today's grandparents grew up listening to baseball games on the radio, watching a featured game (often just one game!) each week in college and professional football, and learning about the personal side of teams and athletes through newspaper columns for stats and scores, reading full-length magazine features, and tuning in for a substantial chunk of the nightly local TV newscast.

Contrast that, just a few decades later, with 24-hour coverage of not only sporting events, but practices, training sessions, press conferences, player drafts, recruiting, and now fantasy and esports—pushing athletes and sporting events into a nonstop maelstrom of celebrity-driven entertainment via both traditional and social media streams.

Since the 1980s, the advent of all-sports national and regional cable television channels; the ability to access national and local newspapers via the internet; the wide-ranging scope and dialogue of sports talk radio and online message boards; and the proliferation of specialty media covering a single sport and/or team have given immeasurable opportunities for the posting of sports-related content.

The variety of social media platforms, and the willingness of athletes and coaches to post to them unfiltered by traditional PR checks and balances, create both opportunities and challenges for organizations and institutions trying to build and enhance a brand.

These options extend the life and scope of news items, as well as "would-be news" and rumors. Where media relations directors once prioritized according to news cycles, print deadlines, and "hits" on the six o'clock news, now public relations staff find themselves responding to items with more immediacy and from a much wider range of sources in order to provide timely updates on topics and stories around the clock. Social media, in-house reporting, and citizen journalists in the blogosphere supply not just more opportunities to share the message, but also a much broader expanse of origination for the patchwork of opinion, fact, and conjecture that make up the diverse coverage of athletics in the 21st century.

A philosophical change in coverage angles has certainly taken place. Where sports were once primarily feel-good, upbeat stories of epic battles and heroes in the making, now, mainstream problems of legal issues, family dramas, and financial affairs are as much a part of the sports report as the tabloids.

Of course, driving and accelerating many of these developments are extensive innovations in technology, enhancing how we collect, produce, and distribute information. Emerging technologies have made it easier to find material, to voice an opinion, to connect with other fans, and to "participate" in sporting events without the need to buy a ticket. Ideas and inquiries that spread through the web quickly become items of interest to the media and public; conversely, the archival abilities of the internet mean no story is ever totally forgotten or lost. The scene is kaleidoscopic, with images emerging with such speed and variety that no one can predict future patterns.

It's easy to chronicle the changes in the sports media industry—yet it's more important to keep in the forefront what hasn't changed.

The goal is still telling the story of teams and individuals as they compete and strive for accomplishment.

Reporting this story—and maintaining the audience's wish and willingness to become involved in its journey and outcome—is the objective at the heart of media relations in all aspects of athletics.

Sports are the ultimate "reality" shows, and their ever-evolving narratives and surprises fascinate us. Finding ways to attract an audience and tell those stories with description, facts, competence, and flair while remaining true to the brand is the ultimate aim of sports media relations today.

Shelly Poe
Assistant Athletic Director for Communications, Auburn University
2006 Inductee CoSIDA (College Sports Information Directors of America)
Hall of Fame
2012 CoSIDA Trailblazer Award

Preface

For the book project, *Media Relations in Sports*, FiT Publishing brought together three authors from different professional backgrounds to work together to produce the third edition of *Media Relations in Sport* in 2010. This newest edition, our third, and the publisher's fifth, brings us together again to offer college students some real concrete ideas about working in the sports communications industry. This book is a product of three authors who consider themselves teachers and scholars, but who also have experiences in the sports industry that bring a unique perspective to this book. We like to think that this book can function at the undergraduate and the graduate level, as well as the working world of sports communications; it is a great resource for the entry-level employee and the mid-level practitioner. Sport communications is one of the common professional components as outlined by the Commission on Sport Management Accreditation (COSMA). This content is a very important part of any sport management curriculum, but this book can also be used effectively in a course offered by universities and colleges with a school of communications.

Brad Schultz is a former sports reporter, where he wore many hats and developed an impressive communications industry skill set; he was an editor, reporter, news director, producer, videographer, and writer. He transitioned to academia where he taught in the School of Journalism at the University of Mississippi (Old Miss). Brad has been a very active writer and presenter in the world of sports media scholarship. Phil Caskey is an adjunct professor in the Sport Management program at West Virginia University and a former sports information director (SID) for the Mountaineers Athletics Department. He worked with many Mountaineer sports, coaches, and athletes during his tenure at WVU. He was a seven-time award-winning writer of feature articles, as judged by the College Sports Information Directors Association (CoSIDA). Craig Esherick is the former head coach for the Georgetown University men's basketball team, where he also played, learned the coaching profession as an assistant coach for John Thompson, Jr., and found time to earn a law degree from the Georgetown University Law Center. Craig is now an associate professor at George Mason University in their sport management program and continues to dabble in the TV industry as a color commentator during college basketball season. This book is written by a former basketball coach, a former sports reporter, and a former sports information director; each of the authors view the sports industry from a different perspective. We think (and so does our publisher) of this as a strength and believe that this book has been put together purposely in a format that is unique to the genre.

There have been many changes in the sports communication business since we first worked together for the edition published in 2010. The biggest change is the development of new technologies and internet-focused media businesses that have helped to spur the rise of social media, both in and outside the sports industry. Chapter 1 outlines the changing communications model, gives students a short history lesson, and helps to set the stage for the rest of the book. Chapter 2 and 3 discuss the continued evolution of print media and broadcast media; this part of the industry has seen titanic changes. Chapter 2 outlines the new skills that reporters must learn to keep up with changing technology and the changing sports desk at newspapers and magazines. Old media gives way to new media and in Chapter 4 the authors review the development of Twitter, Facebook, Instagram, and Pinterest. Caroline Williams, the longtime Director of Communications for USA Basketball offers some helpful tips on how to make social media your friend. Chapter 5 is a review of the job of a sports information specialist with the primary focus being sports information directors who work for intercollegiate athletic programs. This chapter contains some great tips on how to effectively develop a productive relationship with the press. There is also some great advice on working with sports administrators, coaches, and conference officials. Chapters 6 and 7 covers the nuts and bolts, the blocking and tackling of the communications industry; the authors discuss in detail the interviewing and writing skills needed by communications specialists in the sports industry. Chapter 8 is a primer on promotional guides. College athletics departments use these publications to inform the local media, but coaches have a hand in their preparation because they play a big part in their recruitment of high school prospects. Chapter 9 outlines the many events that communications professionals have to manage and offers some suggestions to make those events successful for the team, school, athlete, or coach who must appear at those events. One event covered in Chapter 9 is the press conference—one of the most common media events for professional and college athletic programs. The focuses of Chapters 10 and 11 are two important areas for communications professionals in the sports industry: the publicity campaign and crisis management. Athletes are nominated for awards like Rookie of the Year, All Conference, and Player of the Year in every sport, conference, and league around the world. Who wins the award sometimes depends on which athlete has a competent communications director working on their behalf. Chapter 10 offers some great advice to launch these campaigns. When dealing with high profile athletes, coaches, and athletic programs, the human element is always in play. We humans make mistakes, and sometimes those mistakes can cost athletes their scholarships, cost coaches their jobs, and also cost schools or sports organizations their reputations. Communications professionals can mitigate the damage and sometimes help to rehabilitate the reputations of the school, the athlete, the coach, or the organization. Chapter 11 focuses on strategies to prevent maximum damage in these types of crisis situations. In Chapter 12, the authors discuss the impact of globalization on the sports industry and the opportunities that exist for those who study sports communications. Jason Knapp and Caroline Williams give extensive insight about their respective jobs as NBC Olympics broadcaster and USA Basketball Director of Communications. The book concludes with a discussion of the foundation of media communication in the United States, the First Amendment, along with regulations and ethical standards that guide the professional behavior of those in the sports communications industry.

This edition has end of chapter questions to help develop a deeper understanding of the content as well as recommended exercises after each set of questions. As in previous editions, the Coach's Corner highlights the interaction between the coach and the sport communications professional. Successful media relations professionals should develop productive lines of communication with everyone they work with: coaches, athletic directors, athletes, executives within their sports organizations, and members of the media that cover their teams and organizations. These Coach's Corners help to highlight the importance of those relationships.

The authors' desire is that this book is both illuminating and motivating to the readers.

Acknowledgments

First, I would like to say thanks for the contributions of my two coauthors. This is our third edition working together on *Media Relations in Sports*. Ours has been a very productive partnership. The hard work and expertise of Eileen Harvey, Barbara Dalton, and the FiT Publishing staff is very much appreciated.

At George Mason University, I continue to be motivated by my students and my colleagues in the School of Sport, Recreation and Tourism Management; it is hard to believe I am beginning my twelfth year with Mason. I do some of my best writing in my family room at home and I appreciate the indulgence of my wife, Theo, and my two sons, Nicko and Zack.

— **Craig Esherick**

I'd like to thank my amazing wife, Sarah, for her continued love and support. Many thanks also need to go to my parents, Larry and Joan, my sister, Laura, her husband, Mark, and their four beautiful children, Silas, Lydia, Christianna, and Luke and my youngest sister, Caitlin, and her husband, Joe. I'd also like to thank Sarah's family, especially my in-laws, Darrell and Judy Smith, as well as my brother in-law, Jason, his wife, Nicole, and their daughter, Sadie.

And I have numerous friends, colleagues, and peers both in Sports Information and in education, too many to name, that I thank for their never-ending support.

— **PC**

I would like to thank my coauthors on this edition for picking up the slack I created by my leaving academia. I am also grateful to West Virginia University and FiT Publishing for allowing me to contribute to this project, albeit from somewhat of a distance.

— **Dr. Brad Schultz**

1 | Introduction to Media Relations in Sport

Love him or hate him, Bill Simmons has become the embodiment of what is happening to sports media.

Like many sports fans growing up in the Boston area, Simmons thought he might one day like to become a sportswriter. He wrote for the school paper at Holy Cross, and then after getting a graduate degree from Boston University in journalism he bounced around for a while, eventually covering high school sports for the *Boston Herald* and freelancing for the *Boston Phoenix*. Neither stint worked out and a broke and discouraged Simmons, unable to find a newspaper sportswriting job, became a bartender.

The rest of the story, of course, is much more well-known. Simmons turned to the fledgling internet, where in 1997 his *bostonsportsguy.com* became a hit. By 2001, it averaged 10,000 readers per day—enough to get him noticed at ESPN. At ESPN, he became even more popular, his column grew by half a million unique visitors and more than a million page views each month. Simmons parlayed his success into a podcast, wrote for *ESPN The Magazine*, worked to develop television programs for the network, created the now-defunct *Grantland* website, and eventually anchored NBA Countdown. When he had a falling out with ESPN in 2015, Simmons signed a new deal with HBO, created his own media company, and developed a new website, *The Ringer*. In 2018, he also boasted more than six million followers on Twitter.

Simmons might still be serving drinks in the Boston area if not for the dramatic shift in the sports media landscape that has taken place since the 1990s. Once, newspapers, television, and radio (and to a lesser extent magazines) were the only sports media game in town. If you didn't like what they were peddling as an audience member—too bad. And if you wanted to work in sports media and couldn't break into their ranks, well, that was tough luck too, as Simmons found out in the early going.

But then digital technology happened, the internet arrived, and everything changed. Suddenly, people like Simmons didn't have to go through the media, they could go *around* them. Now, athletes and coaches who had always mistrusted the mainstream media had other options that allowed them to voice their opinions unfiltered. Perhaps most importantly, fans and the audience who had been shut out of the process for decades had a growing voice and myriad options for what they wanted to see.

Technology has been the driving force behind the changes, but certainly economics has played a role as well. Together, they have combined to overhaul the old way of thinking about sports media and usher in a new paradigm.

The Evolution of the Sports Communication Model

Fully understanding how things have changed so drastically requires a closer look at how we define media relations in sport. As the phrase would suggest, there are three key components—media, sport, and how the various parts of the sport communication process relate to one another. That relationship has changed significantly over the years.

The Old Model (1850s–1980s)

There is no precise time to date the emergence of mass media coverage of sports in the US. According to Enriquez (2002), one of the earliest known sports stories was a description of a prize fight that appeared in a Boston newspaper in 1733. Media coverage of sports was fairly sporadic until the middle of the 19th century. Sowell (2008) argues that the birth of national sports coverage began in 1849 when the telegraph was first used to help cover a championship boxing match, and partly for that reason we'll use 1850 as the starting point for the model. By that time, the forces that helped create the mass audiences needed for mediated sports coverage—industrialization, urbanization, and the growth of education—were already under way.

The media during this time were characterized by the traditional mass media that still exist today: first newspapers and magazines, followed in the 1920s by radio and then television in the 1950s. These outlets had exclusive access to the athletes, games, events, and news related to sport. They would distribute this content to large mass audiences through their distinct media. In return, the athletes and events received the important publicity they needed for economic growth and survival. Even as far back as 1950, long-time baseball manager Connie Mack (1950) observed, "How did baseball develop from the sandlots to the huge stadiums? From a few hundred spectators to the millions in attendance today? My answer is: through the gigantic force of publicity. The professional sporting world was created and is being kept alive by the services extended the press."

That publicity made both sports and the media unbelievably rich. As the media helped the sports become more popular, the rights to distribute the content became more valuable, and the fees sports and leagues charged to distribute their product skyrocketed. For example, in 1960 CBS paid $394,000 for the rights to televise the Summer Olympic Games in Rome. NBCUniversal acquired the rights to Olympic Games in 2014, 2016, 2018, and 2020 for $4.4 billion, and extended the deal through 2032 for a staggering $7.75 billion (Futterman, 2014; McCarthy, 2011). The NFL's current broadcast contract, which includes CBS, FOX, NBC, ESPN, DirecTV's "Sunday Ticket," and Westwood Radio, is worth $27 billion (Badenhausen, 2011). Television rights fees for the NFL have increased 10,000% since 1970, which reflects the tremendous audience interest in NFL programming. The 30 seconds of commercial time in the Super Bowl that cost $239,000 in 1967 went for over $5 million in 2018 (Zarett, 2018).

All that money coming in drastically increased the economic power and prestige of sports organizations and athletes. While the effect of free agency cannot be discounted, it has been primarily the infusion of media dollars that have enriched athletes beyond anyone's wildest dreams. In 1969 the average Major League Baseball salary was $24,909. By 1990 the figure had risen to $578,000, and in 2015 it was $4.25 million (Berg, 2015). *Forbes* magazine estimates that in 2018 the 100 top earning athletes from around the world earned $3.8 billion, with nearly a quarter of that coming in endorsements and appearances. Fresh off their $400 million fight, Floyd Mayweather and Connor McGregor were at #1 and #4, respectively, with Ronaldo and Messi in between at #2 and #3. ("The world's Highest-Paid Athletes," 2018).

For its investment, the media had almost total control in shaping the presentation and image of the content providers. While the number of media outlets was still fairly small, the publicity generated by the media was typically positive. Sports reporters could develop relationships with athletes and coaches that often evolved into friendships. As a result, reporters would be reluctant to publish material that would damage the athlete's reputation. There is a story, possibly apocryphal, of reporters covering Babe Ruth during the baseball star's height of popularity in the 1920s. While the team was riding the train between cities, Ruth ran through one of the cars stark naked. Right behind Ruth was a similarly naked woman chasing him with a knife. One reporter who witnessed the scene turned to another and said, "It's a good thing we didn't see that; otherwise we'd have to report on it" (Braine, 1985).

This symbiotic relationship worked well for sports and media, but in many ways limited the enjoyment of the audience. The media completely controlled the content in terms of its amount, scheduling, and distribution. McCombs and Shaw (1972) called this the *agenda-setting* function of the media—their ability to exert a significant influence on public perception through the control, filtering, and shaping of media content. For example, the three New York City baseball clubs banned live radio broadcasts of their games for five years in the 1930s because they were concerned the broadcasts were hurting attendance. More recently, television networks have scheduled event times to maximize potential profit, even if it inconveniences a large portion of the viewing audience. World Series games, even those on weekends, have shifted from daytime to much later at night, in some cases not ending until after midnight in the Eastern time zone. Bear Bryant, the legendary former football coach at Alabama once commented, "You folks (the networks) are paying us a lot of money to put this game on television. If you want us to start at two in the morning, then that's when we'll tee it up" (Patton, 1984).

Technology was also a limiting factor for sports audiences for several reasons. The distribution of sports content has depended on technology, such as radio and television airwaves, and broadcast receivers. During the early stages of development for these technologies, the quality of sports content often suffered. Recalling the early days of sports on radio in the 1920s, pioneer sportscaster Harold Arlin remembers, "Sometimes the transmitter worked and sometimes it didn't. Sometimes the crowd noise would drown us out and sometimes it wouldn't. And quite frankly, we didn't know what the reaction would be; if we'd be talking in a total vacuum or whether somebody would hear us" (Smith, 1987). Television went through similar growing pains. Long-time football director Harry Coyle remembers that "the equipment always kept breaking down. There were always hot smoldering irons laying around for repairs. You could recognize a television guy by the burn marks all over his clothes from those irons" (Halberstam, 1989).

The technology obviously improved, but remember that during this time sports content providers had total control over distribution. The only place to get the content was from the established mass media, which determined all facets of distribution, including how much, when, and where. Even as sports started to become extremely popular on television in the 1950s, there was a limit on how much content could be provided by the three major networks at the time. And into the early 1980s television networks offered no more than one or two games per week, no matter if it was professional football, baseball, basketball, hockey, or college sports. In a broadcast sense, audiences were typically restricted to getting games or information for a few hours on the weekends, which provided great depth, but not much frequency. Fans had the opposite problem with print outlets like newspapers. The information came out daily, but generally not in great depth.

If we consider sports communication at this time as a model, it would look something like what we see in Exhibit 1.1. You can see a solid black line from the mass media to mass sports audiences, which represents the power and control

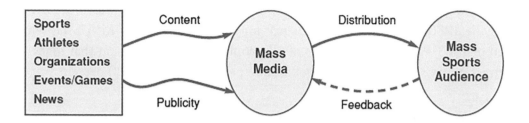

Exhibit 1.1 *Historic Model of Sports-Media-Audience Communication, 1850s–1980s*

these media had in the distribution of sports content. The fainter dashed line from audiences to the media represents a limited amount of feedback and participation. In almost every sense of the word, sports audiences during this time were *passive*. They were participants in the communication process only to the extent that they watched, read, or listened to the content distributed by the mass media. Otherwise, sports audiences had very little input, other than the occasional letter to the editor in the newspaper or an appearance on sports talk radio, and sports radio was very limited. The sports talk format didn't appear until the 1970s and truly didn't catch on until the late 1980s when WFAN in New York became the first all-sports talk radio station in the country (Eisenstock, 2001). Thus, before then, not only could audiences not really talk with the content providers, but they also had a hard time connecting with each other. In many respects, sports audiences were isolated and powerless.

As a result, sports content providers did not look at the audience as comprised of distinct individual units, but rather as a homogenous whole. They were a *mass* audience, defined by sheer size. For print outlets, it meant circulation and for broadcasters it meant ratings, but in both cases the bigger the better. Content providers wanted those big audiences so they could get more advertising dollars. Even today, the economic system is still largely based on this simple principle; it just worked better in the old days because technology limited the amount of sports programming, and content providers had relatively captive audiences.

Mass also meant captive. Audiences tended to congregate around the same type of content simply because they didn't really have anyplace else to go; because of limits in technology there wasn't much in the way of choice in programming. Events like Major League Baseball's *Game of the Week* and the NFL's *Monday Night Football* became extremely popular, in part because they had no real sports competition. When you consider the *most-watched* programs of all-time, the top five are all recent Super Bowls (see Chapter 3). That's no surprise, because more people are watching television today than ever before. But when you look at the *highest-rated* programs in terms of percentage of the audience watching, most of the shows on the list are from the 1980s or earlier. The audience for the last episode of M*A*S*H, which aired in 1983, was more than 77% of all people watching television that night. By contrast, today's top-rated shows get a share percentage around 20 percent.

The New Model (1990s–Present)

Through the 1970s, the sports distribution system remained much as it had since the advent of television—radio and the three major television networks distributed the majority of live sports programming, while delayed coverage of those events was handled by television, radio, newspapers, and magazines. These mass media had a monopoly in terms of agenda setting and gate keeping; they decided all facets of distribution, including the *what*, *when*, and *how*.

The first cracks in this system began showing in the 1970s through the rise of pay cable television. Home Box Office (HBO) began programming in 1972, relying first on a network of microwave relays, then ultimately satellites. It was satellite technology in 1975 that allowed HBO to show its subscribers a live transmission of the heavyweight boxing match from Manila between Muhammad Ali and Joe Frazier; the broadcast networks had to wait for taped copies of the bout before they could show the fight (Kloplovitz, 2015).

Thus, it was the growth of technology that signaled a new era in sports content distribution, especially live satellite transmission. Other important advances included the development of fiber optic cables, which could carry 65,000 times more information than conventional copper wires, and home video recording. In 1977, RCA introduced a VHS version of the video cassette recorder, which soon came to dominate the market (Kloplovitz, 2015). In the following years, breakthroughs in technology would introduce into American homes the personal computer, internet communication, home satellite reception, and digital transmission.

These new technologies had two immediate impacts for sports communication: they weakened the power of the traditional mass media, and they empowered the sports audiences as never before. The "Thrilla in Manila" between Ali and Frazier showed that the networks no longer had exclusive control over sports content, and that control continued to fragment in succeeding years with the growth of new regional and specialized content providers. When ABC still owned exclusive rights to televise almost all college football games, the NCAA limited teams to six appearances over two years. Some of the big-time programs filed a lawsuit, and in 1984 the US Supreme Court ruled that such a plan violated anti-trust laws (Hiestand, 2004). Today, there are literally dozens of national and regional networks that televise college football, increasing the viewing options for the sports audience.

The growth of college football on television is just one example of how the audience has much more choice in consumption. In addition to the television offerings, fans could also listen to the games through several internet and satellite radio services. In some cases, games not available on television could be viewed via live streaming on the internet. And it's not just college football. During a typical week, hundreds of hours of sports-related content are available across a multitude of platforms. Technology has finally allowed production to catch up with demand.

These multiple consumption options caused the sports audience to fragment into smaller niche audiences. Where once there was one mass audience that received the same content from a single provider, technology had created literally hundreds of audiences based on content interest. Under the old model, someone might be labeled a "college football fan," and get one football game a week on national television. That same person might read about the sport in the local paper and subscribe to a general interest magazine like *Sports Illustrated*.

Today, that same fan could more precisely be called a "Big 10 football fan" or "University of Iowa football fan" because there is specialized content devoted to those niche topics. He or she might visit or subscribe to specialized websites or magazines that focus on Big 10 football. This same person might look at the college football television schedule and decide not to watch any of the games, but instead take advantage of games made available over the internet or through the conference's Big 10 Network.

The success of the SEC Network is an example of how sport communication has changed in the new model. Affiliated with ESPN, SECN was created in 2014 as a platform for conference sports of all kinds, with football and basketball considered the main attractions. While the SEC was a bit late getting in the game compared to the established Big 10 Network, it has now surpassed all its other rival networks. In 2015, thanks mainly to the network, the SEC distributed $435 million to conference schools, up from $298 million the previous year. That's $31.2 million per school, more than triple the revenue the schools got the year before (Staples, 2015). Two years later, the total amount was $596.9 million and $40.9 million per school (Kirshner, 2018). Today, almost all conferences have some sort of television network and the University of Texas has its own Longhorn Network, a joint venture with ESPN that will give Texas $300 million over the course of a 20-year contract.

It's important to remember that the demand for sports content did not suddenly appear overnight. People didn't wake up one day and decide they wanted to see two dozen college football games on Saturday instead of one. The demand has always been there; it's just recently that technology has been able to meet that demand through such developments as digital transmission, home satellite reception, and internet streaming. The Big 10, the NFL, the NHL, and other organizations that now have their own sports networks have simply taken advantage of new technologies and economic opportunities that have allowed them to expand their product. In the case of college football and the SEC, the conference signs an agreement that gives the major networks (in this case, ABC) the first choice of what game that network wants to broadcast on a given Saturday. ABC pays the SEC for those rights, which are considered "first-tier" revenues. Up until the 1980s, that was the only money involved, because the major networks were the only distribution channels available.

Today, the SEC can also sell its "second-tier" rights for games ABC doesn't want. These are the games seen on ESPN and its sister networks. Then, the conference has "third-tier" revenue from the games on its own SEC Network. It's a very simple formula in which everyone seems to be a winner—people want to see the games, the technology makes it possible, and the money increases almost exponentially.

Providers also found that customers would pay extra fees for this content when it was not available on broadcast networks. Technology made possible the birth and growth of subscription services, such as MLB's Extra Innings and the NFL's Sunday Ticket. Customers pay an additional fee to receive the games they want to see through cable or satellite channels, which can be extremely lucrative. The NFL Sunday Ticket package has more than 2 million subscribers each paying $300 or more (Schad, 2018). In a similar way, sports leagues are using satellite radio to reach consumers. In addition to dozens of specialized sports channels, Sirius XM satellite radio has a long term deal that could bring almost $1 billion to MLB when the once-renewed contract ends in 2021. The deal calls for Sirius XM to broadcast every MLB game (Smith, 2013).

But audiences are getting more out of the process than just extra programming and content. They are now able to communicate directly with athletes, journalists, and each other. New broadcast technologies such as the internet, Twitter, and other social media such as Facebook have changed the nature of athlete-media interaction, allowing athletes to bypass the traditional media, such as newspapers and television, and take their message directly to fans. In 2018, the website *twittercounter.com* reported that soccer player Cristiano Ronaldo had nearly 75 million followers on Twitter, up from 18 million just five years before. Another soccer player, Kaka, grew his Twitter audience from 15 million to 30 million over the same time period.

Such technology is now interactive and allows athletes to communicate directly with fans, meaning they have the potential to "change the athlete/fan interaction forever" (Gregory, 2009). When basketball star Shaquille O'Neal retired in 2011, he first made the announcement through social media. Since this announcement and his retirement from the NBA, Shaq has built an enormous following on social media. "He had full control of when, where, and how he wanted to make that announcement," said Amy Jo Martin, a social media consultant who works with athletes.

Platforms such as blogs, mobile television, and social media have become the new frontier for content providers looking to find audiences. In 2016, while the NCAA men's basketball championship saw its television ratings fall 37 percent from the previous year, online streaming of the game held steady at 3.4 million (Schwindt, 2016). Live video streaming of the entire tournament has surpassed 14 million hours and continues to increase each year. Certainly, television remains the primary way fans consume sports, but people are increasingly turning to online, mobile, and social media networks.

So when we speak of greater audience empowerment we can understand it partially in terms of better technology and more content offerings. The other part of that empowerment is that audiences have become actual participants in the mediated sport-communication process, and not just in the limited sense of providing feedback to the established media outlets. Not only are audience members much more connected to each other, they are now starting to challenge the mainstream media in terms of creating and distributing their own content.

One part of participation is the interconnectivity fans now enjoy with athletes, journalists, and each other. Social media sites such as Facebook and Twitter have become common tools for fans to comment on their favorite sports stories, athletes, or breaking news. A variety of message board and fan outlets also exist in cyberspace—some run by professional media companies, others by fans who just want a place to talk about their favorite team. A fan of the Ohio State Buckeyes, for example, can belong to any number of interactive message boards, including buckeyeplanet.com, ohiostaterivals.com, buckeyesports.com, buckeyegrove.com, buckeyes247.com, and bucknuts.com, to name but a few. The list does not include the specialized Ohio State message boards attached to media outlets like CBS Sportsline or the *Columbus Dispatch* newspaper.

All of these blogs, message boards, and chat rooms have done more than just given fans a way to talk back; they have created their own distinct social communities of sports fans. Visit any sports message board and observe how certain fans represent themselves (usually with pseudonyms), and the pattern of communication between fans that have developed a relationship. Haag (1996) and Tremblay and Tremblay (2001) noticed this with sports talk radio. Sports talk and these developments on the internet are simply technological extensions of the local sports bar. Instead of gathering at the local watering hole to talk about the game or a favorite player, fans are now gathering around their laptops and cell phones to connect with other fans. That the traditional sports media are no longer required in this process is perhaps the most significant development of the new sports communication model.

These older media are also finding themselves replaced in another way. Historically, newspapers, radio, television, and magazines have been the dominant (and in some cases only) provider of content to sports audiences. But in the new model, technology is making it possible for the content providers, including athletes, organizations, and coaches, to communicate directly with fans.

A younger generation of coaches and athletes seems to have embraced these new methods of communication. NFL running back DeAngelo Williams (2015) has been one of many athletes to embrace social media. "I wanted to be liked, I wanted my opinions to be validated, I wanted to be accepted," he said. "[But] I didn't understand that opening a 24/7 conduit to the fans (and the detractors) meant that I was starting an infinite and immutable conversation—and I certainly had no idea that my popularity would end up being far less important than my ability to connect with people in a meaningful way." Avoiding the mainstream media allows content providers to connect with audiences directly, unfiltered and unedited. Said *Miami Herald* sports columnist Dan LeBatard, "We're fast approaching the day when they (athletes) don't need the media at all. They can just create their own connection to the fan without our help. It's publicity on their own terms" ("Pardon the," 2009). Taking this to an even bigger extreme, former Yankees star Derek Jeter created *The Players Tribune* in 2014 as a way for athletes, coaches, and sports figures to directly express themselves in an online platform with no censoring and minimal editing.

Another growing part of audience participation is content creation. There are now literally hundreds of internet sites created by individuals or groups, and some of them have developed massive followings. The *Bleacher Report* was created in 2007 by four sports fans who had gone to high school together. The site publishes around 1,000 unique sports articles a day written by a variety of contributors, many of them volunteers with no professional training. By 2012, the *Bleacher Report* was making $40 million per year in advertising, leading Time Warner to spend $200 million for its acquisition (Bercovici, 2012). By 2016, the site had an estimated value of $418 million ("How much?" 2016).

The *Bleacher Report* shows how fan-created content can become commercially successful. This is especially true for high school sports. The local high school team might get a few column inches in the newspaper or a few minutes on the local television news, but that has been far exceeded by specialty websites. The leading high school websites, MaxPreps and Rivals, primarily focus on recruiting news and have millions of page views per month. A host of other smaller websites allow fans, parents, and players to contribute video, statistics, and information on almost any sport.

With more sports content now being produced and distributed, audiences that were previously underserved or ignored are getting much more attention, and niche sports audiences have grown tremendously. Under the old model, the mass media typically covered the same sports—a lot of football, basketball, and baseball, with a little bit of boxing, hockey, and horse racing thrown in. These were the sports

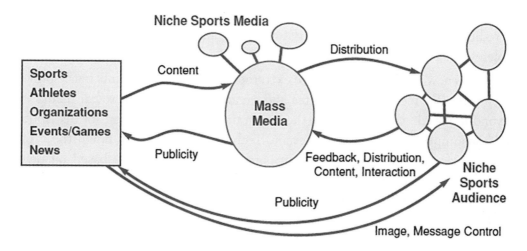

Exhibit 1.2 *Modern Model of Sports-Media-Audience Communication, 1990s–Present*

that appealed to the predominantly white, male, 24–54 year old group of sports fans that consumed most mediated sports. Today, several demographically diverse sports audiences exist.

A prime example is the booming extreme sports market. For years, no one paid much attention to skateboarding and snowboarding, sports that content providers viewed as unprofitable. But ESPN took a chance on televising these events, hoping to tap into their youthful demographic. The result was the X Games, an international gathering of the top extreme sports athletes from around the world, now held during summer and winter, and aired on three ESPN channels in 75 countries. "They came at a moment when a good chunk of young people were getting a little bored with football and baseball, while even more were on skateboards practicing their Ollies in mall parking lots across the country," wrote *Time* magazine (Pickert, 2009). Athletes like Tony Hawk and Shaun White are now household names, and earned millions from clothing, video games, and sporting equipment deals. Several of the extreme events are now contested in the Olympic Games.

Taking all these factors into account—the growth of technology and the corresponding shifts in audience empowerment—it is time to revise that old model of sports communication into a more modern system (Exhibit 1.2). The system still starts with the sports figure, event, or organization itself, although that too has been challenged in recent years. In the case of a typical game or sports story, the media would cover the event and distribute it to audiences across a variety of platforms. Depending on how big the story is, television and newspaper would be involved, as could niche channels and sports outlets. Sports audiences would consume that content then begin the intricate feedback and interactivity process. Fans could comment directly on the event, talk to other fans, athletes, or journalists, and perhaps post their own pictures or video. That kind of discussion can generate incredible publicity for a particular story and make it much more difficult for the athlete or organization to control the message.

In this new model, audiences are extremely *active* as participants in the process. They can offer feedback to athletes and organizations through social media, and beyond feedback, they can create their own unique sports content for distribution and consumption through the internet. Technology has broken down the typical mass audience for sports content into smaller niche audiences, based on demographic factors such as age, income, and interest. Today's traditional content providers, such as newspapers and broadcast television, put much more emphasis on reaching these niche audiences. The audiences are obviously smaller, but since they are more targeted they have strong appeal for advertisers. For example, if you're selling golf clubs you might consider buying advertising in *Sports Illustrated* or a prime-time network show. Those are mass audiences, but the cost is expensive and there would be a lot of waste—that is, a lot of people in the audience would have no interest in the product. Advertising in *Golf Digest* magazine or *golf.com* would reach fewer people, but probably with more success.

The best way to illustrate the change in these communication models is to look at specific examples.

Can You Keep A Secret?

Given the control that athletes and sports organizations had under the old communications model, it was much easier for them to control the flow of information and the coverage of the story. Consider the example of tennis star Billie Jean King's announcement on May 1, 1981, that she was gay. King had long been considered one of the top female tennis players in the world, and her 1973 "Battle of the Sexes" match with Bobby Riggs garnered enormous media attention. However, her private life had never been mentioned in the media and her sexual orientation probably would have remained secret if not for a lawsuit filed by her longtime partner Marilyn Barnett. (Barnett sought half of King's income for the years they were together in the 1970s. A judge later dismissed the suit).

When the lawsuit became public, King decided to hold a press conference and explain her situation. "I felt very violated," she later said. "I felt blackmailed. And yet I wanted to tell the truth. I argued with my publicist and my lawyer for two days so I could do that press conference. They didn't want me to do it, but I was insistent. I did the right thing" (LaRosa, 2009). The media gave huge coverage to the announcement, with major stories appearing in *Newsweek, People, The New York Times, Chicago Tribune, Sports Illustrated,* and a host of other magazines and newspapers. Television and radio also gave extensive coverage to the announcement on the day of the press conference, and in subsequent days. But it's important to remember that the media was reactive, not proactive. Only after King's announcement did the media cover the story, even though some media members may have suspected the truth before then. Audiences were completely in the dark about King's private life until her press conference, and once the announcement filtered through the news cycle, the media moved on to other stories.

The King story is just one example of how sports content moved through the historic communication model. The mass media exercised their agenda setting and gate-keeping functions by deciding how much importance to attach to the story, how much time/space to give to it, how often to let the story continue beyond the original date, and how to distribute the story to audiences. On May 1, 1981, sports audiences most likely heard about the story on radio or television, which were the most immediate media at the time. The story might have rated a minute or so in local and national news programs later that evening, but no channels dedicated solely to sports yet existed. For more in-depth information, sports fans would have to wait until the following day for coverage in the morning newspapers. Fan inter-action and feedback was still limited to writing letters to sports editors or calling sports radio programs.

Flash forward to the fall of 2012 and the case of Notre Dame linebacker Manti Te'o. Of Samoan descent from Hawaii, Te'o surprised the college football world when he chose Notre Dame over a host of other schools. The team was not very good in Te'o's first three seasons, but in his senior year he became a star, leading Notre Dame to an unbeaten record and a berth in the national championship game. In December, Te'o finished second in the Heisman Trophy balloting, a rare accomplishment for a defensive player.

Te'o had an even more compelling personal story. In September 2012, he told the media that both his grandmother and girlfriend had died. Te'o reported that the girl, a student at Stanford University named Lennay Kekua, had died in a car accident after battling leukemia, and that he promised her he would play in her memory. By that time, he had become a symbol of what was right about a sport that had often faced charges of corruption and cheating, and he was portrayed as the shining star of college football on the cover of *Sports Illustrated*.

But shortly after Notre Dame lost in the national championship game in January 2013, the sports website *Deadspin* published a story claiming that Te'o's girlfriend never existed and the entire story about her was a hoax. The story was further complicated by rumors that Te'o himself may have perpetrated the fraud. Ultimately, a friend of Te'o named Ronaiah Tuiasosopo admitted to the hoax, but it was Te'o who saw his reputation and his life unravel. Almost overnight he went from football hero to the punch line of a national joke. "I mean, I can't wait till the day I can turn on the TV again or read the sports page without seeing this story about me," Te'o said. "When I went out and around, I could tell people were looking at me. I could hear them whispering and talking about me. And that's when I really started to know how bad this was" (Zeman, 2013). Instead of portraying him as the shining knight of college football, the national media now took a much different view. The Manti Te'o story was lampooned in national media, in part because public relations specialists did a poor job of staying on top of the story.

The Manti Te'o story is an excellent example of how sports communication takes place in the modern media environment. The story was not broken by the mainstream media, but rather by a relatively new internet sports blog. After receiving an anonymous tip, *Deadspin* reporters Tim Burke and Jack Dickey scoured the internet, focusing on Twitter messages. According to Andy Hutchins (2013) of *SB Nation* (another sports website that relies on fan contributions), "Those aren't things that ESPN or *Sports Illustrated* or NBC Sports' Notre Dame website *couldn't* have done, but they are things the bigger, more respected media outlets *didn't* do, for whatever reason, and that's got to scare a lot of people working at the bigger outlets."

Almost from the moment the story appeared in *Deadspin* it became a media sensation. The mainstream media picked it up, as did bloggers, tweeters, and late-night television comedians. Notre Dame held a press conference to say that Te'o was the victim of a scam, but it only raised more questions than it answered. Those questions were coming fast and furious: Who was behind the hoax? Exactly when did Te'o and Notre Dame know about it? Was Te'o himself involved? As it turns out, Te'o had learned of the scam in December, but steadfastly denied any personal involvement, claiming it was a friend back in Hawaii who was responsible. Te'o did admit to perpetuating the hoax once he learned about it as a means of avoiding embarrassment.

It's not unusual for such questions to be asked in the course of a big story, but it's where the questions were coming from that caused Notre Dame and Te'o to lose control of the story, the message, and ultimately Teo's reputation. Notre Dame might be able to control the information it released, but it could not control the information being exchanged through blogs and social media. Teo's troubles became constant fodder for commentaries on Facebook and especially Twitter.

The lessons from the Manti Te'o story are many and fall into many different categories—the changing nature of personal relationships, the danger of new technologies, the lack of privacy in the new media environment, and so on. In a sports communication sense, perhaps the most important lessons are about who controls the image. Is it fundamentally shaped by the journalists and content providers who cover professional athletes? Or does today's athlete have greater power to define and present his image to the public? In many ways, it's really a discussion about marketing—how content providers market their product (the athlete and the games) so as to draw the largest possible audience, and how athletes market themselves in the minds of the sports consumers. *Forbes* magazine had an interesting take on this perspective.

Marketing Lessons of Manti Te'o

While some experts had him projected as a first-round selection in the 2013 NFL Draft, he fell to the second round, in part because of questions about the scandal. As Te'o continued to rehabilitate his image in the summer of 2013, he might heed the advice offered by *Forbes*:

- *If you lie you will get caught.* In today's digital age it's increasingly hard to get away with lying. You will get caught and the aftermath will be embarrassing.
- *Think through your PR stunts.* The media are a powerful tool for raising awareness and speaking to an enormous audience, but the press giveth and taketh away.
- *Shape the story before it shapes you.* Respond to the story while it's still a low hum, before it becomes a loud roar. Because it will. Also, communicate to the right audience. For example, if a PR crisis begins on Twitter, address it on Twitter.
- *Be real.* Authenticity creates loyalty. Being true to your brand and your audience goes a long way.

From: Pitts, M. (2013).

A Challenging Model

Coverage of the Manti Te'o story is a good illustration of the importance of content in the new sports communication model. In today's technological environment, content is king; the demand for it continues to increase, the ability to store and distribute it constantly improves, and anyone can create it. If ownership of distribution outlets—namely, television and newspapers—was the key to the old model, then content is what drives the new model. That creates several challenges for sports communicators as we head into the second decade of the new millennium. Specifically:

- **How will technology continue to impact sports communication?** Blogging, tweeting, podcasting—the list of new communication technologies continues to grow. It's difficult to predict what the next breakthrough in technology will be, but we can say two things with some degree of certainty: 1) communication technologies will continue to get faster, smaller, and more powerful, and 2) they will continue to empower sports audiences in the communication process. Without a doubt, sports audiences will have greater power in terms of mediated consumption; there will be more to watch, read, and listen to than ever before. But their ability to take part in the communication process should also drastically increase. We already live in a time in which athletes and fans can communicate directly, quickly, and without filter; the balance of power in the original communication model has started to tilt drastically in the direction of the audience and will only continue to do so.

- **What does this mean for the traditional mass media?** Dan LeBatard's statement that athletes "won't need the media anymore" is probably premature, and certainly Manti Te'o needed the media. He took his case for atonement to Katie Couric and specifically her ABC daytime show *Katie*. The interview did wonders for Couric's relatively new show, spiking ratings some 30 percent (Guthrie, 2013), but it did not necessarily have the same positive effect for Te'o. In a similar way, cyclist Lance Armstrong tried to use an interview with Oprah Winfrey in January 2013 to rehabilitate his crumbling image in the wake of charges that he lied about using performance enhancing drugs. Armstrong's case was further complicated by accusations that he may have lied to Winfrey during their interview (Karlinsky, 2013). Even though both Armstrong and Te'o may not have initially succeeded, coming clean to the nation in a televised interview is still very common for disgraced athletes.

But there is a sense that the role of television, newspapers, radio, and magazines are evolving. Their traditional role of communications bridge between athletes and audiences has significantly weakened. Fans can already communicate directly to athletes through websites, Twitter, and other social media, and that relationship is only going to grow. There will always be a role for the traditional media as mass distributor, as long as they control the rights to live events like the Super Bowl. But these traditional media need to rethink their position and how they fit into the evolving sports communication process.

In many cases, the evolution has already started and many traditional media outlets are streamlining and eliminating some outdated areas of their operations. Several local television stations, for example, have made drastic changes to the sports segments that appear in their newscasts. Recent cutbacks have taken place in such large markets as Las Vegas and Baltimore, where time for the sports segment has been drastically reduced or eliminated altogether. "Nobody's tuning in and sitting there in front of the TV

Exhibit 1.3 *Think Before You Tweet Social Media Mistakes and Punishments*

Sports Figure	Social Media Mistake	Resulting Punishment
Greek triple jumper Paraskevi Papachristou	During 2012 Olympics in London, she tweeted, "With so many Africans in Greece, at least the mosquitoes from the West Nile will be having homemade food."	Showing insensitivity to Africans and those suffering from West Nile virus, Papachristou was sent home by the Greek Olympic delegation before the Games even began.
University of Minnesota basketball players Kevin Dorsey, Nate Mason, and Dupree McBrayer	The three players posted an explicit video that involved them in various combinations having sex with multiple females.	The players tried to delete both the tweet and the entire account, but the damage was done. All three were suspended for a game. One commenter on a fan message board asked the obvious question—"HOW CAN ANYONE BE SO STUPID TO POST A VIDEO LIKE THAT TO THEIR TWITTER?????????"
Former Oklahoma receiver Jaz Reynolds	When a gunman opened fire on the University of Texas campus and then took his own life, Reynolds tweeted, "Hey everyone in Austin, TX.......kill yourself #evillaugh."	Oklahoma immediately suspended the star receiver with coach Bob Stoops saying, "Our rivalry with Texas will not come at the expense of dignity and respect." Reynolds sat out an entire season, but returned to play three years for the Sooners.
Ohio State quarterback Cardale Jones	During his freshman season, Jones tweeted, "Why should we have to go to class if we come here to play FOOTBALL; we ain't come to play SCHOOL; classes are POINTLESS."	Embarrassing certainly, but Jones later recanted his statement and became an important contributor to the Ohio State football team. Once listed as a third-team quarterback, Jones became the starter in 2014 and led Ohio State to a national championship.
Disgraced cyclist Lance Armstrong	During the height of Armstrong's doping controversy, he thought he was sending out a direct message to a friend. Instead, he posted his cell phone number for the entire world to see.	Nothing more than a few thousand annoying phone calls and the need to change numbers, but Armstrong's troubles quickly escalated as doping charges proved to be true.
Josh Hader, Donte DiVincenzo, Josh Allen, et. al.	Hader (Milwaukee Brewers), DiVincenzo (Villanova basketball) and Allen (Buffalo Bills) all had breakout seasons in 2018, only to see embarrassing tweets from their past come back to haunt them. In Hader's case, it was homophobic and racist tweets he made in high school, to which he responded, "I was young, immature and stupid."	A painful lesson learned for these three (and countless others out in the Twitterverse): what you say can hurt you, even if it was said many years ago. As media and fans continue to comb through the social media history of athletes, many players are scrambling to purge their accounts. There is apparently no statute of limitations for athletes on social media.

Sources: Chanen & Rayno, 2016; Trotter, 2010; Love, 2015; Lacques, 2018.

for half an hour at 11 just to get the score of the game or a highlight or two," PressBox publisher Stan Charles says. "It's like everybody has been ESPN-ized to death, and there's an awareness of that among the stations" (Zurawik, 2011). Increasingly, efforts are being made to make local sports more interactive and participatory. More and more television stations and newspapers are offering ways for audience members to contribute content, such as with blogs, message boards, and home video.

- **What does this mean for athletes, events, and organizations?** As a positive benefit, the changes taking place give athletes much greater control in shaping their own image. We've already noted how several athletes have their own websites, blogs, and Twitter accounts. These allow the athlete to bypass the mainstream media, which can filter, edit, or reshape the message. "The vast majority of the players I know are more than capable of handling their business," says NFL running back DeAngelo Williams (2015), "and we should have every right to express ourselves in an uncensored way. For many of us, social media represents a chance to set the record straight, to push back against agenda-based narratives pushed by traditional media."

  However, social media has very much become a double-edged sword, and athletes (along with coaches and almost any popular sports figure) have to be much more careful about what they say. There is a long list of athletes who have been fined, suspended, or embarrassed by comments they made on Facebook, Twitter, or Instagram (Exhibit 1.3). Almost all professional organizations—and now most colleges as well—have workshops for athletes on how to manage their social media accounts. Exhibit 1.3 is by no means a comprehensive list, but athletes and coaches have run into some very serious trouble for their (mis)use of social media. In some cases, the offending messages ruined or shortened careers.

Summary

Primarily because of technology, a new model of sports communication has evolved. The old model (Exhibit 1.1) was based on a one-way system in which the traditional mass media (newspaper, radio, television, and magazines) dominated the creation and distribution of sports content. Communication was one-way from medium to audience members, who had a passive, reactive role in the process. But starting in the 1970s, technological developments such as satellite transmission, the internet, and digital communication helped create a new model (Exhibit 1.2). These technological advances have taken power away from traditional media and transferred it to sports audiences. Such audiences now have much more choice in terms of mediated consumption, and they have a greater ability to take part in the communication process. Audiences are now able to create and distribute their own sports content.

This shift has important consequences for all parts of the sports communication equation—the media, the athletes, and audiences. The media must rethink their position relative to audiences and adapt to changing times. Many of the more traditional media have begun using technology to encourage audience interactivity and participation. Athletes can now bypass the media and communicate directly with audiences, but that also has a down side. Audiences can create and distribute their own content, including things that may damage the image of athletes or organizations. It is believed that power will continue to shift away from the mass media and toward the sports audience as the technology continues to develop.

Discussion Questions

1. Does technology seem to be the driving force in modern day sports communication? Why or why not? What other factors play a key role in how sports communication continues to evolve?

2. Critics argue that today's sports reporting is obsessed with scandal and celebrity. Do you agree? What role does that suggest culture plays in the sports communication process? If Babe Ruth were playing today, would he be treated differently in the sports media than he was in the 1920s? If so, in what way?

3. How does economics figure into the sports communication process? Given that media outlets are businesses that need to make profit, how does that influence communication between them and audiences? Between them and athletes?

4. Dan LeBatard commented that eventually athletes might not need the traditional mass media (television, radio, newspapers, and magazines). Would you agree? Why or why not? How might these media evolve in the future?

Suggested Exercises

1. Consider a recent sports story or issue that received a lot of media attention. Detail how this story was/would have been covered under the two models of sports communication.

2. *Sports Illustrated (SI)* is another good example of how today's sports media integrate their content through the web, print, radio, television, and other outlets. Specifically, detail how *SI* is using these various media to distribute content and communicate with audiences. What kind of strategy seems to

be involved? Does it seem like *SI* is trying to reach two (or more) different audiences?

3. *Sports Illustrated* has also created a "vault" of all its content going back to its first issue in 1954. Using the *SI* Vault website (http://www.si.com/vault), analyze how the sports communication process has evolved at *SI* over the years. How is the magazine communicating differently with audiences? Is it possible to determine when this evolution started taking place?

4. In addition to *how* sports audiences are behaving more interactively (creating and distributing content, posting comments to message boards, blogs, etc.), media scholars are also interested in *what* they are saying. Pick a particular blog, message board, or fan website and analyze it for a period of time. What is the content? What are these fans trying to say? What is the tone of the conversation? What does it possibly mean for the sports communication process?

2 | The Print Media

In the 1880s, the German philosopher Friedrich Nietzsche made his famous comment, "God is dead," referring to the loss of absolute morality in the world. As philosophers wrestled with the idea over the decades, it led to a humorous rebuttal from religious adherents long after the philosopher had passed from the scene: "Nietzsche is dead—God."

In the same way today, the argument goes back and forth about the print media, especially newspapers and magazines. Many in the media industry are convinced that "print is dead," and they point to the fact that since 2010 the newspaper business in the US has shrunk by more than half, and in Britain by more than a third (Wolff, 2016). It's an economic argument that sees advertising dollars rapidly shifting to online and digital formats, leaving print editions with fewer readers and declining revenues. Some simply closed shop, as the *Tampa Tribune* did in 2016 after 121 years in the business. Others, like the *Pittsburgh Post-Gazette*, are desperately trying to stay afloat. The same year the *Tribune* folded, the *Post-Gazette* raised newsstand prices to two dollars for a daily paper, despite the fact that circulation had dropped 54% over the past decade (Gallin, 2016). In 2018 the paper announced it was not going to publish a print edition on Tuesdays and Saturdays (PG, 2018).

The problem is that online advertising is not picking up the slack. In the analysis of *USA Today*, "Despite the online world's crowing about advertising growth, and the belief of many publishers that online ad revenue would surely replace offline, the per-view price of a digital ad continues to drop, and ever-more ad dollars are concentrated with Google and Facebook. Now, to boot, there are ad blockers: nobody ever has to see a digital ad. The passing enthusiasm for paywalls as an alternative revenue stream has, other than for a few must-have titles, produced scant revenue as well as falling readership and a collapsing brand awareness for many newspapers" (Wolff, 2016).

These same factors are affecting the print sports media, with the *The Sporting News* as a sobering case in point. The first issue of *TSN* came out on March 17, 1886, at a cost of five cents per issue, or $2.50 for the entire year. Alfred Spink was the founder and publisher, but was having trouble until his brother Charles pitched in. Thanks to the work of the two brothers, *TSN* became so popular that it eventually became known as the "Bible of Baseball."

Although competitors popped up now and then, *TSN* dominated the sports magazine industry until the arrival of *Sports Illustrated* in 1954. Even then, *TSN* remained steady until it too got caught up in the tsunami of changing technology and economics. In 2008, *The Sporting News* debuted what it called the nation's only daily digital sports newspaper, a free edition delivered by a link sent to subscribers via email. More than 75,000 initial subscribers signed up for what was called "the first step in a reinvention of a title continuously published for 120 years; perhaps the ultimate test of how to take part in the transition to online beyond a website" (Kramer, 2008).

However, just two years later, even as subscriptions for the free edition reached 200,000, *TSN* announced a fee of $2.99 for the service. President/Publisher Jeff Price was hired by *TSN* from *Sports Illustrated* where he managed their digital content. He came in with a mandate to make changes. He was quoted as saying that he looks at *The Sporting News* "like a 124-year-old startup" (Hebbard, 2010). Price made quite a change two years later, in December of 2012, when he gave up. After 126 years, *TSN* would no longer offer any printed edition at all and go completely digital in 2013. "Having spoken with many of our longtime subscribers, we recognize this is not a popular decision among our most loyal fans," he wrote. "Unfortunately, neither our subscriber base nor the current advertising market for print would allow us to operate a profitable print business going forward" (Price and Howard, 2012).

The painful lessons of *The Sporting News* are still being played out across the sports media landscape. *Pro Football Weekly* had covered the NFL for nearly half a century when it shut down in 2013. "We built some truly great stuff that you all seemed to love, but try as we might, we couldn't get enough of you to pay what it cost us to deliver it," said editor Hub Arkush (2013). "There comes a time when there is just no more money to lose, and now we are forced to close the doors." At the time of its closing, *PFW* had assets of $143,000 and liabilities of $8.5 million, and its publishers found the transition from print to digital difficult, especially since it came out only once a week. "News and analysis must be delivered in real-time via electronic means, not once per week in a publication that looked and felt more like a newspaper than a magazine," observed NFL writer Mike Florio (2013).

It's a seemingly bleak picture, and a far cry from the time when newspapers and magazines ruled the sports media as the only game in town.

A Look Back—And Ahead

Extensive newspaper coverage of sports began in the late 1800s, due in large part to the newspaper wars taking place in New York. Under the leadership of Joseph

Pulitzer, the *New York World* became one of the first newspapers to create a distinct sports department. To keep up, *The New York Times* began running sports photographs in a special Sunday picture section, and in 1895 the *New York Journal* became the first newspaper in the US to print a section entirely devoted to sports (Wanta, 2006).

Newspaper coverage flourished in the early 20th century and focused mainly on baseball. Reporters played a major role in exposing the Black Sox betting scandal in 1919, and in elevating Babe Ruth to iconic status in the 1920s. Sportswriters of the 1920s created other heroes as well, including Bobby Jones, Red Grange, and Jack Dempsey. In many cases, the sportswriters themselves reached a level of celebrity status; men such as Ring Lardner, Dan Daniel, and Grantland Rice. With radio still in its relative infancy, audiences were almost completely dependent on these writers to learn more about their favorite teams and athletes.

Even as radio and television came onto the scene, print sports reporting did not lose any of its importance. While TV and radio could carry the games live, it was newspapers and magazines that provided the depth, even if fans had to wait several hours to get the information. During the heyday of the Dodgers, Giants, and Yankees in the 1950s, there were nearly a dozen New York papers covering the teams on a daily basis. "Every night at nine we would stand in front of the candy store waiting for the *Daily News* truck to come up," said Brooklyn native and baseball author Donald Honig. "It was like the docking of a luxury liner. Why was this such an important event? Because the details of the Dodger game were in there. We already knew every pitch that was thrown. We listened to the game on the radio. We discussed it for three hours. Now we were going to read about it." (Golenbock, 1984, p. 260).

It was also during the 1950s that sports reporting began to take on a harder edge and leave behind the fawning heroism of previous generations. A combination of cultural and industry forces (primarily competition from television and radio) forced reporters out of their chummy relationships with athletes. One of the leaders of the movement was Dick Young of the *New York Daily News*, who would antagonize players by analyzing, explaining, and describing their weaknesses in great detail. According to sportswriter Michael Shapiro (2000, p. 50), "It's hard to imagine today's (sports audiences) being satisfied with the sort of sportswriting of the era before 1950, before Dick Young made his way from the comfort of the press box down to the clubhouse, shoved his mug in a ballplayer's face and asked, 'What were you doing trying to steal third with two men out?'"

But as the old sports communication model began to give way to the new (see Chapter 1), print reporting began to lose a bit of its luster. A major shift occurred in 1980 when ESPN began broadcasting 24 hours a day, seven days a week. Other cable networks and channels soon followed suit, and sports fans no longer had to wait for the newspaper to get the details they wanted. In part because of more choices and options, the mass sports audience began to fragment into smaller niche audiences. The death of *Sport* magazine, and to a lesser extent the ambitious *National Sports Daily*, were harbingers of bad times ahead for sports publications.

The Death of *Sport* and *The National*

Sport was always thought of as a competitor of *Sports Illustrated*, but it came out only once a month as opposed to *SI*'s weekly publication. Maybe that's why *Sport* seemed to emphasize reflective, in-depth reporting while *SI* stuck more with news. Both magazines focused on quality reporting, vivid color photography, and mass sports appeal, but as the times changed, *Sport* found itself the odd man out. Citing declining advertising revenues, its publisher called it quits in 2000. At the time of its passing, former editor Roger Director said, "*Sport* lurched around searching for the right demographic niche these last years. But there was really only one reader, and he was doing a bit of lurching around, too. He's the one wondering how in so many pages there can be nothing he wants to read" ("Scorecard," 2000).

In 1990, *The National* debuted as the first national sports daily in the country. With a strong stable of writers, headed by editor Frank Deford, the paper had high hopes, but it never got above 250,000 circulation. While Deford blamed the paper's demise on distribution problems, others suggested that "those buying the paper were not regular news-paper readers hungry for more sports statistics, but young men who were rabid fans and spent much of their leisure time watching sports on television" (Jones, 1991).

The disappearance of *Sport* and *The National* continued the transition from the mass appeal sports magazine to the niche publication target-ing specific audiences of sports fans. *Sports Illustrated* is the stron-gest mass appeal sports magazine, but it has also reached out to new audiences.

Print readership was further eroded in the mid-1990s with the rise of the internet, which provided fans with an instantaneous, and almost limitless, store-house of sports information. It also allowed audiences to communicate more directly with sportswriters, and in many cases create and distribute their own

Exhibit 2.1a *Sport Magazine*

Exhibit 2.1b The National Sports Daily

content through such practices as blogging. Blogging and the internet both seemed to grow almost exponentially in the early 2000s. By the end of 2018, the internet had an estimated 3.89 billion users, a figure that has more than tripled since 2005 ("Number of," 2018).

As sports audiences started to turn their attention to the internet, so did advertisers. Print outlets began to find themselves in serious financial difficulty and many—the aforementioned *Tampa Tribune, Rocky Mountain News, Cincinnati Post*—found it easier to quit than fight. Those that decided to stick it out shifted to online resources and advertising, but in many ways that has proven to be fool's gold. "The paywall," says media analyst Michael Wolff (2013), "other than providing a bit more time to wrestle with the underlining problems of newspapers, does not solve any of them."

The paywall refers to a strategy of charging customers to access online content. On the surface it makes sense—if people are willing to pay to buy a newspaper they should be willing to pay to get the same content online. Studies have been mixed as to the effectiveness of a pay wall to increase both circulation and revenue. The pay wall has been experimented with across the industry with mixed results (Senz, 2019). The relatively new sports site, *The Athletic*, uses the paywall model and their editor explained in a letter to current and potential subscribers that this model was their only option in his opinion (Mirtle, 2017). Sports websites connected to larger networks, like ESPN and CNN, can subsidize their writers with other revenue generating options. The ad model for many new or small town newspapers seems to be unsustainable, especially with the competition for online ads with organizations like Google and Facebook (Senz, 2019; Mirtle, 2017).

The problem is that many users expect free online content and simply won't pay for it. That's not an issue if everyone on the internet charges, but there are plenty of sports media sites, including *Sports Illustrated* and ESPN, that offer free access, not to mention all that fan generated-content. Pay sites like the *The Atlantic* may have unique content, but fans have no trouble finding similar content in any number of places. According to *The Economist*, "For most general-interest papers people tend to read the freebies, then leave" ("Up against," 2015). Studies (Anannay and Bighash, 2016) indicate that paywalls generate only one to ten percent of industry revenue. With that in mind, dozens of newspapers have now dropped their paywalls in favor of other models.

One of those new models includes the use of what has been called "big data." When readers access online content, publishers can collect a massive amount of information on them—not only standard identifiers such as age and income, but also shopping habits and lifestyle choices. For example, when you click on some content, a short survey (one or two questions) may pop up, usually related to your spending habits. You can't access the story until you complete the survey.

Media outlets can in turn sell this information to any number of companies looking to target very specific audiences. In 2015, the selling of big data was a $10 billion business for media companies, and a $122 billion business overall. Experts predicted that total revenue for analytical data would rise 50% by 2019 to more than $187 billion (Davis, 2016).

Big data will certainly play a part in the evolving print media environment, but so will paywalls and other approaches, some of which are only now emerging. "Now we're in the digital age, there's no such thing as one model," says Eric Newton, a media professor at Arizona State University. "There are a thousand models, a million models, a trillion models, and one must find the right model for the right place and the right time to reach the people that one is concerned about in the community, through the right means" ("For digital," 2016).

The Dinosaur Still Roams—The Success of Sports Illustrated *in a New Age*

We have already discussed the evolution of the sports magazine. While some have gone out of business (*Sport, Pro Football Weekly*), others have quit publishing in print to focus on digital delivery (*The Sporting News*). Even *Sports Illustrated* is scrambling. Once the unquestioned king of sports publishing, *SI* has seen revenue steadily decrease from $239 million in 2015 to $184 million in 2017 (Kafka, 2018). Circulation has dropped, and with it, the magazine has had to endure a series of difficult staff layoffs. Once the jewel of the Time-Life empire, *SI* was sold to Meredith Corp. and is on the selling block again. "We need to find," said one writer, "someone who grew up reading and loving the magazine, who wants to come in and rescue it" (MacCambridge, 2018).

Terry McDonnell worked at *Sports Illustrated* from 2002–2012, becoming one of the longest serving editors at the magazine. Before he retired to become an author, McDonnell was a Senior Editorial Advisor to Time Inc. He knows the road ahead won't be easy for *SI*, but believes it can come back.

Q: *How does Sports Illustrated succeed in an environment where so many sports publications are struggling?*

McDonnell: We became more aggressive. When I got there the website was run by Turner in Atlanta, which I thought was a mistake. I wanted to bring si.com back to *SI*, and then build and integrate it back into the magazine.

Q: *Is getting on multiple platforms important today for a sports magazine?*

McDonnell: It needs to be done yesterday. All across Time Inc. there was a passive-aggressive civil war between the print and online sides. The print people felt above doing online and wanted to get paid extra for it, while the web people felt they were looked down upon. I forced the integration so we could move to put content on as many platforms as we could. For example, at one time our Swimsuit issue was on seven platforms, including Playstation.

Q: *Why is this so important?*

McDonnell: Revenues are changing so quickly. The dilemma is that advertising print revenue is falling faster than digital advertising revenue is picking up the slack. It's a situation, like they say on Wall Street, that's like "catching falling knives." The mistake is not putting more money in research and development in order to explore other platforms and revenue possibilities. You've either got to find new revenue streams or get full value from the traditional ones.

Q: *How important is it for print writers to understand this?*

McDonnell: Very important. Two writers at *SI* have been models of the digital transition, Tom Verducci and Peter King. Peter was savvy enough to understand what was coming digitally, and he embraced it. His *Monday Morning Quarterback* included notebook material that was too big for the magazine, but just perfect for the website.

Q: *ESPN obviously has a print outlet as well and has integrated on multiple platforms. How does Sports Illustrated compete with that?*

McDonnell: People who have the rights to the games have the most power today. They have the content that people want to see. So in that sense a group like ESPN would be in a better position than a traditional journalism outlet like *Sports Illustrated*.

Relating with Content Providers: Athletes

While economics is understandably an essential part of today's print media conversation, it is a discussion that mainly involves media managers—editors, publishers and the like. Writers and reporters must certainly be aware of the economic picture, but their day-to-day focus is more concerned with creating content, as content providers. Athletes, coaches, and sports organizations play and coach the games, organize the competition, and make the news that sports audiences want to know about. Reporters need access to these people in order to generate content for their readers; the athletes, coaches, and sport organizations need the reporters for promotion and publicity.

When the athlete is playing well and the team is winning, access is easy. Players are always willing to tell reporters how they hit the game-winning home run or scored 30 points in the championship basketball game. The fans are happy because the local team is winning, and the reporters have no trouble filling their pages with feel-good stories and interviews. But just as obviously, access becomes extremely difficult when the athlete is playing poorly, the team is losing, or there is a scandal involved. The fans get angry because they don't want to hear bad news about the local team.

This is especially true of highly involved fans that have an emotional investment in their favorite team or player (Wann, 2006), and there can be a tremendous backlash against reporters who write critically of the local team. The Penn State football scandal came to light in 2011 with a story in the local *Harrisburg Patriot-News*. The paper expected national outlets to pick up the story and turn it into a bombshell. "We were prepared for an onslaught," said *Patriot-News* editor David Newhouse. "Instead, there was silence. In central Pennsylvania, Jerry Sandusky was a secular saint. It sank with barely a ripple. Somehow, [it] was being viewed by the rest of the media as a nonstory. The bombshell had bombed" (Modiano, 2016). The story eventually gained national traction, but people in Pennsylvania and Penn State fans everywhere simply wanted it to go away.

Such criticism can also come directly from the content providers themselves. Under the constant microscope of 24/7 coverage through mainstream media, social media, and even fan reporting, it's not hard for players and coaches to lose their patience. After his North Carolina team beat Syracuse in the 2016 NCAA Final Four, Coach Roy Williams lashed out at the media for what he perceived as critical reporting. "I see our guys in the locker room every single day," he scolded. "You know how many practices we have had? 98 practices. How many of you guys have been to our practices? I would never criticize somebody about something that they know a heckuva lot more about. When I retire in 2035, I want to be an announcer one year, [because] I want to be the only announcer not to criticize coaches" (Webster, 2016).

The increase in the amount of sports media, the speed at which material gets to the public, and the demand for more content to satisfy audiences suggests that the critical reporting will continue. There may have been a time in which reporters and athletes could develop trusting relationships; Roger Kahn covered the Dodgers during the 1950s and admits to making friends with the players (Gietschier, 1994). But for the most part the relationship today is wary at best, adversarial at worst. "We're everywhere," said Bill Plaschke (2000, p. 44). "We surround them as they are preparing for a game; we barely give them room to dress afterwards; and we're not looking to make friends, but front pages." Added former Major League Baseball pitcher David Cone, "We feel like targets. A lot of times [the media are] looking for a reason to get on you. Negativity sells" (Schultz, 2005, p. 25).

Content providers try to control such negativity through various means, including news releases, media guides, and news conferences. They can also limit the time and place of access, which is particularly common on the high school and college level. The schools justify this by saying that the student-athletes are not paid and need to be protected from constant media scrutiny. Prior to a game against Ohio State in 2016, University of Oklahoma quarterback Austin Kendall made some disparaging remarks about the Buckeye defense. After Ohio State won the game, Oklahoma coach Bob Stoops decided that he would begin restricting media access to certain players. "I'm not punishing anybody," Stoops said, "I'm protecting my team. I don't want information out there to other teams from guys that I can't trust to say the right things. I can only put people out there that are going to represent the program and say the right things" (Trotter, 2016).

School administrators, athletic officials, or sports information department staffers serve as filters through which the media must go to get access to players and coaches. There are similar positions within professional sports organizations, but at the pro level access is more often determined by the individual athlete. For the most part, if an athlete doesn't want to talk, he/she doesn't talk. Several athletes, including stars like former NFL running back Marshawn Lynch, became well-known for their refusal to grant media access at particular times.

The print reporter's job is to not only work within the access rules established by the coaches and sport organizations, but also to find access in other ways when necessary. We've already learned how players, coaches, and fans can get upset when the media reports bad news. When that happens, the coaches and teams typically go into "lock down," either refusing to talk to anyone or limiting communication to carefully crafted statements. Former sports broadcaster and now college educator Charlie Lambert observed, "Journalists who cover top-level sport are facing a real challenge. Teams and organizations are so powerful and so wealthy that they want to control everything that is said or written about them" ("Sports journalism," 2008).

Access can be virtually impossible during crisis situations, and reporters must find a way to get beyond the official information and find what they need. As noted in Chapter 1, Lance Armstrong and Manti Te'o responded to crisis situations by only issuing information to the media on their own terms. Baylor University did much the same thing when faced with a sexual assault scandal involving its football players in 2016. The university dragged its feet, trying to sweep the allegations under the rug, until a damning report from ESPN made further silence impossible. "Baylor knew the latest ESPN story was coming," said Jon Solomon (2016) of CBS, "and rather than allowing key people at the university to speak, put out its Title IX coordinator to talk in generalities about improvement. That might limit liability for the moment, but it speaks volumes about your efforts to really move forward." ESPN's report blew the scandal open, costing Chancellor Ken Starr and football coach Art Briles their jobs.

Relating With Content Providers: Audiences

The primary relationship between the print outlet and audiences remains unchanged in that the outlet provides audiences with content. But several other things *have* changed, including how much content is provided, the nature of the content, and how that content is provided to audiences. New technologies are the driving force behind these changes, allowing audiences to take a much greater role in the communication process.

In some ways, the type of content provided by print outlets is not much different than it was 50 or even 100 years ago. The sports event is still the major attraction for audiences and reporters, who spend a great deal of time previewing, analyzing, critiquing, and rehashing live game action. Some reporters specialize in commentary, analysis, or opinion, while others focus on investigative work. Another type of sportswriting is the feature story, a longer form of writing that centers on the emotional aspects of a particular story. Many sportswriters are beat reporters, which means they cover the same story or team over a long period of time. This not only helps them stay on top of potential stories, but also develop a better relationship with athletes and coaches. "That's 90 percent of sports reporting," said longtime sportswriter Bill Plaschke (2000, p. 44), "standing around batting cages and end zones and practice courts, just talking. The best sports reporters are the people who are the best at hanging out."

This is not a textbook on sportswriting and there is no need to go into great detail on the process (if you are interested in the basics of sports reporting see Schultz and Arke, 2015). However, it is important to note that in terms of creating content, the role of the sportswriter has changed in recent years. Under the old model of sport communication, a reporter might cover a particular game then file a story for the next day's newspaper. Thus, the reporter had at least a few hours to gather quotes, process information, and write the story. The reporter might even have time to create an additional sidebar story—a supplemental story related to the game.

Today, the reporter has a lot more work to do and less time to do it. There is still the main game story that will run in the next day's newspaper, but most reporters must now also write for their internet audiences. This could include posting several short updates throughout the game, or in some cases running an ongoing game blog.

A Day in the Life of Today's Print Sports Reporter

Before the age of digital, social media, and the internet, the print sports reporter's job was pretty basic—write a story to appear in the next day's newspaper (or magazine). Writers had plenty of time to kill both before and after the game. Today, of course, the process is much different and more time-consuming. Consider a football game the reporter will cover at 7:30 that night. The reporter begins the day by browsing through the web and social media sites for any late-breaking stories. That might be followed by contributing written material previewing the game to the paper's website, and distributing similar social media messages. During the game the reporter will communicate with readers via social media, and continue to do so after the game is over. In addition to stories for the web and printed versions of

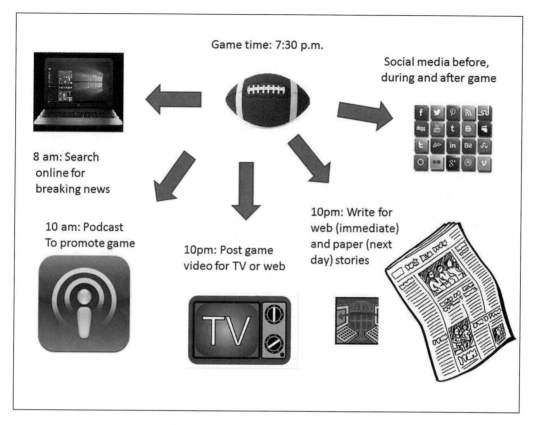

Exhibit 2.2 *Game Day Preparation*

the paper, the reporter might also have to include some video work, either for the paper's website or for local television. Thus, the coverage of a single game requires the reporter to work anywhere from 12 to 16 hours.

Blogging has especially become an important part of the reporter's job because it reflects the growing interactivity of sports media. Nardi, Schiano, Gumbrecht, and Swartz (2004) define a web blog or blog as a web-based form of communication that includes frequent updates and a series of archived entries made in reverse chronological order. It also allows for dialogue and interaction between the blogger (in this case the reporter) and the audience member. Audiences can post comments and sometimes engage in real-time conversations with sports reporters. Blogging has become extremely popular among fans, teams, and players, and many of them have started their own blogs. Athletes and teams find it a good way to present their message to fans, and fans like it because they have a much more active role in the process.

But there is a significant downside. As noted, outlets typically do not pay their reporters extra money for blogging and oftentimes reporters are unsure about what exactly to put in a blog. Because it is by nature personal and subjective, blogging raises issues about journalistic integrity and ethics. In addition, reporters are by nature reluctant to change engrained work habits. For all of these reasons and more, blogging has not been universally embraced by sports journalists.

However, a growing number of sports journalists, mostly young and technologically savvy, have used blogs, podcasts, and a host of other new technologies to reach fragmenting audiences. The modern sports reporter realizes that the audience has much more control and choice in terms of accessing content, and good media relations means creating good relationships with audiences by any means necessary.

Blogged Down

One of the big debates in sports journalism is the role of live blogging. Journalists have the ability to instantly transmit the events of a particular game, but does that transmission devalue the television broadcast of the event or violate rules protecting television rights transmissions? In 2007, a newspaper reporter for the *Louisville Courier-Journal* was ejected from an NCAA baseball game for live blogging game action, and the NCAA only later backed down when the paper threatened a lawsuit. The NFL tried to limit live blogging to 90 seconds per day of audio and/or video of interviews, press conferences, and team practices that may be posted on a website.

However, many reporters and outlets simply ignored the rules, including the *Wall Street Journal*, which in 2009 had one of its reporters sit at home and live blog a game between the Tennessee Titans and New York Jets as a means of testing the NFL's resolve. The exercise also pointed out the league's double standard in trying to limit the blogging of journalists at the stadium while ignoring the blogger at home. As a result, the league has taken something of a "don't ask, don't tell" policy on its blogging; the other major sports leagues and organizations have almost no restrictions.

For those organizations that do try to take a hard line, like the International Olympic Committee (IOC), the problem is one of enforcement. Yes, the IOC could conceivably remove credentials or restrict access, but as attorney Brad Shear noted, "What is the IOC going to do about it? They will ask the athlete (or journalist) to remove the tweet, but once it's been retweeted, once it's been out there online, it's hard to remove" (Merron, 2012).

Blogging Down the Fairway

The PGA Tour has no restrictions on live blogging of events, believing that such coverage helps increase audience interest. This is just a small portion of the golf.com blog on the final round of the 2018 PGA

Championship. The blog ran continuously from 8:30 in the morning to 5:00 that night. Note that live blogging punctuation is not a priority.

4:43: Dustin Johnson keeps on rolling...DJ makes a long birdie putt at 11, his fifth of the day. With that he joins Kyle Stanley at -3, just two shots behind Fowler's lead.

4:40: Rose makes a beautiful stroke with his birdie putt at 8 and sinks it to move to -2. Rahm drops his short one to get to -1. Spieth settles for another par.

4:35: Spieth had to hit his third shot on the par -5 8th from deep rough short and left of the green. He hits a decent one from there to the back collar, but he'll have a tough putt for birdie.

4:33: Patrick Reed (+2) stops the bleeding with a birdie at 9.

4:28: 52-year old John Daly is off to an impressive start. He's made one birdie and two bogeys to go +1 on his first nine.

4:23 Spieth makes his putt at 7 to capture his first birdie of the day. He moves to +1. Rose gets up-and-down for part to remain at -1.

4:21: Koooooooch gets into red numbers with a birdie at 10. -1.

Source: golf.com (https://www.golf.com/travel/2018/08/08/pga-championship-live-blog/)

The laptop or portable computer has become mandatory for the modern sports reporter, and the ability to write and transmit stories directly from the game allows reporters to work faster and keep up with rapidly shrinking deadlines. Computers can also be used to transmit video and audio, and the print reporter could tape game action or interviews using a small camera. This material would then be posted on the newspaper's website as soon as possible after the game. Thus, the reporter might be required to write a story (or two) for both the internet and print editions of the paper, maintain a blog, take digital photographs, and shoot video/audio for posting on the web. The outlet might also want two different versions of the story—one for the web and the other for the next day's newspaper. It all adds up to a lot more work, and usually for not much more pay.

And don't forget the role of social media. Reporters must now connect with audiences and athletes through Facebook, Twitter, and other platforms. Social media adds an interactive dynamic that allows sports communicators to engage in discussions and commentary with athletes and fans. What may have started as a fad has now become an indispensible part of how sports journalists do their jobs (see sidebar).

"R U Able to Talk?"

Text messaging and Twitter have become increasingly more important in sports communication, not only for keeping up with athletes and coaches, but as a way of sourcing, breaking, and promoting their own stories. Below are some examples of how these tools are affecting the way reporters do their jobs.

"I have no clue where he's going or leaning"

—Text message sent to the media from Huntington (W.Va.)
high school coach, Rob Fulford (Bedore, 2013)

Fulford was talking about Andrew Wiggins, the nation's number one basketball recruit, who was set to announce his college choice. Coaches, athletes, and organizations are increasingly using text messages to break stories and communicate with the media, so media members have to pay them careful attention. (Wiggins eventually signed with the University of Kansas). In some cases, tweets or text messages are the only official statements reporters will get on a particular story. "Quoting a text message is no different than quoting from an email," says Liz Norris, who writes for *Sports Business Journal*. "Journalists have been quoting emails for a good 10 years or more. There is nothing wrong with using texted messages as quotes in stories as long as the source is aware that they are texting with a reporter and there is no agreement that the texts are off the record" ("Liz Mullen," 2010).

"I see my tweeting during the game is being talked about as much as the game itself. Not my intention; just bored I guess.

—Tweet sent by former NBA star Kobe Bryant, who was injured
during the playoffs (Conway, 2013)

Now retired, Bryant got into some hot water for his critical comments about his coach and teammates as he live-tweeted during an NBA playoff game. In fact, Bryant's comments became more of a story than the game itself, prompting the star to shut down his tweeting for subsequent games. Media researcher Marshall McLuhan (1964) once famously wrote that "the medium is the message," and that certainly seems to apply in cases where texting and tweeting move from mere delivery systems to stories themselves.

"**@sammcgaw: There are rumors that LSU head football coach Les Miles will step down on Monday after allegedly having an affair with a student. Hmm...**"

—Tweet of Bleacher Nation *contributor, Sam McGaw (Bedard, 2013)*

McGaw's tweet was retweeted 167 times and he picked up some 30,000 followers after posting it. The problem is that the information was based on an internet rumor that turned out to be completely false. Technology allows sports journalists to transmit information in just seconds, which often forces them to release information without checking it out. The result to be first and beat the competition means a lot of rumor, innuendo, and just plain falsehood are presented as fact.

"**Apologies to all involved...I tried to showcase the absurdity of bad journalism...I made a horrendous mistake...**"

—Tweet of Washington Post *reporter, Mike Wise ("@MikeWiseguy," 2010)*

To prove a point about the dangers of tweeting and texting, *Washington Post* sports reporter Mike Wise intentionally sent false information into the public domain with his phony tweet about the possible suspension of Steelers' quarterback Ben Roethlisberger. A number of web sites, including the *Miami Herald* and NBC's *Pro Football Talk*, picked up the story, for which Wise quickly apologized. "I need to take my medicine and move on," Wise said after the paper suspended him for a month, "and promise everybody this will never happen again" ("Mike Wise", 2010).

Covering the Beat: The New Reality

As noted previously, responsibilities of the print sports reporter have increased drastically in the new model of sport communication. Reporting in the new model is quite different and much more time consuming. Consider how a sports reporter for Digital First Media spends his or her day:

On game day, the sports reporter covers the events live, either using a tool such as CoverItLive or ScribbleLive directly, or by live-tweeting and feeding the tweets into the liveblog or by frequently updating a news story or blog. The nature of the liveblog might vary, depending on television coverage.

If the reporter is covering the local professional or big-time college team, and fans are likely to be watching in the stadium or on television, her role is more commentary and interaction with fans than play-by-play. If it's a road game that's not on television, the reporter needs to report more of the action. In either case, it's essential to report big plays and periodic scores (in a game with infrequent scoring, such as football, baseball, or hockey, she probably reports every score; with volleyball or basketball, summarizing runs or noting lead changes should suffice). In the case of high school sports, the reporter needs to decide (and watch the interaction to judge) whether most of the people joining the liveblog are at the game or following it from afar, and blog accordingly.

Fan reaction during the game helps guide the reporter's coverage: The fans can identify a huge issue that she has to address in her game coverage. Or the fan discussion can show the reporter which issues have been thoroughly discussed, helping her choose a fresh approach.

In regular beat coverage between games, the sports reporter must monitor social media accounts of athletes, coaches, and teams, where they might offend or apologize to fans, trash-talk upcoming opponents, or disclose or discuss injuries. The reporter tweets and blogs about stories she is working on. The reporter shoots brief video clips during interviews to embed later in a story or blog post.

When big news breaks, such as an injury, trade, or coach firing or hiring, the reporter hustles to be the first to break the story with a swift combination of tweet, news alert, Facebook update, website bulletin, blog post, and full-blown story.

The reporter will interact live with the community during the week in one or more of these ways:

- Webcast, possibly with other sports writers, sports bloggers, coaches, and/ or athletes.

- Live chat with fans (again, possibly with guests, who don't need to be onsite, so you might bring in a coach or athlete from a team the local team will be opposing soon).

- Combination webcast and live chat with reporter(s) on the webcast and an editor fielding and asking questions from the live chat.

(From: Buttry, 2011)

Summary

The print media dominated sports coverage through the 1950s. Periodicals such as *The Sporting News* and *Sports Illustrated,* along with daily coverage in thousands of local newspapers, helped make the print media essential for sports fans and audiences. However, the growth of electronic media, specifically television and now the internet, has seriously damaged many print media outlets. Many of them are losing money; others have cut budgets or simply shut down. Faced with these challenges, many of the print sports media are turning to new technologies. Newspapers and magazines are getting more involved in online formats and working harder to become more interactive and audience-friendly. On a positive note for newspapers, *The New York Times* reported $790 million in online revenue in 2018 and a total (print/online) subscriber base of over 4 million (Peiser, 2019). The newspaper also added 120 newsroom employees (Peiser).

New technologies such as blogs, webpages, and Twitter, also bring a new set of issues to the print media in terms of access to players and coaches. While players and coaches can now use these technologies to get their messages out unfiltered, in some ways it's now easier for the print media to contact and interview sports newsmakers. Access becomes extremely difficult during scandals and other crisis situations, and the print sports reporter must find other sources to help tell the story.

Technology is also changing the way the games get reported. Laptops, blogs, Twitter feeds, and text messaging make a print reporter's job easier, but also more varied and time-consuming. Instead of producing just one print story for the magazine or newspaper, today's reporter often has to include video, interviews, and a blog for the internet. In addition, the reporter might have to respond to fan comments posted about the story. Thus, the print sports reporter of today is becoming more multimedia oriented.

Discussion Questions

1. At the beginning of this chapter it was suggested that the print sports media are going through difficult economic times. What is your opinion on that? What are the advantages and disadvantages of a print outlet moving completely online (like *The Sporting News)?* If the print media are to survive, how will they do it? What might they look like in ten years?

2. Some print reporters will get thousands of emails after a big story. If you were the reporter, what would you do with all that response? Would you try to answer some or just delete them all? Would you even read them all? How involved should reporters be with their audience in terms of feedback and interaction?

3. Many outlets require print reporters to shoot video, audio, and digital photographs for use on the web. Is this a good idea? Does the modern print reporter need these types of multimedia skills or should someone else be responsible? Why or why not? In the future, is there going to be such a thing as a "print reporter" who is different from a "broadcast reporter?"

4. To follow up on the previous question, should journalism schools now be training students to be "only" print reporters and/or broadcast reporters, or should they be teaching these multimedia reporting styles? If you were going to teach

someone how to be a sports reporter, what would be important for that person to know?

Suggested Exercises

1. Make arrangements to go with a newspaper reporter to a local game (for a high school game it shouldn't be much of a problem getting permission and you might even get to help out some). Observe how the reporter goes about covering the game. How many stories does he/she need to write? How much time do they have? Do they also have to take pictures or shoot video? If the reporter has a few years of experience, you can also ask how this process has changed over the years.

2. We have seen that sports blogs are much different than newspaper stories. Select a newspaper sportswriter who writes for both a blog and the print version of the paper and compare the writing styles. Do they seem to be different? Should they be? Which version seems to be more interesting and why? What does this mean in terms of communicating with readers?

3. After a big game go to a print outlet's website. Over the course of a few hours, see if you can identify the abbreviated story, developed story, and possible sidebar story related to the game. How do these stories differ in terms of style, length, tone, and approach? You might also try to look at two different events on two different levels. For example, how the local newspaper covered a big game compared to *Sports Illustrated*.

4. As a hypothetical example, say the coach of the local high school football team has been suspended by the school for an unspecified violation of school policy. Develop a strategy for getting the access you need to report on the story. How would you try to work through official sources? Unofficial sources?

3
The Broadcast Media

There is a tremendous amount of discussion today about the growing power of "new" media technologies such as the internet, social media, and cellular phones. There is no doubt that such content and distribution platforms are increasing in scope and influence. But with all the focus on interactivity, interconnectedness, and global communication, we tend to forget the traditional broadcast media— radio and television. Television especially remains a powerful presence in the sports media landscape. Even though the ratings dipped from 2012, some 342 million people worldwide watched the 2016 opening ceremonies for the Olympics from Rio de Janeiro (Roxborough, 2016). While that seems like a huge number, it's dwarfed by the audience for the 2014 final of the FIFA World Cup soccer tournament. The match between Argentina and Germany drew a television audience of more than one billion, with another 280 million watching online. The total in-home audience of those who watched at least one minute of the 2014 World Cup was 3.2 billion ("2014 FIFA," 2015). These numbers increased for the 2018 final and the total viewing audience for the 2018 World Cup (FIFA, 2018).

There is no doubt that more and more people are watching these events on laptops, tablets, and even cell phones, just as there is no doubt that the internet has the potential to reach audiences just as big. But in terms of the ability to bring together an audience—to galvanize a nation or even a planet for a singular event—television and radio still hold an important place among sports media.

Radio

Radio and television went through similar evolutionary phases related to sport communication, especially in their early years. The first radio sports broadcast took place on July 2, 1921, and involved a heavyweight boxing match arranged by RCA founder David Sarnoff as a way to promote radio. Later that same year, the World Series went on radio for the first time and again, Sarnoff played a leading role. Recognizing that the new medium needed programming, Sarnoff made baseball one of the cornerstones of the industry. "We had to have baseball in order to sell enough sets to go on to other programming," he later wrote (as cited in Schultz,

Exhibit 3.1 *Advertising Money Spent for Television and Radio in Millions of Dollars, 1949–1956*

Year	Radio	Television
1949	571	58
1950	605	171
1951	606	332
1952	624	454
1953	611	606
1954	559	809
1955	545	1,035
1956	567	1,225

Source: Robert J. Coen, McCann-Erickson, Inc. (as cited in Sterling, 1984).

2005, p. 173). By the end of the 1920s, Cubs owner William Wrigley had his team's games on *five* different stations and reportedly said, "The more outlets the better; we'll tie up the entire city" (Hilmes, 1997).

Live sports programming helped radio become a rich and powerful mass medium through the 1930s and 1940s. Network links carried the events to every corner of America, which provided advertisers with the mass audiences they needed to make radio extremely profitable. By 1935 CBS, NBC, and Mutual were all broadcasting baseball on a national basis. In 1937, rights to broadcast the World Series on radio were worth $100,000; in 1949, Gillette signed a seven-year, $1 million deal to become the exclusive radio sponsor of the World Series and All-Star games ("Broadcasting," 1949).

But that was the high-water mark for network radio sports. By the 1950s, television had successfully shown that it had the technology to broadcast live sports and could attract enough audience to interest advertisers. (Ironically, a demonstration of television's viability was provided by Gillette, whose sponsorship of a televised boxing match in 1946 reached 100,000 viewers in just four cities). By 1958, television had far surpassed radio in terms of advertising revenue (see Exhibit 3.1).

Sports radio networks still exist today, and remain attractive for their local advertising revenue. For example, you can see in Exhibit 3.2 the extensive reach of the St. Louis Cardinals radio network, which includes stations as far away as Hawaii. Such broadcasts are valuable to the Cardinals in terms of connecting audiences with local advertisers.

Local (spot) advertising has traditionally been the largest part of radio advertising and still is, but recent years have seen a decline due to growth in mobile and

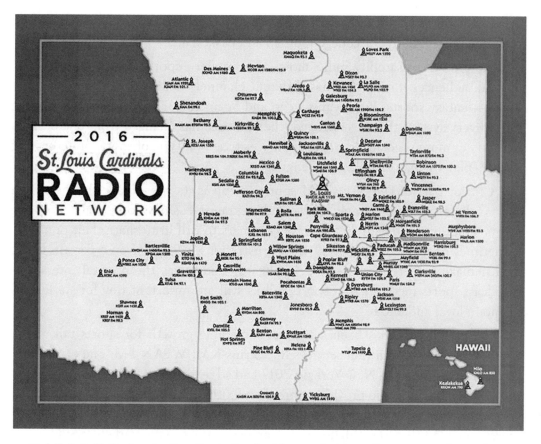

Exhibit 3.2 *St. Louis Cardinals Radio Network Area. Fans can still get free, over-the-air signals of live sporting events through outlets like the St. Louis Cardinals radio network. The Cardinals have built an impressive network of more than 130 stations in ten states, mostly across the Midwest, but also reaching as far as Hawaii.*

digital platforms. Digital now accounts for 7.5% of radio station ad billings, which may not seem like much, but it rose 13% in 2018 to nearly $800 million (RAB, 2018). Such growth is reflective of the fact that satellite radio has become extremely popular in carrying live sports programming. For example, those St. Louis fans that live outside the coverage area of the Cardinals radio network have shown a willingness to pay to get access to the games.

The dominant satellite radio provider is the merged Sirius XM company, which gives listeners access to NFL, MLB, NBA, NHL, and NCAA games, along with other sports programming, in exchange for subscription fees that range up to $16 per month. Analysts say that Sirius XM has around $1.2 billion in revenue and essentially has doubled its expected growth, from 12.9% to 22.9% (Barnes, 2016). In 2016, Sirius XM signed a new five year agreement to extend its broadcast rights.

The deal gave the company even more games to offer on its satellite and mobile platforms, particularly for college football and basketball.*

The growth of satellite radio shows how modern sports radio caters to fragmented audiences. Sirius XM has different channels dedicated to—among other topics—fantasy sports, European soccer, and Spanish language sports. It's not just the delivery system that has changed; the audience has changed from one of mass interests to more specialized niche audiences based on type of sport, preference of format (play-by-play or talk), and language.

A major part of the Sirius XM sports lineup is its sports talk channels. The sports talk format is extremely simple and inexpensive: show host(s) talk about the sports issues of the day and encourages listeners to call in to share their opinions. Sometimes people call in to vent their frustrations, comment on a certain topic, or just make sure their voice is being heard. Radio was the original interactive broadcast sports medium, and sports talk is still an important way for stations to maintain loyal audiences.

The past decade has been a time of incredible growth for sports talk radio, and not just on subscription services like Sirius-XM. WFAN-FM, one of the top-ranked radio stations in New York, in 2017 had ad revenues of $41 million ("Radio's top," 2018). ESPN Radio provides more than 9,000 hours of talk and event content annually, reaching 32 million listeners a week on 600 nationwide stations, including more than 375 full-time affiliates and clearance in the top 25 markets. ESPN is also heavily invested in digital formats, as its radio programming is available on Sirius XM and on ESPNRadio.com ("ESPN," 2018).

In an era of multiplatform content, sports radio has surprisingly reached back into television. The popular Dan Patrick Show, for example, airs on hundreds of radio stations and satellite radio, but there is a television version that also runs on the NBC Sports Network. It has become quite common for television stations to pick up such programming, not only because of their popularity, but because the shows are so inexpensive to produce. Like Dan Patrick, Paul Finebaum has versions of his call-in radio show that are available on television (SEC Network) and podcasts. Finebaum parlayed a radio background to become one of the most popular sports media figures in the US.

---

* Westwood One (a division of NBC) is the major network carrier of live over-the-air sports programming, and its events include the Super Bowl, NFL games, and several NCAA sports.

Paul is Doing More than Fine

Now considered the expert on college football, especially in the Southeastern Conference, Paul Finebaum has become an unlikely multimedia sports star. He started as a columnist and investigative reporter in Birmingham, and then branched out to create his own syndicated radio network. Finebaum joined the new SEC television network in 2014, and the television version of his call-in radio show has become one of the most popular programs on the channel.

A third major platform for radio content has emerged with the podcast. Podcasts are essentially long-form audio—extended interviews, conversations, or analyses that go into greater depth afforded by typical radio programming. In 2016, *Sports Illustrated* debuted a trio of podcasts, including one hosted by NFL reporter Peter King, and the following year ESPN created a podcast version of its *30 For 30* documentary film series. "Podcasts can succeed in ways that sports talk radio can't," said Bob Dorfman, a sports marketing analyst. "Although they can't match the immediacy and participatory nature of sports talk radio, they can deliver superior storytelling, deeper analysis, and richer interviews" (Heine, 2016).

Sports programming will play a big role in the future of radio. "Sports talk radio is a local programming platform," said Scott Becher, an executive with Federated Sports and Gaming. "While other formats tend to be national and more competitive with satellite radio, it's much more difficult for a sports fan to get a daily fix for their local teams other than in sports talk. Local still matters" (Ourand, 2012).

Television

National and International Level

Fans may be able to call into their local radio station and talk sports for hours. They may also be able to see live streaming of sports on the internet or take part in the web's many live sports chats, blogs, or forums. The newspaper also comes to the front door every day with detailed sports stories, features, and pictures. But none of these media have dominated the sports communication process like television. Television is still the unquestioned and unchallenged leader in terms of delivering sports content to audiences, both big and small. Live sports on television cuts across race, gender, and all of the other demographic categories. Sports are dramatic and unpredictable. Burke Magnus, the Executive VP for Programming and Scheduling, had this to say about the content that is the backbone of his network: "Sports is platinum, premier content and there will be always a lot of suitors for it" (Spangler, 2018). Those suitors that Magnus is keeping an eye on lately are companies like Facebook, Google, Verizon, and Amazon.

The first telecast of a Major League Baseball game occurred on August 26, 1939, but featured only two cameras. Reception was fairly poor, but hardly anyone seemed to notice—only about 400 sets existed in New York to pick up the signal. *The New York Times* noted, "Television set owners as far away as 50 miles viewed the action" between the Reds and Dodgers from Brooklyn ("Ebbetts Field," 2001). Other sports programming suffered similar handicaps. Pro football also televised its first game in 1939, which consisted mostly of fuzzy camera shots of the player with the ball. Cameramen were frequently faked out, and on several occasions announcers had to invent intricate lateral passes to explain why the home viewer could not see the ball. Coverage slowly improved but even by 1948, in a broadcast of the college football game between Oklahoma and Texas on WBAP-TV, the bands that performed at halftime had to stay in between the 35-yard lines so as to remain in range of primitive cameras.

Initially, the cost of a television set was too much for the average American family and most sports were watched at the local tavern. Boxing and wrestling predominated during this early period, not only because they appealed to the blue-collar tavern crowd, but because the action could fit neatly onto the television screen and be covered with only one or two cameras. By the mid-1950s television technology had improved, the cost of the sets had come down, and television quickly made its way from the tavern to the home. Sports played a major role in the growth of television, particularly the NFL Championship game of 1958, in which the Baltimore Colts beat the New York Giants in overtime. "I still think the biggest game we ever had was the Colts' win over the Giants," said former NFL Commissioner Pete Rozelle. "I think that was the first game that got television coverage across America. It reached fans who had never seen pro football before" ("Tint of," 1994).

Television sports exploded throughout the 1960s, as the three major television networks—ABC, CBS, and NBC—dramatically increased their production and distribution of live sports content. The networks jockeyed with each other for exclusive broadcast rights for popular events such as the Olympics, NFL, MLB, and the NBA (CBS was the first network to broadcast the Olympics in the US, but the rights eventually passed to ABC and now NBC). The competition dramatically increased the amount of sports on television and the rights fees to broadcast those events. Network competition helped increase the value of television rights fees, but the Sports Broadcasting Act of 1961 (SBA) also played a vital role. Up until that time teams were required by anti-trust law to individually negotiate their own television rights deals. The Act removed the anti-trust restriction and allowed leagues to negotiate as a whole on behalf of their member teams (and distribute the money equally in a revenue-sharing plan).

The NFL was the driving force behind passage of the SBA and today has one of the richest rights-fees packages among all sports leagues. The average yearly NFL television earnings are more than the yearly average of the television rights of the NBA, MLB, NASCAR, NHL, PGA, NCAA basketball, and Summer Olympics *combined*. "No other franchise delivers ratings the way an NFL game does," said former CBS Corp. Chief Executive Leslie Moonves (Flint, 2011).

Televised sports content was controlled by ABC, CBS, and NBC until more competition came along in the 1970s. Ted Turner's WTBS began distributing Atlanta Braves games through national cable, and suddenly the networks began to lose their power. More content providers emerged, and in the late 1980s media mogul Rupert Murdoch attempted to create a fourth national network. One of the keys to the eventual success of the Fox Broadcasting Company was its acquisition of NFL television rights in 1993. Fox outbid CBS for the rights to televise National Conference games, spending $1.6 billion for four years. "Having NFL football really made us a network," Murdoch said (Sandomir, 1997); in 1998 CBS got back in the game with an eight-year, $4 billion deal to televise American Conference games (Stewart, 1998).

We discussed earlier in this chapter the huge audiences pulled in by mega events like the Olympics and World Cup. But other traditional big events, like the World Series and Indy 500, have not fared as well. When the San Francisco Giants clinched the World Series in 2012, the climactic game was seen on television by fewer people than that evening's episode of *Dancing With the Stars*. In terms of the share rating—the percentage of people watching television at the time tuned into a particular program—sports numbers for events like the World Series have declined (Exhibit 3.3). The World Series has suffered a significant decline in both television ratings (how many people are watching) and shares (a comparison of how the event does against other television shows on at the same time).

Exhibit 3.3 *Decline in World Series Game Television Ratings*

Year	World Series Teams	Rating*	Share#
2015	Royals—Mets	8.7	16
2014	Giants—Royals	8.2	14
1997	Marlins—Indians	19.5	29
1987	Twins—Cardinals	24.0	41
1977	Yankees—Dodgers	29.8	53

* Rating refers to the percentage of all television sets watching.
# Share refers to the percentage of sets turned on and watching at that time.
Source: World Series ratings (2015).

The problems of the World Series indicate how the sports media audience has fragmented in recent years. When the Dodgers and Yankees met in the 1977 World Series there were essentially three television stations available—ABC, NBC, and CBS. NBC, which had rights to the games at that time, got a whopping 53 share (53% of all television homes watching at the time), in part because there really wasn't any competition. In today's multi-channel television universe, the World Series must compete against hundreds of other programs, as well as movie rentals, video games, Netflix, and other entertainment options.

Even as the World Series continues to lose viewers, Major League Baseball continues to make more and more money from its television rights fees. In 2012, MLB signed a contract extension with Fox and Turner Sports worth just under a billion dollars per year through 2021. How does that make sense? The answer lies in new broadcast sources such as satellite, pay-per-view, and subscription, along with emerging new platforms, such as mobile and social media.

Sports programming commands some of the highest fees from cable and satellite providers. ESPN, for example, charges each cable and satellite subscriber more than seven dollars ($7.21), compared to non-sports channels such as Fox News, which charges $1.41 (Wile, 2017). Even though ESPN continues to lose subscribers (12 million in six years) and has gone through a series of staff layoffs, there is a difference between subscribers and viewers, and "the number of viewers for ESPN appears to be as strong as ever" (Gaines, 2017).

DirecTV pays the NFL $1.5 billion per year for the Sunday Ticket program and charges just under $300 per subscriber for a season package, but a series of recent problems—declining NFL ratings, the national anthem controversy, and DirecTV's price-gouging charging for additional services—have caused DirecTV and its parent company, AT&T, to struggle (Ozanian, 2017). Internet-related streaming services provide another vein of revenue, primarily catering to fans who live outside the broadcast coverage area of their favorite teams.

At one point, the sports media figured the best way to maximize revenue was to own a sports franchise. Thus, at different times during the 1990s and 2000s, the Chicago Tribune company owned the Cubs, Disney owned the NHL Ducks, and Ted Turner's broadcast empire owned the Atlanta Braves. Those relationships have ended and the relationship has been turned around. Today, sports teams are creating their own networks in order to gain revenue through both advertising and cable fees. The Yankees have led the *Forbes* ranking of baseball team valuations every year since 1998. The team's 20% ownership in the YES Network, which televises Yankees games and other sports programming, gives the team baseball's highest cable rights fees ("New York," 2016).

The success the Yankees enjoyed with YES has spurred other teams and leagues to create their own networks. A lot of people laughed when the Big 10 Conference began the Big 10 Network in 2006, wondering if anyone would bother to watch volleyball and field hockey matches, but after five years of struggle the network became profitable. That prompted other conferences to follow suit, and in 2014 the SEC Network debuted to almost instantaneous success. The following year, the SEC broadcast rights fees jumped from $210 million to $312 million—a nearly 50% increase (Berkowitz, 2016).

The creation of these channels and internet sites not only means more money, it means that teams, leagues, and even individual athletes can more directly control the flow of information in the sport communication process. It could also suggest significant consequences for the traditional broadcast outlets—television and radio—which now find themselves in uncharted territory. In a sports sense, the main function of national television and radio outlets is the distribution of popular content to audiences. That will change when one of two things happen: 1) the content becomes too expensive to distribute or 2) technology makes it possible to distribute the content in a different, better way.

We are already starting to see a change in regards to new technologies. While television—whether at home, with friends, or in a public setting such as a bar—continues to dominate in terms of sports consumption, digital platforms such as mobile television and social media are becoming dramatically more popular with audiences.

US Media Sports Consumption—The Digital Revolution

Television is still the dominant platform for audiences to watch sports content, and 96% of fans consume sports on TV. But thanks to new technologies, other platforms are growing quickly, including mobile and social media. They are not yet ready to challenge broadcast television, but the tipping point may not be far away.

Adults in US who claim to follow sports	70% (168 million)
Fans who consume sports on television	96%
Fans who consume sports on a mobile device	42%
Fans who have paid to watch sports on TV in the last year	34%
Fans who consume sports online	68%
Fans who use a second screen while watching sports on TV	45%

Fans who follow sports on social networks

Facebook	70%
YouTube	40%
Twitter	24%
Google+	16%

Source: The Global Sports Media Consumption Report, 2014

Mobile television has become increasingly popular as a way of consuming sports for many of the same reasons radio was popular in the 1950s—its portability allows for consumption virtually anywhere. Mobile also has the added advantage of allowing the user to multi-task while watching. For example, someone might be watching a game on a smartphone, while at the same time talking with someone, texting, sharing on social media, or interacting through an internet site. In a 2018 Google survey, 30% of self-identified sports fans said they now watch live sporting events on tablets or smartphones, while 80% said they juggled multiple screens while watching sports. That includes accessing data and messaging fans on a phone while watching the game on television (Booton, 2018). "Mobile will eventually become the predominant screen," predicts Bob Dorfman, "I'd say within 10 years" ("Why TV," 2016).

Online and social media sports consumption has grown even faster, with social media usage more than doubling between 2011 and 2015. Social media platforms are still used primarily for interacting with people, but more and more they have become a live streaming vehicle. In the summer of 2016, the NBA streamed nine pre-Olympic basketball games on Facebook, and later that fall debuted two live streamed basketball shows on Twitter. The NFL also broke ground in the fall of 2016 by live streaming its Thursday Night Football games on Twitter. "As your audience diversifies, as their viewing habits diversify, your distribution models have to follow," said Elizabeth Lindsey of the Wasserman Media Group. "You went from prime time broadcast to cable. You went from online viewing to mobile apps. Now we're getting to social" (Castillo, 2016).

Local Level

While the national broadcast sports media go through a time of great uncertainty, the situation is even more drastic for local television broadcasters. The same forces affecting the national media are also at work on the local level, but local broadcasters do not enjoy million-dollar revenue opportunities. In addition, the national media are also taking over many of the functions of the local broadcasters. Thus, there is a serious concern that local sports television may not survive, at least in its present form.

When we speak about sports television at the local level, we're talking about two main functions: live production of local sports, and regularly scheduled broadcasts of sports within the local newscast. Both functions are in danger; national media and even audience members are starting to take over production and distribution of local sports content, while economic conditions have seriously threatened the role of sports within the local newscast.

In Chapter 2 we talked in some detail about the distressing financial picture for the print media, and the situation is somewhat similar for local broadcasters. Viewership of local television news (including the local sports segment) continues to decline in almost all time slots and for almost all demographic areas. The main problem for local television is the younger viewing group (under 30 years of age), which has turned to alternative digital platforms, such as online and social media, to find its news. A study in 2016 found that in the 18–24 year old age group, 28% listed social media as their main news source, compared to 24% for television (Wakefield, 2016).

Local television is trying to make up for those losses online, but it is a risky and uncertain move. Stations are still unsure how to transition broadcast content from the television to the computer screen, and how to make money from it. Total online revenues for local television increased 12% in 2015 to $900 million, and by 2020 are expected to reach $1.6 billion. But online revenues "still account for a tiny portion of the total ad revenues—an estimate of just 5% in 2015, and this share is not expected to grow much over the next five years" (Matsa, 2016). Over-the-air advertising remains the main economic engine for local television, and that engine is starting to break down.

Unsure how to create additional revenue, many local stations have turned to cutting costs, and that includes sports programming. Some have simply eliminated sports from the local newscast or drastically reduced its time allotment. Where sports used to get four to five minutes in the newscast, that time today is more likely one to two minutes. There are several understandable reasons for the reduction, including the fact that interested sports fans can easily find the content they're looking for online, at ESPN, or in any number of accessible outlets. Research also consistently shows that the average local news viewer does not care that much for sports. A survey by the Radio and Television News Directors Foundation indicated that only 31% of viewers said they were "very interested" in the sports segment, while 32% said they were "somewhat interested" ("Journalism and ethics," 1998). But 72% expressed an interest in the weather. "Sports is extremely polarizing," said television news consultant Brent Magid. "The majority can either take it or leave it, or despise it" (Greppi, 2002).

Those committed to local sports broadcasting are searching for new ways to make it more viable. "Sports is the single most unifying aspect in most, if not all, of our communities," says former television news director Kevin Benz (2011). "Unfortunately, we are not generally good at covering it."

How to Fix Local Sports—and Local Sports Communication

Everyone agrees that local sports broadcasting is in trouble, but not everyone agrees on the solution. One term that keeps popping up is *relevance*—making local sports more important for the audience and giving viewers a reason to watch. As local stations struggle with how to do that, here are some suggestions from television people around the country:

- *Make it local.* Before the days of ESPN and the internet, local sports broadcasters used to include many national highlights and scores. But all of that information is now easily accessible and audiences that tune into local sportscasts have probably already seen it. Thus, the emphasis today for local sportscasts is localism. "I haven't broken it down to say sports is running the audience off," said Ron Comings of KLAS in Las Vegas, "but some local sportscasters haven't adapted to the change in the media environment and turned enough attention to local sports, which won't be seen anywhere else" (Bornfeld, 2009).
- *Have conversations with viewers and include them in the communication process.* This is where social media such as Facebook and Twitter can become essential. These tools make the audience members feel like they play a part in the story process, and that gives them a greater reason to watch. It's not just a matter of posting material on different platforms, but also engaging viewers in real-time conversations. "It's absolutely crucial to engage," says reporter Jonathan Betz of Al Jazeera America. "There's no point in doing it if you're not going to engage. You just can't put a link on the Facebook page and ignore it. People want to talk to you, not only about the story but the behind the scenes aspects of it. They want to know all the nitty gritty about it. If someone comments, you really should comment back. If they tweet, you've got to retweet."
- *Manage sports the same way you manage news.* This means no double standard for news and sports, which often happens when the sports section is left to rip and read national scores and

highlights. "Get out of the studio and into the community," says Kevin Benz (2011) a former news director in Austin, Texas. "You do stories on local athletes and teams with great story-telling, characters and themes. You cover hard sports journalism like steroids in high school and graduation rates among local college athletes. In short, you make sports relevant to your local audience every day."

- *Look for new audiences.* Yes, research suggests that the main audience for sports is men, but that doesn't mean it's the only audience. In fact, newer tools such as Twitter and Facebook are opening up sports for traditionally underserved audiences such as women and older viewers. Research suggests that these audiences actually are taking part in sports communication on a larger scale than traditionally believed (Schultz and Sheffer, 2011).

Benz is referring to the traditional concept of local sports broadcasting—an anchor sits on a desk, reads a few stories, shows a few highlights, and then calls it a day. In an era of multimedia platforms, digital options, and social interaction, that approach simply doesn't work anymore. Today's local sports broadcaster must not only appear on television, but must engage audiences in a variety of different ways and on different platforms.

As just one example, let's consider sports director Scott Saville at KCRG-TV in Cedar Rapids, Iowa. Of course, Saville's main job is to anchor the sports segments on KCRG, which he does at 6 pm and 10 pm. Sometimes, Saville has help in putting these shows together, including photographers, producers, and videographers, but in smaller markets the sportscaster often does most of the jobs himself. He then sits on the anchor desk and delivers that information twice a day for anywhere from two to four minutes per segment. Once upon a time that workload was considered enough.

But in today's media environment, Saville must do much more than simply talk from a set. Like many sportscasters, Saville has branched out into other media platforms. This includes hosting a local talk show called *Iowa Live*, which runs on both the station website and KCRG radio. The production allows Saville and KCRG to provide more in-depth and detailed content that cannot fit in the few minutes allowed on the television sportscast. This is yet another reason that the internet is becoming a preferred medium for accessing sports content.

Saville also has accounts on both Facebook and Twitter, and uses them in a variety of ways. Some of it is simply engaging audience members in conversation. For example, in September 2016, Saville used his Facebook account to give away tickets to a University of Iowa football game. The giveaway not only promoted fan conversation and interaction, but also helped promote awareness and attendance for the *Iowa*

Live show, where the tickets would be given away. The idea is to get viewers to feel closer to the sports personality (at least in a social media context), and thus build audience for television sports segments. This type of parasocial interaction between television viewers and personalities has been well documented (Allen, 1988).

In addition to creating conversations, Saville also uses his social media to promote his work on other platforms, particularly stories that aired on television. One of his Facebook posts was a link to a story he had done on a local athlete that competed in the Paralympics. The link displayed a story on the athlete (voiced by Saville) that ran earlier in the television sportscast. While social media is becoming more popular for streaming sports material (Saville posts links to the *Iowa Live* show on both Facebook and Twitter), sportscasters continue to use it to promote cross-platform content (Schultz and Sheffer, 2010).

Another use of social media, and perhaps its most common, especially in the broadcast media, is as a means of breaking news. Saville will often tweet short breaking news items, such as recognition for local athletes, updated scores, or images. For an important game, like the annual football rivalry game between Iowa and Iowa State, Saville tweeted constantly before (pictures and accounts of tailgaters, and players warming up), during (more photos and updated scores with information), and after (post-game reaction and additional information, such as an Iowa player proposing to his girlfriend).

Saville has correctly recognized the need to take the local sports segment "outside the box" in order to reach new audiences. Those audiences are now active participants in the process of sports communication and their role in growing. Not only are audience members now discussing sports stories, they also have the technical ability to create their own content.

The most obvious example is YouTube, which continues its phenomenal growth after more than a decade in existence. The user-generated content site has more than a billion users—almost one-third of all people on the internet—and everyday people watch hundreds of millions of hours and generate billions of views. Much of the sports content on YouTube is simply fluff, but some of it is impossible to ignore. Sports videos, many of them shot by viewers, pull in an aggregate audience in the tens of millions, and since advertisers follow audience, YouTube's revenue increased from an estimated $12 billion in 2016 to an estimated $20 billion in 2018 ("YouTube," 2019).

YouTube is but one example of how audience members are generating and distributing their own sports content. High school sports, especially as they relate to college recruiting, have become a popular and lucrative area of user-generated content. MaxPreps (maxpreps.com) has become one of the leaders in coverage of high school athletics by getting local coaches, players, parents, and freelance writers to

Tweets	Following	Followers	Likes
4,927	458	1,975	487

Scott Saville @SavilleSez · Aug 29

Mid-Prairie dedicating football season to former player

Mid-Prairie dedicating football season to former player

Mid-Prairie is dedicating its football season to Colton Allen, who lost his life back on June 6th.

kcrg.com

🗨 1   ↻   ♡ 25

Scott Saville @SavilleSez · Aug 29

Athlete of the Week: Abby Flanagan

Athlete of the Week: Abby Flanagan

Exhibit 3.4 *Scott Saville's Twitter account shows various ways social media can be used by sports reporters. (Courtesy KCRG-TV9)*

contribute content. Founded in 2002, MaxPreps was acquired by CBS in 2007 and now includes schedules, standings, and statistics for each of the 16,225 high school football teams in the US.

Sites like MaxPreps and Rivals (which primarily focuses on recruiting) present both a threat and an opportunity for the established broadcast media. The threat is that such content is a direct challenge to traditional providers, such as television and radio. If audiences can find the content they want on sites like MaxPreps, it makes them less likely to tune into the local sports segment.

The opportunity arises for traditional outlets to increase their audience reach by partnering with these new content providers. After nearly going bankrupt, Rivals was acquired by Yahoo! in 2007 for a reported $100 million. In 2005, Fox Sports bought another high school recruiting site, Scout.com, for a reported $60 million. Fox turned around and sold Scout to NAMG in 2013 and CBS acquired Scout's assets out of bankruptcy in 2017 (Spangler, 2017). *Acquisition* is not the only road to expansion. In 2013, CBS Interactive, 247Sports, and MaxPreps partnered together to become more visible in high school football and basketball recruiting coverage.

In terms of live event production, it seems unlikely that the average sports consumer would be able to produce something that would be able to seriously compete for either large audiences or advertising dollars. But the people shooting these events and posting them online to YouTube, MaxPreps, or some other outlet aren't necessarily interested in making money; research (Schultz & Sheffer, 2009) has shown that these "citizen journalists" are far more interested in making themselves heard and sharing their work with others. Even as some professional outlets have begun to pay for amateur content—Fox-owned stations in several local markets are experimenting with a plan to pay $50 per story and $20 per photo that makes it to air—the money obviously isn't much (Baig, 2016).

The technology already exists for amateurs to create very specific sports programming that could potentially reach an audience of millions, but may interest only a few hundred, such as a local high school game. But if those few hundred watch on YouTube rather than the local television channel, that could spell trouble for the established media.

The answer may be some sort of *partnership* between the broadcast media and motivated fans, especially if local stations can get audience members to contribute the material to the station website instead of somewhere else. This would be an arrangement similar to the freelance or stringer arrangement that newspapers have successfully used for a long time; the person contributing the content would get a nominal fee and the station would have more content (although typically at lower quality) for its local audiences. Because of the cost savings benefits it's not out of the question that one day a station could depend entirely on citizen sports journalists for all of its content. That may seem a bit far-fetched, but in the new media environment all the old rules are slowly being rewritten.

Summary

In terms of media relations and the sport communication process, what do all these changes mean for the broadcast media?

Although still dominant, the role of the broadcast sports media is changing. From their traditional role as one-way content provider and distributor, television and radio must now become more interactive and consumer-friendly, especially if they hope to attract newer, younger audiences. These are not your grandfather's media anymore. He may have grown up listening to the game on the radio or more likely watching it on television, but today's younger audiences have found newer ways to experience mediated sports. Simply producing and distributing the content in hopes that large audiences will watch doesn't always work in today's media environment. The older media must accommodate and incorporate these newer media as a means of attracting new audiences and involving them in the communication process.

The broadcast sports media must change because technology is changing the way people communicate. Media theorist Marshall McLuhan believed in a technological determinism in which each new media technology fundamentally changed cultural practices. According to McLuhan (as cited in Griffin, 1997), "Family life, the workplace, schools, health care, friendship, religious worship, recreation, politics—nothing remains untouched by communication technology." Are blogging and Twitter merely fads or do they hold the potential to fundamentally alter our cultural practices? In some cases, overuse may be an issue. During the height of the Twitter craze *Sports Illustrated's* Cory McCartney (2009) noted, "Everyone is tweeting … but just because some coaches are showing how hip they are by opening a Twitter account doesn't mean *every coach* should be living life 140 characters at a time. West Virginia's Bill Stewart set the hip factor back decades with this tweet: 'Driving at 4:15 a.m., I was listening to *Little Deuce Coupe* by the Beach Boys. Talk about getting pumped up early in the morning.' Thanks, Twitter. Now coaches have officially entered the TMI Age." Even so, 15 years ago very few people had cell phones; now they are virtually an indispensable communication tool that shapes how we work, play, and live. If blogging and tweeting don't catch on, history tells us something better eventually will.

New technologies are making it more difficult for the broadcast media to control information in the communication process. The internet, blogging, tweeting, message boards, fan forums, and the like have drastically reduced the gatekeeping and agenda-setting functions of the media (see Chapter 1). Fans can communicate with the media, with each other, and even directly with athletes. There are more and more cases of athletes using Twitter even during games. In 2015, University of Texas player Kris Boyd had to apologize after tweeting during halftime of a game against TCU. "In no way did I intend to be disrespectful or disloyal," Boyd said. "I deeply regret my actions and want to reassure everyone that I am 100 percent committed to this team and program" (Dixon, 2015).

The future of broadcast sports may be through citizen participation. With a few exceptions, sports ratings are down, stations are losing money, and broadcast corporations are facing bankruptcy. The economic realities of today's competitive media environment may shift more of the burden of content production and distribution to the consumer. This is not to say that the Super Bowl will one day wind up as a home video distributed on YouTube, but it's a common practice for businesses to shift costs to consumers (think of the self-checkout lines at the grocery store, for example—you're doing their work for them at no cost). It makes economic sense for outlets to let audiences shoot and contribute sports content—the audiences are usually highly motivated, they have the technology to do it, and it costs them virtually nothing other than the time they put in. The quality may suffer a bit, but that certainly hasn't stopped YouTube from becoming a multi-billion dollar media empire. Today's broadcast media are learning the YouTube lesson—letting the audience take part in the process works on multiple levels, most especially economically.

Discussion Questions

1. One of the main issues in broadcast sports media today is the growth of subscription and/or pay-per-view programming. If a mega event like the Super Bowl could be sold on a pay-per-view basis for around $75 do you think audiences would go for it? What would be the advantages and disadvantages of such an idea? Will we eventually see a time in which *all* sports programming is pay-per-view? What would that mean for the future of sports advertising?

2. It is very easy today for anyone to take a handheld (or smaller) video camera, go shoot highlights of the local high school game, and post the material online. Do you see this kind of "citizen sports journalism" as the future of the sports media? Why or why not?

3. You are the general manager of a local radio or television station. Discuss some ways in which you can make your sports content more relevant to local audiences. As you think through your options be sure to consider the economic, cultural, and technological issues that might affect your ultimate decisions.

4. A University of Texas player tweets during halftime of a game; other players have their own blogs and websites. How do these types of things change the

dynamic of media relations between athletes and fans? Between fans and the media? Media and athletes?

5. Do you agree with McLuhan's vision of technological determinism? How would it apply to our discussions of sport media and communication?

Suggested Exercises

1. Record a live sports event either from radio or television. As you review the game make a note of how the content provider is trying to

   • include audience members in the communication process,

   • incorporate new media technologies such as blogging or twittering,

   • address economic concerns (which don't necessarily have to be through advertising), and

   • reach out to new audiences such as casual fans.

2. Use the same approach as in #1, but do it for the sports segment of the local television newscast.

3. Pick a particular athlete and analyze the content of his/her blog site or web-page. What is the nature of the material? What is the athlete trying to do with the communication? Why?

4. You can also analyze the sports content on citizen journalism sites like Fan Media Network (http://www.fanmedianetwork.com). Do you think sites like FMN could eventually replace the traditional sports media? How would you assess the content posted by average sports fans on the FMN site in terms of its quality and interest/relevance for sports fans?

4 | Social Media, Twitter, and Technology

Sports and the media have changed dramatically since the newspaper, telegraph, and magazine days of the 1800s and the days of radio in the early 1900s. What would those who worked for the sports media in the early 1900s think of streaming video, blogs, Twitter, Instagram, Snapchat, the iPhone, YouTube, and Facebook? Would Ring Lardner send out better tweets than Grantland Rice? How do you think Edward R. Murrow or Walter Cronkite's podcast would compare to listening to them live on the radio? Do you think Howard Cosell would have been a blogger or a tweeter? What type of Facebook page would Damon Runyon have had?

Every year, every month, sometimes every week, there seems to be a new innovation that can make a sports journalist's job simpler but at the same time make it easier for a professional athlete, sport organization, or sports information director to bypass the beat writer and talk directly to the sports fans of the world. The 45th President of the United States, Donald J. Trump, has turned his tweets into "breaking news." Newspapers and their sports departments have been shrinking, yet advances in technology create new platforms for sport communication professionals and opportunities to reach a global audience. One of those platforms is Twitter. In 2013, Twitter hired a new head of sports partnerships. His job was to develop Twitter's sports business (Ourand, 2013); Twitter now has a much expanded partnership operation and live-video team. Twitter has deals with Live Nation Entertainment, Major League Baseball, the PGA Tour, and Major League Soccer, just to name a few (Spangler, 2018). Facebook recognized the power of sports to generate engagement and they too have invested heavily in sports content. The social media giant is slowly building out its presence in the sports media industry, signing deals with Major League Baseball, NCAA men's basketball conferences, Major League Soccer, the English Premier League, the Champions League and Fox Sports (Spangler). Major college athletic departments have created new positions, such as director of digital communications, social media coordinator, and digital broadcasting director. The National Basketball Association operates a large number of Twitter feeds, including those for the WNBA (@WNBA), the NBDL (@NBAGLeague), the NBA Store (@

NBAStore), and NBA Cares (NBACares), along with many country specific Twitter accounts (e.g., @NBAIndonesia, @NBAChina, @NBABrazil, @NBAAustralia). All of this new media needs content and sports communications professionals to update each website, Facebook page, and Twitter feed. The league has a plethora of opportunities for communications professionals in their communications department, content management department, media operations department, and the NBA Digital/ Turner Sports partnership. There are also a large number of opportunities with each NBA franchise for aspiring sports industry professionals with a communications background. As will be discussed in Chapter 12, there are opportunities overseas too with the NBA and with other sports organizations.

Forty years ago, a family's television viewing options were ABC, NBC, CBS, and a local over-the-air broadcast station. Fast forward to today and the choices are endless. Sports fans don't need a television to watch video; they can watch an NFL game or the World Cup on their phone, iPad, Mac, or home computer. Watching sports events and games are now supplemented by interactive features that allow the audience to tweet, Snap, or post about the event using their smartphone, tablet, or other device that can access the internet. Twitter and Facebook now produce their own video content. They have become sports channels themselves. Fans have many choices for news and entertainment, and to view video, and there also has been an explosion in sports networks. A typical lineup for a local cable package may include ESPN, ESPN 2, ESPNU, CBS College Sports, the Big Ten Network, SEC Network, NFL Network, NBC Sports (now owned by Comcast), and Fox Sports 1. Many college sports conferences have established networks to stream their own content. Each one of these networks is staffed by a large group of sport communication professionals, some of whom are former newspaper reporters. Others write for newspapers and double-dip as reporters or on-air talent for the networks. Many of these networks have also expanded their presence on the web, which signals greater demand for competent communication professionals to provide stories, videos, news updates, and podcasts.

The dramatic growth of the internet and the movement of advertising dollars from television and newspapers to the web have caused a sea change in these industries. People still appreciate good writing and commentary, but where they go to find that information has changed. In 1995, only 15% of adults in the US used the internet, but by 2018 that number had increased to 89% (Mills, 2010; Pew, 2018). It has been estimated that at the beginning of 2018, over 4 billion people have access to the internet around the world; this figure includes 95% of the people who live in North America and 85% of Europeans (Internet, 2018). Fans don't just connect to their favorite sports page via a laptop or personal computer. They now have smartphones or tablets (iPad, Samsung Galaxy, Kindle, Nook, Google Nexus, etc.) that permit them to find articles by their favorite sports writer while riding on a bus to the office, or they can watch that same writer who moonlights on ESPN or the SEC Network on that same smartphone or tablet. The mobile share of web traffic has increased from 0.7% in 2009 to 52.2% in 2018 (Kemp, 2018). It is estimated that in early 2018, there are 8.49 billion telephone subscriptions worldwide (Kemp). In the US, a survey conducted by Pew Research found that 95% of American adults own cell phones and 77% of those Americans own smartphones, capable of surfing the internet (2018). To further demonstrate the importance of mobile phones to the average American, a different survey indicated that almost 92% of Americans keep their mobile phone within three feet of them, 24 hours a day (Filoux, 2010). According to the Center for Disease Control (CDC), which has been tracking phone ownership since the early 2000s, less than half of the households in the US have an operational landline telephone; landlines are moving towards extinction, just like the phone booth (Blumberg & Luke, 2018).

In the following sections, we will examine some of the latest innovations that have affected how sport media professionals and athletes alike communicate with sports fans. We will focus our attention on the developments in the world of social media, and will then examine how a few communications professionals who have worked in professional sports, college athletics, US sports federations, and the Amateur Athletic Union (non-profit sports organization) use social media in their professional capacities.

Social Media

Twitter, Instagram, and Facebook

Twitter, Instagram, and Facebook are three of the more popular social media sites around the world. These sites are fashionable brand building opportunities for teams, leagues, athletes, and communications professionals in the sports industry. Facebook reached one billion monthly active users worldwide in late 2012, and crossed the two billion user barrier in June of 2017 (Facebook, 2018). During the same reporting period in 2017, Twitter had 326 million monthly active users (Number, 2018). Instagram is the late bloomer of the three, but this photo sharing site has overtaken Twitter, with 800 million monthly active users during this time period (Most, 2018). Sports organizations use social media for a variety of reasons: to increase fan loyalty, grow their businesses, develop new partnerships with sponsors, and improve sales or overall revenue.

Twitter was established in 2006 as a social media tool by Biz Stone, Evan Williams, and Jack Dorsey (Johnson, 2009). When the tool was first introduced, communications sent out on Twitter used just 140 characters to send messages (tweets) over the internet. Users were able to draw up a profile limited to 160 characters on the site and a user picture can be posted. They could choose who to

Exhibit 4.1 *Facebook and Twitter Monthly User Stats*

	Facebook	Twitter
Introduced	2004	2006
2010	608 million	100 million
2014	1.35 billion	241 million
2018	2.167 billion	328 million

Source: Newsroom, 2018 and Number/Twitter users, 2018

follow on Twitter, as well as use the retweet (RT) feature to send out tweets they have read that they think will be of interest to their followers. Twitter has developed a very smooth interface with many sports websites, allowing the user to tweet out an article with a few taps on a screen or the keyboard. Tweeting from all types of smartphones has become effortless. The hashtag (#) component to this social media site allows the user to comment on a hot topic or have their tweet (with the hashtag) easily identified by those who want to find tweets about a particular topic. There is a trending topics capability now that permits users to involve themselves in popular discussions immediately.

There have been many applications developed over the years to make the Twitter experience easier and also more engaging for users. Twitter added a function that allowed users to send a six second video clip through Vine, which was introduced in 2013. Vine is no longer supported by Twitter, but users still have the ability to use video in a variety of forms. Twitter has added many features that have made it easy for advertisers to use this social media platform more advantageously. One of those features is Twitter Analytics. In 2017, Twitter doubled the number of permissible characters on tweets to 280. Software and apps have been developed to enhance the Twitter experience on iPhones, Android-supported products, and other devices. Twitter lists make it easier for communications professionals and reporters to follow a select group of athletes, teams, or reporters who cover the same sports beat. Those with Twitter feeds can tweet in more than one language, which is perfect for World Cup stars who have soccer fans all over the world. The former Pope, Benedict XVI, had separate Twitter feeds in Arabic, English, German, Italian, Portuguese, French, and Spanish. A direct message (DM) feature was introduced that permits a user to send a tweet to just one follower. Those who like to post their tweets to Facebook now have a button supplied by Twitter that makes it very easy to do this.

Facebook was started in 2004 by a Harvard student as a way to meet fellow students on campus. That student, Mark Zuckerberg, expanded to other Ivy League campuses and now Facebook is a widely popular social forum used by the young and old. With its popularity, Facebook has also found a way to generate revenue as the company reported earnings of $40.7 billion in 2017 (Facebook, 2018). Users can post a profile and photos to their Facebook page, and there are privacy settings

Exhibit 4.2 *Instagram Monthly User Stats*

2010	Introduced
2013	90 million
2017	800 million
2018	1 billion

Source: Number/Instagram users, 2018

that can be used to share some information while keeping others private. Users can update their status, such as changes on the job, a recent marriage, or the birth of a child. Facebook provides users with the ability to share content, to "like" a post from a "friend," and to comment on the posting of a photo, a story, or a change of status.

Most sport organizations, teams, leagues, and businesses in the sport industry have Facebook pages. Many athletes also have a Facebook page that they use for developing their brand and interacting with fans. Sport communication professionals post content to these sites in order to create a conversation around their organization, but also to drive traffic back to their organization's website. Facebook has created applications that enable easy connectivity with smart phones, tablets, and most sport organization websites. An icon at the beginning or end of most news articles permits easy posting to Facebook.

Instagram was the brainchild two Stanford grads: Kevin Systrom and Mike Krieger. This social media site, introduced in 2010, provides the user with a simple method to repurpose digital photos and then share those photos on multiple platforms. There is an Instagram app for iPhones and the Android operating system. The company has become a favorite of many sport organization websites, as well as social media platforms operated by these teams, leagues, conferences, sport federations, and other businesses. The company reached the magical one billion monthly active users mark in 2018 (Considine, 2018). Instagram was purchased by Facebook in 2012 but Systrom and Krieger are still very involved in the leadership of the enterprise. The company introduced Instagram Stories, which permits users to share video and photos together while also being able to add text, stickers, and icons. Like Facebook and Twitter, Instagram has become a very popular venue for athletes to speak directly to their fans, build their personal brand, and also promote companies they sponsor. International soccer stars like Beckham, Renaldo, Messi, Gareth Bale, and Neymar dominate the list of athletes with the most followers on Instagram (Most, 2018). LeBron James is the lone basketball player and American to break the top 10 as of mid-2018 (Most).

With this rise in the use of social networks such as Twitter, Instagram, and Facebook, media companies, college athletic departments, professional sports teams, leagues, and other sport organizations have, with varying degrees of success and emphasis, attempted to take advantage of this popularity and build audiences with these tools. Many sports journalists use Twitter and Facebook to post stories or informational updates, and to comment on games, athletes, teams, and other events during the course of the day. Journalists have many reasons to follow athletes, coaches, and team executives. They can keep up with breaking news, develop story ideas, and even get quotes for stories. When journalists tweet, they are most often trying to find breaking news, connect to fans, and promote their work on other platforms (Schultz & Sheffer, 2010). Twitter allows reporters and athletes to connect to readers and fans outside of their geographic area too; Twitter is global. Some journalists use Twitter to contact sources for a story and Twitter has also become a great way to get to know other sports reporters you can follow, or who you would like to follow you (Swasy, 2017). One cautionary note echoed by Shi Davidi, a Toronto-based sports reporter, is that reporters and other sports communications professionals in the sports industry need to understand that the Twitter experience does not represent all readers or all sports fans (Aguilar, 2017). The Twittersphere is passionate, but there are other opinions out there. As but one example, Facebook is regularly (monthly active) used by more than five times as many people as Twitter.

The communication arms of all of the major professional sports leagues use Facebook, Twitter, Instagram, and other social media platforms to create interest in their games, teams, events, and leagues. College athletic departments use them to promote their programs; these platforms are used by the marketing and the sports information departments. Facebook and Twitter have upgraded their technology to make it easier to post and add pictures and video. Instagram is based on the sharing of photos but with the advent of Instagram TV (IGTV), this platform now enables users to post video up to 60 minutes in length. This creates new possibilities for communications professionals who have access to video production studios. This also might be a budgetary rationale for some sports organizations in the upgrading of video production and the hiring of staff who have these skills. There are many social media sites that can be used to promote teams, athletes, sports organizations, and brands with smartly produced video. With the establishment of the ACC Network, conference schools have invested heavily in this very proposition, to the tune of an estimated $100–120 million worth of studio and production facility upgrades, along with equipment purchases (Smith, 2018).

Athletes and coaches at every level of play have become active in using social media. The information they provide has created news opportunities for reporters, but has also created controversy because tweets and posts are viewed by some as an attempt to avoid the mainstream media outlets. *USA Today*'s Thomas Emerick wrote that Twitter gives athletes even more power "to circumvent the modern sports writer [and to leave] journalists further out of the brawl" (Twitter, 2009); this theory has been supported by empirical research (Sanderson & Kassing, 2012). Some members of the Italian and English speaking media had announced that they would no longer report the updates that cyclist Lance Armstrong tweeted because the seven-time Tour de France winner had refused to speak directly to the press during the 2009 Tour of Italy/Giro d'Itlaia (Taciturn Armstrong, 2009). Golfer Tiger Woods posted a message to the media and public on his own website months before he had a press conference or submitted to one-on-one interviews with the Golf Channel and ESPN in early 2010. Woods attempted to use his website to shape the public debate about the state of his marriage and the many published reports about his personal life. Many in the press resented this tactic and even the late Arnold Palmer, one of the great golfers and sports icons of all time, thought Woods needed to get out and talk to the media (Ferguson, 2010).

Caroline Williams—Director of Communications—USA Basketball Advice

Social:

First and foremost: stop and think before you post. That goes for both the professional account(s) you may use and your own personal accounts. If it gives you pause, if there's even a chance it could be taken the wrong way, reword or do not post.

USA Basketball currently uses: Twitter (@usabasketball, @usab3x3, @usabyouth), Instagram (@usabasketball, @usabyouth), Facebook (usabasketball, usabyouth), and YouTube (therealusabasketball) on a regular basis.

USA Basketball's general rules about following accounts: Are they connected somehow to basketball or are they a heavy influencer, such as Kevin Hart, who is a known basketball fan? We follow USA Basketball athletes and coaches (both junior and senior team athletes), basketball federations, the USOC and other Olympic-related accounts, basketball media, university basketball accounts, NBA, WNBA, G League teams, etc.

Do:

- Respond to fans/followers on a regular basis.
- Be respectful of opponents.
- Be respectful of others.

- Think before posting. And then think again. And then make sure you proof it before you go live. And check it once more. Once you post something, it's out there forever.
- If you're working with a team on an account, try to use a common voice and style that aligns well with your team or brand.
- Use video and imagery.
- Keep posts positive.

Don't:

- Don't be overly bullish about a 78-point victory.
- Don't put other teams down.
- Don't disrespect a tournament's host country (or your host institution).
- Don't post personal and/or private information that might have been heard at a team meeting unless you make sure the athlete or coach is okay with it.
- Never post a rumor about something —always stick to the facts.
- Don't be afraid to own up to a mistake.
- Don't treat the team account as if it were your own.

Common Mistakes:

Posting too much or too little. Obviously, there will be times when you have to break this rule. On game days, for instance, will have more items to post. On a daily basis, however, once a day on Instagram or about five a day on Twitter are generally accepted targets. Your followers don't want to be spammed, nor do you want them to forget about you.

Not tailoring posts to each platform. How a tweet is written should be very different from your Facebook post. Same message, different delivery.

There are many athletes that have not had the benefit of the advice offered by Caroline Williams. Tweets by athletes have sometimes drawn the ire of fans and management. Kevin Love of the NBA's Cleveland Cavaliers, formerly with the Minnesota Timberwolves, tweeted that his coach Kevin McHale had been fired before the move became official (Pucin, 2009). Former NFL wide receiver Chad 'Ochocinco' Johnson announced on his Twitter feed during training camp that the Bengals' first-round draft choice, Andre Smith, had just signed. When this turned out to be false, Smith's agent had to use Twitter to refute Ochocinco (Wilner, 2009). Tweets by Wayne Rooney and Jack Wilshere, two stars of the

English Premier League, drew the ire of the UK Advertising Standards Authority. This regulatory body felt that their tweets were really Nike ad campaigns and they did not clearly disclose this to their followers (Holt, 2013). Two potential 2012 Olympians, one from Greece (Paraskevi Papachristou) and the other from Switzerland (Michel Morganella) were kicked off their national teams because of racist tweets. Recently discovered tweets made by several MLB players (Trea Turner/Nationals, Josh Hader/Brewers, and Sean Newcomb/Dodgers) before they became major leaguers were the subject of multiple apologies when these tweets were circulated to a much wider audience. The most embarrassing of these episodes involved Hader, who had just appeared in the 2018 MLB All Star Game. He was confronted with these tweets by a large group of reporters in the locker room soon after the game. There are many lessons that can be learned from all of these examples. One lesson is that communications professionals can be valuable advisors to the athletes, coaches, and other executives they work with. Providing a second opinion before a tweet is being sent, or chats from time to time about the proper conversations to have on social media can prevent some of these problems, but not all of them. A sincere, public and direct apology is a very good idea, if offensive behavior on social media is discovered (also see Chapter 11: Crisis Management). Sports fans are, for the most part, willing to give someone a second chance, but the offending party must *deserve* that second chance.

Twitter has become a great source of breaking news for fans, reporters and news organizations. NBA All Star Joel Embid is very popular on Twitter. He has not only posted some very funny tweets, but also provided new information for reporters covering the Philadelphia 76ers. It is a good bet that all local reporters who cover the 76ers in Philadelphia follow Joel Embid on Twitter. When the former General Manager of the 76ers, Bryan Colangelo, became involved in a Twitter fiasco that cost him his job, Embid's tweets reacting to news updates became news themselves. Manu Ginobli, the San Antonio Spurs legend, announced his retirement on Twitter; so did two-time NBA champion, David West, formerly of the Golden State Warriors. Tweets by LeBron James reacting to tweets by the 45th President of the United States have also become news for sports reporters covering the NBA. In fact, many NBA players have made news on Twitter reacting to tweets by President Trump. Singer Carrie Underwood has had some newsworthy Tweets while watching her husband Mike Fisher play hockey for the Nashville Predators. One tweet in particular was probably not appreciated by members of the NHL Officials Association.

"This game is being called so insanely awful, I can't even..."

—Tweet sent by Carrie Underwood during Nashville Predators game against the Pittsburgh Penguins (@carrieunderwood, May 31, 2017)

Twitter and Facebook can be valuable resources for fans who want to find game times, to see how their favorite team did in their last game, to view updates while a game is being played, or to just feel connected to a favorite player or team. These social media sites also can be used by the local beat writer to follow their assigned teams, to learn what a player is up to, as well as to find new story lines about the leagues they cover. Many of the professional athletes in leagues like the NBA, NHL, the Premier League, La Liga, and the NFL follow their colleagues on Twitter. Reporters also follow their colleagues on social media. The aforementioned professional leagues and college leagues in the US, like the Big Ten, SEC, and Pac 12, also post video highlights of recent games on their Facebook pages, as well as references to their main website to try and encourage friends to log onto the website. Each of these organizations use their website as a promotion for e-commerce opportunities, like the purchase of T-shirts, jerseys, game tickets, and hats. Sports information directors working for these leagues are charged with managing the websites and the social media the leagues deploy to develop interest in their game. From a management perspective, it is a good idea for all communications professionals to maintain a dialogue with the revenue-producing side of the house. Members of the ticket sales office, sponsorship department, and the marketing executives might have some interesting ideas that can be implemented on the team's website, Facebook page, Twitter feed, or Instagram account.

Twitter and Facebook updates from a league like the Big Ten, the Ivy League, or the NBA are written by communications professionals hired by each of these leagues. The posting of these stories, video, audio, and photos is a full-time job. Many of the leagues also have a full time staff member hired to produce interesting content for their networks and all of their websites (e.g., NBA Entertainment and NFL Films). Well-written tweets, interesting stories written by league-employed communications professionals, and eye-catching pictures and video all serve the marketing interests of these sports leagues. However, the communications professional is also writing and posting for the benefit of the large press contingent that follows these leagues, their players, owners, and coaches. An interesting tidbit tweeted by an NBA communications professional can generate two or three stories written by the local beat writer in Chicago, New Orleans, or Dallas, where franchises are located. In many cases these same stories will be posted on several different Facebook pages, and also mentioned in tweets by NBA sportswriters and fans. The NBA may not have directly monetized a particular event or story, but the reader has maintained interest in the product through well-written pieces by sports writers or by members of the NBA Communications office. Many of these stories, photos, highlights, or video productions find their way to Facebook pages in China, Europe, or South America, and they help to make these athletes, teams, and organizations global brands.

The goal of creating loyal readers is why Twitter and Facebook are used by news-papers like the *Washington Post, New York Times,* and *USA Today*. Each one of these media companies wants to attract readers on multiple platforms. As one example, the *Washington Post* sports department has multiple feeds on social media, written and updated by sportswriters and editors. Soccer Insider, Wizards Insider, Redskins Insider, WashPostHS, Terrapins Insider, and Capitals Insider are all *Washington Post*-hosted Twitter feeds that help inform fans and readers but also, hopefully, drive readers to the newspaper or to its website. The global editor for Reuters, Dean Wright, sees social media like Twitter and Facebook as a good thing. "If great storytellers use those platforms to display their knowledge, access, expertise, and abilities, I think that is a marvelous advance" (Emerick, 2009).

In a 2010 study, reporters were asked open-ended questions about how and why they used Twitter (Schultz & Sheffer, 2010). Their number one reason was to break news and the number two reason was to promote their own media outlet. Other rea-sons cited were to connect with the audience, to become better journalists, and also to provide opinions about news of the day. But a follow-up study found that more than half of reporter tweets included personal commentary (Sheffer & Schultz, 2010). In a study of more than 2,700 tweets from reporters at over 50 newspapers, it was found that the use of Twitter by reporters to share the content of others can increase engagement with their own news organizations (Artwick, 2013).

Twitter has proven to be invaluable as a tool for fantasy football participants. The ability to follow tweets from players all over the league, from reporters that cover each team, as well as from communications professionals of each team and the NFL all permit the fantasy football aficionado to marshal plenty of information every week to establish a competitive roster (DiFino, 2009). Many well-known media outlets have established fantasy football experts to report regularly on Fantasy results each week. The NFL Network, ESPN, NBC, and CBS have assigned reporters to provide regular updates and advice to football fans who put together fantasy football teams. Many writers and fantasy football experts have set up their own websites in an attempt to monetize their expertise in this area.

Twitter has made the NFL Draft interactive. Agents, players, fans, teams, and the league all tweet and respond to each other during, before, and after the NFL Draft. College coaches on Twitter offer tweets of congratulations to play-ers that were just drafted (Borelli, 2009). Several teams actually announced who they had drafted via Twitter, before NFL Commissioner Roger Goodell had made the announcement on TV. For the 2013 NFL Draft, a gentlemen's agreement was reached between the reporters that work for the two networks covering the draft: ESPN and the NFL Network (Deitsch, 2013). The reporters not on the air agreed not to report any draft results until after the commissioner had announced each team's selections. Many fans had criticized this practice in previous drafts, opining that they wanted to hear the picks from the commissioner on television. This practice by reporters continues to be a concern, especially of the networks who have the rights to the draft broadcast. The NFL has also asked reporters for networks who televise regular season games to ask their NFL beat reporters to wait until the pick has been announced before tweeting about a draft decision (Johnson, 2017).

During the 2018 Winter Olympics you could find a list of 117 participants with Twitter accounts, posted by NBC and titled Winter Olympians 2018. Many websites for colleges, conferences, professional teams, and leagues compose a list of social media, enabling fans and reporters to follow athletes and coaches, along with the official social media sites of each team. Twitter was a very popular social media site during the 2012 London Olympics. There were a total of 150 million tweets from the beginning of the opening ceremonies to the end of the closing ceremony (Szalai, 2013). While Usain Bolt ran his gold medal winning race in the 200 meters, there were 80,000 tweets per minute, and while the Spice Girls were performing during the closing ceremonies there were 116,000 tweets per minute (Szali, 2013). There were 103 million tweets sent about the Winter Olympics in PyeongChang (Cohen, 2018). Seventeen-year-old snowboarder Chloe Kim grew her Twitter following by 320,000 during the course of the games (Cohen). The three most popular moments on Twitter during the 2018 Winter Olympics involved athletes from Japan; the women's curling team gold medal victory and the performances by skaters Yuzuru Hanyu and Shoma Uno (Cohen).

Social Media in China

Twitter, Instagram, YouTube, and Facebook are censored by the Chinese government, which has opened the door for Chinese companies to operate in the social media space. Some of the more popular social media sites in China include WeChat, Sina Weibo, Youku, and Tencent QQ. Sina Weibo is a microblogging site like Twitter, but also has some Facebook similarities. The NBA signed a deal with Sina Weibo in 2017 to provide the Chinese social media site with exclusive content and highlights produced by the NBA for the Chinese market (NBA, 2017).

Exhibit 4.3 *China Social Media Monthly User Stats: January 2018*

We Chat	1.06 billion
Tencent QQ	803.2 million
Youku	580 million
Sina Weibo	431 million

Source: Kemp, 2018.

Youku is the Chinese version of YouTube. This site was acquired by Tencent QQ and is accessible on PCs as well as mobile phones. ESPN signed a deal with Tencent in 2016 to provide content, including some NBA owned by ESPN (Huddleston, 2016). WeChat has some similarities and functionality to Facebook, Instagram, WhatsApp, and Skype. A study was conducted and published in *Communication and Sport* in 2017 researching the social media habits of sports journalists in China (Li et al, 2017). The authors found that much like their counterparts in the US, sports journalists in China use social media as a news-gathering device (Li). The most popular Chinese networks for the 133 reporters who participated in the study were Sina Weibo and WeChat (Li).

With the massive audience in China, American companies like Twitter and Facebook continue to hold out hope that one day they will have access to users of social media in China. As of the publishing date of this book, these companies have a lot of work to do, or in the alternative, the Chinese government will have to make a 180 degree change in their philosophy. Providing Chinese citizens with unfettered access to conversations on the web does not look promising in the foreseeable future.

Google+, Linked In, Snapchat, and Pinterest

While Twitter, Instagram, and Facebook have the lion's share of the social media market in the sports industry, there are other players in this space that have garnered quite a bit of activity from social media users around the world. These sites are used by many in the sports communication industry and only time will tell if one of these players supplants the big three. It is also true that we could be talking about four or five other social media ideas very soon, with the rapid change occuring in the technology space.

Google+

Google Plus was launched by the online behemoth in 2011. Many describe this application as a social media layer to everything Google. Those that use YouTube, Gmail, Android, Google Calendar, and Google Search now have a social media platform as well. Google+ users can upload personal information, a profile picture, and photo albums. Google purchased photo sharing application Picasa in 2004 to interface with Google+. Tabs in Google+ are appearing on more and more sites, enabling easy sharing of news stories. Users can connect with Twitter, but also offers various privacy settings to limit access to the posted content. Google has created some interesting add-ons to this social media service. Google+ Circles are a way to organize others with whom you are sharing into groups; for example, friends, coworkers, fantasy football team members, New England Patriots fans, and family. This device permits you to see content you have shared that is also being shared by those in your circle. You can also create a Google+ Community by a particular issue or topic, for example, college football or English Premier League.

Google Hangouts Chat allows a group of people—either social or professional—to chat online in a restricted environment. Multiple languages are supported and presents an opportunity for businesses to use this tool for project-based work, or even for sports communications officials to edit the same document. Google Hangouts Meet is a videoconferencing tool aimed at professionals, but it has other uses as well. Google Hangouts on the Air was a feature established by the company for discussions that were designed to be public and accessible by anyone with an internet connection. Former President Barak Obama used this feature as part of a conversation with Americans in conjunction with two of his State of the Union addresses. These Hangouts on the Air were very much like Town Hall Meetings, but they were held online. Former Vice President Joe Biden also used Hangouts on the Air to lead a discussion about solutions to gun violence in the United States. *The New York Times* used this feature to discuss the Supreme Court decision upholding the constitutionality of the Affordable Health Care Act (dubbed Obamacare). After the White House had released its second climate action plan, a Google Hangout on the Air was conducted by the Energy Secretary Ernest Monzi and EPA Administrator Gina McCarthy. They answered questions about the President's plan, as well as talking with the audience about the topic of climate change. Google has since migrated this content to YouTube and encouraged everyone to use YouTube for this purpose moving forward.

Many sport organizations have established a presence on Google+. The content they post is very similar to content that can be found on team, league, and other sport organization websites—photos, news stories, and video interviews. Google Hangout has been used as a cross- marketing device, along with a video conferencing opportunity, by athletes and their sports marketing partners. One can also find some Google Hangout videos posted to various Google+ sites.

Many of the big four professional league teams have their own Google+ websites and a typical site is offered by NBA's Los Angeles Lakers. There is a video interview with a reporter who covers the Lakers, discussing the 2018–2019 schedule. There are multiple interviews with members of the Lakers summer league team and also highlights from some of their games. The former Head Coach, Luke Walton, was interviewed about his views about the team as it was shaping up over the summer, and there were also interviews with the summer league coach, Miles Simon, and the General Manager of the Lakers, Rob Pelinka. The Lakers communications staff posted video of newly acquired player LeBron James' first workout at the Lakers practice facility, along with highlights from an NBA Africa exhibition game where two Lakers participated during the summer (Luol Deng and newly acquired player Javale McGee). A montage of former Laker Kobe Bryant's many 40-point games was also produced by the Lakers communications staff. A nice feature of Google+

is the fact that once video is posted to this site, it will also appear on the Lakers YouTube page. The Google+ site for the Lakers has almost one million followers.

The Real Madrid Google+ site featured coverage of the USA Tour that the team embarked on during the summer of 2018. Photos and video from the tour were included. Real's communications staff posted starting lineups for the games on the tour. Several posts announced the acquisition of new players for the 2018–2019 season, including their new goalie, Thibaut Courtois. Content was posted during the 2018 World Cup with photos showing Real Madrid players participating for their home countries during the tournament. There was a video tribute to the departing coach, Zinedine Zidane. There are many photos celebrating the 2018 UEFA Champions victory in Kiev. Real Madrid also announced on their Google+ site that Ronaldo would be leaving to play for Juventus. The Real Madrid site had over 7.6 million followers, which is quite a contrast to the million followers of the Lakers Google+ website.

The official NFL Google+ site features highlights from the 2018 preseason exhibition games, video from tryout camps in Europe for pro prospects, features on the NFL Draft, and tributes to several former NFL stars. There were posts from the Pro Bowl, the most recent Super Bowl, and many videos from press conferences during the course of the season. The site also had highlights from the American Flag Football League (AFFL), which features many former NFL players like Chad Ochocinco and Michael Vick. This site had over two million followers by the end of August 2018.

In response to a security breach of the Google+ site at the end of 2018, Google executives made a decision to shut down the consumer version of Google+. Business and enterprise customers continue to have access to Google+, but by the middle of 2019 Google had shut down the version used by individual customers. Low usage, no growth, and the data breach were all factors in this decision.

LinkedIn

LinkedIn is a social media platform that is primarily used by professionals to post bios and resumes online. The company was established in 2003 and continues to grow, with 500 million users reported by the company in 2018. LinkedIn went public in 2011 and has been very popular on Wall Street. LinkedIn has been the subject of many acquisitions rumors; ultimately Microsoft purchased LinkedIn for $26.2 million in 2016 (Lunden, 2016).

Once becoming a member of LinkedIn, the user can join groups (communications professionals in sports) with similar interests. Members, called "connections" can also recommend other connections for particular skillsets, such as writing, social media expertise, or sports broadcasting. LinkedIn can be used as a search engine for business contacts in a particular field; for example, college sports communication. LinkedIn services are available in multiple languages. Members can post business references, while human resource departments can use LinkedIn to search for a pool of potential employees—such as professional teams looking for someone who can sell season tickets. Prospective employees can easily forward their LinkedIn profiles to employers when asked for a bio or resume. For students looking for a job, this social media website can be a valuable resource. LinkedIn has also added a service called LinkedIn Resumé Builder that is a resource for members just starting out or changing careers who want to tweak their resume for employers in a new industry.

The company has added many premium services that have boosted revenue. There is a tool called Sales Navigator for members in sales business who are prospecting for new customers. This tool could be helpful to the sport communication professional that has started a new business. A newly minted sport communication graduate can pay an extra fee under the heading of Job Seeker, which gives their resume an extra boost within the LinkedIn community. There is a service for employers who are hiring. This premium service provides data from LinkedIn members that fit a certain profile. The service could be very valuable to a company like the SEC Network or Fox Sports 1, that is looking to build out a sports presence for their network due to recent expansion. For sport communication businesses, like CBS Sports, NBC Sports, ESPN, and *Sports Illustrated* looking to staff their marketing department, LinkedIn has two solutions. The first is a bank of data on potential employees with marketing expertise, easily searchable within the LinkedIn membership. There is also a premium service called Marketing Solutions, which can further enhance the marketing efforts of these companies. There are many groups sport communication professionals can join to establish a larger network and for professional development. For those looking to develop skills, the site offers LinkedIn Learning. Members who pay a subscription fee can watch training videos under the professional development on the subjects of business, creative, and technology.

LinkedIn has established a service for high school students and parents of college bound students called University Pages. If a high school student is interested in studying communications, journalism, or sports management, LinkedIn can provide information about alumni from selected schools that have these majors. Students can see where these professionals now live and work. A similar feature also exists for graduates interested in a particular company. The Company Pages on LinkedIn provide job seekers more information about businesses or sport organizations. LinkedIn also provides members access to blogs of LinkedIn Influencers, like the Dallas Mavericks owner Mark Cuban, Microsoft founder Bill Gates, and former President Barak Obama, as well as many members of the media industry. This move by LinkedIn had an immediate increase in page views. The site saw a 63% jump in the first quarter of 2013 (Kaufman, 2013).

Snapchat

Like Instagram, Snapchat was developed by students from Stanford and debuted in 2011. The site enables users to share photos and text that disappears after 10 seconds. They have developed other user options, like Snapchat Stories that can be created and will remain on the site for 24 hours. Through Snapchat Discover, users can view partner-created content, such as news articles, game highlights, and short video clips. Teams, leagues, and other sports organizations who have established agreements with Snapchat can post videos of events, team practices, and short clips from games. The NFL developed a partnership with Snapchat Discover. Content is produced from video supplied by the league, or Snapchat will post Snaps and short video clips sent by Snapchatters. The user generated content is then repurposed by NFL Media. This arrangement with the NFL includes content from the Super Bowl, the NFL Combine, and the NFL Draft. The NBA has produced short videos on the site to promote their league. The strategy of the NBA and NFL is to try and reach a demographic that might not be watching their games on a regular basis. The Snapchat user audience has historically trended younger than any of the other social media sites popular with the major sports leagues.

Fox Sports and Snapchat collaborated during the 2018 World Cup on two different ventures. One was a series of videos professionally produced by Fox exclusively for the Snapchat audience. The other arrangement consisted of highlights, photos, fan reactions, and Snaps from Snapchatters mixed with content produced by Snapchat editors.

Pinterest

This social media site was launched in 2010 and by early 2018, had acquired an estimated 175 million unique monthly visitors (Aslam, 2018). Much like an online collection of bulletin boards, Pinterest gives the user the ability to "pin" or share images and content onto "boards" they create and organize. Each user's main "board" or page contains groups of boards organized by user-identified subject; in each board, each pin contains a collection of images typically linked to a website, blog, or other online source. Like Twitter, Pinterest users can follow users or specific boards, and can comment on specific pins. When a user pins content or a photo, other Pinterest users can view those images and comments, and can click on the pin to display the source website or related content. Pinterest users have the ability to re-pin an image they found on other Pinterest boards to share that content on their own board and followers. Pinterest users can create private boards for their own viewing or shared boards that display pins to followers. Research into Pinterest users reveals that many more women use this social media website than men (Aslam, 2018). This is an opportunity for sports businesses that are attempting to attract more women as customers and fans. Just as some sports organizations might use Snapchat to reach the 18 to 24-year-old demographic, Pinterest can be an opportunity for communications professionals to reach female sports fans and generate new fans of their teams and leagues.

Many sport organizations have developed an official Pinterest website. The Boston Red Sox official Pinterest board promotes the purchase of Red Sox gear in many of their more prominently placed pins. The site contains boards with photos from Fenway Park and a separate board with photos from their spring training facility in Florida, which is sponsored by Jet Blue. There are many pins of photos of former players, tributes (boards) to former players in a series of related pins, and pins of multiple photos from their World Series celebrations and victory in 2013 World Series. There is the obligatory series of photos of the Hall-of-Famer Ted Williams, as well as the future Hall of Famer, Big Papi, David Ortiz.

The South Sydney Rabbitohs of the National Rugby League in Australia have a famous fans board on their Pinterest site. Celebrities like Russell Crowe, Jimmy Fallon, Jay Leno, Oprah Winfrey, and others appear in pictures pinned to this board. There are a total of 14 boards on the Rabbitohs site, including a Rabbitohs pets, legends, Christmas, and baby membership. Just like the Red Sox Pinterest site, there is also a board promoting Rabbitohs merchandise.

News organizations also have developed Pinterest sites. *Sports Illustrated* has developed a Pinterest site with a total of 20 boards with pins featuring the covers of the *SI* Swimsuit issue (of course!), an NFL board, an NBA board, an MLB board, and a college football board.

The key for sports organizations as it relates to Pinterest is what can be gained by posting photos to the site and managing and updating the content on a regular basis. If a sports organization has a staff of two in their communications department, a decision must be made as to how many of these social media sites deserve their attention. What will be the return on investment when staff time is being spent on Twitter, Facebook, Snapchat, Pinterest, and any of the many other social media sites available to the sports fan who also has a limit in terms of engagement?

Insight from Communications Professionals

College and Professional Sports

Stephen Czarda was the Managing Editor for the Washington Redskins communications department, and the sports communications director at UNC-Greensboro Athletic Department, is now with the Wake Forest SID office in charge of social media. Czarda started as an intern for the NFL franchise's website five years ago and slowly worked his way up to Managing Editor. He holds an undergraduate and master's degree in sport management from George Mason University, where he is also an adjunct professor.

Q. How has social media changed the sports industry?

Czarda: Social media has given fans the opportunity to interact with players, staff members, and even the teams themselves in ways that weren't previously available. Additionally, social media is at the forefront of all team coverage, along with news.

Q. What social media platforms did you use in your position with the Washington Redskins? What do you do now as a college sports information director?

Czarda: I used my own personal Twitter account that was primarily focused on Redskins content, but I also had access to post on the team's social media accounts on Facebook, Twitter, Instagram, and Snapchat. As an SID at UNC Greensboro, we use three of these platforms. We don't do much with Snapchat. We focus our Facebook content more towards families of players and alums. Instagram content is focused on the current players and prospective student athletes. Twitter is used for news.

Q. What is the biggest mistake you see communications professionals make on social media?

Czarda: I think there's a fine line between creating a unique online identity that can interact with fans against one that either posts too frequently or is venturing into areas fans aren't following them for on a daily basis. It is difficult to stay on one side of this line, but if a reporter can add just a little bit of personal flair without going overboard, it will benefit their following.

Q. What is the official NFL Policy as it relates to Twitter and other forms of social media?

Czarda: NFL policy regarding Twitter and other forms of social media is constantly updated. Each team and the league have official Twitter feeds, and many players also have their own Twitter accounts. The communications professionals for every team are available to advise the players as to their social media activity and the NFL has a large staff in their communications office to not only post on social media but also advise teams. The NFLPA has a communications office available to members of their union and during rookie orientation; the use and abuse of social media is a topic that is discussed with all incoming players. Agents for the players in the league provide advice regarding social media and Twitter; some players hire their own communications professionals to handle their social media activity.

National Football League – Social Media Rules

Effective Date: May 4, 2016

Welcome to the rules for the official social media accounts of the NFL! These pages are a place for NFL fans to get news and updates, discuss their favorite teams, the season, and all things NFL. These "Rules" govern all social media accounts operated by the NFL, the National Football League, its Member Clubs, NFL Ventures L.P. and each of their respective officers, directors, agents, employees, representatives, and licensees (collectively, the "NFL Entities" or the "NFL").

By posting or reposting ("Posting") comments, photos, visuals, videos, or other materials ("Your Content" or "User Content") to social media web sites and applications owned/operated by the NFL, including, but not limited to, Facebook, Twitter, Instagram, Vine, Snapchat, or similar sites ("NFL Page(s)"), you agree that the NFL can use Your Content— including any names, voices, images, and performances that content contains—for any purpose. Further, by Posting Your Content on an NFL Page, you grant the NFL a perpetual, non-exclusive, irrevocable, fully-paid, royalty-free, sublicenseable, and transferable worldwide license in any and all media (now known or hereafter devised) to use, reproduce, distribute, display, perform, modify, and create derivative works based upon Your Content for any purpose, including advertising and promotion, without notice, attribution or payment. You also waive any moral rights associated with Your Content. You certify that you are the original author, creator, or owner of Your Content, and that you have the right to Post it. You also certify that you have acquired and hereby grant to the NFL all necessary rights for the NFL to depict anyone who appears in Your Content , and that the NFL's use of Your Content in accordance with this license will not violate or infringe upon anyone else's rights.

User Content does not necessarily reflect the opinions or ideals of the NFL Entities or the entities and/or individuals that operate the NFL Pages, and the NFL does not endorse any opinions expressed by fans on the NFL Pages. The NFL does not represent or warrant the accuracy of any statement or product claims made on the NFL Pages and is not responsible for any User Content on the NFL Pages.

We may revise these Rules from time to time. The Rules are governed by the laws of the State of New York without regard to or application of its conflict of law provisions or your state or country of residence.

Source: NFL.com/help/social-rules

Q. *Do fans have WiFi access at FedEx Field?*

Czarda: All stadiums in the NFL have WiFi access as fans have become more interconnected with each other and the league through social media. Fans want to experience the in-game entertainment, but they also want to post on social media about actually being at the game while also checking things like their fantasy football teams.

Q. How do you use Facebook with your fan base and the press?

Czarda: While reporters tend to use Twitter as their go-to source for news, Facebook reaches a different audience and, in particular, an older crowd. Facebook also tends to have more positive responses on posts in comparison to Twitter and Instagram.

Q. Give us an example of an NFL player or a member of the Redskins who you think makes great use of social media and explain why you think that player is using this medium so well.

Czarda: I think one player that has done a tremendous job maximizing his own personal brand on social media is running back Derrius Guice. Considered a first-round talent entering the 2018 NFL Draft, Guice slipped to the second round because of reported character issues before the Redskins selected him. Early on in his time with the Redskins, Guice became a fan-favorite because of not only his constant interaction with them, but because he was posting things like himself buying his mother—who raised him as a single parent—a new car and raising money for philanthropic efforts.

Q. How can communications professionals use humor on social media to engage the fans and the media?

Czarda: I think it's important to showcase individual personality, especially in the form of humor when it is appropriate. Gone are the days where cookie-cutter communication such as simply posting a box score will allow a reporter to stand out.

Q. How many Twitter sites does someone in your position usually have to monitor? Is there ever time for sleep for a communications professional in this day and age of 24/7 news and tweets?

Czarda: One tool that really lends itself in a favorable manner to reporters and in-house media members is TweetDeck. This platform provides real-time updates on tweets of followers along with the ability to monitor certain hashtags and lists. In the NFL, for example, teams tend to create lists of the other teams in the league to see what they're posting.

Q. Any other examples of teams or leagues who do a really good job with Twitter?

Czarda: The NBA does a phenomenal job of utilizing social media platforms, particularly Instagram. With a "digital-first" mindset, NBA teams push highlight reel plays while also allowing their players to showcase their own individuality. In turn, NBA players tend to have a much higher following on social media than NFL players. For example, as of July 2018, LeBron James had more than 39 million followers while Tom Brady had 4.2 million followers.

Q. *What advice do you give to athletes in regards to social media? Do teams work with their athletes to help them handle this medium?*

Czarda: Athletes should use social media to promote their own brand in a positive way. Athletes should be able to showcase who they are as a person beyond the playing surface, but keep content positive, clean, and engaging. This, in turn, can lead to potential sponsorship deals and extra income for the professional athlete. While team and social media employees will help out and provide advice if asked, they don't normally run individual personal accounts for the players.

Q. *What advice would you have for coaches who are on social media?*

Czarda: Similar to athletes, find ways to interact with other users but don't open up yourself too much to criticism and remember to block out any negativity.

Q. *What is the single best tweet or social media post you have seen and why? Best use of Instagram?*

Czarda: It is truly a difficult task to pinpoint one social media post in particular; there are many athletes who have been creative. I will say that those that are popular have the same traits: engaging, organic, and unique.

Q. *Talk about how you work with the marketing department, ticket sales, suite sales, etc. to coordinate your social media strategy. Do you have any suggestions in this area for young professionals just starting out in the industry as to how they should coordinate with other parts of their organization?*

Czarda: I think young professionals should be open to feedback from other departments, but should still stand strong on what they believe will be engaging content. Of course, every department has goals they must hit that are both unique to that department but also company-wide goals as well. Work with those departments to find out what exactly their goals are, but also find ways to create synergy so that any social media and digital media obligations are engaging.

Q. *What social media should all communications professionals be using and why?*

Czarda: I think from a professional outlook, professionals should be using Twitter to not only follow breaking news, but see how reporters present their coverage and how they interact with their followers.

Q. *How do you deal with negative comments on social media? Advice for our students in this area?*

Czarda: I think the biggest thing is determining what form of negativity it is. Is it someone voicing a concern with a critical tone or is it someone simply being negative? If they're constructively giving feedback, respond and try to create an open dialogue. If they're just "hating," however, just ignore. Social media feedback shouldn't be a driving force in how you view your own work.

Q. *Do you write a blog? How can that be used to get the message out to the fans and the media? Name a few good sports blogs you follow—can be outside the NFL too.*

Czarda: While I do not write for a blog outside of my professional obligations, I think following depends strictly on what you're looking to read. If it's something that is a quick-hitter of sorts, *Bleacher Report* has a lot of unique monthly visitors. But if something more satirical is what you're seeking, *Deadspin*, and *Barstool Sports* could be places to go.

Nonprofit Sports Industry

Cody Norman received his undergraduate and master's degree from George Mason University (Fairfax, VA). He was a sports public relations intern at Walt Disney World (Lake Buena Vista, FL) and then became the Public Relations Manager for the Amateur Athletic Union (AAU) at their headquarters on the Orlando Walt Disney World property. AAU is one of the largest, nonprofit, volunteer, multi-sport event organizations in the world. The organization has been in existence since 1888 and formed their partnership with Disney in 1996.

Q. *What are your duties with AAU and how long have you been with them?*

Norman: I have been with the AAU for three years. We have about 30 AAU national championship events that our office manages, most of which are in the Orlando area. My main role is finding ways to get media—both traditional media and non-traditional influencers—to positively talk about our events. I talk to our event managers, sport chairs, coaches, and team contacts to find unique human interest stories about our athletes and coaches that might make their trip to AAU national championship events improbable or interesting. I write the press releases, media advisories, and blog posts, and pitch media on covering our athletes and our events. Other duties include representing media while they are onsite, scheduling photographers/videographers to shoot stories, fulfilling credential requests, managing social media accounts, and creating communications calendars for the organization.

Q. *What did you do for Disney before this AAU job?*

Norman: I spent one year as an intern on the Disney Sports public relations team prior to being hired as the public relations manager at the AAU. My team at Disney managed all the public relations efforts for events at ESPN Wide World of Sports Complex, the runDisney business (manages themed weekends around half-marathon and marathon road races), and Walt Disney World's recreation program. That included finding and pitching human interest stories or news stories to the appropriate media outlets, building media lists, repping media at events, writing and distributing press releases, scheduling photo/video opportunities, and managing the Disney Sports News media website. My team also handled any photo

Exhibit 4.4a *US Olympic gold medalist Laurie Hernandez poses for media during the 2017 AAU James E. Sullivan Award presentation at the historic New York Athletic Club in Manhattan. (Photo courtesy of AAU).*

or video opportunities with sports celebrities at Disney Parks and supported the larger Disney Parks public relations team on any property-wide initiatives, like Star Wars Weekends, Frozen Summer Fun, and the opening of an expansion at Disney's Animal Kingdom Park.

The ESPN Wide World of Sports Complex has a large indoor arena, a 9,500 seat baseball stadium (Atlanta Braves partner), a separate large baseball complex, two indoor fieldhouses, a softball complex, youth baseball fields, a track and field complex, and other multi-purpose fields.

Q. Describe how you use social media in your role with the AAU.

Norman: Social media and public relations efforts go hand-in-hand. We use social media at the AAU to start and maintain conversations about our national championship events. We take and post photos of record-breaking performances, photo finishes and other extraordinary accomplishments by our athletes. At our AAU Girls Junior National Volleyball Championships, the largest volleyball tournament in the world, we activate on social media with a photo booth onsite at the Orange County Convention Center.

Q. What are some mistakes you see communications professionals and athletes make with their use of social media?

Exhibit 4.4b *NCAA Men's Basketball Champion Joel Berry III is interviewed by members of the New York media during the 2018 AAU James E. Sullivan Award presentation in New York City. (Photo courtesy of AAU).*

Norman: Communications professionals and athletes often forget that everything on social media is forever. People are too quick to respond emotionally to critics or negative events and think that just because they've deleted a post, this means the world will never see it again. Young people, in particular, have to be very careful about things they are posting to their social media accounts. The news about Josh Hader (MLB player with the Milwaukee Brewers) is just the most recent in a long list of rising athletes who were discovered to have posted something derogatory, racist, sexist, or just downright embarrassing on their social channels when they were young people. Age is not an excuse for ignorance, especially in a media cycle that focuses so much on negative issues.

Q. Do you have tips for students in college now to prepare them for jobs where social media will be part of their inventory of responsibilities?

Norman: Social media is becoming a stronger focus for PR professionals every year, especially as more and more journalists use it as their primary means of communication. College students should know the difference between using social media for personal communication and using social media for professional communication. Remember, again, that everything you put in a public space is forever—and that is still true if you have your profile set to private. Also, college students should

Exhibit 4.4c *Elite athletes from across the country collide each year at the AAU Junior Olympic Games for the largest youth track meet in the United States. The Games have produced some of the most accomplished track and field athletes in history, including Carl Lewis and Jackie Joyner-Kersee. (Photos courtesy of AAU.)*

take the time to learn the intricacies of social media, and understand how they can leverage the various tools and platforms to build relationships. Although face-to-face communication is becoming rarer, the foundation of a PR position will always be relationships.

Q. *What hardware and software do you use on the job?*

Norman: I use an iPhone and a combination photo/video camera. I also use editing apps like Canva, which makes professional-looking graphics from a phone, and iMovie, which allows me to edit video in a timely manner for social media use.

Q. *What is the number one skill students should develop while in college?*

Norman: The number one skill every student should develop in college is the ability to develop relationships. Hardware, software, social media platforms, and communication strategies change regularly, but you have the greatest chance of success at the next level if you are able to build genuine relationships with mentors, peers, and other resources in your field.

Exhibit 4.4d *Track and field phenom Brandon Miller (O'Fallon, Missouri) has won nine gold medals at the AAU Junior Olympic Games, the largest annual youth track meet in the United States. Miller set the 15–16 year old boys 1500 meter record with a time of 3:58.10. (Photo courtesy of AAU).*

Exhibit 4.4e *The AAU Girls' Junior National Volleyball Championships, held annually in Orlando, includes teams from more than 10 countries each year. The champion of the international division is matched against the champion of the United States for a world championship that airs live on ESPN+ on the final day of the event. (Photos courtesy of AAU.)*

Q. *Where do you see the media relations/communications/sports information career heading in the next 5–10 years?*

Norman: The media relations/communications/sports information career is becoming increasingly focused on social media. Social media is a lower-cost marketing option, so more and more businesses are allocating marketing dollars to advertising on social media. Professionals in these positions will need to know how to target specific groups with social media ads, as well as how to effectively cut through Facebook's changing algorithm to ensure the organization's content continues to be seen by the largest possible audience. Communication with reporters and journalists will likely be almost entirely on social media and sports information professionals will have the benefit of taking their team's stories direct-to-consumer with a robust social media strategy.

Soccer Club in Europe

Koen te Riele is the press officer and communication manager of PEC Zwolle, which plays in the premier football division (Eredivise) in the Netherlands. PEC Zwolle

Exhibit 4.4f *Nine-time Olympic gold medalist Carl Lewis speaks to members of the media at the AAU Junior Olympic Games. Lewis's The Perfect Method has partnered with the AAU to provide youth athletes with a proven and measurable way to achieve their goals. (Photos courtesy of AAU.)*

has gone through some growing pains and name changes over a 100-year history of competition. The city of Zwolle is located on the Ijssel River, east of Amsterdam. Mr. Riele has been with PEC Zwolle for six years and has been a fan of the club since he was six years old.

Q. What are your official duties with the club?

te Riele: I'm responsible for all the communication, so I make sure there are new website articles and social media updates every day. Together with my department (three guys in total), we also make match programs for every home game, club magazines (twice a year), business magazines (twice a year), and the one and only PEC Zwolle newspaper every summer. Besides, I also arrange all the interviews with players, the coach, and the board during the week and after the games we play. And, of course, we monitor everything (on- and offline) that is said about the club.

Q. How do you use social media to do your job?

te Riele: The use of social media is very important in our communication strategy. It's a good tool to influence the public opinion by using the right words and pictures/graphics. Also, social media is important to show the values of the club. PEC

Zwolle is known as a transparent, ambitious, and enterprising club. We want to express these values through social media.

Q. *Do your players and coaches also use social media?*

te Riele: Some of our players use social media. They are mainly active on Instagram, Snapchat, and some of them on Twitter. Our coach is on Twitter and our board members also.

Q. *What skills are important to learn for young people who want to start a career in media and communications for a team in soccer leagues in Europe?*

te Riele: First of all, you need to be sports minded. It is also important to be stress-resistant, and you have to interact well with different types of people; players, for example, are from a variety of different social backgrounds. You also need to be creative, because sometimes it's a hard job to make good content, like when the results are disappointing. On the other hand, when the team is winning you've got too much good content and you need to be a decision maker.

Q. *Who are the major media outlets who cover your team and your league?*

te Riele: FOX Sports and NOS (Dutch public broadcast corporation) are the biggest outlets on television. The NOS is also the biggest outlet on the radio. Then there are many newspapers and magazines like *De Telegraaf, De Volkskrant, Voetbal International,* and *NRC* [NRC Handelsblad] who write daily about football. And, last but not least, our local news reporters visit twice every week (the match and training before the match): *De Stentor, RTV Oost,* RTV Focus, and Sportief Zwolle.

Q. *What is the procedure for interviewing players after games?*

te Riele: After the game, journalists can pass on their requests to me. I will get the right players out of the dressing room and make sure they are good to go. Because the interviews take place 10 minutes after the game, some players are emotionally still in the match, depending on the result. So I always check, with a little chat, if they're ready for a good media performance.

Q. *Do you or a member of your staff provide media training or advice for your players?*

te Riele: I'll talk every few months with the team about social media and interviews. Sometimes about a specific topic like attitude/body language in front of the camera, sometimes in general. As well I talk with players individually. Because I see all the interviews, I can give the players tips and tricks.

Q. *Does your team or league have rules about the use of social media?*

te Riele: The club has a social media protocol, with do's and don'ts about the use of social media. For example, the rules are about the moments of posting (not the night before a game), about what is good to say (appreciate the fans, talk about the team-effort) and what you don't say online (for example: the referee is rubbish). In my experience, players and board members respect the protocol, it's a good guide.

Summary

With all of the talk about the death of newspapers and good sports writing, it appears that new media and the constant advances in technology may actually enhance the market for the sports story teller. With more avenues to tell stories, the opportunity for a citizen journalist to break through and become a paid blogger for an aggregator like Yahoo, Fanhouse, Bleacher Reports, or the Huffington Post is much greater now than it was a few years ago. This certainly presents pressures for the media to constantly produce interesting content. Both the reader and television viewer have a greater number of places to find innovative, ground-breaking stories. With all of the new sports networks being created, there is a constant need for those skilled in talking about sports on the air, as well as those who are good at producing written content.

It remains to be seen if this new media can create stories with the depth that magazines and newspapers can produce; a tweet is only 280 characters. It is also a continuous concern as to the reliability and accountability of this new generation of communication. Is the information produced accurate, well-sourced, and transparent? Still, the old media must stand behind their stories and be accountable for inaccuracies and bad reporting. A member of the Twittersphere that has no connection to a media company does not bear the same responsibility for mistakes, but mistakes made on social media, can be just as harmful.

Athletes, coaches, sports information personnel, and organizations that regularly use social media have created both opportunities and obstacles for sport journalists. News has been created by many of these tweets but there is a concern that the media has been bypassed. Athletes and coaches should be careful, however, that they take these communication devices seriously. A well thought-out plan is always the best way to proceed. Twitter can be a great way to build community. Those giving advice to athletes using social media should not discourage the use of social media; a better avenue is to educate them as to the strengths and weaknesses of all these new applications and websites.

The speed with which innovation takes place in the communications industry can be dizzying. Cisco produced a router that can download data equal in size to all of the books in print at the Library of Congress in one second. That would qualify as fast. Innovation has caused the broadcast networks and their employees many sleepless nights; the newspaper industry has had their problems, too. Who is to say that the next new media invention will not create countless new jobs in the sport communication industry?

The key for today's students will be to constantly improve their communication skills while also understanding that the ability to engage and retain their audience will be important to market survival. A strategy of making use of Twitter or Instagram with your daily reporting duties may be necessary to maintain and build an audience. Learning new skills relative to video may attract another group of readers to your website or blog. Just as those in the sport communication industry had to adjust to the emergence and popularity of radio and television, they have to be ready for emerging technology and be ready and willing to adapt. Predictions that the sky is falling have been heard before, but we are still here.

Discussion Questions

1. After reading this chapter, what do you think of the future of newspapers? Do you read a newspaper? Where do you regularly look for information about your favorite sports teams or athletes?

2. Do you think social media has helped or hurt the newspaper business? Is social media more valuable as a marketing tool than a communication tool? Do college students spend too much time on social media?

3. Will the eBook development help the publishing industry? Do you think more young people will want to read if books and other publications are made more available in electronic formats? Do you use the eBook option in your classes?

4. Do you think social media have encroached on the privacy of today's athletes and coaches? How about the privacy of the communication professional? Is it a good thing that some athletes are tweeting about their personal lives? Does social media permit people to hide behind the internet?

Suggested Exercises

1. Go to the Facebook page of the local newspaper in your area. What types of stories are they posting on the site? Compare their posts to the paper's website and the print newspaper.

2. Join Twitter and become a follower of a team, an athlete, and a reporter that covers that team. How regularly do they tweet? Compare and contrast their tweets for news value, fan value, and commercial value.

3. Watch an athletic event streamed to your smartphone or your computer. Compare your viewing experience with that of watching the same type of event on TV. Do you think streaming is going to replace TV, or is the TV experience so much more enjoyable that this will never happen?

4. Watch a news program or sporting event and observe how they integrate Twitter into the conversation. Go on Twitter and tweet out comments about the program or sporting event.

5. Compare and contrast the views on social media of Caroline Williams, Cody Norman, Stephen Czarda, and Koen te Riele. What advice would you give to athletes if you were asked to give a seminar to a college athletic department on how to effectively use social media?

5 | Sports Information Specialists

Amy Ufnowski's typical day is anything but typical. The eighth-year ACC (Atlantic Coast Conference) Director of Communications thrives off expecting the unexpected and, depending on the season, sport, and time of year, she's busier than most in a profession that is anything but a traditional 9 to 5 job.

"There isn't a typical day in this profession," Ufnowski said. "Every single day is different. The day goes by so quickly because it's a constant output of work."

But don't think that bothers her in the least. She thrives on being one step ahead of the athletes, coaches, and media as she tirelessly works to promote the ACC.

"Expecting the unexpected in season is sometimes the most exciting part of the job," Ufnowski said, who worked at Marquette University for eight years prior to joining the ACC, "You can't forecast on a day-to-day basis what is going to happen because it's out of your hands. Game days are great. You can be the worst team in the league and have a huge upset and vice versa. I love the atmosphere around games. It's unpredictable and that's what makes the job worthwhile, because something great has happened to a team or a player."

On any given day in season, Ufnowski will be writing press releases, working on game notes, pitching stories to the media about the teams she covers, working with the SIDs of her member institutions to promote those student-athletes, working with her coaches, and generally working to promote the ACC in any way she can. Out of season, there's still work to be done, but on a much less hectic schedule.

So why does she work in a field few have heard about but many would love to be in; one in which you must be willing to sacrifice personal and social time to get the job done?

"It's the thrill of pitching stories and having that pitch be accomplished by an outside entity," Ufnowski said. "I think what we do is like sales. You're selling your team and great human interest stories. I like to get those out there and have our players put out in the best light possible. If I'm obnoxious or not, with the media, it still all comes down to building relationships with local, regional, and national media and pitching those stories and getting the most positive information out about the ACC."

The sports Ufnowski has overseen in her job throughout her career seem endless: men's soccer, wrestling, basketball, tennis, volleyball, women's soccer, lacrosse, swimming and diving, and men's hockey. And her career has taken her from the US Olympic Training Center in Colorado Springs, Colorado, to the University of Denver, to Marquette, in Milwaukee, Wisconsin, and now to the ACC.

With a bachelor's degree in exercise and sport sciences, with an emphasis in sport management, and a minor in business administration, Ufnowski is now working towards a master's degree from Marquette.

"I don't know if this is my career for the next 30 years of my life," she admits. "But I wanted to see how far I could get within college athletics."

Having read a first-hand account of what it's like to be involved in sports media relations, a grasp of the different entities of the sports mass media introduced in Chapters 1–4, we turn now to an in-depth look at the world of the sports information specialist.

What's in a Name?

They go by many different names: sports information directors (SIDs), sports media relations practitioners, communications director, sports information specialists, or simply a public relations (PR) specialist. Despite the different names or acronyms, it's what they do on a daily, weekly, monthly, and yearly basis that bring notoriety, prominence, recognition, and a continual, and hopefully, positive brand name to a sport organization, an athletic department, a specific team and its coach, and most importantly to the athletes and student-athletes that are the backbone and foundation of the organization.

At the collegiate level, a group of sports information specialists created an organization in 1957 called the College Sports Information Directors of America (CoSIDA) in an attempt to bring some uniformity and standards to the profession.

"Previously, sports information directors, as a group, were a part of the American College Public Relations Association, but most SIDs at those ACPRA meetings felt that a separate organization was needed. There were 102 members at the original meetings; since that time, CoSIDA has grown to over 2,400 members in the United States and Canada. The association is designed to help the SID at all levels. It is the desire of the members to have the profession take its rightful place on the decision-making levels of college athletics. Everything done is geared to this objective." (CoSIDA.com)

CoSIDA is an important organization that represents the best interests of SIDs at all levels of college athletics. A national convention is held yearly, and all members are encouraged to attend to discuss growing trends and new topics that affect the industry. CoSIDA also asks its members to abide by its Code of Ethics.

Confidentiality is directly related to ethics. In the fast-paced world that is sport communications, especially at the collegiate level, the SID will be privy to information that is confidential with regard to a student-athlete's health and private matters (information that is protected under the Student Privacy Act), information that is not for the public or media's consumption (time-sensitive material), and behind-the-scenes or inside information. In collegiate athletics, academic records, personal and family matters, and injuries are some items that should be kept confidential unless the student-athlete specifically allows release of such information. At the professional level, sports information specialists should adhere to their organization's policy regarding the release of injuries and other such sensitive information. It is of the utmost importance that the SID is honest and trustworthy with confidential information, respecting the athlete and the organization.

CoSIDA Code Of Ethics

In order for the Sports Information Director to serve their institution and the College Sports Information Directors of America most effectively, s/he should observe these basic tenets:

- Always be mindful of the fact that s/he represents an institution of higher learning and that exemplary conduct is of paramount importance.
- Intercollegiate athletics is an integral part of the total university program, not the dominating force. Promote them accordingly and not at the expense of other areas.
- Policies of the institution, its governing board, administration, and athletic hierarchy must be acknowledged and supported, whether or not the Sports Information Director agrees with them.
- A challenge of controversial policies should be resolved within the appeals framework of the institution. No public forum should be encouraged or developed. Internal problems, such as disagreement over policy, should not be "leaked" or in any other way exploited.
- Loyalty to the athletic administrator, his/her aides, and the coaching staff is imperative. No confidence should ever be violated, regardless of how apparent or insignificant it might appear. Above

all, avoid criticism of staff members. Administrators and coaches should be encouraged to answer questions from the media honestly and accurately. In the event they choose to avoid a sensitive question or area for any reason, it is incumbent upon the Sports Information Director to honor the "no comment" by refraining from any subsequent "briefing" session with the media, particularly in an informal atmosphere where misuse of the intonation could be most damaging to all concerned.

- Respect for athletes and their values should be encouraged. The confidence of an athlete must not be violated, particularly as it pertains to information regarding academic, disciplinary, and health information. To release this type of information without the athlete's permission is a violation of the Family Privacy Act of 1974. Also it is highly unethical to falsify weights, heights, and other personal data.

- Relations with the media must be established and maintained at a high professional level. Fairness in the distribution of information is paramount, regardless of the size or importance of the publications or stations. Student media must be accorded the same privileges and rights of the commercial or noncampus media.

- Operation of all facilities in which members of the media may be in attendance should be professional in all aspects. Cheerleading in the press box, for example, is gross and undesirable. Other distractions, such as extraneous descriptive and unrelated announcements, should be discouraged.

- Criticism of officials is totally unethical, either before, during, or after a contest.

- It is essential that the Sports Information Director be cognizant and observant of all institutional, conference, and national governing body regulations as they pertain to his/her functions within the framework of his/her institution.

- It is incumbent upon a Sports Information Director to take immediate and appropriate action when he/she has knowledge of a fellow/sister Information Director who has violated the CoSIDA Code of Ethics, institutional, conference, or national regulations.

- Participation in organized gambling activities is discouraged.

- Endorsement of products or commodities which reflect a conflict with regular duties is not in the best interests of the institution or the profession.

- Lack of cooperation by members of CoSIDA in not responding promptly and accurately to requests is deemed irresponsible, hence unethical.

From: College Sports Information Directors of America © 2019 CoSIDA Code of Ethics.

A career or profession as an SID can be extremely gratifying because you have the opportunity to work with some of the finest athletes in the world, and some of the most brilliant minds in the coaching profession. At the collegiate level especially, SIDs have the opportunity to make a positive impact in the molding of young people, namely student-athletes. Know that no two days are alike and be prepared to expect the unexpected. After all, it is the world of public relations, and dilemmas rarely arise at a moment of our own choosing (see public relations dilemmas detailed in Chapter 11). And there are certainly days when the SID will look down at the clock and wonder where the time went.

"Like many sports careers, there are few typical days for SIDs, who may spend a morning editing a future media guide, an afternoon welcoming media for a team day, and an evening tracking statistics in the press box during a game. If you're a sports junkie who enjoys the idea of working closely with a team, coaches, and athletic department, as well as the media that cover the teams, sports information positions could prove rewarding" (Angst, n.d.).

Being a part of a winning program with continual, annual success creates new avenues for being creative in promoting your team or organization. The SID builds myriad types of skills such as time management, communication, teamwork, and multi-tasking capacities regardless of a team's success. Conversely, losing teaches humility and character. Try covering a team that perpetually loses and it will certainly teach the SID ways to bring about creative public relations practices and skills while attempting to remain positive; there are always silver linings to everything. And because SIDs interact with so many people driven by a competitive nature, conflict is sure to arise during losing times, thus helping to build effective problem-solving skills.

So what exactly is the sports information profession and what does the SID do? Simply put, a sport organization's SID is usually the first contact a media member, a fan, an opposing team, or even an alumnus has with the sport organization. They are the liaisons between those respective entities and the sport organizations. They work very closely with the coaches as a member of their support staff. And it's imperative to leave the most positive lasting impression possible with whomever they come across, because ultimately the bottom line of the job is to create a memorable and lasting positive image of their sport organization.

SIDs are like puppeteers, pulling the public relation's strings from the behind-the-scenes, allowing the flow of positive information to reach media that covers the team, its coaches, and athletes, without gathering their own fanfare. And the contemporary reality that technology presents today allows the successful SID to utilize a multitude of platforms to garner attention from both the media and the general public (i.e., Twitter, Facebook, Snapchat, Instagram).

Whatever the mode or means achieves the utmost coverage is the path one must choose in order to be the most successful and creative SID. Sometimes it's a thankless job, and very seldom will the SID be congratulated for actually doing the job at hand and doing it well. The trick to knowing great work has been achieved is seeing one's coaches and particularly student-athletes receiving the recognition they deserve through whatever medium it may appear—be it a feature story in a local paper, a taped interview that runs on the nightly news, or a regional or national award bestowed on an athlete based on the SID's nomination of that respective athlete. Recognition of a job well done may come from a media member using a note, story idea, or just having a positive influence from dealing with the SID. Very few people remember or acknowledge a job well done, but a mistake has a lasting impression and will most definitely be brought to one's attention.

An easy way to recognize what a SID does is to compare it to that of being a doctor on call, but instead of his/her office being a hospital or an operating table, the place of work is an athletic facility or playing field. In a contemporary 24-hour news cycle, breaking news never sleeps; whether it be positive or negative, proactive or reactive, messages and assistance need to be delivered to the media and the general public in a timely, organized fashion. Hence, SIDs are always ready to spring into action at a moment's notice, which is why they can most often be found in the office, especially when their athletic teams are in season. It's not out of the ordinary for a sports information specialist to work 60–70 hours in a week during the season. Think about it. The profession ultimately revolves around the team's sporting event. And when, typically, are those events? They're not at 2 p.m. on a Tuesday afternoon (unless it's a mid-week baseball game). They're in the evenings, and during the weekends, when contests are scheduled at many different times, ranging anywhere from mid-morning to late in the evening. So, it's easy to see why the work week for a SID can sometimes span all seven days of the week and easily double the working hours of a normal profession. Now throw in the social media responsibilities in a now 24/7 news cycle, and one could argue that the SID is never truly "off the clock," even in the off-season.

Coach's Corner by Craig Esherick

The relationship between a coach and his/her sports information director (SID) or director of communication is an important one. Your communication professional has the ability to provide the press with valuable background information when the coach (or sports administrator) makes decisions that might seem unpopular or ill-advised at the time. Media relations professionals, like assistant coaches, should be aware of the head coach's philosophy or, in a similar vein, their sports administrator's vision for the organization. Coaches should spend time with their communications professional, talking about their sport, how they perceive their role as coaches, and what strategies they prefer; this background enables the SID to form an accurate picture of the coach as a professional. That picture of the coach will be what the press sees when they talk to the organization's director of communication. A knowledgeable SID can set the stage for a great relationship with the members of the media.

Sports communication specialists should also be encouraged by coaches to sit in on practices, training exercises, and film sessions. The director of communication should meet the coach's family and spend time with assistant coaches or other important members of the team/organization. They should be comfortable around all of the athletes; this is true at any level (college, national team, professional sports). Remember that the SID will be a trusted advisor for these athletes when they are working with the media. Postgame interviews with the press take place during the emotional highs and lows of a season. A relationship based on trust between the player and the SID helps to manage the ups and downs of a season, which promotes a positive image for the player, coach, team, and ultimately for the school or sport organization.

Coaches experience many of the same emotions as athletes before, during, and after contests. The coach also has the added pressure of the job insecurity associated with the coaching profession. A good working relationship between the coach and SID will benefit the coach during these emotional times. A smart SID can sense when a coach is on edge after an emotionally charged game. A few quick thoughts about how to handle the impending questions can help refocus the coach to the task at hand of discussing the game or event rather than focusing on any frustrations of that contest. The director of communication who knows the coach can also sense during interviews when a well-timed interruption can prevent the coach from saying something that under normal conditions the coach would not have said. Many experienced media relations professionals who work for teams in the NBA and the NFL have saved their coaches penalty fines with a timely joke or cautionary comment.

The communication professional and the coach should discuss how to handle news conferences, how the press should contact the coach, the policy for locker room interviews, and other procedural issues relating to media access. Setting the ground rules early will help the interaction between a coach and SID grow into a productive and professional partnership. Developing a relationship based on mutual trust will allow a good SID to offer advice the coach may not want to hear. It is a long season. No coach is perfect—and the SID may have to remind the coach of that from time to time.

Essential Skills

So what is required of a SID? "There are three simple rules to follow to be well on your way to being successful: 1) communicate well; 2) get along well with others; and 3) be a leader" (Shutt, 1998, p. 5).

Again, communication is the backbone of the industry. Working well with co-workers, coaches, athletes, and media is of the utmost importance because you can't do your job on your own and being a team player will make life much easier for you. And there's a great cliché that comes from the military: "Lead, follow, or get out of the way." That phrase couldn't be truer in this profession. Grab the proverbial bull by the horns, step forward, and assume the responsibility bestowed with open arms. Get the job done, but don't hesitate to delegate to one's subordinates to help with the completion of one's tasks.

In addition to the three key components listed above, what follows is a look at some of the more specific skills required of a SID.

Effective Writing Skills

The skill set required to be a SID is extensive, and the backbone of it all is successful, creative, and excellent writing skills using the Associated Press (AP) style. If you're not a good writer, then sports public relations may not be for you. That said, if you're not already a great writer, you can acquire those skills via practice and patience. But know that a professional cannot succeed without a thorough understanding of the parts of speech, sentence structure, grammar, spelling, punctuation, and theme development, etc.

The ability to understand and use proper grammar and AP style while writing on deadline is arguably the most important aspect of the SID's job. The SID's writing will be seen and viewed by many in both news story and news release form, and it will be in many different types of work, such as news releases, news stories, tweets, social media posts, game notes, media guide text, feature story writing, internal organization communication, speech writing for the coaches and student-athletes, and various other forms of writing.

News Releases

The lifeline and arguably the most important job the SID will have is writing news releases. A news release, which is very similar to a news story written by the print or broadcast media, represents *hard news* and utilizes the inverted pyramid comprising the 5Ws and the H (who, what, where, when, why, and how). When a sporting event has concluded, the SID will write a news release and distribute it to the media for those who weren't there in attendance. The story is also usually placed on the athletic department or sport organization website. The mechanics of how to write news releases will be discussed in detail in Chapter 7.

Game Notes

A conglomeration of quick points, story lines, anecdotes, statistics, trends, historical information, records, updated profile information, and more, is compiled on a game-by-game basis by the SID and used by the media to assist with game stories and the SID's own news releases.

Media Guide Text

Regardless of the sport he/she is responsible for overseeing, the SID is the chief executor of a media guide, which includes writing and editing the entire body of its text. While creating a media guide will be discussed in detail in Chapter 8, the media guide is arguably the first-ever glimpse into a program or a sport organization. In it will be rosters, schedules, bios of players and coaches, historical information and records, last season's statistics, and myriad other information fully promoting the sport from both a recruiting and media coverage standpoint.

Contemporarily speaking, media guides are accessible in print, but also as an online entity through the school or organization's official website.

Feature Writing

Very similar to writing news releases, feature writing uses the *soft news* angle to tell a story about athletes, coaches, or administrators. The SID usually writes features for the department's game-day program, the department or organization's website, and smaller media outlets that may utilize a feature story that focuses on a hometown athlete or coach.

Keen Visual Skills

This skillset is almost just as important as having effective writing skills. The SID needs these skills for understanding basic layout, design, and presentation of media guides, game notes, and other public-facing materials, like pamphlets, brochures, etc. that will emanate from his or her office. The SID will also need great visual ability when it pertains to the department or organization's website to know what will be visually appealing to the reader.

Strong Speaking and Interviewing Skills

Not only does the SID work with the general public, always presenting the best foot forward for the organization with great customer service skills, but he/she will also need excellent speaking skills for opening press conferences, pitching and selling story ideas to the media that cover the athletes and teams, and doing the same with the administration. There will also be times when the SID will act as an interviewer with coaches and athletes when writing news releases and feature stories and they need quotes to enhance the information they're providing.

Effective Problem-Solving Skills

As is fully explored in Chapter 11, there are certainly going to be public relations dilemmas. Some of the most trying times while being the SID involve crisis management in the most unlikeliest of times. Therefore, a good SID will be able to think on his or her feet in high-pressure situations in an attempt to deflect as much as possible any negative publicity for the athletes, coaches, program, department, and organization.

Good Interpersonal Skills

You can't do this job by yourself. It requires organization and teamwork. In many cases, SIDs have subordinates and delegation is key to being an effective leader. Good leadership starts at the top and trickles down through the ranks. Know that no SID's job can be done on one's own, so being a true team player is also vital to his or her own success. Outside of the organization, the SID must foster a professional and amicable relationship with members of the media and have a knack for creating and maintaining a social media presence.

Responsibilities of the SID

Now that the SID's necessary skills have been explained, what are the areas where skills are put to use?

Game Management/Game Day Media Operations

Depending on the sport and the amount of media coverage it receives, game days and the days leading up to them may be hectic. And once the game is over, there's no rest for the weary. The SID will turn right back around and repeat the same process all over again in preparation for the next event. The game itself is the premiere showcase for the job, and it will be a culmination of all the hard work and positive endeavors leading up to and following the event.

Interviews

When a member of the media wants to speak to a coach, an athletic department employee, or a student-athlete, that media member will contact the sports information director to set up an interview. Traditionally, the unwritten rule of the business is to expect 24 hours to process the interview request. At the collegiate level, the SID is dealing with many different schedules, such as classes, study hall, practice, and strength conditioning, so it can take time to fulfill the request based on a student-athlete's hectic schedule.

Of course, there will be interview opportunities pre- and post-game day. Postgame simply entails a press conference with the coach and requested players. Pre-game usually consists of interviews a few days prior to a game that will ensure proper coverage prior to the contest.

It also falls on the SID to not just assist with the setup of the interviews and seeing them come to fruition, but it is a key responsibility to "coach up" the athletes prior to the interview itself. The SID deals with all types of athletes—some who love the limelight, others who view the interview as a chore or task, and those who avoid the media at all costs, simply because of shyness. It is the duty of the SID to assist in any way possible, which could include sitting in on the interview with the shy athlete, or acting as a mediator if an interview could turn precarious. It's not out of the realm of responsibilities for the SID to limit questions for an athlete that can only give a few minutes of their time.

At certain schools or sport organizations, handbooks are created and given to the athletes as it pertains to dealing with the media and how to always represent the organization in the best manner. The handbooks (such as the NFL player's handbook) are used as a tool or reference for athletes to consult in how to work with the media. For an example of such a handbook, see the end of this chapter for a portion of West Virginia University's *Media Relations Handbook* given to all student-athletes each year.

Working with Athletes and Coaches

One of the most appealing truths of working as a collegiate sports information director is the daily interaction with student-athletes. The SID is ultimately in the business of shaping and molding a portion of a young person's future. The SID will get to know their personalities, their strengths and weaknesses, as they pertain to interviews and public appearances. And by working with them, the SID will work closely with coaches when it comes to nominating student-athletes for national awards, such as All-America status, Academic All-America status, and all-conference accolades.

Articulate and punctual student-athletes will oftentimes be requested multiple days during a week or month for interviews (depending on the sport), so it's imperative that the SID work to alleviate the media pressures imposed on those athletes by creating a workable schedule to fulfill those requests. Study hall, strength conditioning, practice, and classes have their time-consuming rigors. The effective SID will be able to juggle the student-athlete's hectic schedule with interviews desired by the media.

Working with coaches has the same principles as working with athletes. The SID is ultimately helping promote the team or school and working closely with the coach is a necessity. In season, the SID will be in constant daily contact with the coach, fulfilling interview requests, getting quotes for his/her own requirements (i.e., news releases), and working for the betterment of the athletes. The effective SID will create a working interview schedule for the coach, especially in season, when the coach's time is in high demand. Out of season, the SID will still be in touch with the coach, depending on the sport and the coach's schedule, on a daily or weekly basis.

Working with the Media

The effective sports information director cultivates an open and honest relationship with members of the press and the community. The relationship is based on trust and mutual respect. The SID understands the push for details on a big story among competitive media and forgives the overzealous reporter who becomes a bit too pushy on occasion. The journalist recognizes the administrative constraints on the SID and accepts limitations placed on release of information, albeit grudgingly.

Both sides understand the give-and-take nature of the business. The SID provides a little more information on one story and expects the journalist to follow up on a lukewarm story idea in return at some point. As payback for the same deal, the reporter, on the other hand, expects the SID to deliver a useful nugget of information (at the very least) for a major breaking story under deadline and competitive pressures.

The key to working with the media is to always be truthful and honest in all situations. That will build credibility and rapport as the working relationship cultivates.

WVU Media Relations Handbook

The following is an excerpt of the West Virginia University Media Relations Handbook that is presented to Mountaineer student-athletes at the beginning of each season.

10 Important Highlights when Interacting with the Media & Social Media

1. *Interviewing is a learning experience.* You'll learn as you go and gain more comfort with time.
2. *Remember who your audience is.* Most interviews end up in print, audio, or video for the public. Mountaineer fans, alumni, fellow teammates, your coaches, and your opponents to view.
3. *Always be on time.* If something comes up, let your athletics communications contact know.
4. *Never give out your personal cell phone number.* The athletics communications office will never do so either.
5. *Never agree to an interview unless it has been coordinated through athletics communications office.* This helps to avoid contact with unauthorized people and keeps you safe and your team safe and compliant with NCAA legislation.
6. *Nothing is "off the record."* Even if the talk is friendly, it can be repeated and used by reporters as a "reliable source."

7. *If you can't say something nice, don't say it at all.* Use your best judgment in representing yourself, your family, your teammates, your coaches, and your university.

8. *Answer personal questions at your own comfort level.* You are not required or expected to answer questions of a personal or family nature unless you feel comfortable doing so.

9. *Good media relationships can give you a positive public image for a lifetime.* What you say, how you say it, and how you handle the interview will go a long way in what people think about you, your teammates, your coaches, and WVU.

10. *Be sure a speaking engagement, banquet, or other function is permitted.* Before you agree to it—check with your coach, athletics communications contact, or the compliance office to be sure the event is NCAA compliant so you don't put your eligibility at risk.

Guidelines for Social Media

- *Be smart* about what *photos* you upload or are tagged in.
- Set *privacy settings* to limit access to those who are not your friends.
- Remember *hashtags* and anything you tweet is open to interpretation—*be selective*.
- *Media members* can *follow your every move* and turn *what you say and do* into *story ideas*.
- Represent yourself, your teammates, your coaches, and WVU in a positive light.

Remember: It is a privilege to have media request you for an interview, so represent yourself and WVU the best you can. After all, you are the spokesperson representing your team at that moment.

Get to know your athletics communications contact. S/he handles

- Processing all interview requests.
- Writing press releases, feature stories, and media guides.
- Updating and maintaining the school's official website: WVUsports. com.
- Compiling team statistics.
- Nominations for conference and national athletic and academic awards.
- Select travel to road contests.

- Hosting the media on game days and subsequent postgame interviews.
- Updates your team's social media accounts.
- Monitors your social media accounts.

The DOs and DON'Ts of Interviews

Do:	Do Not:
Be confident & positive	Be sarcastic or lose your cool
Respect your opponent	Be negative or say something that your opponent can post in the locker room to use against you
Praise your teammates and coaches	Be arrogant
Make good eye contact	Have an attitude
Speak slowly, articulate, and concise	Use fillers or slang
Be patient; questions may get repetitive	Hide. A few minutes with the media is better than nothing at all
Be available	Forget your image; your actions are always being observed
Think before you speak, keep it simple, and focus	

Courtesy of West Virginia University.

Working with the Conference/League Office

Just as the SID is a representative of his/her respective organization or team, the conference or league in which the team or organization belongs also employs a Sport Information Director to oversee the entire media operation for that conference or league. For instance, West Virginia University belongs to the BIG 12 Conference, and members of the league staff are SIDs who promote the entire 10-team conglomeration. In the professional ranks, the same hierarchy holds true. For instance, Major League Baseball has publicity directors who promote the entire league, while also working with each team's public relations specialists. Team SIDs will work closely with league SIDs when it comes to helping them prepare their media guides (when they need a team's vital information), when they select weekly league player-of-the-week awards (typically the team SID will nominate players based on weekly performances and after getting approval from the head coach), and

Exhibit 5.1 Big 12 Conference Staff Directory

Commissioner	Bob Bowlsby
Deputy Commissioner	Tim Weiser
Senior Associate Commissioner	Tim Allen
Senior Associate Commissioner	Dru Hancock
Senior Associate Commissioner, General Counsel	Kelvin Smith
Senior Associate Commissioner, Football	Edward Stewart
Associate Commissioner, Communications	Bob Burda
Associate Commissioner, Championships	Dayna Scherf
Associate Commissioner, Men's Basketball & Game Management	John Underwood
Chief Financial Officer	Steve Pace
Assistant Commissioner, Events & Human Resources	Brad Clements
Assistant Commissioner, Governance & Academics	David Flores
Assistant Commissioner, Compliance	Keri Mendoza
Director, Technology and Video Services	Bret Ayers
Director, Digital Content and Strategy	Will Gulley
Director, Media Services	Joni Lehmann
Controller	Catrina Gibson
Associate Director, Championships	Maria Swanson
Assistant Director, Compliance & Governance	Jessica Hamm
Assistant Director, Media Services	Russell Luna
Assistant Director, Video Services	Justin Nusser
Coordinator, Multimedia Design	Robert Rosa
Digital Correspondent	Brittany Graham
Digital Correspondent	Aaron Pryor
Digital Correspondent	Christine Williamson
Executive Assistant to the Commissioner, Manager of Executive Affairs	Melanie Ellis
Administrative Assistant	Regina Everett
Administrative Assistant	Tracy Hunt
Administrative Assistant	Christina Monjarraz
Administrative Assistant	Valerie Rocha
Communications Coordinator	Rachel Coe
Championships Assistant	Carson Hadaway
Will Hancock Communications Assistant	Sam Thomas
Student-Athlete Programs Assistant	Michelle Woods

when compiling the sometimes daily and always weekly updated conference statistics. Those statistics begin with a team's statistics compiled by that team's SID, who submits them to the conference or league, and the league office creates the master daily or weekly conference-wide file.

When it comes to the season's conclusion and it is time to nominate players for conference and national awards, the conference/league SID will assist in the nominations of athletes for everything from All-America or All-Star status to individualized, sport-specific awards.

Historian/Record Keeper

The SID is also the chief statistician for their respective sport and is the keeper of all things as it relates to the organization's historical records. As each game is completed, for whatever sport, the statistics are compiled and used to create and update new and existing records for the team and individuals.

In the offseason, SIDs are always researching records that will help enhance the future coverage of their teams. And the longer they are with the team they're covering, the more of a historical authority they become.

Rules/Compliance Awareness

While a SID is responsible for myriad tasks, one of the most important jobs is to be aware and keep up-to-date with all rules and regulations that are in effect as it relates to the team or organization. This is especially important, and often difficult, for SIDs at the college level because the NCAA has an abundance of intricate rules. One of the biggest factors as it pertains to rules compliance for SIDs to be aware of national signing day, when prospective recruits become members of the collegiate program. It is imperative to be up-to-date on the rules as it pertains to announcing those signings, as well as any other pertinent up-to-date rules that affect day-to-day tasks.

A golden rule of thumb when it comes to compliance: when in doubt, contact your compliance director. Lack of knowledge or ignorance isn't an excuse.

Travel

If SIDs travel with their respective teams, and most of them do, they'll take their SID show on the road. While technology has made the SID's job away from the office much easier (prior to the internet, SIDs had to call in scores and key facts and stats from road games), the job must still be done while away from home.

Traditionally, the SID of a visiting team will rely heavily on the host SID to assist in coverage, especially as it pertains to getting postgame information out to visiting media members if the visiting team and SID are departing the venue as soon as the contest has concluded. This also includes getting post-game box scores to coaches and players prior to the fulfillment of any post-game interview requests.

On the road, and because technologies are far advanced, SIDs can write their post-game releases and send them out to their media contacts immediately upon the conclusion of the game. Good SIDs will have their statistics file to update their master stats, and if there are any interview requests for the coach or athletes, they will facilitate those.

In some sports, such as basketball, the SID is traditionally the visiting score keeper, sitting beside the official scorers, or working closely with them during the game should any discrepancies arise. And while scoring, many are also writing their post-game news release that will appear on the school or organization website, as well as updating their organization's social media presence as the game progresses and concludes.

Social Media

The rapid growth and ever-expanding realm of social media has become another integral part of a SID's job. Simply, social media is an ever-growing presence in all levels of athletics. When utilized effectively and efficiently— and as a key ally for a SID to further promote their product—the benefits of a key tweet or Facebook post can be immeasurable. Conversely, the power of social media's immediacy and the potential (lack of) oversight and control issues it brings can be a nightmare for sports PR practitioners. Far too many times, national highlight sportscasts or media reports begin with social media controversies because it fuels the general public's need for controversy. In the grand scheme, it is important to remember that the news cycle doesn't sleep in our fast-paced, 24-hour news cycle. The internet never sleeps, and news now breaks and is known with the snap of two fingers. Therefore, it is imperative that the effective SID utilize social media when appropriate for the desired positive responses, yet have strong oversight, or rules, for athletes to adhere to in order to prevent controversies in the public realm.

Various Other Responsibilities

The best way to classify this is as "all other duties/responsibilities as assigned." From writing speeches for coaches and athletes, to helping a colleague research or expand their record book section, there are countless other activities the SID is expected to complete in the overall promotion of the organization. Other ways to assist the media include helping obtain photographs and credentialing the media for sporting events. The credentialing process begins with the media agency or personnel applying to cover the sporting event; the SID either grants or denies the request. If the request is granted (all SIDs should have a clearly outlined policy for granting credentials, usually detailed in a media guide, so that no questions of favoritism arise) the SID is responsible for creating a seating chart for the media for the upcoming event.

Pros and Cons of the Job

As the saying goes, there are two sides to every story. That holds true as it pertains to being the SID of a sport organization. While there are plenty of rewarding moments, there can be times of frustration as well, just as there is in any profession. So let's examine some of the pros and cons to working in the sports information specialist profession.

First, being the SID means you'll get to travel. Depending on the level of your organization or team, travel could be local, regional, nationwide, or even worldwide. At the small college level, SIDs may only travel within a specific region, unless tournaments or post-season play leads to further destinations. At the largest colleges, SIDs trail blaze the country while they travel with their respective teams, especially for holiday tournaments, bowl games, and other post-season events. In some cases, teams will take international training trips (such as a summer tour) to destinations across the globe. At the professional level, sports information specialists travel much more frequently and the trips are usually further from home and can often last more than a week.

As mentioned earlier, SIDs at the collegiate level have a hand in molding the life of their student-athletes. That can be very rewarding and advantageous for many SIDs because they are ultimately having a positive impact on someone's future and life.

Sports information specialists also traditionally get various free perks, whether it be team apparel or complimentary tickets to sporting events for family and friends. Water cooler talk also abounds for SIDs. As mentioned earlier, a lot of times the SID is privy to inside information, typically hearing information before the general public. And there's something to be said for being the first to know. Remember, though, that confidentiality must be kept.

Lastly, you'll get out of it what you put into your work, and for many in the profession, it's a lifelong enjoyment of promoting the school or organization that employs them.

Now, what are some of the cons of the profession? Just as travel was a perk, it can also be taxing and make for a long year or season of constantly being on the go. As previously detailed, SIDs put in long hours that almost always include working late nights and weekends. That makes it difficult to have a normal social or family life in-season in this profession.

Lastly, winning and losing marks the best of times and worst of times. If an organization or team is not very successful, the stress levels can reach peaks for SIDs as the frustration level of players and coaches increases. It's important to keep an even keel and remember that a job has to be done win or lose.

How to Become a SID

Now that you have a core background into the sports information specialist profession, how do you become one? First, you volunteer your time immediately with the sports information department at your school in any way, even if that entails being a press row worker (stat runner), and don't take "no" for an answer. If you're a writer, continue to improve your writing ability and enhance your knowledge by covering as many different sports as possible, because that expanded knowledge will be beneficial when it comes to being assigned various sports as SID.

Tips for Young Sports Information Specialists

1. Learn the philosophy of the athletics program, its missions, its goals, its structure, its personnel, and its athletes—past and present. Doing so will only make your job a lot easier.

2. Know as much as possible about the coaches and the athletes; keep a biographical file, statistics, and pictorial data on each. Also, maintain alumni files if space allows. You'll be called upon to track down information at a moment's notice, so having these at your fingertips is a must.

3. Learn the local media, their missions, their target audiences, their structure, and their personnel. Doing so will only assist you in pitching story ideas and the overall promotion of your organization.

4. Know your business. The SID must understand what is going on in the athletic world, the entertainment world, and the media in order to guide journalists to write and tell upbeat, positive stories.

5. Define your public relations target market. Know who should receive information about the athletics program to ensure maximum success. Failure to do so would be a grave waste of time.

6. Learn the production and printing deadlines of local media, and time announcements to attain maximum benefit. Obviously, broadcast media can "break" a story almost immediately. Not so with the print media, which have strict copy and publication deadlines, although most print publications do have websites where they post breaking news.

7. Encourage coaches and athletes to grant interviews, to return media telephone requests, and to take an active part in the publicity thrust. Guide those who are ill-prepared or inexperienced so they will present a positive image and reflect the appropriate view of the university.

8. Identify and suggest good feature stories and personality profiles to the media, whether the stories concern a volleyball player, a cross country runner, or the star quarterback. This all comes from items 1 and 3.

9. Know what types of information and messages are likely to generate the most media interest. Also, recognize the potential results from an organized public relations program focused on athletics.

10. Exhibit courage in crisis situations. Be tactful and informative in times of coaching changes, protests, boycotts, drug problems, or any other potentially awkward situations. Be proactive and honest at all times.

11. Remember that credibility, integrity, versatility, and service are the characteristics that define successful sports information directors. An outgoing personality is an asset to any SID, but can never replace in-depth knowledge of the school's program or consistent and quality information about the program.

Summary

The SID is arguably the most important cog in turning the wheel of the athletic department or sport organization, especially when it comes to promoting its coaches and athletes. The SID is the lead link and liaison between the media, the general public and the athletes and coaches as it pertains to publicity and promotion. During constant interaction with the players, coaches, and media, as SIDs promote their team or organization, they must maintain a professional standard of confidentiality, integrity, and ethical conduct.

There are several essential skills that SIDs must possess, but the core of the profession is being able to write well, especially under deadline pressures. It's also important to have keen visual skills, strong speaking and interviewing skills, problem-solving abilities, and good interpersonal communication skills.

There are numerous responsibilities that fall under the direction of a SID, including overseeing game management, facilitating interviews and press conferences, maintaining a team or organization's social media presence, working with league or conference SIDs, compiling statistics, and maintaining knowledge of important rules and regulations.

There are several pros and cons to the profession, as with any job, ranging from travel and free perks to working long hours, especially in season. But all told, it's a rewarding profession for those who have a knack for writing, have great time management skills, and a desire to work towards the overall positive thrust in creating and molding the positive image of organizations, coaches, and athletes.

Discussion Questions

1. In your opinion, what is the most attractive part of a SID's daily workload? Why? In your opinion, what is the least desirable? Why?

2. What are some of the facets of the job that would come easy for you and, conversely, where would some of your added attention be targeted or needed?

Suggested Exercises

1. Choose your favorite team. For its next contest that is about to be played, assemble some pregame notes that you would hypothetically distribute to the media that cover that team. Find some player anecdotes, historical nuances and records about to be broken that would enhance an SID getting coverage of his or her team.

2. Interview a local collegiate coach and ask about his/her needs from his/her SID. Report back your findings to your class.

6
Developing Interviewing Skills

Interviewing looks so easy on television, but sticking a microphone in someone's face and trying to get a good answer can be extremely difficult. The good interviewers—the professionals who make it *look* easy—actually spend a lot of time in preparation. How the interview ultimately turns out depends a great deal on the time spent before the cameras (or tape recorders) ever begin to roll.

Before the Interview

There are several things a sports interviewer needs to consider before sitting down to actually conduct the interview. Primarily, the interviewer must determine issues, such as method, audience, agenda, theme, setting, stakeholders, and access. *Method* is simply how the interview will be conducted, either in-person, over the phone, or by some other way such as email or text messaging. In situations where there are physical distances involved, or simply sometimes for speed and convenience, interviews will take place over the phone or by email. There is nothing wrong with these methods, but the lack of direct contact sometimes results in answers that are misunderstood or taken out of context. An impersonal interview may also cause the interviewer to miss the subtleties and nuances that go with face-to-face conversation. In this regard, a phone interview is preferable to an email contact, but the in-person interview is the best of all and should be the method used whenever possible.

Audience refers to who will be watching or listening to the interview; it has become especially important in an age of niche sports content where there are potentially dozens of different audiences even for the same media outlet. For example, a local television station may have a sports segment in its noon, 5 pm. and 10 pm newscasts, but all three shows have vastly different viewer demgraphics. (Research suggests that more women and casual fans are watching at noon and 5 pm compared to other newscasts).

The interviewer needs to consider the type of audience, because that will help guide the tone and direction of the interview. LeBron James may appear on *60 Minutes* one night and Jimmy Kimmel the next, but the interviews will be much different because the audiences and their expectations are different. The *60 Minutes* audience expects hard-hitting questions, while the Kimmel audience expects more entertainment. If the interviewer does not understand the audience and its expectations, it can cause some difficulties.

A Thorny Rose for Gray

In October 1999 before a World Series game, NBC sports reporter Jim Gray conducted a live interview with former player Pete Rose. Rose clearly thought the interview was about his inclusion in baseball's "All-Century Team," but Gray focused the interview more on Rose's alleged involvement with gambling on baseball and his attempts to lift his lifetime ban. The interview created a firestorm of controversy, as many thought Gray went too far in his questioning. "It was very venomous, a lot of anger," said Gray, who received death threats and hate mail. "A lot of people were upset. An NBC switchboard operator told me, 'This makes O.J. Simpson look like … nothing'" (Martzke, 2004).

Jim Gray: Pete, the overwhelming evidence that's in that report … why not make that step tonight?

Pete Rose: This is too festive a night to worry about that, because I don't know what evidence you're talking about. I mean, show it to me.

Gray: We don't want to debate that Pete.

Rose: Well, why not? Why do we want to believe everything he says?

Gray: You signed a paper acknowledging the ban. Why did you sign it if you didn't agree?

Rose: But it also says I can apply for reinstatement after one year. If you remember correctly in the press conference … as a matter of fact, my statement was I can't wait for my little girl to be a year old so I can apply for reinstatement. So you forgot to add that in there.

Gray: You applied for reinstatement in 1997. Have you heard back from commissioner Selig?

Rose: No. That kind of surprised me. It's only been two years. He has a lot on his mind. I hope to someday.

Gray: Pete, it's been ten years since you've been allowed on the field. Obviously, the approach you've taken has not worked. Why not take a different approach?

Rose: You say it hasn't worked … what do you exactly mean?

Gray: You're not allowed in baseball, not allowed to earn a living in the game you love, and you're not allowed to be in the Hall of Fame.

Rose: That's why I applied for reinstatement and I hope Bud Selig considers that and gives me an opportunity. I won't need a third chance; all I need is a second chance.

Gray: Pete, those who will hear this tonight will say you've been your own worst enemy and continue to be. How do you respond to that?

Rose: In what way are you talking about?

Gray: By not acknowledging what seems to be overwhelming evidence.

Rose: You know, I'm surprised you're bombarding me like this. I mean, I'm doing the interview with you on a great night, a great occasion, a great ovation, everybody seems to be in a great mood and you're bringing up something that happened ten years ago.

Gray: I'm bringing it up because I think people would like to see … Pete, we've got to go; we've got a game.

Rose: This is a prosecutor's brief, it isn't an interview and I'm very surprised at you. I am, really.

Gray: Some would be surprised you didn't take the opportunity. Let's go upstairs to Hannah. Congratulations, Pete.

Source: Courtesy NBC/MLB

The public uproar following the interview forced Gray to go on the air the next night and apologize; not for his line of questioning, but for "taking some of the joy out of the moment." Gray was vindicated in 2004 when Rose publicly admitted that he had not only bet on baseball, but had bet on his own team while manager of the Cincinnati Reds. NBC Sports Chairman Dick Ebersol said, "Rose owes an awful lot of people an apology, especially to Jim for the pain and humiliation Rose's lying put him through in the World Series" (Martzke, 2004).

Rose's interview brings up another important consideration, that of *agenda*. For 15 years Rose lied to any and all reporters who directly asked him whether he had bet on baseball, as was alleged in the 1989 report that led to his suspension from the game. "I feel he has embarrassed me," said veteran sportswriter Roger Kahn. "I must have asked Pete 20 times, 'Did you bet on baseball?' He would look at me, blink his eyes and say, 'I didn't bet baseball. I have too much respect for the game'" (Dodd, 2004). Interviewers must understand that the people they talk to have a reason for talking, whether it's to promote their own self-interests, deny damaging information, or achieve certain goals. When Rose finally did come clean about his gambling in January 2004 he had two main goals in mind—to sell more copies of his newly-released autobiography, and to try to lift his lifetime ban from major league baseball. "For the last 14 years I've consistently heard the statement: 'If Pete Rose came clean, all would be forgiven,' said Rose. "Well, I've done what you've asked" (Dodd, 2004). According to sportswriter Hal McCoy, who covered Rose for 31 years, "When it became clear he wouldn't get in (to the Hall of Fame) unless he admitted it, he admitted it" (Dodd, 2004).

Interviewers can't do much in dealing with an agenda other than to recognize it and try to push through it. No athlete or coach is going to volunteer difficult or damaging information, which is why interviewers have to keep asking the questions, even if they may be unpopular or even controversial. Regarding the Gray-Rose interview, sportswriter Michael Shapiro observed, "What if Gray had not pushed Rose? What if he had reduced himself, as so many of his colleagues have, to the role of asking, 'So, big fella, heckuva night, huh?' Reporting is neither about deference nor is it always about asking nicely. It is about finding out. We need, we want to know, be it profane or sacred" (Shapiro, 2000).

As an interviewer you must also learn to recognize your own agenda. In other words, there is no such thing as a completely objective, unbiased interview, because every interviewer has his or her own set of personal values, beliefs, and opinions. For example, consider the December 2002 interview between Bryant Gumbel of HBO's *Real Sports* and Martha Burk. At the time, Burk and the National Council for Women's Organizations were pushing for the Augusta National Golf Club to admit female members. Burk and the NCWO tried all kinds of ways to pressure Augusta National, including a threatened protest at the Masters golf tournament. (The tactics failed at the time, but in 2012 Augusta National did admit its first female member). The following was part of the exchange between Gumbel and Burk:

Bryant Gumbel: I heard it characterized to me one time as whereas women are arguing about wanting to pay the tab at the restaurant, African-Africans can't even get in the restaurant … and that's a big difference.

Martha Burk: Well, women can't even get in Augusta.

Gumbel: But most Americans can't.

Burk: But not because of an immutable characteristic. At least theoretically, you as a man have the ability to get rich enough, powerful enough, or a good enough golfer to get in Augusta. I, as a woman, do not have that chance. That is the difference; that's the essence of discrimination.

Gumbel: We're talking about maybe one or two rich, privileged women.

Burk: Yeah, we are.

Gumbel: So, why all this hoopla to afford one more privilege (*voice rising*) to some already privileged women?

Burk: Would you have asked this question at Shoal Creek, Bryant … for heaven's sake! Would you say, "Why are we doing this to let one rich, African-American man who's already got it made into the Shoal Creek Country Club?" (*Under pressure from*

Civil Rights groups, the private Shoal Creek Country Club in Birmingham, Alabama added its first black member in 1990 prior to its hosting the PGA Golf Championship).

Gumbel: But you don't worry about your safety on this, do you?

Burk: No, I don't worry about my personal safety.

Gumbel: See, that's (*voice rising*) … another difference between race and gender discrimination.

Burk: What? (*voice rising*)

Gumbel: If you were fighting race discrimination, yes, you would be concerned about your safety at all times, because people do get shot over it. Nobody gets shot over women's rights.

Burk: Well, I disagree.

Gumbel: Nobody gets beaten or lynched over women's rights.

Burk: What do you think rape is, Bryant? It's a hate crime against women.

Source: HBO/*Real Sports*, December 16, 2002.

The entire interview lasted about 20 minutes, but in just this short section you can see the background Gumbel brought into the interview. As a black man, Gumbel had a completely different perspective on the issue, compared to Burk. In addition, Gumbel is an avid golfer and a longtime member of the private, all-male Burning Tree Golf Club in Bethesda, Maryland. Ross Greenberg of HBO Sports called the interview "an unbelievable case study in journalism. Ideally, you want a journalist with nothing in his background to ask the questions that need to be answered. However, there's a personal life to every journalist in America. We all have certain things in our private lives that raise our level of consciousness" (Sherman, 2002).

Dealing with personal agenda can be a tricky hurdle for any interviewer. The best suggestion is not necessarily to eliminate any personal feelings (which is impossible anyway), but rather to acknowledge and try to control them. Many people suggested Gumbel would have been better off disclosing his membership either before or during the interview with Burk, and Greenburg later admitted that doing so might have prevented "an unnecessary and ill-conceived conflict" (Raissman, 2002). Good interviewers also put themselves in the place of the person being interviewed and try to see things from that perspective. That doesn't mean agreeing with the other person, but rather playing the role of "devil's advocate," with respect for the other position. An interviewer should never ask questions simply to make a point or promote a cause, but at the same time you can't let the person you're interviewing do the same without being challenged.

Good examples of this were the interviews of 49ers quarterback Colin Kaepernick during the summer and fall of 2016. Kaepernick ignited a media firestorm by kneeling for the national anthem during a preseason game, a practice he continued in succeeding weeks. After one game, Kaepernick faced several media members in the locker room. A condensed version follows:

Question (Q): What are you trying to accomplish?

Colin Kaepernick: Ultimately, to bring awareness and make people realize what's going on in this country. There are things that people are not being held accountable for and that needs to change. This country stands for freedom, liberty, and justice for all, and it's not happening for all right now.

Q: How has this progressed to the point that you're making a stand like this?

Kaepernick: It's something that I've seen and felt; wasn't quite sure how to deal with it originally. It is something that's evolved. As I've gained more knowledge about what's happened in the past and what's going on currently. It's things that have gone on in this country for years and years and haven't been addressed, and they need to be.

Q: Will you continue to sit?

Kaepernick: Yes. I will continue to stand with the people who are being oppressed. When there is significant change and I feel that flag represents what it's supposed to represent, and this country represents people the way it's supposed to, then I'll stand.

Q: Specifically, what would you like to see change before you stand?

Kaepernick: There's a lot of things that need to change. One specifically is police brutality. There are people being murdered unjustly and not being held accountable. Cops are getting paid leave for killing people. That's not right.

Q: So many people see the flag as a symbol of the military. How do you view it and what do you say to those people?

Kaepernick: I have great respect for men and women that have fought for this country. I have family and friends that have fought for this country. They fight for freedom; they fight for the people, for liberty and justice; for everyone. And that's not happening. People are dying in vain because this country isn't holding their end of the bargain up.

Source: KTVU/August 29, 2016

Obviously, those asking the questions had feelings—either supportive or critical—about what Kaepernick was doing. Yet, they did not let those feelings interfere with the objectivity of the interview. The one question that could have been interpreted as critical was about the military, and it was asked in such a way as to not discourage Kaepernick from answering. Had the questioner asked, "Don't you feel like you're insulting the military by doing this?" Kaepernick likely would have responded critically or not answered at all.

The *theme* of the story simply refers to what the story is about. Every story should be reducible to one sentence—"The Cougars rallied heroically to win the game," or "John Smith is an inspirational athlete who won't let cancer ruin his career." It sounds overly simplistic, but not establishing the theme of the story before the interview causes all kinds of problems. If you fail to clearly identify a one-sentence theme for the story then the interview can become a rambling, unfocused mess. A clear theme can help the interviewer determine whom to interview and what to ask.

Coach's Corner with Craig Esherick

I have been interviewed by many reporters—after games, a day or two before games, over the phone while I am sitting in my family room at home, during the off-season, on camera, and in the hallway moments after we've just won or lost a key conference or tournament game. Most coaches understand that reporters have a job to do and are often working on a tight deadline. But whatever the situation and especially when being interviewed by someone I have never met, I want to know that the interviewer respects what I do for a living and who I am as a person. Context is everything when you ask a coach or other sports administrator a question.

A question asked on the first tee of a charity golf outing is a little bit different than a question asked right after a heart-breaking loss to end a tough season. The level of emotion involved and the many thoughts swirling through the coach's head at that moment have to be factored into the question.

Let me provide an example of two possible questions that could be asked of a basketball coach at a post-game press conference, following a loss that came down to the last possession of the game:

[1]"Coach, can you take us through the last possession of the game and talk about what you and your team were trying to do on that last play?"

[2]"Coach, why couldn't you get a better shot at the end of the game, especially since you called timeout right before that last possession?"

Unless the reporter is intentionally trying to damage his/her relationship with the coach, or is trying to incite an angry response, the phrasing of the first question is much better. That's the question that will enlighten the audience without alienating the coach. Opting to ask the question phrased the second way will set a tone for the relationship with the coach that will ultimately prove unproductive and the coach might be so angry, he won't bother to answer the question. Everyone loses in that scenario.

As a college coach, I never thought it was a good idea to criticize a player in the press. The relationship between a coach and athlete at the college level requires *the coach*, in my opinion, to shoulder most of the blame for mistakes made by the team. This is also true if you are a coach or an athletic director for a high school, middle school, or youth league team. Interviewers should respect this dynamic and not attempt to coerce a coach or athletic director into saying something negative about a player. Professional athletes and those competing at the Olympic level, however, may not be deserving of such protective treatment. I also believe that most coaches, no matter the level of play, would prefer to criticize their players in private or at least in a setting that is less public than a press conference.

I always thought that my players (college athletes) deserved to be treated *by the fans and the press*, as students who are in school and play a sport, not as professional athletes who are paid to train and perform at a high level. I feel very strongly about this, and I know that many in the press would feel the same way if their own student-athlete (son or daughter) were being interviewed by a colleague in the media.

It's also courteous of interviewers to understand that student-athletes are not as experienced as coaches at being interviewed, so questions should be posed in a manner that don't intentionally lead them to say things they will later regret. This consideration should especially be extended when interviewing players immediately after a big game or championship event, when emotions are often high and the athletes haven't had an opportunity to calm down and gather their thoughts.

An experienced communications professional can help the coach, athlete, and sports administrator develop a comfort level with the media.

Exhibit 6.1a *Diane Roberts, from CBS affiliate WUSA9, interviews George
Mason University head basketball coach, Dave Paulsen.
(© Art Pittman/George Mason Athletics.)*

Exhibit 6.1b *GMU player interviewed by CBS affiliate WUSA9.
(© Art Pittman/George Mason Athletics.)*

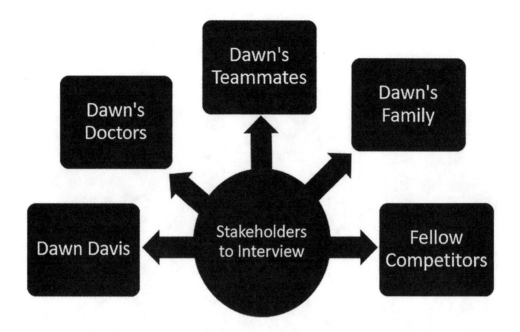

Exhibit 6.2 *Stakeholders for Dawn Davis, Paralympic Athlete Story*

Mock interviews can help those in your organization put their best foot
forward in an interview or at a press conference. Practice makes athletes better on the court/field but also better in the interview room; the
entire enterprise improves when all parties are prepared to put their
best foot forward on both sides of the interview.

Let's consider the story of a Paralympic athlete. It's important to identify the
theme as precisely as possible, so in this case it might be "former track star shows
courage in returning to competition after a tragic accident took both her legs." The
reason we want as much specificity as possible with the theme is that it will help
determine who to talk to and what questions to ask. (A less focused theme such
as "Dawn Davis is a Paralympic athlete" doesn't really help clarify these issues).
The theme should also reflect what's newsworthy about the story; what makes it
interesting or relevant to the audience. It's not just that Dawn Davis is a Paralympic
athlete, but rather that she has shown incredible courage, determination and perse-
verance after a devastating accident.

The focused theme then leads us to determine the *stakeholders* in the story. The
stakeholders are the people related to the story who might contribute something to
it, such as background information or an interview. As you can see from Exhibit 6.2
there are several potential stakeholders for the story including Dawn Davis herself,
doctors, teammates, family, and fellow competitors. A long format story such as a

magazine feature might include all of these stakeholders, but because of time and space restrictions more than likely, you'll need to whittle down this list to just two or three.

This is why having a focused theme is so important. Because the theme is about Davis showing courage, we can narrow down our list of potential stakeholders. The fans, and other athletes might be interesting interviews, but they don't really contribute to the main theme of the story. (In a sense, all of the other competitors have shown courage, which takes the story in a different direction.) That leaves us with three groups of stakeholders to interview, including Davis, her doctors, and possibly her family. It also helps us figure out what each of these stakeholders is going to contribute to the story and what questions to ask them. Instead of fumbling around trying to come up with good questions, the theme leads us to the appropriate questions to ask. The list of questions should, by no means, be exhaustive, but you really don't need to ask more than a few questions from each stakeholder.

Setting refers to where the interview will take place and how much time the interviewer will have. In some cases, this decision is completely out of the hands of the interviewer, who may only have a quick few minutes to talk with a player on his way from the locker room to the field. News conferences (see Chapter 9: Event Management) and locker room interviews (typically where the athlete or coach is interviewed after a game) are examples where the setting is dictated. These types of events are attended by dozens of reporters if not more (think Super Bowl Media Day) and intimacy is all but impossible. That's one reason athletes and coaches are much less likely to open up or give interesting comments in these group settings.

A good example is the February 2009 interview between freelance political blogger Ken Krayeske and former University of Connecticut men's basketball coach Jim Calhoun. Krayeske wanted to talk about Calhoun's large salary (a base of $1.5 million per year; more than the university president or athletic director) in the midst of an economic recession. But Krayeske chose a post-game news conference to ask his questions, and after Calhoun tried to defuse the situation with humor the exchange soon became testy:

Ken Krayeske: Considering that you're the highest-paid state employee and there's a $2 billion budget deficit, do you think …

Jim Calhoun: Not a dime back. (*Laughter.*)

Krayeske: Not a dime back?

Calhoun: Not a dime back. I'd like to be able to retire some day. I'm getting tired.

Krayeske: You don't think $1.5 million is enough?

Calhoun: I make a lot more than that.

Krayeske: You do?

Calhoun: What was the take tonight?

Krayeske: What's the deal with Comcast worth?

Calhoun: You're not really that stupid, are you?

Krayeske: Yes, I am.

Calhoun: My best advice to you—shut up.

Krayeske: Thank you. That's very polite of you.

Calhoun: No, it wasn't polite of me; I want you to shut up. If you want to talk to me outside, I'd be more than happy to.

Krayeske: If these guys covered this stuff, I wouldn't have to do it. (*Other reporters at news conference begin to audibly groan and complain.*)

Calhoun: Quite frankly, we bring in $12 million a year for this university. (*Then, Calhoun's volume really increased.*) Get some facts and come back and see me. Get some facts and come back and see me. Don't throw out salaries or other things. Get some facts and come back and see me. We turn over more than $12 million to the University of Connecticut, which is state-run. Next question (Borges, 2009).

The issue is not whether Krayeske had a right to ask the questions (although some suggested that he obtained his press credential fraudulently), but he should have realized that Calhoun was not going to offer any meaningful answers in that particular setting. A more appropriate setting would have been a one-on-one interview, which is not conducted in the aftermath of a game. At the same time, there's no guarantee that Calhoun would have agreed to such an interview; Krayeske probably realized that and figured he better ask his questions while he had the chance.

(The Krayeske-Calhoun interview also brings up the issue of *access*. We talked about this at some length in Chapter 2 and don't need to go into much more detail here. Obviously, there are going to be situations where interview access is more limited, such as when a player, coach, or organization is dealing with bad or embarrassing news. Access is usually much freer on the professional sports level, where athletes and coaches typically decide for themselves when and where they want to talk. College, and especially high school, athletes are more protected and access is more difficult. Many times, access to an interview will have to be arranged through a sports information person. This is why news conference and locker room interviews are so common—those are the places where the athletes and coaches are most available.)

Another type of setting is the onfield interview, which usually takes place before or after a game, and sometimes at halftime. Before a game or during halftime the interviewer will have a few seconds with a player or coach for some quick analysis, while the end of the game interview focuses more on reaction. In some cases, these interviews can be unintentionally revealing. In the heat of the moment many players and coaches have cursed (on live television) or said something they later regretted.

In order to prevent such incidents and maintain control of their agenda, many teams and schools have banned onfield interviews in favor of controlled news conferences, which take place after players and coaches have had a chance to cool down.

While the reaction interviews after a big game are sometimes compelling, most onfield interviews are bland and uninteresting. Coaches and players keep their comments intentionally plain, in part because the questions are pretty boring. It's hard to come up with a great question when the team is running on the field and a coach only has 20 seconds to talk. The "celebrity" sideline interviews with former players are similarly uninspired, except for the rare occasions when things go terribly wrong. One of the most famous sideline interviews of all time, a December 20, 2003 interview between ESPN's Suzy Kolber and former New York Jets quarterback Joe Namath, stands out mainly because of Namath's drunkenness (he later apologized to Kolber and admitted he had a drinking problem):

Suzy Kolber: Joe, it's been a tough season for Jets fans. What does it mean to you now that the team is struggling?

Joe Namath: I wanna kiss you. I couldn't care less about the team struggling. What we know is we can improve. Chad Pennington, our quarterback, missed the first part of the season, and we struggled. We're looking to next season, we're looking to make a noise now and ... I wanna kiss you!

Kolber: Thanks Joe! I'll take that as a huge compliment ... [*Namath in background: YEAH!!!!*] Joe Namath, part of the four-decade team. We'll see these guys at halftime.

Source: "Top 10," 2004.

To the extent that the setting can be controlled it should be as comfortable for the interview subject as possible. A comfortable, familiar environment automatically puts the subject at ease and makes it more likely that he or she will open up with good answers. Newspaper reporter Gary Cartwright covered the Dallas Cowboys during the Tom Landry coaching era, and in the setting of the locker room or press conference, Landry was often considered reserved and controlled. But interviewing the coach one time when Landry was at his desk, Cartwright observed, "Landry was relaxed, more than I had ever seen him, strangely relaxed considering it was less than three hours before game time, perversely relaxed for a man who detests small talk and was now being bombarded with it" (Cartwright, 1973).

In the case of our story with Dawn Davis, the best place for the interview might be her office or her home. If possible, avoid a setting, that would be unfamiliar or uncomfortable, such as outside with the sun shining in her eyes.

Once the elements of audience, agenda, theme, setting and stakeholders have been determined, the interviewer will likely need to do some additional research and background work. Each sports story has its own unique information that not even the most knowledgeable interviewer can be expected to know. Fortunately, the internet makes it very easy to access background information, especially related to facts and figures. For more personal information the interviewer might want to contact those with an intimate knowledge of the subject matter. In regards to the Dawn Davis story, a quick search of the internet should provide important information such as age, records set, and details of the accident. In other cases where such information is not readily accessible, a few phone calls to relevant stakeholders might be necessary.

Doing the required background research (the "leg work" as older journalists would say) is just as important to the interviewing process as developing the proper theme. The information learned during this process will help the interviewer more sharply focus and frame the appropriate questions. In addition, knowing about your interview subject puts him or her more at ease during the actual interview. People are more likely to open up and give more insightful answers when they can respect and trust the interviewer.

As a corollary, not doing research puts the interviewer at an obvious disadvantage. ESPN's Roy Firestone was reminded of this lesson when he interviewed then-Indiana basketball coach Bobby Knight in the spring of 2000. Knight had come under tremendous pressure amidst allegations that he once choked a former player during practice. A videotape of the incident had circulated in the general media for quite some time, but Firestone never bothered to view the tape and could not question Knight about it. As a result, Firestone came under criticism for not approaching the subject and being too 'soft' on the coach.

One of the last things the interviewer may want to do before the interview is create a list of questions, which has both advantages and disadvantages. On the plus side, having a list of questions forces the interviewer to focus and narrow down the most important topics he or she wants to address. In some cases, an interview can digress and get off track, and a list can help make sure that the interviewer returns to cover the essential points of the story. However, a list can also make an interview seem scripted and stilted. Instead of an honest conversation, the interview turns into an interrogation where the interviewer is rattling off questions that seem to put the respondent on the defensive. There's also the temptation of not listening to the answers and focusing on the next question on the list. This can lead to some major embarrassment for the interviewer if the respondent says something unexpected. Instead of writing out the questions in the form of a list you might consider using an index card that includes some short reminders about important topics.

At the Interview

The best thing that the interviewer can do at the interview is create an atmosphere of trust and confidence that helps the respondent speak more freely. As we have noted, this is extremely difficult in news conference and locker room situations that include dozens of reporters or more. In those situations, the athletes and coaches have a natural tendency to get defensive and speak more guardedly no matter what the interviewer does. That's why the answers from news conference and locker room interviews often seem cold and uninspired.

If the interviewer has the chance to get a more intimate one-on-one interview there are several strategies for building trust and rapport. The best approach is to already have established a trusting relationship with the person being interviewed. If the coach or athlete knows the interviewer and realizes that he or she can be trusted, not only will it be easier to get access, but the answers will also be more honest and open. This is obviously a long-term strategy that can take months or even years to develop, and it works especially well for beat writers who cover a team or player on a regular basis. However, there are more sports media today than ever before and the sheer number of reporters all wanting interviews makes this a difficult proposition.

It is possible to create a certain level of trust even in an interview situation where there is no established relationship. Again, conducting the interview in a place that is comfortable for the interview subject is important. It also helps to engage in what can be called a *pre-interview*, which is nothing more than idle chit-chat with the subject before the real interview begins. Talking about the weather, favorite hobbies, or family is a great way to relax someone and get him or her to feel more at ease. If you see several bowling trophies on the mantle of her office you might ask her about them and how she got involved in bowling. A pre-interview doesn't have to last long and it can give the broadcast reporter something to talk about while the equipment is being set up. But be sure the interview subject always knows when the real interview starts and his or her comments are officially on the record.

The order of questions can also help put the interview subject at ease. Assuming there is enough time, the interviewer can help "warm up" the subject by asking easy questions first. (As already noted, this does not work in certain situations where time is more limited). Easy questions at the beginning help the interview subject relax, so when the harder questions eventually come he or she is more inclined to answer. Asking tough questions right off the top might work for *60 Minutes*, but it runs a higher risk of the interview subject refusing to answer. If the hard questions are asked at the end and the subject refuses to answer at least you have some quotes/sound bites you can use. Sportswriter Bill Plaschke put this into practice when he interviewed former Major League Baseball player Spike Owen after a game. Owen had hit his first home run of the season in the fourth inning, but committed a costly error in the ninth that lost the game. "Standing in front of several reporters afterward," noted Plaschke, "my first question to Owen was about the home run.

Relaxed after talking for a few minutes about the homer, Owen was revealing and insightful when answering my next question about the error" (Plaschke, 2000).

Trust is also a two-way street, which means at the very least you should respect your interview subjects. That doesn't mean you have to like them or even agree with them, but you will have a better interview if you respect their position and point of view. It could be argued that provocateurs like Howard Cosell and Jim Rome (see v 5-2) were highly successful because of a lack of respect for their interview subjects, but they are the exceptions rather than the rule. Plaschke (2000) correctly observes that "you catch more flies with honey" than you do with vinegar, which is another way of saying that in the long run it usually doesn't pay to be intentionally difficult or argumentative—unless you're Jim Rome.

The Sacking of Rome

Jim Rome has created a successful career on sports radio and television as the interviewer-provocateur: someone who purposefully tries to agitate and goad interview subjects. To Rome, the interview is spectacle and the idea is not always to get good answers, but to create good television. It's debatable whether the interview Rome conducted in 1994 with then-NFL quarterback Jim Everett qualifies as "good television," but that it is still talked about 20 years after the fact says something. During his interview with Everett on the ESPN show *Talk2*, Rome kept calling him "Chris," as in former tennis great Chris Evert. The name was an implication that Everett lacked toughness—a serious criticism for an NFL quarterback. Rome continually denies that the interview and ensuing studio melee were staged:

Jim Rome: Jim, good to have you on the show.

Jim Everett: Good to be here, Jim. Thank you.

Rome: Check that. Chris Everett, good to have you on the show.

Everett: You know what? You've been calling me that for about the last five years and…

Rome: Two years actually, Chris.

Everett: Let me say one thing. In that game … how many sacks did I have that we came back and won?

Rome: How many sacks did you have?

Everett: Yeah … how many sacks?

Rome: You see, this was back in 1989. You may have even been Jim Everett back there, but somewhere along the way Jim, you ceased being Jim and you became Chris.

Everett: Well, let me tell you a little secret … that, you know, we're sitting here right now, and if you guys want to take a station break, you can. But if you call me Chris Everett to my face one more time...

Rome: I already did it twice.

Everett: You'd better … if you call it one more time, we'd better take a station break.

Rome: Well, it's a five-minute segment, on a five-segment show. We've got a long way to go.

Everett: We do.

Rome: We've got a long way to go. I'll get a couple of segments out of you.

Everett: It's good to be here with you though … because you've been talking like this behind my back for a long time now.

Rome: But now I've said it right here, so we've got no problems then.

Everett: I think that you probably won't say it again.

Rome: I'll bet I do.

Everett: OK.

Rome: Chris.

[*Everett tosses aside coffee table and attacks Rome until restrained by studio personnel.*]

Source/Courtesy: ESPN

It's also important not to go too far in the other direction and let the interview subject control the interview. This is more difficult that it sounds for several reasons. Sports figures can be very intimidating figures, whether because of their personalities or the circumstances surrounding the interview. Few sports journalists (other than people like Jim Rome) want a confrontational interview, but sometimes they simply can't be avoided. In those situations, the reporter needs to keep calm and remain on theme or the interview will just turn into a shouting match. It's hard to retain composure when someone is shouting at you, but experienced interviewers have learned not to become part of the story.

The following exchange took place in September 2012 between WEEI Radio reporter Glenn Ordway and Red Sox manager Bobby Valentine. The Red Sox were in the midst of a miserable season that would see them finish in last place, so Valentine was understandably testy. Ordway was interviewing Valentine long distance, as the team was on a west coast road trip. After some initial pleasantries, Ordway got to the theme—accusations that the team had given up.

Glenn Ordway: Let's get it out on the table. People back here are talking an awful lot about you … You do get the impression that people think maybe you've kind checked out. Have you checked out of this?

Bobby Valentine: What an embarrassing thing to say. You know, if I was there I would punch you right in the mouth. How's that sound? Sound like I checked out? That's something a comic strip person would write. How could someone in real life say that?

Ordway: I did say that; let me expound on that. Because you were late at a ball game last week. Podsednik bats third and when people are asking you about it you don't seem to have an answer.

Valentine: That pisses me off. Whoever wrote that knew what happened. They knew my son was coming to see me for the first time this lousy season; I got to see him on the road and his flight was late. I was waiting in San Francisco for his flight to come in and reported to my coaches that I was going to be a little late. And to say that I was late is an absolute disgrace to their integrity, if they have any.

Ordway: Do you feel like you're coming to the ballpark every day and putting in your best effort, and do you feel like the players are putting in their best effort?

Valentine: I just told you … when you said what you said, you should apologize to me for saying that I came late.

Source: WEEI Radio (http://audio.weei.com/a/62126258/bobby-valentine-job-has-been-miserable-but-part-of-my-life-s-journey.htm)

What's interesting about the interview was that it was part of Valentine's radio contract; he was being paid by the station to appear weekly with hosts Ordway and Michael Holley. So despite all the trust and rapport that had built up between the men over the course of the season, the interview quickly degenerated into confrontation. Credit Ordway and Holley for not pandering to Valentine and ignoring the difficult questions, but rather acting as sports journalists even at the cost of Valentine's anger. Note also that they did not set out to provoke Valentine, but simply asked the hard questions that their audience wanted to hear. (It's important to remember that Ordway and Holley could afford to be a bit combative with Valentine because they weren't risking a loss of access. The manager was contractually obligated to appear with them once a week).

After the 2003 NCAA basketball championship game, Bonnie Bernstein of CBS got a short interview with losing coach Roy Williams, then at Kansas. Speculation was rampant at the time that Williams would soon leave KU to coach at North Carolina, but Williams had refused to comment until after the game:

Bonnie Bernstein: Very understandably you didn't want to address this issue during the week, but many people out there, with the game over, want to know what your level of interest is in the North Carolina job.

Roy Williams: Bonnie, I could give a flip about what those people want. As a journalist you have to ask that question and I understand that, but as a human being … all those people who want that answer right now are not very sensitive.

Bernstein: If they offer you the job, though, would you be willing to take it?

Williams: The guy in your ear that told you that you had to ask that question … as a journalist, that's fine … but as a human being, that's not very nice … and I've got to think that in tough times that people should be more sensitive. I don't give a **** about Carolina right now. I've got 13 kids in that locker room that I love. (*Walks off*).

Bernstein: Coach, thank you.

Like Jim Gray with Pete Rose, Bernstein received some criticism for the timing of her comments, but still maintains that "if I had to do that all over, I would do it the same way" (Hruby, 2005). In Gray's case, the problem was one of agenda; Rose kept trying to focus the interview on his All-Century Team honor, while Gray kept pushing him to talk about his gambling. Gray, Bernstein, and Ordway deserve credit for trying to maintain control of their interviews and keep them focused on the main theme. It may have been more "sensitive" for them to change their line of questioning, but not necessarily good sports journalism. And like Gray, Bernstein was also somewhat vindicated when less than two weeks after the interview Williams became the head coach at North Carolina.

Questions, Questions

Now we're down to the essential part of interviewing—figuring out what questions to ask. It sounds like a difficult proposition, but it's actually pretty simple if we have carefully figured out our audience, agenda, theme, setting, and stakeholders. Those decisions tell us who will be watching/listening and what they expect from the interview, who we should interview, and most importantly, the main focus of the story. We can now add another important consideration—what kind of answers we want.

Don't confuse expected answers with scripted answers; we're not trying to get the interview subject to say a particular thing or give a preordained response. Many young journalists make the mistake of writing the story ahead of time then trying to goad the interview subject into giving a certain quote or sound bite. The needed portion would then be crammed into the story, which is an approach that works about as well as jamming a square peg in a round hole. When we talk about expected answers we're talking more about what the stakeholder will contribute to the story based on the theme. Refer back to our hypothetical story on Paralympic athlete, Dawn Davis. Based on the theme, we already know what we need Davis to contribute—some kind of responses that show how she showed courage and determination in overcoming a terrible accident. The specific answers Davis gives to these questions don't matter as long as she addresses the topic. So if we asked her, "How do you feel about returning to competition after the accident?" it's immaterial if she says it's wonderful, disappointing, or something in-between.

However, there are certain ways to frame such questions to get more meaningful answers. In this context, meaningful suggests an answer that not only supports the theme of the story, but also is memorable and has an emotional impact. Those are somewhat difficult concepts to define, but perhaps an example from our Davis story will help:

Q: Could you tell me a little more about the accident and what happened?

A1: "Two years ago I was driving alone at night when my car got hit by a drunk driver. The accident caused the amputation of both of my legs just above the knee."

A2: "I'll never forget that night two years ago when I got hit by a drunk driver. I could see it coming, but couldn't do anything to stop it. It was like it was happening in slow motion or like I was watching it in a movie. Only when I woke up later in the hospital did I realize that this was no movie, but it was real—and happening to me."

Hopefully, you consider the second answer much more interesting and memorable. That's because it relates to the personal perspective of the interview subject; she is telling us something only she can relate from her own experience. You get these kinds of responses by asking certain kinds of questions—"how" and "why" questions as opposed to "who" and "what." "Why is this important to you?" and "How do you feel about this?" are examples of questions that force the respondent to think and come up with more personal responses. In a sports context we hear the same question after every big game—"how do you feel?" It may seem like a dumb question (after all, players on the winning team are certainly going to be happier than players on the losing team), but it's the simplest, most direct way to get a personal answer.

In terms of getting good responses, "who" and "what" questions (along with questions that can be answered "yes" or "no") are not very strong. However, that does *not* mean you shouldn't ask them. Such questions are very important in terms of getting information you need to fill in background in the story. But the answers to such questions should not be used as quotes or sound bites, especially if you have something more meaningful. If possible, avoid using information (the "who," "what," and "when" information of the story) as quotes or sound bites; the best responses come from the "how" and "why" questions.

As we discussed a bit earlier it often helps to ask somewhat easy questions at the beginning of the interview to help the respondent relax and loosen up. For our story on Dawn Davis asking the question about the accident could trigger painful memories and isn't a great question to start on. Consider something like, "How did you first get interested in track?" that will be easy for her to answer and help her open up a bit. Even if you don't intend on using the answer to the question in the story (and in this particular case, you probably wouldn't), it's still advisable to start easy and save harder questions for later. The issue then becomes what should follow the opening question. We talked earlier about having a list of questions and one could be used in this case. But as already noted, using a list runs the risk of a scripted, interrogation-type interview. Consider these approaches for the Davis story:

Questions from List

Q1: Could you tell me a little more about your track career and how you got interested?

A: "I wasn't a very athletic kid, and in fact was sick quite a bit. But I saw that movie *Forrest Gump*, where he goes on to run even with leg braces. I figured if he could do it, maybe I could to."

Q2: You decided to become a sprinter and try for the Olympics. How disappointing was it not to make it?

A: "Very disappointing. I trained very hard to my event for four years, and then to just miss—to come in fourth in the qualifying trials—really set me back. At that point, I felt like quitting and never running again."

Q3: It was coming home from the trials that you had your accident. Could you tell me a little more about that?

A: "I'll never forget that night two years ago when I got hit by a drunk driver. I could see it coming, but couldn't do anything to stop it. It was like it was happening in slow motion or like I was watching it in a movie. Only when I woke up later in the hospital did I realize that this was no movie, but it was real—and happening to me."

Q4: At what point did you make the decision to try and run again?

A: "Well, for a long time I wasn't even sure I was going to be able to walk. But after I got my artificial legs and took my first steps it was like the adrenaline started up again. I got that same old feeling and knew I had to get back in competition."

Q5: It took you three long years of rehab to get back. How difficult was it?

A: It was incredibly difficult because the progress was so slow and incremental— sometimes only inches a day. But my doctors and family were great cheerleaders. Whenever I got down they just picked me right back up. I owe them a lot."

Questions without a List—The Conversational Approach

Q: Could you tell me a little more about your track career and how you got interested?

A: "I wasn't a very athletic kid, and in fact was sick quite a bit. But I saw that movie *Forrest Gump*, where he goes on to run even with leg braces. I figured if he could do it, maybe I could to."

Q: Do you mean you had leg braces as a kid?

A: "No, but I had about everything else. The usual like chicken pox and tonsils, and then even stuff that doctors couldn't even explain. I was in and out of hospitals so much they almost held me back a year in school. Finally, about the time I reached high school I got well enough to try out for the track team."

Q: It was there that you set several national high school records for the 100-meter dash. At what point did you think you could make the Olympics?

A: "I never really thought much about it, but my coach kept on me to try out. I had seen the Olympics on television and just didn't think I was that kind of world-class athlete."

Q: Why not?

A: "I don't know; maybe from how sick I was as a kid. I guess I thought that really great athletes are born, not made. My coach convinced me otherwise and I began a long training program."

Q: You trained for four years to get your shot at the Olympics and just missed out. How disappointing was that?

A: "Very disappointing. I trained very hard to my event for four years, and then to just miss—to come in fourth in the qualifying trials—really set me back. At that point, I felt like quitting and never running again."

Q: Did you feel that same way after your accident?

A: "Well, for a long time I wasn't even sure I was going to be able to walk. But after I got my artificial legs and took my first steps it was like the adrenaline started up again. I got that same old feeling and knew I had to get back in competition."

Q: And you stuck with it despite a three-year rehab process. How difficult was it?

A: "It was incredibly difficult because the progress was so slow and incremental— sometimes only inches a day. But my doctors and family were great cheerleaders. Whenever I got down they just picked me right back up. I owe them a lot."

We call the second approach conversational because the interviewer takes time to listen to the answers and adjust the questions accordingly. When Davis mentions that she didn't consider herself a world-class athlete, the skillful interviewer notices and asks a follow up question. The interviewer using a list simply keeps going to the next question and misses the opportunity to follow up. (Notice also that in some cases these follow up answers are the best, most personal responses). A good interview is like a conversation, which implies listening, dialogue and feedback. In some extreme cases, a particular response might take the interview in a completely different direction. The interviewer should not be afraid to explore these possibilities, even if it changes the theme of the story. It might be that the response creates a new, better story idea.

Taking a conversational approach can also be effective when the interviewer has to ask difficult questions. Questions can be difficult for any number of reasons; they may be potentially damaging, embarrassing, or conflict with the respondent's agenda. But a conversational interview can help draw out the respondent and make these potentially difficult situations more successful. One strategy is what interviewers call the *golden moment*, which refers to the interviewer being quiet and letting the respondent fill in difficult dead spaces. Many interviewers tend to talk too much (experts suggest that if you're talking more than 10% of the time in an interview you're talking too much) and they want to fill up all the quiet moments with their own words. Instead, when the interview hits a dead spot after you've asked a question simply sit back and say nothing. This *golden moment* is a nonverbal signal that the respondent should keep talking, and it works surprisingly well. Veteran radio and print reporter Joyce Davis noted, "It is amazing when you shut up how much you get. My normal way of interviewing would be to ask you a question, then as soon as you shut up give you another … really pick at you a lot. I tried to ask a question … then say absolutely nothing. That was very hard. The person will come up with deepest things if you just let them fill those silences" ("Dealing with," 1993).

Conclusion

Getting sports interviews can be extremely frustrating, intimidating, and exhausting. Some players and coaches can be very uncooperative, and even the most cooperative of them have usually heard all the questions before. It is a constant challenge for the sports reporter to get access to the people he wants to interview, create an atmosphere conducive to good interviewing, and finally ask the questions that result in memorable answers. There is no magic formula, other than preparing, working hard, and trying to earn the respect of the athletes and coaches you need to interview.

As a final thought, always stay focused on the end result—good answers. In other words, don't spend too much time worrying if your questions are phrased perfectly, whether you asked a dumb question or how you appeared on camera. Most of the time your questions aren't even going to be used in the story. If you have to ask a few dumb questions or stumble over asking a certain question, so be it. As long as you get the insightful, memorable quotes or sound bites you need, you have done your job.

Discussion Questions

1. NBA's player Kevin Durant has been scheduled to give interviews to both Bryant Gumbel of HBO's *Real Sports* and Stephen Colbert of *The Late Show*. How do you think the interview questions will differ? What specific questions do you think each interviewer would ask?

2. How do you think the Martha Burk-Bryant Gumbel interview would have been different if someone else had been the interviewer? How would it have been different if the interviewer had been Katie Couric? Oprah Winfrey?

3. For the same story you have to interview three different athletes; one says he can only do it by phone, another prefers email and the third has agreed to a sit-down personal interview. Will your approach to these three interviews differ? Do you think the answers you will get will be different? Which do you think would be the more compelling interview and why?

Suggested Exercises

1. For each of the following situations identify the appropriate theme, stakeholders, and agendas. Develop a list of questions you would want to ask the people related to your story:

   a. Local 80-year old man trains to run in this year's Boston Marathon.

   b. Football team reunites 25 years after winning championship.

   c. Popular area basketball coach rumored to be leaving to take another job at a rival school.

    d. Local high school player sets state record for most home runs.

    e. School district declares star player academically ineligible the week before the championship game.

2. If possible, arrange an interview outside of class with a local athlete or coach. (If not possible, pair up with someone in class and interview each other outside of class). For the interview, work on

    a. choosing the appropriate setting

    b. establishing a level of comfort

    c. conducting a conversational interview related to the theme

3. Write down (or otherwise record) the responses from the interview. What were the best answers? What type of questions led to these good answers?

4. Bob Costas has developed a reputation as one of the best sports interviewers of all time. Access one of Costas's sports interviews, either online or on television, and analyze it in terms of the principles we've discussed. What makes it such a good interview? What makes Costas such a good interviewer?

7 | Developing Writing Skills

Purpose and Function of Writing

Writing is much like athletics. Some individuals possess innate qualities that facilitate development of the skills required—a creative imagination for writers, for example—but it takes a lot of practice to excel at a craft or a sport. Any good writer will tell you that the secret to success is practice, practice, practice.

An aspiring sports information director (SID) does not have to be "a born writer." However, anyone in the business of sports information must learn the fundamentals of good writing and practice them diligently to develop proficiency in the craft. A professional cannot succeed without a thorough understanding of the parts of speech, sentence structure, grammar, spelling, punctuation, and theme development. A knowledge of writing techniques—use of description, direct quotations, and rhetorical devices such as analogies, similes, and metaphors—is also helpful.

Although creativity is an asset, writing for the media is more like theme or report writing than creative writing. James Stovall, author of *Writing for the Mass Media*, draws these distinctions between writing for the media and other forms of writing:

- *Subject matter.* Writers for the mass media must take on a wide variety of subjects, including news stories, feature stories, advertisements, letters, editorials, and more.

- *Purpose.* Writing for the mass media has three major purposes: to inform, entertain, and persuade.

- *Audience.* Mass media writing is often directed to a wide audience, and this fact dictates not only the subject matter, but also the way in which something is written.

- *Circumstances of the writing.* Writing for the mass media often takes place in the presence of others who are doing the same thing. The writing is frequently done under deadline pressure, and often several people will have a hand in writing and editing a particular item for the mass media. (2009, p. 8)

News Terms

advance—a story written before an event, such as a preview

alternative structure—any one of several literary formats, including a circle and an hourglass, utilized to organize information in a story

5Ws and H—the six questions (who, what, when, where, why, and how) that all news stories must answer

feature release—a news release that spotlights or features a particular athlete

follow—a story written after an event, such as coverage of a game or an update to an earlier story

game advance—a news release that offers a preview of an upcoming game

header—information at the top of a news release that provides contact information and suggested release time for the story

hometown release—a news release about an athlete that is sent to media in the geographical area in which the athlete lives

inverted pyramid—a story format in which the writer organizes information in descending order of importance

lede—the first sentence or paragraph of a news story

news peg—a phrase or sentence that connects the story to the most important news element or news event

tieback—a phrase or sentence that explains how a story relates to an earlier news event

weekly preview/review—a weekly schedule of all the organization's athletic teams

Various Forms of Writing

SIDs, like an artist, have many different pallets from which to write about their venue, teams, athletes, and/or organizations.

A news release is very similar to a news story written by the print or broadcast media. Both may emphasize the hard news angle of a story, such as the announcement of the selection of a new coach, a scholarship recipient, or a new facility. Both also may take a soft news approach, as in a personality profile of the new coach. In simplest terms, hard news generally centers on issues, events, actions, and their consequences. Soft news usually revolves around people, such as athletes and their connection to the event or issue.

The purpose of a news story, however, is significantly different from that of a news release. The primary objective of a news story is to inform, that is, to present information in a fair, objective manner. A secondary function, though no less important, is to entertain, so the sports journalist works hard to inform and entertain an audience. The primary intent of a news release is to persuade (i.e., to present the organization's message or image in the most favorable light). Secondary functions may be to inform, to entertain, and in some cases, to educate. So the SID strives to use information to persuade—to enhance indirectly the image of the organization in the public eye—rather than simply to inform for information's sake.

In his book, *Becoming a Public Relations Writer*, Ronald D. Smith says all public relations writing seeks to influence a reader in some way:

> **All public relations writing is an attempt to influence people in some way. If you aren't trying to make an impact on your readers, why write? Without intending to affect readers in some way, you're just wasting time, because you won't produce anything useful… . As a writer, you have a particular effect in mind when you write. You want to increase your public's knowledge and understanding about something, you want them to feel a certain way about this information, and you probably want them to respond to that information in a particular way. (2008, p. 7)**

Sports information specialists usually structure news releases like news stories, with some modifications, to enhance their publication or broadcast prospects. Hard news stories generally follow a simple but rigid straight news format designed to deliver key information quickly, whereas soft news stories may take a variety of creative or feature approaches that emphasize the people in the story as much as the information.

The most common structure for hard news is called the inverted pyramid because it places the most important information at the top and the least important at the bottom. The lede of the story quickly summarizes the basic news elements: who, what, when, where, why, and how (known as the 5Ws and H in journalistic jargon). It emphasizes the most important element of the news and presents the details of the six elements in descending order of importance. The story does not have a conclusion, but ends with the least important detail:

- Most Important Information or Element
- Quick Summary of 5Ws and H

- Most Important Details
- Less Important
- Least Important
- No Conclusion

The information or "news" drives the story in the inverted pyramid. The structure is effective for two reasons. First, it quickly delivers the information readers are most likely to want. Even those who do not read more than a couple of paragraphs will obtain a quick summary of the facts, with emphasis on the most important details. Second, the story is very easy to trim if it is too long to fit the space allotted on a newspaper page or the time allotted on a newscast. The journalist sacrifices only the least important—and least read—details.

(LEDE) MORGANTOWN, W.Va. (January 9, 2019) (WHEN AND WHERE) – West Virginia University officials (WHO) announced today the hiring of Neil Brown as the school's 35th head football coach. (WHAT)

WVU President Dr. E. Gordon Gee, in conjunction with Director of Athletics Shane Lyons, officially signed Brown to a six-year, $19,050,000 contract. (HOW)

Brown has spent the last four years as the head coach at Troy University, compiling a 35–16 record, including 3–0 in bowl games. The Trojans posted a 31–8 record (.795) over the past three seasons, tying for the highest winning percentage nationally among non-Power 5 schools. Troy has won 17 of its last 20 games and 22 of its last 26. After directing the Trojans to the 2017 Sun Belt Conference Championship, Brown was honored as the league's coach of the year. (WHY)

The inverted pyramid approach is most appropriate for stories such as announcements, meetings, and breaking news, because the reader does not already know most of the basic information. Sports information specialists most often use the inverted pyramid approach for game advances, news releases, and announcements. Sports information personnel also use the inverted pyramid style on stories they submit to the news media immediately following a game.

Journalists use a number of variations of or alternative to the inverted pyramid for soft news stories in which the basic information will not "hook" the reader. For example, the reader already may know the basic details—the 5Ws and H—of last week's football game, so the journalist looks for an entertaining angle to encourage people to read further in the story. The journalist often starts with a literary device that emphasizes the drama, the suspense, the irony, or some unusual or intriguing facet of the topic. The story may open with a narrative lead, a re-creation of a key play, an anecdote, a quotation, an ironic twist, a question, or some other common literary technique that engages readers.

The rest of the story also may take a variety of forms, depending on the technique utilized in the beginning. A story that opens with a scene-setter might relate the rest of the action in chronological order. A story that begins with a re-creation of the turning point in a game might move from one key play to another. A story that features the star player might move from one key play by the star to another. Such stories generally require more description and detail than do stories that follow the inverted pyramid format. They also require greater creative writing skill.

No matter what technique the writer uses, stories that follow the alternative structure do have several common organizational elements. They use a literary device to establish a theme or focal point and then follow with a news peg or tieback. A *news peg* connects the story to the most important news element like the first sentence of a story written in the inverted pyramid style. It also may summarize the 5Ws and H to remind the reader of the basic news details. A *tieback* explains how the story relates to a previous news event (i.e., it ties the opening back to the original news announcement or news event). The body of the story adds details in a logical order and wraps up the story with a conclusion that reinforces the theme. The alternative styles may take more of a circle approach in that they "come full circle," or conclude with the emphasis on the same point as the beginning.

- Feature Opening—Theme
- News Peg or Tieback
- Points in Logical Order
- Conclusion—Reinforce Theme

Alternative approaches put greater emphasis on the people and the drama of the event. As a result, they usually contain more description that recreates the scene or event, and more quotations that give voice to the "characters" in the stories. They are most effective for stories about athletes in which most readers already know the basic information, or the news details are secondary to the person or theme of the story. Journalists utilize alternative styles most often on personality profiles, human-interest features, and follow-up stories—stories printed a couple of days after an event. The alternative styles are also becoming more prevalent by newspaper writers for game stories, because by the next morning, most fans already know the essential details of the game from TV, radio, and internet coverage. Sports information directors use them for feature releases and weekly reviews or previews.

A journalist actually can use either or both approaches to tell the same story. Here's an example of an inverted pyramid lede and an alternative lede and news peg on the same story:

Inverted Pyramid

> JACKSONVILLE, Fla. – Casbaugh State University's men's basketball team used a 41–8 run in the first half and never looked back, holding Riptide state scoreless for more than 11 minutes, en route to a 79–42 victory over the Man-O-Wars in opening round action of the Preseason NIT Friday night, in front of 3,581 fans, at the CSU Coliseum.
>
> CSU shot 56.3% from the field (18–32) in the first half and forced 14 Riptide turnovers in taking a 43–13 first-half lead. Casbaugh State's defense held the Man-O-Wars to 3–22 shooting in the first half and just 30% (15–50) for the contest.
>
> For the game ....

Alternative

> JACKSONVILLE, FLA. – Casbaugh State felt the pressure early.
>
> Nearly 3,600 fans filled the CSU Coliseum to watch Casbaugh State's season opener against Riptide State in the Preseason NIT, Friday night at the CSU Coliseum. Riptide got out to an early 5–2 lead in the opening minutes, while CSU tried to find its offensive rhythm.
>
> Twelve minutes later, however, the Mules led by 20, 34–14, and all was right by the partisan crowd.

Broadcast journalists use a modified and abbreviated inverted pyramid approach to most news stories. Because listeners or viewers are hearing the story rather than reading it themselves, stories for broadcast often open with a catchy word, a phrase, or a sentence designed to catch one's attention—to give the ear time to listen for the important element. The rest of the story is written in a conversational style, just as in telling a story, but generally follows the inverted pyramid style.

The TV or radio story emphasizes the same basic news elements of a newspaper story. Because of time limitations and the emphasis on immediacy in broadcast journalism, a story may cover only the who, what, when, and where. The accompanying video in TV news may provide the details in a couple of highlight film clips. In fact, the video, or visual images from the video, serves as the attention grabber.

Radio reports generally cover only the results and, if time permits, some quotes (sound bites) from the coach or a player who starred in the game. Broadcast news reporters have to write stories to fit a specific time allotment. According to Kohler (1994), most radio stories are 10 to 45 seconds long, 25 to 110 words. Most TV news stories run 15 seconds to 2 minutes, or no more than 300 words. That means broadcast journalists often do not have time for the why or the how unless those are the most important angles of the story.

When writing for online entities, discretion is at the hands of the sports organization. Some will simply cut and paste their news release to their website. Others will expand that writing with a more feature style. Stories can go longer online due to the unlimited space on the internet, but the 5Ws and the H should still be adhered to in order to get one's message across in a limited amount of time.

News Releases

Sports information specialists can enhance the possibility that a newspaper, a radio station, or a TV station will use the information in a release by writing in a style similar to news formats. Of equal importance is providing the name and telephone number of a contact person a reporter can call for additional information or clarification.

An editor will rarely run a news release without making some changes in style, structure, content, or length for policy or space reasons. For those who do, it's imperative that the SID be on top of his/her writing game because—in the fast-paced world, especially on deadline, of sports journalism—a well-written story may just appear verbatim in the next day's paper.

From a structural standpoint, the SID must pay close attention to two primary elements of a release: the header and the story. The header at the top of the page identifies the organization and provides other information useful to a reporter or editor. The story, of course, is the release.

Headers

The header on a news release generally includes the following information:

1. College or team name and address—to identify the sender.
2. Contact person—the SID or the person who wrote the release.
3. Telephone numbers—day, night, and fax, if desired.
4. Release date—a requested publication or broadcast date. "For Immediate Release" means the media are free to use the information whenever they wish. "Embargoed until 7 am Aug. 18" or "Not for release until 7 am Aug. 18"

Exhibit 7.1 *USA Basketball's Jerry Colangelo, Head Coach Greg Popovich and Utah Jazz star Donovan Mitchell at post-game press conference. (Photos courtesy of Andrew D. Bernstein/USA Basketball.)*

indicates a preference not to print or broadcast the information prior to the specified time. However, the "embargo" is not legally binding on the media. It is only a polite request.

Public relations firms often attempt to embargo or to dictate a release time out of a sense of fairness. They hope to give the media outlets a chance to release the information at the same time, to nullify any competitive advantages. However, differences in newscast times and newspaper deadlines make it impossible for all of them to release the information at the same time, although if it is an important news item the media outlet will usually put the release on its website. Public relations personnel may also send information they plan to reveal at a press conference to the media in advance so the media can gather background and other details. The objective is to give reporters a head start on a story that might be released on their deadline.

Use embargoes carefully. Remember, the media are under no obligation to honor them. Some reporters do not honor them, as a matter of policy. They argue that their job is to disseminate news as soon as they are aware of it. Competitive pressures lead others to break embargoes. They can get the jump on the competition as well as on the story by breaking an embargo before a press conference.

Story

Although a good news release is similar to a news story, it contains additional elements designed to serve the purposes of the sport organization. Two parts of the story are optional:

1. *Suggested headline*: A newspaper will seldom use a headline suggested by the sender. Reporters do not write the headlines at most newspapers. Copy editors write the headlines to fit a given type size and space dictated by page-design considerations. However, the headline may give a reporter or editor a quick idea of the subject matter.

2. *Dateline*: The dateline identifies the city in which the release originates. It is printed in all-capital letters, followed by a dash (—), at the start of the first sentence. Newspapers traditionally use datelines on stories that originate from cities outside their circulation areas. From the perspective of the SID, a dateline quickly gives the media a clue to the proximity of the sender.

The majority of news releases follows the inverted pyramid structure but may add a concluding paragraph that provides direction on how to obtain additional information. The most common structure contains the following components:

1. Lede (5Ws and H)

2. Details

3. Background

4. Sport organization tag

The lede starts with the element most important to the audience, or the readers. For example, a release announcing an award would emphasize the "who."

JACKSONVILLE, FLA.—Casbaugh State junior running back Joe Smith has been named the Eastern Atlantic Player of the Week for his efforts in guiding the Mules to a 70–63 victory over Riptide State, last weekend.

The lede also zeroes in on the strongest news characteristic. Although journalism texts offer anywhere from five to eight criteria, most include these six: timeliness, proximity, prominence, impact or consequence, the unusual or odd, and conflict. The sports information specialist can improve the publication or broadcast prospects of their news releases by emphasizing the same elements.

Emphasizing the timeliness would be effective in the lede on a story announcing the selections on an all-star team.

PROVIDENCE, R.I.—The 2018 CoSIDA/*ESPN The Magazine* all-District II academic first team was announced today and Casbaugh State junior point guard Michelle McKinney was named to the team for the second consecutive season.

The SID most likely will focus on proximity in a hometown release. Note how the SID might change the Michelle McKinney release sent to the Baltimore Sun.

JACKSONVILLE, FLA.—Baltimore native and Casbaugh State junior point guard Michelle McKinney was named today to the 2018 CoSIDA/*ESPN The Magazine* all-District II academic first team for the second consecutive season.

Prominence would be significant in a release announcing a speaker or a new employee.

JACKSONVILLE, FLA.—Former Mule All-American Mike Taylor was introduced today as the 35th men's lacrosse coach at Casbaugh State University.

Emphasizing the impact or consequences might be effective in the lead on a story about the upcoming season.

JACKSONVILLE, FLA.—Casbaugh State University's women's basketball team's 2018–19 season schedule was released today and will feature 14 games on national television, a first in program history.

"We are excited that our young ladies will be on national television so many times this season," Head Coach Joe Smith said. "It's a testament to the rise of our program and will certainly help in the recruiting efforts next season."

The odd or unusual might catch the attention of editors and readers in a news feature.

JACKSONVILLE, FLA.—Just call him the "Diamond in the Rough." For senior Casbaugh State University men's swimmer Justin Taylor, when he's not in class or practicing with his nationally ranked teammates, he's preparing for his internship next summer in the South African diamond mines as part of his major's study abroad program.

Conflict could come into play in a story about resignations, conference alignments, or suspension of players for rules violations.

MIRAMAR, Fla.—Riptide State University soccer coach Jack Johnson today announced the indefinite suspension of four student-athletes for a violation of team rules.

The body of the story should begin with details that elaborate on the basic news elements in descending order of importance. Obviously, the first details should provide amplification of the news element emphasized in the lede. The writer should put times, dates, and other specific information in the body.

A story that leads with the announcement of the selection of a coach, for example, should go on to provide more information on the coach's experience, coaching record, reasons for accepting the job, quotes, etc. Background on the circumstances that led to the search for a new coach, on the outgoing coach, and on the team's record for the season would follow. Newspaper editors who do not want to run the entire story or do not have space for all of it can easily eliminate the background, the information that followers of the team will already know.

An announcement about ticket sales, scheduling, or other matters about which readers might want additional information should close with a paragraph that tells them how to quickly find it.

Times for all Casbaugh State University basketball games will be announced at a later date. Season tickets for all 18 home games are on sale at the CSU Ticket Office at the CSU Coliseum, online at CSUGame.com, or by calling 1-800-CSU GAME.

An alternative lede uses a literary technique to emphasize the theme or news element of a story. It incorporates the peg or tieback that explains the news connection.

JACKSONVILLE, FLA.—Northwest Dakota A&M gave Jackson Taylor a second chance. Now Northeast Arkansas State is doing the same.

Five years after initially turning down an offer to coach NEAS, Taylor resigned after one year at Northeast Arkansas State, which hired him after a year away from coaching, to return to his alma mater and coach the Mules.

The body of an alternative story is similar to that of an inverted pyramid. However, it flows in a logical order appropriate to the style. Because the emphasis is on people, the story may contain more direct quotations from those included in the story. The writer must be careful to attribute the direct quotation to the speaker. The story may close with a direct quotation, an example, additional details, or a technique that reinforces the theme.

Types of Releases

Different types of releases naturally lend themselves to an inverted pyramid or alternative style. News releases fall into five broad categories.

Game Advance

A game advance release is a preview of an upcoming game. The story is designed to provide basic details on time and ticket information, as well as a rundown on team records, star players for both teams, series records and information, and quotes from the coaches about the matchup.

For the news media, the release provides useful information about the game for readers. From the perspective of the SID, the advance may help to stir interest among readers and to draw a crowd.

A game advance is sometimes written in the style of a feature story (i.e., an alternative approach). One popular supplement is a fact box, which is a format that lists basic facts (similar to the 5Ws) in a brief and punchy writing style. This technique makes it easy to find the primary information. The reporter or editor who receives the advance (fact box) can immediately gather information of importance.

If written in essay or narrative form, the release should take the inverted pyramid form, with the most important information on top and the least important on the bottom. All releases must contain the basic news components. For example, an advance on a football game should include the following:

1. What is the event? (conference game, nonconference)

2. Who is participating? (teams, players, etc.)

3. When will the event take place? (date and time)

4. Where will the event take place? (stadium and city/state)

5. How do they match up? (records for each team, style of play of both teams, strengths and weaknesses, an assessment by coaches/players)

The story should give information about which radio or television stations, networks, internet sites, or cable outlets will broadcast the game, and include the time. Other important details on both teams are injuries, notes, and statistics on key players, the coaches' records, team records, and notes and statistics on the rivalry. The advance may also include a brief preview of the style of play of both teams. Further notes about the sender's team and athletes should be included.

The timing of the release of a game advance is most important. It should be in the hands of the media five days in advance of the event for football and, depending on the schedule, two days in advance for other sports that may have more than one contest per week.

Hometown Release

A hometown release is a story about a student-athlete that is sent to the media in the player's hometown. Weekly newspapers that do not have the staff or resources to write stories about players or teams outside their circulation area often will run a hometown release as submitted.

Hometown releases generally are no more than six or eight paragraphs and follow the inverted pyramid style. They identify the athlete, the sport, and any honors earned. They could also list the student's major field of study and a cumulative grade point average if noteworthy.

A hometown release includes a brief background of the high school the student attended and athletic achievements there. Information about the parents or guardians and other family members also goes into the release. A photograph is included, if possible. Most sports information departments shoot photographs of all team athletes on media day or at the first practice for use in releases.

Feature Release

A feature release is intended to spotlight a student-athlete. The student does not have to be the most visible or talented athlete on campus. The SID can highlight some unusual or interesting facet of the athlete, such as hobbies or academic activities.

Because the emphasis is on an athlete rather than an event, and the purpose is to entertain as well as to inform, most feature releases use an alternative lede. The first paragraph must "grab" the reader immediately. A feature release should include the basic news details, such as the student's sport and performance. The body might follow the inverted pyramid style, or it might develop an interesting angle. In either case, the presentation should be "bright" and "tight," because the primary purpose is to entertain.

Types of News Releases

Game advance

Hometown release

Feature release

News release

Weekly review/preview

News Release

The basic news release is newsworthy because it provides information that most readers do not yet know. It may announce the hiring of a new coach, the signing of an outstanding high school athlete, the firing of a coach, or the groundbreaking ceremony for a new facility.

The release often supplements information announced at a news conference. The emphasis on timely and new information calls for an inverted pyramid approach and a concise explanation of the details. The release also may include quotations from appropriate coaches or university officials that elaborate on the news or put the significance of the announcement into perspective.

Weekly Review/Preview

The weekly review or weekly preview is a necessary evil for sports information directors. This type of release amounts to a weekly schedule of all the institution's athletic teams. It gives a summary of the records, opponents, and key players, as well as an upcoming preview of events to come during the week.

While somewhat taxing to formulate (the assistance of graduate and student assistants and interns is key) the entire review/preview can be sent via email as a PDF file.

Audience Awareness

Regardless of the type or structure of a news release, it should conform to strict media standards of accuracy, clarity and brevity. A media organization's credibility and professional reputation depend, to a large extent, on the accuracy of news reports. A reporter who consistently submits stories with errors or inaccuracies will not last long with a newspaper, magazine, radio, or TV company. Likewise, a sports information specialist who consistently submits releases with errors will soon find that no one in the media will trust or use any of the information.

Accuracy means the story is correct in every detail. To ensure accuracy, the sport information director (SID) must double-check to make certain that all times, dates, numbers, and other details are correct. The SID should check the spelling of all names, addresses, and titles; take care to list the titles of (or to otherwise identify) all people in the story, and to attribute all direct quotations and statements that contain opinion. It's also imperative that someone else edit the story. There may be glaring errors or omissions that the writer just doesn't see since s/he has been working on the material constantly. A fresh set of eyes will certainly help.

The writing style should be clear and concise. Remember, both the media and sports information specialists are writing for a mass audience. The reading ability of members of the audience may vary widely; some may not read at more than a sixth- or seventh-grade level. To reach the broadest audience possible, the journalist or SID must write in a simple style that is easy to understand.

Stories with short, simple sentences, shorter and simpler words, and short paragraphs are the easiest to read and understand. Numerous studies have shown a correlation between sentence length and readability. The longer the sentence is, the fewer who can understand it in its entirety. Journalists disagree on the optimum sentence length, but sentences averaging 15–25 words will pass most readability tests. In addition, journalists prefer one- and two-syllable words to longer ones that are more difficult to understand. The SID should avoid the use of jargon or technical terms the reader might not understand. For example, a story referencing a new Division I transfer in football who is eligible to play immediately would require some in-depth explanation why the recruit is eligible to play immediately.

Long paragraphs are a barrier to readability. Readers mentally interpret long paragraphs as dull and tedious, so journalists arbitrarily limit stories to two or three sentences per paragraph.

Print journalists generally use third person and past tense; broadcast journalists favor present tense because of the emphasis on immediacy. The SID should avoid using "we" or "you" in stories.

The SID should be particularly careful with both opinion that is not attributed and interpretive adjectives. They compromise the objectivity of the story because they suggest bias in favor of one viewpoint. It is better to forget the self-serving praise. The SID should avoid the use of superlatives and interpretive adjectives; for example, "Matt Smith, the best player in the conference, is approaching a school record." Clichés ("a classic game," "a coach on the field") should also be avoided. An editor will purge all of them, or pitch the release in the trash.

The SID can make certain a story conforms to news style by stocking the office with reference guides used by the media. Here are some of the most popular:

- *The Associated Press Stylebook.* The stylebook provides guidelines on news style for titles, addresses, numbers, dates, etc. It also includes tips on word usage, grammar, and punctuation. One chapter is devoted exclusively to sports and is usually updated every year. There is a also a section on social media criteria. This stylebook is a must for any SID or PR practitioner and is often referred to as "the journalist's Bible."

- *Broadcast News and Writing Stylebook.* The guide not only offers tips on style, but also addresses ledes, endings, and story forms for both radio and television.

- *The Elements of Style.* This book has served as the authority on grammar, spelling, style, and usage for years.

Common Errors

No matter the form a news release takes, these common errors should be avoided to ensure releases are more likely to be accepted for publication or broadcast.

Lack of Newsworthiness

The story fails to emphasize the most important news element or buries it in the middle of the story.

Wrong:

Casbaugh State University will play a basketball schedule this season, including 13 teams that appeared in postseason play.

The Man-O-Wars will play 10 non-conference contests and face the usual 18 league members in Northeastern Atlantic play.

Coach Jackson Taylor will lead CSU when the season kicks off.

Right:

Veteran coach Jackson Taylor, CSU's 21st men's basketball coach at Casbaugh State University, announced Monday that he and his Man-O-Wars will face 13 teams that appeared in postseason play last year, and a schedule that includes 28 contests, 18 of which are in Northeastern Atlantic Conference play.

Lack of Objectivity

The story promotes instead of reports. It sounds like a sales pitch for the school instead of an objective news story.

Wrong:

Riptide State leads the country in fewest points allowed, through 19 games this season, allowing just 61.7 points per contest.

Unfortunately for the Man-O-Wars, they are only averaging 49.6 points a game themselves but are a scrappy, hard-working squad that gives their all every game. But they just can't seem to buy a bucket or get the right call from the officials when the time arises.

"I don't think the officials like me or my team," Coach John Armstrong said. "If they did, we might have won a few more games."

Right:

Despite leading the country in fewest points per game allowed, the Riptide State Man-O-Wars are off to their poorest start in school history.

Opponents are outscoring the RSU by nearly 12 points per contest and are still looking for their first victory 19 games into the season. Poor shooting has hurt the Man-O-Wars all season. They are only connecting on 29 percent of their attempts while the opposition is shooting 46 percent.

The Eight Most Common Mistakes in New Releases

1. Lack of newsworthiness
2. Lack of objectivity
3. Too many superlatives and interpretive adjectives
4. Self-serving quotations
5. Emphasis on the obvious
6. Lack of a local tie (on out-of-town releases)
7. Unnecessary background
8. Too wordy

Too Many Superlatives and Interpretive Adjectives

The story attempts to create hype by using superlatives and interpretive adjectives rather than letting the subject matter speak for itself.

Wrong:

Sharpshooting guard Chip Glass has been uncanny this basketball season.

With the touch of a safecracker and the precision of a diamond cutter, he has led Cincinnati Poly to a break-even season, standing at 12–12 at the three-quarter mark of the campaign.

Glass will duel Curly Grimes of Indiana Tech when the two teams meet Wednesday night, and while Grimes is a first-team all-conference selection, Glass is better, according to CinPoly coach Sam Cameron.

"I will take Glass over Grimes every day of the week," Cameron said. "Everyone should come out and see for themselves that Glass is the best guard."

Right:

Arguably the two finest guards in college basketball will face each other Wednesday night at Riverfront Arena when Cincinnati Poly meets Indiana Tech.

CinPoly's Chip Glass will trade shots with all-conference choice Curly Grimes when the Polys hope to snap a five-game losing streak.

"It will be interesting to see the guard matchup," said CinPoly coach Sam Cameron. "Each is a skilled player, and they both know how to score lots of points in a basketball game."

Self-Serving Quotations

The direct quotations aim at self-promotion instead of at explaining and providing perspective on the subject matter.

Wrong:

"I firmly believe we have the finest college basketball team in all of Division II," said Baltic University coach Kelly Smith.

"We have great shooters, we are quick, and we play tenacious defense. I say we have it all and it's a shame we are only 5–12 this season. We have so many injuries, and they have hurt our chances."

BU will try to snap a nine-game losing streak tonight when the Overseas take on Wharton University, which is 19–1.

"We have played a much tougher schedule than Wharton, and we are a better team than the Stockbrokers," added Smith.

Right:

Baltic University will try to snap a nine-game losing streak tonight when the Overseas play host to Wharton University.

BU, which is 5–12, has not won since defeating Baker Barber College, 112–111, on Nov. 11. Wharton, meanwhile, is 19–1.

"We have our job cut out for us, and we know it will not be easy, but the Wharton players put their shorts on one leg at a time, just like we do," said BU coach Kelly Smith.

Emphasis on the Obvious

The story leads with information the reader already knows or with obvious information that does not encourage the reader to go further.

Wrong:

Jane McIntyre, of Hoboken, N.J., plays on the Ashoil University basketball team.

Right:

Jane McIntyre has been the unsung hero for the Ashoil University women's basketball team this season.

McIntyre, the only player from Hoboken, N.J., on the Eagles, leads them in steals and blocks and her calming influence on the court has helped carry Ashoil to a 12–0 record going into conference play.

Lack of Local Tie (on Out-of-Town Releases)

The story does not quickly make clear that some aspect of the story has a local connection (proximity).

Wrong:

Release sent to *The Plain Dealer* in Cleveland:

FORT WORTH, Texas—The Texas Christian women's basketball team will play host tonight to Baylor for the BIG 12 tournament championship.

The Lady Horned Frogs are led by sophomore Becky Lane of Houston, who has averaged 25.4 points per game this season.

Right:

Release sent to *The Plain Dealer* in Cleveland:

FORT WORTH, Texas—Sophomore Becky Lane of Cleveland, Ohio, will lead the Texas Christian Lady Horned Frogs into tonight's BIG 12 championship women's basketball game against Baylor.

Lane, who attends TCU because her aunt lives in suburban Fort Worth, averages 25.5 points and 12.7 rebounds per game for the Frogs.

Unnecessary Background

The story contains too much "old news" at the top of the story, obscuring the new or important elements.

Wrong:

Freshman Jane Schmidt came to Miami University on a basketball scholarship with plenty of previous acclaim.

She was a middle school phenomenon before she starred in high school, when she was named an All-American, and then played a key role for a team that won the Amateur Athletic Union (AAU) 16–18 title. Now in her first year at Miami she has continued her solid play with a 22.1 scoring average.

Schmidt exceeded her scoring average with 25 points last night as the Lady Hurricanes defeated Georgia 77–71 in the first round of the NCAA tournament.

Right:

Jane Schmidt, who has been one of the nation's top women's basketball players the last four years, scored 25 points last night to lead the University of Miami to a 77–71 victory over Georgia in the first round of the NCAA championship tournament.

Too Wordy

Long sentences filled with clauses that cover two or three ideas confuse and lose readers.

Wrong:

Johnny Jones, who is from Paducah, Ky., is one of the finer young golfers in the nation who play on Wednesdays and Fridays during July and August in preparation for the National Junior Golf Championships.

Jones, who is a southpaw, and James Johnson, another teenager, will compete with Bill Brown, who has a very good game, and George Green, a former standout basketball player from Athens, Ga. This group, which has a combined age of 98 years, is, as a group, quick on the draw, and each one, when the climate is right, can putt with the tour professionals.

These young golfers from the Midwest also are very good students, and several of them, when not playing golf, work out in karate classes. This helps them develop the arm strength needed to be good golfers. His long drives are one of the reasons Jones is one of the favorites in the tournament and the person many pros think will win.

Right:

Johnny Jones, a smooth-swinging teenager from Paducah, Ky., is the odds-on favorite to win the National Junior Golf Championships.

The primary competition Jones will face for the trophy include James Johnson, Bill Brown, and George Green. All four are good putters, but the long drives of Jones is what many professionals believe sets him apart from the rest of the field.

Distribution of Releases

Two considerations figure into the decision about who should receive a news release: the news organization and the target audience. A news organization's story selection depends on its mission and audience. That is why *USA Today* offers a comprehensive sports section every day, whereas the *Columbus Dispatch* seldom sends sports reporters outside the state. Similarly, a news organization shapes its coverage to meet the interests of its viewers or readers. College athletics are big in the Midwest; pro sports are the draw in New York City. Stories on local athletes are more interesting than information about athletes outside the circulation/coverage area.

A Cleveland, Ohio, sportswriter will have little use for a Texas Christian University football review/preview, or a feature release about a women's basketball player at Louisiana State University. Unless the athlete is from Cleveland, or LSU plays an Ohio team, the information in the release likely will offer little or no benefit to the Cleveland media. Sending the release is a waste of the SID's time.

It is imperative for the sports information specialist to know the sports reporter and the editor or director who supervises sports coverage for each of the local media. It is also important to know the types of sports and the types of stories each uses most frequently. Finally, it is helpful to keep directories in the office that provide names, addresses, and emails of sports editors and directors to whom the SID might send hometown releases.

The personal contacts make it possible for an SID to keep postal and email lists up-to-date and use them to their best advantage. In trimming the list to get the most out of releases, the SID can determine who is sincerely interested in receiving a specific kind of release. It would also be beneficial to update the contact list every year. The SID should ask if the sports department still wants to receive releases, if the names, email addresses, and other contact information are accurate, and what types of releases they will consider running. The use of email has now become the most prevalent method in submitting news releases, particularly in conveying news with a tight time frame.

The SID should be careful not to overwhelm the local media in the primary target market who regularly cover the school. Too much of a good thing can work against the SID, too.

Simply put, the SID or public relations director must know the target market and the media market, then use common sense about the distribution of releases. It is also important to note that a proactive sports information director will be up-to-date with the latest trends in social media and when, where, and how to harness the 24/7 news cycle to the best of one's ability, with the medium (Twitter, Facebook, etc.) that would be the most effective.

In every case, the SID should send the release to a specific person. Releases addressed to generic titles like Sports Editor are often treated as junk by journalists. Sending the release to a specific person takes on added importance in fax releases and electronic communication because releases of every type may pour into a common pool.

Timing is another critical factor. If the information arrives too early, it may be leaked early, or wind up buried at the bottom of a pile of submissions. If it arrives too late, it is worthless to the media and the sport institution.

Summary

Writing is the sports information specialist's backbone and lifeblood. There are myriad forms of writing, from feature stories to game notes to social media posts. One of the main responsibilities is that of the news release, a prepackaged story distributed to the media with the intention that they will pass the information on to the public. Because releases are the most common form of information distributed by sport organizations, strong writing skills are essential to success for SIDs.

News releases are similar to news stories, although their primary objectives differ. News releases attempt to persuade—to create a favorable image of an athlete, a team, or a sport organization. News stories attempt to inform—to present a balanced view of a topic to readers or viewers. They also entertain. The structure of a news story depends on the information or entertainment value of the story. The inverted pyramid puts emphasis on the information in the story, pushing the most important details to the top. Alternative structures emphasize the human-interest angle or entertainment features. They are used most often when readers already know most of the basic facts, or when the news value is minimal.

A sports information specialist can increase the chances that the media will use a news release by writing in a style similar to that of journalists. Game advances, hometown releases, and news releases follow a standard format—lede, details, background, and where to call for more information—built on the inverted pyramid model. Feature releases and weekly reviews/previews often will take an alternative approach. The SID will add information at the top of a release that provides contact information to reporters seeking additional details. The SID can request that the media withhold publication or broadcast of the information until a specified time, but the media are under no legal obligation to honor an embargo.

The most effective releases emphasize the characteristic that makes the story newsworthy, whether it is the announcement of a new coach, or the success of a media outlet's hometown athlete. Because the media reach a broad, mass audience, effective releases also are clear and concise. Short sentences, simple language, and short paragraphs are the most readable. Guidebooks such as *The Associated Press Stylebook* provide direction on how to write according to news style. The most important consideration for every release is accuracy. The SID must check and recheck every name, date, number, and fact to maintain credibility and cooperation among the media.

SIDs maintain up-to-date mailing and email lists and information on the types of releases specific news organizations use. SIDs also pay close attention to deadlines and the timing of releases. A release that arrives too late is of no value. The SID who knows the target media, the target audience, and news structure can write a release that emphasizes the same elements a sportswriter would emphasize. A well-written release may be utilized by both print and broadcast media in different locales, with little alteration.

Discussion Questions

1. When making an announcement, plea, or request in the form of a release, how do you persuade your audience to take the action you desire?

2. What are the criteria used to determine what angle will be taken when preparing to write a news release? Create an illustration and discuss it.

Suggested Exercises

1. Write four one-page releases (hometown, feature, news, and weekly review/preview).

2. Apply a readability formula to a story you have written and determine the reading level at which you write.

3. Using the AP style book, create a mock social media post using social media guidelines for one of your releases in Exercise 1 above.

8 | Creating Promotional Guides

A sports organization's image is one of the most important aspects to its success. How the organization is perceived and portrayed is very important and vital to ensuring success in its future endeavors. A positive image portrays success. That perception starts with the organization's director (i.e., athletic director in college, general manager, owner, or president in the professional ranks), and it trickles down through the department hierarchy to and through the sports information specialists.

Part of the organization's image is portrayed through its promotional guide, and creating and maintaining that guide is arguably one of the most important duties of the SID. While their names have evolved through the years, as well as their content, length, size, and even method of delivery, these guides are still recognized as one of the foundations of the SID's profession. Some sport organizations still refer to them as promotional guides. Others refer to them as recruiting guides, media guides, information guides, virtual guides (if online), or just *guides*, because they now serve many different purposes.

Most, if not all, are now completely accessible via a school/sport organization's website and are highly interactive, fulfilling both recruiting and promotional functions.In its online version, the guide is unlimited and not constrained by NCAA printed material guidelines; guides are in full color, and the flashier the better. Chock full of history, video, statistics, bios, etc., these guides will sometimes be the first look a recruit, announcer, fan, sponsorship target, or parent has with a school or sport organization.

In the 1960s and 1970s, media guides at the collegiate level were nothing more than a handful of pages, especially for football, usually in a small booklet or pamphlet format that included the most vital of information about an individual sport: schedule, roster, basic profile information, a brief outlook of the upcoming season, and any pertinent records.

Today, primarily because technology has evolved so much, these informational guides have been transformed to serve many different purposes: providing a basis of information to the media (which was the original concept in the development and creation of media guides), serving as a tool by coaching staff in the recruitment of prospective student-athletes, and generating income and interest for fans and their team or organization. Regardless of the intended audience, it is still the SID's responsibility to make the guide fully functional and up-to-date.

In a contemporary guide, all sorts of information fulfills the needs of its audience:

- schedule
- roster
- coach bios
- player bios
- conference/league information
- historical records, such as single-game, season, and career records for both individuals and teams
- the previous season in review
- the upcoming season's prospects and notes
- opponent information
- honors and awards
- basic information about the organization (e.g., at West Virginia University it is an in-depth look into the entire university and the city of Morgantown)
- basic information for the media (e.g., SID contact information, directions to athletic facilities, radio and television affiliates, and rules and regulations pertaining to obtaining interviews with coaches and athletes)

Simply put, it's a one-stop point of reference for everything that a recruit, a coach, a member of the media, a sponsor, or a fan would need to know about that organization or team.

The Basics of a Promotional Guide

A college coach looks at the media guide not only as a means to impress the media, but also as a tool to recruit potential players and their parents. The media guide often becomes the first look a potential recruit will have of the school and campus the coach represents. While it might be called a media guide, the publication is often a handbook for recruits and their parents to learn about the coaching staff, check out photos of the locker room, and get a view of campus life through an array of photos and descriptions of students, staff, and faculty. Given the online techno-logical innovations in the production of these publications and depending on your budget, a media guide also can have many short audio and video clips of players and coaches. These online versions can truly bring 'someone to life' and present a very positive impression to your audience.

Members of the media who cover college athletics sometimes need to be reminded of these dual purposes. So while several pages of the media guide outlining pricey renovations to the weight room might seem like a waste of time to reporters, it is of great interest to the high school player looking to bulk up for the move from prep star to college standout (and potential professional athlete).

And this is where communication between the coach and his or her sports information director (SID) is key. A well-informed SID is an invaluable asset to a coach. A SID who understands the recruiting process (i.e., when the recruiting contact period begins and ends, when the signing period starts, and when letters of intent are due) can also be instrumental in setting up the media guide's publishing schedule to take full advantage of this process. The SID who understands the needs of his or her coach will take the time in the offseason to gather current photos and images of the campus, community landmarks, members of the team, and write interesting feature stories or captions that enhance the recruiting value of the media guide. A list of the games that will be televised is always a great handout to a parent, coach, or recruit. For the professional team's communication director, the TV schedule is a great way to help add sponsorship dollars to the bottom line.

For the college setting, recruits and their families want to know if any former players are playing in the pro ranks. A page or two of pictures featuring alums that are in the NBA, MLB, MLS, NFL, or other professional leagues can grab the attention of a recruit. A story on a former player that is playing professionally or a list of the "Players in the Pros" is also effective. For media guides that are produced by professional sports teams, the audience will be fans, reporters, and corporate sponsors. The media guide is an attempt to make each athlete appear likeable to the fan and the sponsor, and each player's bio should present an interesting personal story that could lead to a feature article by a local or national reporter. The media guide for an organization like USA Basketball or USA Track and Field is prepared for a national and international audience.

The cover of the media guide is equally as important as what is inside. Are the players featured on the front or should the coach be on the cover this year? Which athletes and how many, should appear on the cover? Is one player a potential Player of the Year? Should that player be featured in a video embedded in the online version of the media guide? Is there a theme for the upcoming season? Is there a new building on campus or a landmark in town that carries special meaning or have recruiting or promotional value? Did your team win the Super Bowl, the World Series, or the NCAA Championship last year? Do you have an athlete that is an Olympic medalist? The answers to these questions and others will influence the final product but it all begins with good communication between the coach and

SID. Additionally, with the emphasis on "going green" there is more consideration given to publishing material strictly online. Producing some video clips that help the media, fans, sponsors, and recruits get to know the players is a great way to use video to enhance an online media guide.

Finally, in relation to a college athletic team's media guides, it goes without saying that many high school players, parents, and coaches are keenly interested in a school's academic reputation, its offerings, graduation rates, and other metrics of success. The media guide is a great place to feature a signature academic program or discipline, to promote an elite faculty, and highlight the achievements both on and off the court or playing field of the student-athletes.

There's little question that a well-designed, lively, and informative media guide can be a college coach's best friend when selling the program to recruits. A well-designed media guide for a professional sports team or national sport federation can be a great tool for the marketing and communication department to drum up sponsorship interest, to aid in selling season tickets or to create feature news stories about players or coaches.

> **"The SID ... is in charge of all aspects of the media guide from planning, writing, layout, proofreading, the bid process where applicable, budgetary considerations and production" (Shutt, 1998).**

Depending on the structure of the organization, most SIDs are in fact their own writer, planner, editor, designer, and point of contact in terms of production and costs. However, some institutions or sport organizations have their own sports publication department that works closely with the SID, decreasing the SID's workload and assisting with the production, layout and design, advertising, and overall structure and presentation of the entire package. Despite the structure in place and its impact on the creation of the informational guide, the SID is still the "editor in chief" and is responsible for ensuring that the project comes to fruition.

While ensuring that the guide meets the needs of the audiences, the SID must discover how much of the guide will be devoted to recruiting, how much to the players and coaches, the record book, and overall basic information about that specific sport and/or sport organization's entire department or program. By today's standards, they are all of equal importance, so deciphering the most important aspect may be a moot point, especially without limitations in size in its online form.

How much of it will be a conglomeration or crossover of both, fulfilling a multitude of needs all in one swoop? While all those questions are kept in mind, the SID will also continue to work closely with the coaches or sport organization executives to ensure the eventual finished product is to their liking.

Once the blueprint for the guide has been developed and the SID knows exactly what content is going into the guide, the SID must also comply with rules implemented by the NCAA for printed guides.

> **"NCAA rules currently allow institutions to print a recruiting brochure or promotional guide, but not both. The publications are limited to one color (except for the front and back covers) and may not exceed 8.5 x 11 inches in size or more than 208 pages in length. Schools typically devote the front half of the promotional guide to recruiting information and the back half to records, historical data, and key player and coach biographies more relevant to media covering their athletics teams."** (McKindra, 2009)

Note that these guides are rarely ever started or created from scratch (unless an institution or sport organization begins to sponsor a new sport). They are usually an evolution from the previous year's version. And, as the previous season unfolds, updated information is kept in the SID's Word files of the guide—keeping track of pertinent game-by-game information for players and coaches bios, and updating any team records or game, seasonal, and career marks set by the organization's players. It is imperative to point out, again, that the guide evolves from the previous entry to meet the demands of all its audiences.

It should also be pointed out that guides at the professional sports level are just that, actual promotional guides. There are no recruiting tools, but they are simply full of factual information that the media use at their convenience. There are no page-count limitations (more on that later in this chapter) and the guides are usually smaller pocket guides such as 5.5 x 4.25 inches, or about one quarter of the size of traditional collegiate guides that are 8.5 x 11.

What follows are some key components the SID must be aware of before developing the guide.

Budgeting

The budget generally is determined by university administrators (or in the professional ranks, by front office personnel). The SID receives an annual allotment for publications and supplements that income through advertising. The SID, in concert with public relations or athletics administrators, decides how to divide the publications budget among various sports. Higher-profile sports will have a larger guide with wider distribution, necessitating a much larger publications budget than lower-profile sports.

Advertising

The more advertising the SID can acquire for promotional guides, the more attractive the guide. Consequently, the sports information office may solicit advertising to supplement the budget allotment. The advertising rate depends on the cost of production per page, and the number of pages earmarked for advertising. The SID at a larger university or organization may have an advertising manager to oversee solicitations of advertising; however, sports information personnel will proof the ads (i.e., read them and note any corrections needed).

Written Content

The sports information director, director of communications, or public relations director oversees all the written material in the guide, and does so while paying close attention to the needs and wants of the coaches and the sports organizations personnel. Sports information personnel will write most, if not all, of the information and compile the statistical sections. That written content will then be edited by everyone in the SID's office to ensure there are no grammatical or spelling errors or factual mistakes.

Photographs

The sports information or public relations director also arranges for all photographs. The SID selects action pictures from the previous year and arranges for new head shots of coaches, team members, and athletics officials. A staff photographer, a freelancer, or a studio photographer may shoot the pictures. These photos are archived in the SID's permanent files and can be referenced for future guides, historical picture requests by media members, or to supplement photographs in future guides.

Keep in mind that all photos for the printed guide must be in black and white. There are no color restrictions for an online guide.

Art and Graphics

The SID will arrange for all charts, drawings, and illustrations, or will obtain and review initial art and graphic designs with members of the current staff and the coaches to ensure the look is appropriate and accepted. The artist may be a volunteer, a member of the art department, an in-house professional, or a hired studio artist.

Page Design

The page design may be created by members of the sports information or public relations staff, personnel in the college printing services office, printing company employees, or outsourced to a paid graphics designer. As in the case of advertisements, the SID or sports information staffers read and mark corrections on proofs of all pages.

Page Limitations

In 2005, the NCAA mandated that all print media guides, regardless of the sport, would no longer exceed 208 pages in length. The rules were set in place to create an even playing field as it pertained to recruiting prospective student-athletes. Consider why these restrictions were imposed. If you're the SID at a major Division I institution, chances are your operating budget for your promotional guide would almost seem limitless. In knowing that, promotional guides, prior to the 2005 NCAA mandate, were astronomical in size, especially when it came to major, traditional football and basketball powers (e.g., Missouri's 2004 football guide was 614 pages). If bigger is better, then potential student-athletes might have made their decisions to attend a school based on the size of its promotional guide, at least in theory, since their first encounter with said school might very well be by looking at a 600-plus page guide.

Now, consider those same recruits who might be getting recruiting attention from smaller Division I schools that don't have as large a budget for their guides. The smaller schools just couldn't compete because of budgetary limitations, hence the rules that took form in 2005.

So under the 208-page restriction, the SID must choose what goes in a guide and what does not. For smaller varsity/Olympic sports (such as soccer, baseball, lacrosse), however, those promotional guides will rarely reach the full 208 pages, freeing the SID from determining what information will not appear in the guide. But for major sports, such as Division I football and basketball, it is imperative that the appropriate information that is included is balanced to meet the needs of the varying audiences: recruits, media, and the general public.

Information that is left out—and there will be information that doesn't make the promotional guide's final print version cut—can easily be placed in a supplement to the actual guide. That information can be bound and distributed to serve as an accessory. Information that may appear in the supplement includes additional all-time records that are important, but not the most important or they would be in the guide itself.

Supplements are usually created for sports such as football and basketball, where information outpaces space allotted in 208 pages. The smaller varsity/Olympic sports will have plenty of room to contain all of that information in their own guides.

Printing

Most colleges contract with professional printing companies for multicolor, magazine-style guides. Local print shops or university printing services often can handle small brochures. The SID or an athletics department administrator negotiates the printing contract or oversees competitive bidding for the contract.

Once those areas are recognized, it is important for the guide to include every detail about the players, coaches, team, and sport organization that will aid the media in their coverage of the team. Because the media often work under intense deadline pressure, they may need to check a record, a past score, or a player's hometown. The more easily they can find the information in the promotional guide, the better the promotional guide will have served one of its purposes.

Note, however, that printing costs have decreased as new technologies and online display evolve new ways to present the guide. Simply put, hard copy needs are not what they used to be.

Mandatory Content of Promotional Guides

Many promotional guides take on the personality of its author and sport organization. Some have used movie themes consistently through the guide, while others use "team themes" created by the coaching staff (e.g., research Tennessee women's basketball and its yearly publication). Others will use the guide as a tie-in with the preseason promotion and publicity of an All-America candidate.

Some guides will also use all of its allotted pages, using filler content, such as an overview and outlook of the institution and an in-depth listing of the organization's entire staff. Others will fill space with advertisements from the organization's sponsors. While these are nice to add if space is available, there are mandatory and essential functional sections of a promotional guide that must be included.

Table of Contents. The table of contents usually appears in the opening pages of the guide and includes a complete list of the contents of the guide, with page numbers, from the front to the back of the publication.

Schedule. The schedule should be as up-to-date as possible with a list of every game that includes the opponent, date, location, starting time, and, if available, television information.

Alphabetical and/or Numerical Rosters. Every guide, regardless of sport, should contain an alphabetical roster that lists every member of the team. It may be beneficial for some sports' promotional guides to also include numerical rosters. The rosters will vary slightly depending on the sport and whether the guide is for a collegiate, professional, or national team, but essentially they should include

2016 U.S. OLYMPIC WOMEN'S BASKETBALL TEAM ROSTER

• Alphabetical Roster

NO	NAME	POS	HGT	WGT	AGE	TEAM	COLLEGE	HOMETOWN
5	Seimone Augustus	G/F	6-0	166	32	Minnesota Lynx	Louisiana State	Baton Rouge, LA
6	Sue Bird	G	5-9	150	35	Seattle Storm	Connecticut	Syosset, NY
10	Tamika Catchings	F	6-1	167	37	Indiana Fever	Tennessee	Duncanville, TX
14	Tina Charles	C	6-4	198	27	New York Liberty	Connecticut	Jamaica, NY
11	Elena Delle Donne	G/F	6-5	188	26	Chicago Sky	Delaware	Wilmington, DE
13	Sylvia Fowles	C	6-6	200	30	Minnesota Lynx	Louisiana State	Miami, FL
15	Brittney Griner	C	6-8	199	25	Phoenix Mercury	Baylor	Houston, TX
8	Angel McCoughtry	G/F	6-1	160	29	Atlanta Dream	Louisville	Baltimore, MD
7	Maya Moore	F	6-0	176	27	Minnesota Lynx	Connecticut	Lawrenceville, GA
9	Breanna Stewart	F/C	6-4	175	21	Seattle Storm	Connecticut	North Syracuse, NY
12	Diana Taurasi	G	6-0	163	34	Phoenix Mercury	Connecticut	Chino, CA
4	Lindsay Whalen	G	5-9	169	34	Minnesota Lynx	Minnesota	Hutchinson, MN

• Numerical Roster

NO	NAME	POS	HGT	WGT	AGE	TEAM	COLLEGE	HOMETOWN
4	Lindsay Whalen	G	5-9	169	34	Minnesota Lynx	Minnesota	Hutchinson, MN
5	Seimone Augustus	G/F	6-0	166	32	Minnesota Lynx	Louisiana State	Baton Rouge, LA
6	Sue Bird	G	5-9	150	35	Seattle Storm	Connecticut	Syosset, NY
7	Maya Moore	F	6-0	176	27	Minnesota Lynx	Connecticut	Lawrenceville, GA
8	Angel McCoughtry	G/F	6-1	160	29	Atlanta Dream	Louisville	Baltimore, MD
9	Breanna Stewart	F/C	6-4	175	21	Seattle Storm	Connecticut	North Syracuse, NY
10	Tamika Catchings	F	6-1	167	37	Indiana Fever	Tennessee	Duncanville, TX
11	Elena Delle Donne	G/F	6-5	188	26	Chicago Sky	Delaware	Wilmington, DE
12	Diana Taurasi	G	6-0	163	34	Phoenix Mercury	Connecticut	Chino, CA
13	Sylvia Fowles	C	6-6	200	30	Minnesota Lynx	Louisiana State	Miami, FL
14	Tina Charles	C	6-4	198	27	New York Liberty	Connecticut	Jamaica, NY
15	Brittney Griner	C	6-8	199	25	Phoenix Mercury	Baylor	Houston, TX

2016 U.S. Olympic Women's Basketball Team Staff

Head Coach: Geno Auriemma, University of Connecticut
Assistant Coach: Doug Bruno, DePaul University
Assistant Coach: Cheryl Reeve, Minnesota Lynx
Assistant Coach: Dawn Staley, University of South Carolina
Team Physician (Brazil): Lisa Callahan, Hospital for Special Surgery
Team Physician (domestic): David Walden, Colorado Springs, Colorado
Athletic Trainer: Ed Ryan, Colorado Springs, Colorado

USA National Team Staff

Court Coach/Opponent Scout: Jen Rizzotti, George Washington University
Court Coach/Opponent Scout: Jamelle Elliott, University of Cincinnati
Video Coordinator: Kevin DeMille, George Washington University

USA Basketball Staff

CEO/Executive Director: Jim Tooley
National Team Director: Carol Callan
National Team Assistant Director: Ohemaa Nyanin
Chief Media Communications Director: Craig Miller
Communications Director: Caroline Williams
Communications Manager: Jenny Maag

Pronunciation Guide

Seimone Augustus (SI-moan)
Tamika Catchings (tuh-MEE-kuh)
Sylvia Fowles (fouls - as in a foul shot, but plural)
Angel McCoughtry (Mc-CAW-tree)
Maya Moore (MY-ah)
Breanna Stewart (bree-ANN-uh)
Diana Taurasi (tuh-RA-zee)
Geno Auriemma (oar-ee-EM-uh)

NOTE: *Ages listed are as of Aug. 5, 2016.*

Exhibit 8.1 *2016 USA Women's Basketball Team Roster.*
(Courtesy of Andrew D. Bernstein/USA Basketball.)

Exhibit 8.2 *Sample Pronunciation Guide*

First Names:		Last Names:	
Akeema	uh-KEEM-uh	Bussie	Bus-E
Asya	Asia	Repella	Re-PELL-uh
Ayana	Eye-yahn-uh		
Korinne	CORE-inn		
Madina	Muh-DEAN-uh		
Tonia	Toe-Knee-uh		

name, height, weight, position, age, class, experience, hometown, and high school or college.

Pronunciation Guide. The pronunciation guide is a must for those who provide radio or television coverage of the team . If an athlete's name is pronounced differently than it appears on the roster, or is one that may create problems, it is important to provide the phonetic spelling of the name.

Last Year's Results. The previous year's results will play a vital role in the coverage of the contemporary team. Therefore, a capsule of each game or event in the previous season, including both individual and team statistics, is required. Results will also include the entire compiled statistical results, such as season highs and lows, statistical trends, player and team seasonal averages, and scores/results from each contest.

Season Prospectus. The upcoming season can be discussed via a brief overview of the previous season and a general preview of the upcoming season. The overview should include comments from the head coach. The growing trend with this section is shifting toward quick hitter information broken down into short paragraph notes.

Quick Facts. Quick facts are the first glimpse into a program or sports team, including information about the institution/organization and the team, the location of the organization, head coach, and key elements about the current team, such as starters returning and lost, and contact information for the SID.

Biographies of Coaches. A complete biography of the head coach is required, including an up-to-date coaching record with any notable achievements, all-time great victories, players in the professional ranks, etc. Biographies on assistant coaches, athletic trainers, strength and conditioning coaches, and other key support personnel are helpful, but not vital. Photographs of the coaching staff help dress up a promotional guide and create a favorable impression.

Player Profiles. Arguably the "meat" of the promotional guide is the player profiles section, which is especially pivotal in the preseason prior to competition. This section contains a detailed profile of each player, including photographs and statistics for each season the athlete has performed for the organization. The bio will also include season-by-season statistics and individual career game highs. Due

2018 WVU Cross Country Quick Facts

UNIVERSITY INFORMATION
Location: Morgantown, W.Va.
Enrollment: 31,442
Founded: 1867
President: E. Gordon Gee
Director of Athletics: Shane Lyons
Nickname: Mountaineers
Colors: Old Gold (PMS 124) and Blue (PMS 295)
Conference: Big 12

COACHING STAFF
Head Coach: Sean Cleary *(12th season/26th overall, West Virginia '92)*
Assistant Coach: Erin O'Reilly *(6th season, West Virginia '93)*
Graduate Assistant: Clara Santucci *(West Virginia '10)*
All-Americans under Cleary: 15 by eight individuals
Mid-Atlantic Region Coach of the Year: 2004, 2007, 2008

CROSS COUNTRY HISTORY
Season of Cross Country: 41st
First Year of Cross Country: 1978
NCAA Championship appearances: 9
(1997, 2000, 2004, 2007, 2008, 2009, 2010, 2011, 2013, 2014)
NCAA Championship Top-10 Finishes: 5
(2007-9th, 2008-4th, 2009-6th, 2011-8th, 2014-8th)
Individual NCAA Qualifiers: 23
NCAA Mid-Atlantic Team Champions: 2004, 2008
Big East Team Champions: 2007
Atlantic 10 Team Champions: 1994

TEAM INFORMATION
2017 NCAA Mid-Atlantic Regional Finish: 7th
2017 Big 12 Conference Finish: 4th
2017 All-Mid-Atlantic Region: Amy Cashin, Maggie Drazba
2017 All-Big 12: Amy Cashin, Maggie Drazba
2017 Academic All-American: Amy Cashin *(First Team)*
Letterwinners Returning/Lost: 8/5
Newcomers: 11

MEDIA INFORMATION
Graduate Assistant/Cross Country Contact: Joe Mitchin
Email: jmitchin@mail.wvu.edu
Office: (304) 293-2821
Cell: (330) 933-2084
Fax: (304) 293-4105
Website: www.WVUsports.com
Twitter: @WVUXCTF
Facebook: /WVUXCTF
Instagram: @WVUXCTF
Associate AD/Communications: Michael Fragale
Assistant AD/Communications: Bryan Messerly
Director of Football Communications: Mike Montoro
Director of Digital Media: John Antonik
Digital Media Manager: Grant Dovey
Director of Athletic Publications: Joe Swan
Associate Director of Athletic Communications: Shannon Wolfgang
Associate Director of Athletic Communications: Ashley Bailey
Assistant Director of Athletic Communications: Amy Salvatore
Assistant Director of Athletic Communications: Charlie Healy

2018 WVU Cross Country Roster

Name	Height	Class	Hometown/Last School
Marianne Abdalah	5-4	r-Fr.	Pittsburgh, Pa./Vincentian Academy
Antigone Archer	5-4	r-So.	Southlake, Texas/Southlake Carroll
Abby Colbert	5-5	r-So.	Shephardstown, W.Va./Jefferson
Amber Dombrowski	5-4	Fr.	Morgantown, W.Va./Morgantown
Katherine Dowie	5-7	Fr.	Carisbrook, Victoria, Australia/Ballarat Clarendon College
Jillian Forsey	5-4	r-Sr.	Stephenville, N.L., Canada/Stephenville
Samantha Hatcher	5-2	Fr.	Morgantown, W.Va./Morgantown
Olivia Hill	5-5	r-Jr.	Scott Depot, W.Va./Teays Valley Christian
Hayley Jackson	6-0	So.	Lusby, Md./Patuxent
Linda Jebet	5-3	Fr.	Kapsabet, Kenya/Kapsisiywa Secondary
Candace Jones	5-5	r-Jr.	Bristow, Va./Patriot
Peyton Kukura	5-5	Fr.	Morgantown, W.Va./University
Hannah Lipps	5-5	Fr.	Romney, W.Va./Hampshire
Malina Mitchell	5-6	Fr.	McDonald, Ohio/McDonald
Andrea Pettit	5-4	r-Jr.	Morgantown, W.Va./Morgantown
Avigail Radabaugh	5-6	Fr.	Morgantown, W.Va./Morgantown
TaShala Turner	5-5	Fr.	Morgantown, W.Va./University
Mikenna Vanderheyden	5-7	Fr.	Mount Brydges, Ontario, Canada/Strathroy Collegiate Institute
Bree Warren	5-7	So.	Belgrave, Victoria, Australia/Monash University
Sarah Wills	5-7	r-So.	Morgantown, W.Va./University
Charlotte Wood	5-7	Fr.	Bracebridge, Ontario, Canada/Bracebridge-Muskoka Lakes Secondary

Exhibit 8.3 *WVU Cross Country Quick Facts.*
(Courtesy of West Virginia University.)

BREANNA STEWART

Forward/Center • 6-4 • 175 lbs
Seattle Storm
Connecticut '16

USA Basketball Highlights

• **Honors:** 2011 & 2013 USA Basketball Female Athlete of the Year, 2013 FIBA U19 World Championship MVP, 2012 FIBA Americas U18 Championship MVP, 2011 All-FIBA U19 World Championship Team.
• **Gold Medals:** 2014 FIBA World Championship, 2011 and 2013 FIBA U19 World Championships, 2012 FIBA Americas U18 Championship, 2010 FIBA U17 World Championship, 2009 FIBA Americas U16 Championship.
• **Silver Medal:** 2015 Pan American Games.

Professional Highlights

• **Drafted** No. 1 by the Seattle Storm in 2016.

Collegiate Highlights

• **NCAA Final Four Most Outstanding Player:** 2013-2016; first woman to earn four Final Four MOP honors and fourth freshman in history to earn the honor.
• **NCAA Regional Most Outstanding Player:** 2013, 2015, 2016; first woman to earn three Region MOP awards.
• **National Player of the Year:**

college and one in high school
• **CoSIDA Academic All-American second team:** 2015.

USA Basketball Notes

• After winning five gold medals in international competition at the junior level, the two-time USA Basketball Female Athlete of the Year was called up to the USA National Team for its 2013 October minicamp in Las Vegas.
• Competed for the USA National Team during its 2015 European Tour, and averaged 7.8 ppg. and 4.5 apg. as the USA earned a 4-0 slate.
• Member of the 2015 USA Pan American Games team that captured the silver medal with a 4-1 record at 2015 Pan American Games in Toronto, Canada.
• Took part in the 2015 USA Women's National Team training camp May 4-6 in Las Vegas.
• Member of the 2014 USA Basketball World Championship Team that compiled a perfect 6-0 record en route to claiming gold at the FIBA World Championship in Istanbul and qualifying the U.S. for the 2016 Olympic Games; helped the USA compile a 4-1 exhibition record.
• At the opening tip of the 2014 Worlds, became the USA's youngest World Championship Team member (20 years, one month) since Kara Wolters (18) in 1994.
• One of three athletes compete on two USA U19 World Championship Teams (Alexis Jones, Morgan Tuck).
• Has won five gold medals and an overall record of 35-1 at age-based FIBA World (U17, two U19s) and FIBA Americas Championships (U16, U18), whlie also helping those teams to an overall 6-1 exhibition record.
• Earned MVP honors at the 2013 FIBA U19 World Championship in Klaipeda and Panavezys, Lithuania; among the 16-team field ranked fourth for scoring (16.9 ppg.), second for free throw percentage (.897) and first for 3-point field goal percentage (.583).
• Was the youngest member and only

National Player of the Year in 2014 (Associated Press, Naismith, USBWA, Honda Award for Women's Basketball, ESPNW); 2015 (Associated Press, Naismith, Wade Trophy, USBWA, Honda Award); and 2016 (Associated Press, Naismith, USBWA, Honda Award for Women's Basketball and WBCA); only athlete, male or female, to win four Naismith Trophies after winning three in

high school athlete on the 2011 USA Pan American Games Team (2-2), becoming just the second high school basketball player to ever compete for the USA in the Pan Am Games basketball competition; started all four games and averaged team-highs of 15.3 ppg., 11.3 rpg. and 1.1 bpg. Among all participants in the eight-nation field, ranked fifth for scoring, second for rebounding, third for field goal percentage (.500), and first for free throw percentage (.885) and blocked shots.

 # 9

Professional Notes

• Drafted No. 1 by the Seattle Storm in 2016 and earned May and June Rookie of the Month honors.

College Notes

• In four years at Connecticut, compiled a 151-5 (.968) record, including a 38-0 mark in 2015-16 and a 40-0 mark in 2013-14; won four straight NCAA titles; and the 2014, 2015 and 2016 American Athletic Conference regular season and tournament crowns.
• Finished her career as UConn's all-time leader with 414 career blocked shots; is second on the Huskies' all-time scoring list with 2,676 points; and is fourth on the all-time rebounding list with 1,179.
• As a senior in 2015-16, started in 36 of 37 games played and averaged team highs of 19.4 ppg., 8.7 rpg. and 3.4 bpg. while shooting 57.9 percent from the floor and 42.6 percent from deep in 29.1 mpg.
• During UConn's 2016 NCAA Tournament run, averaged team-highs of 20.3 ppg. and 11.0 rpg. while shooting 56.6 percent from the floor, 89.3 percent from the free throw line and 47.8 percent from 3-point.
• Consensus All-American first team (2014, 2015, 2016).
• Full Court Press Freshman All-American first team (2013).
• AAC Player of the Year and All-AAC first team (2014, 2015, 2016).
• AAC Tournament MVP (2014, 2016)
• AAC All-Tournament Team (2014, 2015, 2016).
• All-Big East Conference honorable mention (2013), Big East All-Freshman Team (2013) and Big East

Exhibit 8.4 *2016 USA Women's Basketball Team Player Profile. (Courtesy of Andrew D. Bernstein/USA Basketball.)*

to the nature of sports, player profiles have a short lifespan; however, the media frequently use them for reference.

History. This section will include a history of each series with every opponent on the schedule, in the form of a series records. Some guides also include a detailed history of the sport organization from inception to present day, noting great moments throughout its existence. They can be rather detailed and written in flowing paragraph form or broken down into a series of bullet points.

Honors and Awards. The honors and awards section is a complete list of all honors and/or awards that the players and coaches have received throughout the program or sport's history (e.g., all-conference accolades, major academic honors, honor roll information, all-tournament players, players of the week, All-America honors).

Team Records. The team records section is a statistical rundown on the season-by-season record of the team and individuals, dating back to the first year of the program. From those, career records are created and maintained. A good SID will also compile opponent records.

Stadium or Arena Layout. Key information about the stadium or arena in which the team plays is also important. A diagram and information are interesting, if not essential, and will prove helpful information to both the media and fans.

Media Information. This section explains how members of the media obtain credentials, the procedures to be followed by broadcast media, parking information, working media room facilities, and interview request procedures pre- and post-event. Contact information, such as mailing addresses, phone numbers, social media accounts, team website, and email addresses, for the sports information specialist are also compiled in this section.

Production Schedule

We've already discussed that the SID/media relations professional is the chief operating officer for the guide. Keeping that in mind, it is imperative for the SID to establish a timeline for the entire project to be completed, by creating and maintaining deadlines so the promotional guide is printed and delivered prior to the season's first game, or sometimes even a month or so prior to the start of competition. A lot of the production schedule depends on when the coaching staff or organization executives want the finished printed product in hand or posted online

By knowing the final delivery dates, the SID can work backwards from that point, setting deadlines for writing copy, editing by members of the staff and the coaches for their overall approval (especially biographies), pulling photographs, setting the budget, selling advertisements (if necessary), and having the look and feel

Exhibit 8.5 *GMU Volleyball Web Guide.*
(Photo courtesy of George Mason University.)

of the guide created by graphic designers or in-house colleagues. Typically a guide will need to be sent to the printer about three weeks prior to the desired delivery date, so plan accordingly using that basis.

Once a season is completed, the SID can certainly update the entire record book section, if it hasn't already been done during the course of the season. A season review, coach biographies, and the history section can also be updated, which would include honors and awards for players and coaches. From there, the SID will create long-term deadlines for updating player information, especially for newcomers, writing the preseason outlook/notebook, and generally working on the guide every day to ensure the deadlines are met.

For football, the guide information may be used for the spring prospectus, thus the SID has four months (pending a bowl game or playoffs) to finalize the specifics. Should a spring prospectus not be warranted, the football SID should allot five to six months of continuous promotional guide work to ensure the tangible product is in hand by its deadline, which is usually a month and a half prior to the start of season.

For basketball, the guide may be requested for the conference media day, thus bumping up the deadline. If the SID is continually updating information in-season, approximately two or three months should be reserved for producing the guide. For varsity sports guides, a couple of weeks would be the normal timeframe for completing a guide.

Game-Day Programs

In most instances, the SID is responsible for—or at least will assist in—the creation of the game-day program. Why is this included in a chapter about producing a promotional guide? Because the same steps that are used in creating a promotional guide are also necessary in the formation of the game-day programs that are sold, primarily at football and basketball events. While the game programs are heavy on advertisements, the sports information specialist still plays a primary role in its production. The programs typically include feature stories on contemporary athletes, coaches, and administrators, oftentimes written by the SID, updated player and team statistics as the season progresses, and updated schedules and results.

For football, a new game program is published and sold for every home contest. Much of the program will remain unchanged from game to game (these pages are known as *standing pages*) but sections described earlier (i.e., player features, statistics) will be changed and a new cover will be used. For basketball, because home games are often played more frequently than once a week, the same program could be sold for a two- or three-game span with all the same information, just different opponents and updated rosters and statistics.

For smaller varsity sports that have programs, a flip card with rosters and an athlete feature will suffice, and that responsibility will usually fall to the SID.

Summary

Promotional guides are the look and feel of a sports organization and serve many functions, from recruiting future student-athletes (at the collegiate level) to assisting the media during sporting events as it pertains to media coverage. Guides are a single source for assisting the media with everything they need to know about that sports entity.

The guide is comprised of essential information about a team, including player and coach bios, information on the sport organization, records, a history section, opponent information, and other general pertinent information that is a reference point for the media to cover that team. The guide does have size restrictions at the collegiate level, which aims to create an equal playing field for schools with varying budgets to fairly recruit prospective student-athletes.

The SID is the ultimate point person in the guide's production and will oversee the writing, advertising, photograph selection, and overall content considerations for the entire project.

Guides differ between the professional and collegiate level. Professionally, the guides are not bound by the same regulations as that of the collegiate level, such as the 208-page limit and coloring. Professional guides are usually a smaller trim size, but bigger in page count, and they lack recruiting information that can be found in the collegiate guides.

Done properly, the guide will represent a key cog in an organization's overall PR machine and will be a vital tool in portraying the organization's overall positive image.

Discussion Questions

1. In your opinion, what is the most important part of a school's informational guide? Why? Conversely, what are a few items that could be omitted from the guide? Why?

2. As technologies continue to shape the future of promotional guides, do you think there will eventually be no need for a guide at all? Defend your argument.

3. How does a team's media guide add to the allure of the program in other departments? How does it help with recruiting, marketing, ticketing, and sponsorship?

Suggested Exercises

1. You are a SID for a very small Division II school and you have a limited budget for your football guide. Due to financial restrictions, you are only able to produce a 48-page guide. Create an outline for the guide consisting of all the essential items and the order in which they will appear.

2. After much research and fact finding on your favorite collegiate or professional athlete, write a sample promotional guide bio. Remember to provide as much useful information as you can to assist the media with the coverage of the athlete.

3. Log on to the college athletics website for a school in the ACC or the Big Ten conference and compare and contrast the media guides for two men's and two women's sports teams.

9

Event Management

Event management for a sports information director encompasses a wide array of duties that can be categorized into three primary events:

- game management/game-day operations
- press conferences/media days
- special events

They all have some similarities while each also possesses unique aspects. Regardless of whether it is an actual game or a different occasion, all eyes will be on the SID's organization during the event. That is why it is of the utmost importance for a SID to excel at preparation, organization, and communication, all while being a hospitable host.

Game Management/Game-Day Media Operations

When fans of any sport, regardless of level, attend a contest, they typically enter the venue shortly before the game starts, enjoy the show, and then leave in a timely fashion upon its conclusion. What they typically do not realize is the amount of behind-the-scenes effort that is required in order to host the event without a hitch, especially from a publicity standpoint. Enter the SID.

Depending on a SID's sport and the coverage that it receives, the days leading up to and the day of the event may be very hectic. And once the game is over there's no rest for the public relations specialist, who must turn right back around and repeat the same process all over again in preparation for the next event. The game itself is the premier showcase for the SID and will be a culmination of all the hard work leading up to and following the event.

For SIDs that cover football, there are numerous tasks that must be accomplished in order to effectively host a successful game day. Many times the actual game is an after-thought. You read that right. There are times where so many things need to be accomplished leading up to kickoff that the actual game itself is nowhere near as stressful. It's very similar to the long-time cliché in sports that practices are sometimes more difficult than the games themselves.

There are three types of operations as it pertains to hosting a sporting event: pregame, in-game/game-time and postgame.

Pregame Preparation

Weeks before the season-opener it is imperative that the SID ensures the press box/ press table is functional: stocking of media guides for both his/her school and the opponent, seeing that enough accessories are ready (paper, pencils, working copy machines), and ensuring the internet (wireless and hardwire) is available for the media that will be using it either via wireless or Ethernet connections. The SID will also plan for the food that will be served in the press box/press row during the season. A SID's budget will dictate many of the decisions regarding food but meals for each home game are determined well in advance.

The press box/press row food for the professional ranks often includes treating the media to sit-down dinners before games and snacks at halftime. High-profile Division I schools often do so as well. Small schools can provide niceties, too, without stretching budgets. Small colleges typically offer coffee, soda, and donuts in working media areas. Others, with a bit more money to spend, add hot dogs, pizza, or submarine sandwiches to the pregame fare. The budget should be the guiding factor in formulating the menu. Remember, the press area is a workplace, first and foremost—not a restaurant.

An in-season game work week begins on a Sunday (when a traditional Saturday game is played) when the SID will update the team statistics from the previous day, nominate any of his/her players for conference, regional, and national players of the week awards (should any be worthy), assist the coaches with any media responsibilities (e.g., conference calls or press conferences), and prepare the weekly game notes for the upcoming game.

The game notes, as mentioned in Chapter 5, are usually a conglomeration of key statistical trends, notes on players to watch, the team's season statistics, updated player information that supplements the media guide that came out at the beginning of year, and any and all other pertinent information the SID believes belongs in the notes. If a SID's game notes are very good, they'll make it in some form to the television, internet streaming, or radio broadcast during the contest. For example, in 2007, former West Virginia University fullback Owen Schmitt, a future NFL draft pick of the Seattle Seahawks, who spent his career also with the Philadelphia Eagles and Oakland Raiders, was known for his bruising playing style. During his career, Schmitt mangled and broke numerous facemasks on his helmet. The WVU sports communications department inserted a running counter of his career broken facemasks in its game notes. During numerous WVU football games that were broadcast, announcers frequently referenced Schmitt's number of broken face-masks when discussing his toughness, which was a direct result of good work by the SID of including an interesting and useful tidbit in the game notes. A similar storyline developed as Clemson, 2018 Football National Champions, inched closer to setting a single season NCAA record for wins in a season. That was achieved in the National Championship victory against Alabama. During the days leading up to kickoff, the SID will issue credentials to any local, regional, or national media that request to attend and report on the upcoming game.

The sports information staff should develop a written policy for working press credentials. The SID can avoid confusion and mute complaints by including in the media guide and on the back of the credentials themselves the policy and proce-dures for arranging credentials.

The policy should address eligibility for credentials, limits per media or other organization, and arrangements for travel companions. The eligibility requirements should specify what types of publications or broadcast media are not eligible for credentials. For example, a university might choose to exclude gambling publica-tions; obscure and noncredible internet-based publications; free publications, such as advertising tabloids; and publications that do not regularly cover sports events. The policy should explain how the university will handle requests from scouts (i.e., general admission, VIP, or working press credentials). It also should explain accom-modations (credentials or tickets?) available for any spouses. Most college and pro-fessional organizations do not give working press credentials or seats in the working press area to spouses, though some do provide guest tickets and special seating sec-tions depending on the event and seating availability.

The credentials policy should spell out differences in press passes for reporters, photographers, announcers, videographers, and other broadcast personnel, as well as the limit for each media organization. The SID may set limits on the number of reporters and photographers from a single media organization based on the print, internet media, or broadcast company's size, coverage area/audience, and proximity to the school or city.

Newspapers and magazines typically send a beat reporter and a photographer to a college or professional game. They also may want to send a columnist or general assignment reporter and a second photographer to games between rivals and games with postseason playoff impact. A radio station usually will send a two- or three-man crew—a play-by-play announcer and color man, and sometimes an engineer/techni-cian that takes care of the equipment. However, a television production crew may need upwards of 25 press passes—including two for talent (announcers), one for a statisti-cian, one each for a director and a producer, two or three for videographers (camera people), and perhaps a couple for technicians in the truck (who might need to come and go in the stadium/arena). Credentials may also increase from these media entities that now require online streaming or media entities whose sole capabilities are online streaming. This may also include in-house operations within a sports organization.

The credentials policy should specify the work areas to which each person with credentials has access. The press pass or working credential issued to each person should provide direction—by written or color code—that aids university officials monitoring access. For example, a football pass might enable reporters to walk around freely in the press area, in the locker rooms, and on the sidelines for a football game. Colleges and professional teams often issue armbands to photographers that define access to the field, the court, and/or the locker rooms. The passes and armbands might limit access strictly to the field or only to the press box.

The SID is in charge of issuing credentials and keeping a running count to avoid overbooking the work space, realizing that establishing a cutoff point and sticking to it is more important than trying to accommodate everyone who wants a credential. The cutoff policy can create conflicts with a journalist denied a credential, but the media organizations at the bottom of the priority order are the least important to the school or team. Assigning a reporter to a seat behind a pole or crowding everyone to squeeze in a few more journalists may cause greater relationship problems with those media organizations that regularly cover the team. It is better to deny access to low-priority journalists at the outset than to provide substandard work space and assistance to all. Media organizations recognize that space is limited, particularly for high-profile events, and accept decisions of the host organization when those decisions are backed up by printed policy.

The SID should assign a staff member to prepare the credentials, each of which should include the name of the individual and the organization represented.

From his/her master credential list the SID will create that week's seating chart for the press box or press row. The seating chart is compiled based on space availability and the demand for the upcoming event. Usually the better seats in the facility (i.e., between the 40-yard lines at football or between the foul lines in basketball) are given to the media that frequently cover that organization on a daily basis. Visiting media can be added around the core media and the seating chart will go from there. Professional scouts should not be seated with the media or with the statistics staff. Rather, they should have their own areas. For away games, if applicable, the SID will compile a list of media that cover his/her organization and are requesting credentials and submit that to the host SID rather than having the visiting media contact the host SID individually to request credentials.

Also during game week, a schedule of interview availability for the organization's coaches and players should be distributed so that any of the media planning to follow the SID's organization that week are aware of interview opportunities.

The SID will also ensure any technical concerns are addressed: making sure the statistics crew personnel are in place for the upcoming contest and that an internal press box announcer has been secured. The SID must arrange for spotters as well as runners, who act as utility infielders, performing whatever chore is needed. Lining up the SID's staff and any press box assistants (stat runners, etc.) is a must as the job of this magnitude can't be done alone. He/she will also want to ensure the media has the opportunity to file/post their stories via the internet (be it via Ethernet or wireless) from the press box/row.

Game Management Staff

The primary personnel needed for serving the media during game management are as follows:

Sports information director: The sports information director serves as the controller and troubleshooter. The SID should act as overseer and manager rather than performing a specific job.

Statistical crew: The most important permanent unit of the press box/row team is the statistical crew, which may consist of several people for football and around three to four for men's and women's basketball. The stats crew for football should consist of one play-by-play typist, spotters for both sides of the ball and a spotting coordinator. The spotters advise the typist on the name of the ball carrier, the tackler(s), yardage gained or lost, and down and distance to go for a first down. For all sports the tasks are similar but they may be accomplished with far fewer members of the stats crew.

The SID may supplement the basic crew with specialists who keep drive and tackle charts, information that aids in identifying the star performers as well as the statistical differences in the game. Many times those are requested by television and radio. A drive chart is a schematic drawing of a football field that shows the starting point and progress on each play of a drive. A tackle chart is a compilation of the number of tackles, sacks, fumble recoveries, and interceptions by each player on the defense.

A basketball crew consists of a play-by-play typist; a spotter who records points and fouls for players for each team; a spotter who tracks rebounds, turnovers, and assists; and a spotting coordinator.

Duplication/copy specialist: The duplication specialist makes the predetermined number of copies of statistical information, ranging from quickie stats at halftime to books of final statistics.

Runners: The runners distribute duplicated materials and other information to everyone seated in the press box. Football runners pass out "quickie" stats (summaries) after each quarter of a football game, halftime statistics, and final statistical packages. The same holds true for basketball, but on the collegiate level, quickie stats are provided at halftime.

Pool reporter: The SID may assign one assistant to each locker room to gather quotations from players and coaches to distribute to the media. SID assistants can type the quotations and deliver them to the duplication specialist.

Score requests person: This person is responsible for handling all national phone and email requests that arrive during a contest. This person can also tweet out scores at each media timeout, halftime, and at game's conclusion. National media will want score updates and other information often in order to pass it on to its customers.

News conference aids: The SID may assign an assistant to bring players and coaches from each team to the designated room for the news conference. The visiting SID usually handles his/her requests. The SID may rely on assistants or volunteers who perform other duties during the game, as long as the duties are completed by game's end.

Media spotters and runners: A radio station sometimes will request a spotter, especially for football, although many radio crews will provide their own spotter. Television production crews frequently will request a couple of runners—a statistician and someone to manage the cords for videographers who move about the sidelines. The same will hold true for basketball.

The SID should ask about personnel needs when radio and television media request credentials. It also is a wise policy to keep a volunteer or two on standby if media interest is high, to handle any last-minute requests. Merle Levin, a former SID at Cleveland State University, says student volunteers are acceptable if they are "absolutely dependable." A dependable pool may be found in the university's communication, journalism, sports administration, sport management, and/or electronic media departments. Many of those may be knowledgeable about the media's needs as a result of course work and previous field experience.

Hospitality and concessions: The SID should assign a volunteer or two to assist with food and other amenities. The volunteer can advise food service personnel of supplies running low, spills, etc. In many cases, the caterer or university food-service people will take care of this responsibility.

While budget and the pool of volunteers available may limit personnel resources, the SID should keep in mind that efficiency is inseparable from the size of the press-box staff. Mistakes are more likely to happen if people are assigned multiple duties, particularly if the timing for different responsibilities is tight. Service is more likely to falter if flexibility is limited by insufficient personnel at the site.

The SID also should bear in mind that efficiency is inseparable from preparation. The SID should train statisticians ahead of time, even if that involves practice with videotapes. Sports information personnel should schedule volunteers well in advance and call to confirm their participation a couple of days in advance of the game. A walk-through and check of equipment is also good practice.

Remember, a satisfied reporter is likely to speak highly of the accommodations. Word of mouth inside media circles spreads like wildfire because good and bad news can spread immediately with social media and tweets.

If the contest is on television, Thursday or Friday of game week sees the television talent and director/producer meet with some of the team's notable players and its coaches to follow up on story lines they may have found in the SID's game notes. It's a unique opportunity to further promote the athletes and the team and all of this is arranged through the SID. As mentioned previously, the information the announcers acquire in those meetings is used in the subsequent broadcast.

On the day of the game, the SID should arrive no later than two to three hours before the start time to assist with any media issues that may arise. Those would include myriad tasks such as checking the starting lineup with TV, setting up press row for a smaller sport, passing out the game notes packets and media guides, and assisting the statistics crew with preparing the game file. Sometimes seating chart issues arise and the SID has to think on his/her feet (e.g., two media members that don't get along are seated beside each other). The SID will also field questions for story ideas from the media and assist in facilitating those story lines.

For away games, the SID should meet with the public address announcer and any radio, TV broadcasters, and video streamers to ensure pronunciation of their players is accurate.

In-Game Operations

Once the sporting event has begun, the well-prepared SID has the school, conference, and NCAA (should it be a collegiate game) record books readily available should any statistical feats from the contest set new standards. And if that happens, the internal and external public address announcers, television (if the game is being broadcast), and the home radio broadcasters should immediately be informed so the general public and the media are aware of the record-breaking information. Game notes should be readily accessible for player game-, season-, and career-high marks that may be achieved. An on-going tally of notes should also be kept and distributed to the media after the contest's conclusion. In-game, a contest's statistical play-by-play and box score from each quarter is distributed to the media via the SID's support staff to ensure the media is able to effectively cover the contest. Other responsibilities would include the gathering of coach and player names for postgame interviews, being on call should an injury occur and the media request information about the injury, and generally just being available. Some games go on without a hitch. Others that may be high-scoring, record-breaking affairs will keep the SID's nose buried in the record book. For smaller sports that don't receive the same amount of coverage as football or basketball, the SID will be responsible for writing the postgame press release, and the good SID will constantly be writing as the contest goes on in order to have the release ready as soon as possible following the outcome of the contest.

Also in-game, and with today's technology, the sports information department can tweet up-to-the-second records and notable achievements, as well as blog— post photos and short videos to social media outlets—the same information. Both are unique ways of keeping the fans roped in tight to the organization by giving them quick and interesting insight they might not receive until well after the game

Postgame Duties

The primary duties of a SID in the postgame involve managing the head coach's press conference, win or lose, and bringing the requested players into the press conference once the coach has finished. For football, there are usually two areas, one for the visiting team and players and one for the home school, because the event will have so much media coverage. For basketball and other sports, traditionally the visiting team's coach and requested players appear first in the interview room, followed by the home team's coach and requested players.

Postgame is arguably one of the most challenging aspects of the job on game days. It can be a stressful time, especially if media are on deadline and the head coach is slow in wrapping up his postgame chat with his/her team. Should the SID's team lose, his/her players rarely want to be interviewed, yet the media still have a job to do. In these situations, it is imperative to let the student-athlete who is resisting the interview know that true character is shown in both good times and in bad. The media will respect players even more if they speak after a loss, especially if, when times are good, they are more than willing to be in the limelight. Now is the time the athlete would best utilize the tips and strategies the SID gave the athletes for being interviewed. By heeding the lessons taught by the SID and knowing that all eyes are on them at that very moment, giving a great interview will only give the athletes, team, and organization a lasting, positive image.

The quotes from the entire press conference should be recorded, transcribed, and distributed with the contest's entire statistical package to the media as quickly as possible after the game. A press release/news story needs to be written for the organization's website and for immediate distribution to members of the media that were unable to attend the contest. The press conference, if streamed or recorded live, should also be disseminated through social media, should the organization utilize this option.

The final statistical packages for football games typically consist of these items:

- A scoring summary.
- Team statistics, including first downs, net yards rushing, net yards passing, total yards, etc.
- Individual statistics, including rushing, passing, pass receiving, punting, field goals, and returns.
- The contest's starters, on both sides of the ball, for both teams.
- Individual defensive statistics, including tackles (assisted, unassisted, and tackles for losses), quarterback sacks, fumble recoveries, fumbles forced, pass interceptions, and passes broken up.
- A drive chart showing the starting field position and time, and end result of the drive for each team.
- A participation chart showing each player that performed during the contest.
- A play-by-play rundown from coin toss to final play.

The final statistical packages for basketball contests typically consist of these items:

- Final Box Score, which includes starters.

- First and second half play-by-play.

- First half box score.

For SIDs in charge of basketball, the same process is to be used when it comes to pregame, in-game, and postgame management. The big difference, though, is that the entire process is usually repeated two to three times a week because basketball games are played more frequently, so the turnaround time for game notes, interview requests, credentials, etc., is far shorter and the SID is under constant pressure for five months during basketball season.

For varsity or Olympic sports that don't receive the same amount of attention as football and men's and women's basketball, the same responsibilities are still required. The tasks may vary depending on the media coverage of those sports and the frequency of which the sport is played. The most noticeable difference with other sports is that the SID is usually self-sufficient and will probably be the lone official scorer if it's baseball or soccer, or be a part of a statistics crew if needed. There may be no press box food, like with football or basketball. Instead, snacks may be provided, which would have a minimal impact on the overall budget. For sports that require a crew, such as a public address announcer and scorekeeper, etc., the SID will be charged with securing those workers. As previously stated, the SID may find dependable workers in the university's communication, journalism, sports administration, sport management, and/or electronic media departments. There usually isn't a lack of eager undergraduate or graduate students at a university or college to assist as a volunteer worker. In many cases, people have to be turned away, depending on the school and sport.

Event Management on the Road

When the SID is on the road with the team—depending on the sport—many of the same principles described above will generally apply. The SID may keep the statistics, assist with a radio broadcast, run the postgame press conference (should there be a need), and deliver the event's statistics and press releases to the media outlets that aren't in attendance. It is imperative that the news of the event still make it into the hands of the media that cover the team but do not travel to the event. Host SID's may assist in the coverage, but the growing trend, especially with technology advancements such as wireless air cards and wireless internet, is that the visiting SID has now become self-sufficient.

Do's and Don'ts in Press Box

There is a must, do, and don't list regarding press boxes. While some of these are a bit-outdated, they serve as an excellent start for the SID to focus on when it comes to game-day management:

Must:

- Have adequate space for working media

- Must have internet Access/WiFi capability

- Be functional before making it fancy

- Be heated in cold climate

- Keep nonworkers out of working area

- Have adequate area for service and statistical crews and equipment

- Have an electrical outlet at every seat

- Have adequate space for home and visiting coaches' phone booths

- Have adequate space behind writers for traffic

Do:

- Have food service available

- Have adequate toilet facilities for men and women

- Have water fountains

- Have adequate storage space for stats crew materials

- Have easy access to field and dressing rooms

- Have adequate communications between stats crew and working media

- Have adequate lighting, power, and telephone cables and outlets

- Install a bank of telephones throughout the working media area to assist writers filing a story

- Have specially designed television booth and camera spaces

- Have conduit of sufficient size to handle television cable

- Have an elevator

- Have social media guidelines available

Don't:

- Have poles, pillars, posts, or lattice-work windows that obstruct view

- Have so many entrances to the press box that policing is a problem

- Mix scouts and other necessary fringe workers with working media

- Lead VIPs and other nonworkers into the working press area

- Put food bar in main stream of press-box traffic

- CHEER—there is NO CHEERING in the press box, as an unbiased working environment it must be present and maintained. This is arguably the most important press box rule.

The last point is especially important to mention. The press box/press row is a working environment, home to SIDs of both organizations, the working media, press box assistants, and other members working to make the game go off without a hitch. It is imperative that it is kept a work place and no cheering will be allowed as it is an unbiased work place. Any violators will be removed from the premises.

The responsibility for running a clean and efficient media work area belongs to the sports information or media relations staff. The press table is the "office" for the working media. To be of real service, the sports information staff must efficiently provide the materials and assistance the media need to perform their jobs. Good intentions and "I'm sorry" mean nothing to the football announcer who just stumbled through player identifications for four quarters because no pronunciation guide was available. What makes a difference is anticipating every problem that might arise and resolving it quickly.

When the games begin, the SID or public relations director is the managing partner in the working relationship between media and sport organizations. The press table or press box is the work area. "Work area" is the operative phrase. The space reserved for the media at athletics events is a work area, not a social club or party room. Press boxes are not places for VIPs and friends of the university to watch the contests and enjoy free food and drink. That is not to say the press box should be off limits to everyone but the working media; it is to say that the sports information staff should restrict access and eliminate any activity that is not work related.

The press box can double as a mini-dining room for the working media, and no one will complain if university administrators and special guests share the refreshments. However, the SID should seat them away from the areas in which the media will be working during the game. After the game, staff members should ask outsiders to leave, because the press box, press table, or media room immediately turns into a very busy and hectic place—like a subway station when the train arrives. Everyone scrambles to get to work quickly.

At no time is the partnership between journalists and sports information personnel under greater pressure and strain than during postgame. The sports information staff often must cater to the needs of a large group of media with diverse interests. Broadcast journalists must deliver their stories live. Many print reporters must file stories within 20 to 30 minutes after completion of the game. All must work quickly in a setting with little margin of error and few advantages of the home office. Finishing the job before the deadline takes precedence over social graces and professional amenities.

Even during hectic times, however, remember that the SID's overall responsibility is to always create a favorable image of the organization and team. So it's imperative for SIDs to ensure that in the days and hours leading up to a game, they are fully prepared for the event. After all, games are arguably the most important opportunity to convey the most positive image of the organization.

News Conferences and Media Days

The most common types of managed events, outside of game days, are news conferences and media days. Sport organizations set up news conferences to make major announcements (usually positive) such as trades, signings of new players or coaches, changes of ownership, and details on a new facility. They use media days primarily to kick off a new season. Reporters who attend can interview coaches and players. College conferences also organize media days prior to the start of a season. Each college sends a coach and selected players to a joint media day, giving the media access to representatives of each team in the conference. Reporters can gather information, media guides, and pictures they can use in stories throughout the season.

News Conferences

News conferences are one of the most important means through which sport organizations communicate with the media and the public. Managed events, such as news conferences, enable sport organizations to distribute the same information to large groups of reporters at the same time. However, the announcement must be worthy of a news conference. News conferences also give the media the opportunity to ask questions and to obtain information from key players, coaches, and team or athletics department officials at one location and at one time.

On the professional level, most news conferences concern the hiring and/or firing of front office personnel or coaches; player trades or signings; injuries and other personnel matters; and ticket, stadium, and franchise issues. Professional sport organizations are more likely than colleges or high schools to schedule news conferences to address negative issues such as the punishment for a player who violates the organization's substance-abuse policy.

Colleges and universities typically call news conferences to make announcements in high-profile sports such as football, men's basketball, and women's basketball. News conferences may also be necessary in other sports if there is a large enough following (e.g., Florida in baseball, UCLA in women's gymnastics, and Iowa State in wrestling).

High school administrators seldom arrange a news conference for anything other than the introduction of a new coach or administrator or the signing of their student-athletes to colleges/universities.

Planning the News Conference

Planning a news conference is a team effort that may involve many administrators, coaches, and sports information personnel. The roles and responsibilities vary according to the makeup of the sport organization. A team owner may instruct the public relations director to arrange a news conference when the owner fires a general manager (GM) or manager. The GM may order a news conference to announce

Exhibit 9.1a *Otis Livingston, George Mason University point guard, being interviewed after a home game at Eagle Bank Arena. (Photo by Rafael Suanes, George Mason Athletics.)*

Exhibit 9.1b *Head Men's Basketball Coach Dave Paulsen of George Mason University during a postgame press conference. (Photo by Rafael Suanes, George Mason Athletics.)*

a trade. The media relations director may organize a press conference to introduce new draft choices to the local fans and media. The president of a university or the athletics director may request a news conference to announce the hiring of a coach or the announcement of a large donation to the department.

The sports information or public relations director must work with administrators to create a chain of command and a roster of responsibilities for news conferences. The document should spell out the roles and responsibilities of each person in the chain. It should specify who decides when to call a news conference and what information to release, who makes the physical arrangements, who prepares the information released at the meeting, who makes the announcement, and who answers questions.

Typically, sports information personnel begin notifying the media of a news conference as soon as possible, usually a day in advance. The objective is to give reporters sufficient time to make arrangements to attend the meeting, but not enough time to gather enough information to "break" the story before the announcement. In an age of high-intensity investigative reporting by the media, keeping the name of a coach or other major news absolutely secret is almost impossible. In all probability, the media have speculated for days on the most likely candidates for a coaching position, but the sports information or public relations director still should make an attempt to keep the information confidential until the formal announcement. But even if a media outlet does get a "scoop" and reports the information that was planned to be announced during the news conference, the sport organization should go ahead with the news conference—including providing the news release, biographical information, and statements from relevant university or team personnel.

Here is a list of suggestions for SIDs to follow in organizing effective news conferences regardless of the size of the organization.

- Make certain the announcement is newsworthy.

- Inform all members of the media. The timing of the invitations should allow reporters enough time to arrange schedules, but not enough time to find out and to report the particulars of the announcement.

- In the case of a "blockbuster" announcement, issue verbal invitations three to five hours in advance of the news conference. Blockbuster announcements would include the naming of a coach, the completion of a trade, or a decision to build a new stadium. In the case of a "soft" announcement, such as a groundbreaking ceremony for a new stadium, the SID should mail, fax, or email invitations three to five days in advance.

- Make certain that sufficient parking space is available close to the meeting room.

- The room for the news conference should be large enough to handle the crowd but small enough to create an atmosphere of intimacy and importance. A handful of reporters in a large room has a hollow feel, perhaps creating an impression that not many reporters showed up or felt the announcement was important enough to attend. The announcement should be made on the organization's own turf—campus, stadium, office, gymnasium, or conference room.

- The facility should be attractive and functional. Provide an adequate number of chairs and easy access to restrooms along with WiFi access and passcodes. Also, make certain sufficient working space is available to reporters. You should incorporate the institution's name and logo in the backdrop or place them on the front of the speaker's podium.

- Remember, the SID's job is to put the university or organization in the public eye. One of the simplest and most effective ways to do so is to display the institution's name and logo in such a manner that they appear prominently in photographs or video clips from the news conference.

- Make the media feel welcome by offering refreshments, such as cookies or donuts along with coffee, tea, and soft drinks. Do not serve alcohol. In today's society, news conferences are work sessions, not social get-togethers. Do not spend more than you can afford on refreshments. If a modest lunch fits into the budget, a meal is more than acceptable to members of the media. Coffee, soft drinks, and pastry generally are sufficient, however.

- Provide the media copies of the news release. The release should supply all basic information but not all the details.

- Allow enough time in the schedule for media questions. Do not let the question-answer session run longer than 30 minutes.

- Supply photographs to the print media if they will enhance coverage.

- Following the news conference, allow 15–30 minutes for additional one-on-one interviews, which are typically needed by TV and radio reporters. If you let the questions continue for more than 30 minutes, you may infringe on the time available to media representatives to prepare their stories for publication or broadcast.

- The SID should always remain available after a news conference in order to facilitate any further interview requests and answer any questions.

Media Days

Media days are popular and effective publicity-generating events for Division I universities and for professional teams. In Divisions II and III in most parts of the country, media days usually are limited to college football and/or basketball. Colleges and conferences may organize media days for other sports depending on the visibility of the sport in a particular area.

The sport organization gives the media the red-carpet treatment on these days, so careful planning and attention to detail are essential. A poorly organized media day can be a disaster and can result in poor public relations that may take a long time to overcome.

The fall, or football, media day is the first opportunity each year for reporters to visit a college campus or professional team's facilities and interact with the athletes in person. In the case of a conference, the fall media day gives journalists a chance to meet new coaches, athletic directors, and sports information directors, too. Of particular importance is luring journalists new to the school or conference beat. There is perhaps no better opportunity to treat the journalist to a taste of the school and to begin to establish a favorable one-on-one relationship.

Exhibit 9.2a *GMU Head Basketball Coach Dave Paulsen being interviewed by WTOP Radio sports reporter Jonathan Warner. (Photo by Rafael Suanes, George Mason Athletics.)*

College conferences also arrange media days prior to the start of the football and basketball seasons. Such events typically include a luncheon, comments from the men's and women's coaches for each team, opportunities for interviews with coaches and selected players, and announcement of the results of preseason voting on the top teams and players in the conference. Gifts are usually given out to the media as a "thank you" for attending the event.

The Big East Conference had one of the most well-known and respected media days for its football and men's and women's basketball days prior to the conference falling apart due to conference realignment. For the eight-team football league, the media day centered around a clambake in Newport, Rhode Island, which created a unique atmosphere for coaches and players to mingle with the media.

For the former 16-team basketball league, the men's Big East Conference media day held its day at Madison Square Garden, the world's most famous arena and the site of the conference's postseason tournament. For the women's media day, the Big East Conference used ESPNZone in Times Square as its venue, offering a unique setting.

Media days are memorable experiences for the media, coaches, and players alike, and it has created great rapport between coaches, players, SIDs, and the media, while also garnering plenty of positive exposure for the league.

Exhibit 9.2b&c *Former NBC affiliate, current ESPN Sports reporter Dianna Russini interviewing GMU Head Men's Basketball Coach Dave Paulsen. (Photos by Rafael Suanes, George Mason Athletics.)*

Exhibit 9.2d *Former NBC affiliate, current ESPN Sports reporter Dianna Russini interviewing GMU Head Men's Basketball Coach Dave Paulsen. (Photo by Rafael Suanes, George Mason Athletics.)*

Planning the Media Day

As in planning for a news conference, preparing for a media day is a team project. The planning, however, starts much further in advance and involves more people because of the multi-faceted nature of the event. The media day amounts to multiple announcements and interviews all rolled into one package.

The planning typically starts many months in advance. As in the case of news conferences, the effective sports information or public relations director must develop an organizational chart that spells out responsibilities for administrators, coaches, and others. The plan should include a budget and a timetable that lists deadlines for completion of specific tasks and dates for particular steps, such as the date for mailing out invitations. Here's a rundown on the most important steps in the process.

1. Choose a date and a starting time.

2. Choose and reserve a place to hold the event.

3. Choose and reserve a caterer if the school or the facility selected does not have one.

4. Determine the schedule of events for the day.

5. Announce the media day and send out invitations, preregistration forms, and maps.

6. Prepare a preregistration list and add names as they come in.

7. Prepare information packets (press kits) for the media and for others who attend.

8. Prepare a biography sheet on the coach(es) who will attend.

9. Notify the caterer of the final count for the meal.

10. Create a checklist of duties to be performed the day of the event that include social media regulations, internet access, and connectivity.

Typical Media Day Timetable

Nine months (before the event) — Begin the planning process.

Two months — Announce the media day. Send a memo to coaches, sports information personnel, and other athletics officials to provide the date, time, and agenda of the media day. Also release to the media the date, time, and agenda. (If a reporter calls earlier for planning purposes, it is OK to tell the reporter about the event.) Arrange for preparation of composite photo sheets for distribution at the media day. It usually takes a month to get back an order.

One month — Send invitations and event schedules, preregistration forms, and maps to print and broadcast media, coaches, and sports information directors. The invitation can be as simple as a sentence atop a preregistration form or as formal as a printed invitation. The preregistration form should include

- A place for the person to respond yes or no
- A place for the person's name and affiliation
- A deadline for preregistration
- A person to whom to return the form
- An address to mail or email, or telephone number to send the form by fax.
- A map with written directions

One week — Call the caterer or food service director with the final count for luncheon or brunch.

Send an email message to selected TV stations. Send another reminder message three days before the event. Call two days in advance to ask if someone will attend. The more persistent you are with the television media and through social media avenues, the more likely you are to get results.

Special Events

A special event encompasses in-house promotions tied to scheduled games or sport seasons as well as one-time events in which the host team/organization may or may not participate. Both are promotional, designed to enhance the image of the sport organization, and/or to increase revenues.

Colleges and cities collaborate on bids to host conference tournaments plus preliminary and championship rounds of NCAA regional or championship tournaments and meets in men's and women's basketball, swimming, wrestling, track, gymnastics, golf, tennis, etc. At the professional level, special events embrace everything from all-star games to sites for professional tour events or league championships, such as the Super Bowl.

The common denominator among special events is promotion. The objective of an in-house promotion or a single, special event is to advance the financial goals of the sport organization and/or sponsors. An in-house promotion for a game may aim at generating media interest in a team or sport in hopes that increased publicity may result in additional ticket sales.

Although boosting attendance and revenue at events may not be the direct responsibility of the SID, the marketing function and public relations thrust often mesh in staging special events. As in many other aspects of the business of sports, marketing and promotions specialists may lead the way in identifying target audiences and determining the best ways to reach them.

The marketing and public relations functions vary according to the type of event. The university development or professional marketing departments play the larger role in events with a heavy emphasis on identifying audiences, conducting advertising campaigns, and selling tickets and sponsorships. Promotions and marketing people generally handle direct mail, telemarketing, personal contact, group ticket discounts, game-day promotions, and paid advertising or sponsorships. For example, a university promotions specialist or athletics director would most often negotiate the sponsorship of an invitational tournament and halftime giveaways/contests by local businesses. Those assigned promotional duties also would oversee individual game promotions. For example, they would take care of a promotion that promised free admission to a college women's basketball game to youngsters wearing T-shirts from the university-held sports camp the previous summer or the first 50 students to attend the game would be provided with free pizza from a university sponsor.

The sports information or public relations departments play the larger role in events with heavy emphasis on generating publicity and assisting the media in information delivery. The emphasis on media management is why the sports information department takes the lead in news conferences and media days. The objective of each is not to sell tickets, but to deliver information through the media that will heighten interest and indirectly boost ticket sales. Likewise, the sports information office will play a significant role in the awards banquet, postseason playoff events, and all-star games.

Special events essentially can be categorized as either informational or promotional activities. Informational activities are directed primarily by sports information personnel and include news conferences, media days, news releases, awards banquets, postseason playoffs, all-star games, programs for special events, tournament press operations, tournament all-star teams, and awards. Promotional activities are directed primarily by marketing personnel and include opening day festivities, single-game promotions, ticket discount promotions, advertising campaigns (posters, flyers, billboards, etc.), tournament sponsorships, halftime giveaways, and contests.

Planning the Special Event

When an amateur organization, an institution, or a team decides to stage a special event, everyone must get involved: coaches, athletics directors/general managers, business managers, marketing/promotions directors, advertising managers, sports information directors, and even the athletes. Successful events are the result of well-coordinated efforts by specialists in a variety of fields. Each specialist contributes expertise in one area of a multifaceted plan.

The planning process for a special event is similar to the preparations for media brochures or media days, but it is far more extensive. It calls into play all the skills and functions of the sports information specialist—for example, news releases, managed news events, media brochures, interviews, and press-row operations. Planning news releases, news conferences, and other pre-event publicity is part of the job, but the SID may have to think in multiples, scheduling releases and news conferences over a one- or two-year period to maintain public interest and to coincide with the start of ticket sales, selection of teams, etc.

Planning for a special event is a multifaceted process. The primary planning concerns, in order of importance, are as follows:

1. Scope and size of the event

2. Budget

3. Planning committees

4. Operations manual

5. Timetable of duties and activities

The first considerations are the scope and size of the event. They will dictate the budget, the number and nature of planning committees needed, and the timetable for performing duties. The second consideration is the budget. The budget will have a bearing on everything from advertising efforts to promotional activities to paid staff to media operations. If existing budget resources may limit the scope and size of the event, organizers should create a fundraising or sponsorship committee to come up with additional financial resources. The event itself should dictate the budget, not vice versa. If the event is billed as a special attraction, the final product cannot be sophomoric if it is to send a positive message. It must be special. Organizers should consider the financial obligations before deciding to host an event, not afterward.

Creating planning committees and assigning responsibilities follow development of the budget. The budget will identify the paid staff members. Organizers then can determine the number of volunteers needed. The organizers or executive committee will delegate responsibilities to each committee. Individual committees will decide how much volunteer help they will need and how they will fulfill their assigned responsibilities. Each will come up with an organizational chart, complete with group and individual assignments and responsibilities.

Once the budget, organizational structure, and human resources are in place, the real work of planning can begin. All planners must become "detail conscious." Lack of attention to details can destroy a major event. In this case, an old cliché proves true that states that big things can only be accomplished by attention to little details. Paying close attention to details can make an event successful because planners are anticipating and preparing for snafus that might occur.

Preparing a timetable for completion of duties and activities is an effective way to organize details, in three respects. First, it can serve as a logistical tool, identifying needs and the timelines to fulfill them. Second, a timetable can double as a calendar of activities that ensures that organizers keep the event in the public eye in the months and days leading up to the event. Marketing personnel and sports information staff can time advertising efforts, promotional gimmicks, news conferences, and news releases to appear at regular intervals. The calendar of activities also provides a checklist or deadlines that aid organizers, planners, and volunteers in time management.

Third, a timetable facilitates the coordination of the work of all committees. Putting together the timeline requires adjustments within committees, to mesh their efforts with the overall plan. Development of the timetable helps the promotional unit and sports information personnel to coordinate advertising and news releases in particular.

Effective planning and preparation may ensure that a special event runs smoothly, but they will not guarantee a large audience. Promotion and publicity are the keys to building excitement for a special event and boosting spectator and media participation. Promotional activities should be structured much like a seven-course dinner—they should start with appetizers and work up to a sumptuous main course. In short, each activity should create a hunger for more that entices the media and fans to attend.

The promotional activities and publicity plan should be established early in the planning process. They should be incorporated into the operations manual and/or timetable, and they should be structured in such a way that they periodically remind the public of the upcoming event, its significance, and its entertainment value.

Publicity serves a dual purpose. First, it provides both the public and the media with information about the special event. The nature or significance of the event alone may be sufficient to attract spectator and media interest. Second, publicity complements promotional activities. It calls attention to activities and entertaining aspects of the event. In that respect, the objective of the publicity is to drum up fan and media support.

Promotion aims at selling tickets. Although promotional activities may incorporate publicity and information materials, the primary objective is to persuade people to attend the event.

Key Components of a Publicity Plan

Media list

Announcements

Timed releases

Interviews

Dinner

Press packet and program

Publicity

One way or another, organizers should work to maintain a steady stream of publicity about the event. News releases, features, and news conferences should build until the final advances are written and broadcast on the day of the event. Here are the key components of a typical publicity plan.

Media List

Sports information directors use their working media list for local special events, such as awards banquets or game promotions. They expand the list to include the appropriate media in geographical areas for regional or national events. Sponsoring organizations such as the NCAA, USGA, LPGA, and NFL, provide hosts with media lists and telephone numbers.

Announcements

The SID should send out an announcement for any special event when plans are finalized. If time allows, sports information specialists also should call a news conference to announce the event. They should invite print, broadcast, and any online journalists (bloggers, social media) media members who are involved and potentially interested in the event. The news conference should be timed to get maximum coverage especially now in a 24/7 news cycle.

Sports information directors do not always send out releases or call news conferences for annual events or game promotions. They may send out a release covering all the promotions for a sport or team for a year; they may distribute a release with a list on a monthly or weekly basis; or they may include information about the special promotion in game advances or notes releases. However, any one-time or special event, such as a playoff game or a tournament, should receive special treatment, meaning an announcement and a press conference, if possible.

Timed Releases

The publicity plan should include a schedule for releases to selected media. The releases must be newsworthy to be effective. The most effective timed releases are those that relate to details of the event or information about the event. Timed releases include stories about the teams involved, features on the athletes competing, and announcements about the program speakers. Stories on teams and players always should include photographs. Every release should include the pertinent facts of the event: date, time, and location, along with ticket prices and locations of purchase.

The plan should also include the appropriate social media approach to coincide with the timed release.

Interviews

If possible, periodically arrange telephone or in-person interviews with the top athletes for the local media. Such interviews are most popular among the media and most effective for the host organization in the month prior to the event.

Media Day

A media day prior to the event can generate a load of publicity. The sports information or public relations director can draw a good audience by including participants in the event on the program. Setting up a round of golf or other activity involving participants may lead to photographs, social media posts, or video on the local TV news as well.

Dinner

Sport organizations often schedule a welcome ceremony, including a dinner, the night before a major special event, such as a tournament. The dinner provides an opportunity to orient the media and the participants; it also may generate additional media coverage on the opening day of the event.

If organizers are hosting a dinner, they should establish a menu equal to the status of the event itself. In the case of a professional championship game, a full sit-down meal is in order. If it is a small college basketball tournament, pizza is satisfactory.

Press Packet and Program

Depending on the time they are distributed, press kits and programs may not produce much pre-event publicity. However, they provide useful information for advance stories immediately preceding the event, and they unquestionably help reporters prepare accurate and thorough stories once the event begins.

The number and scope of publicity efforts should correspond to the stature of the event as well. A single release may be sufficient for an awards banquet or a game promotion. A full-scale campaign may be more appropriate for an event with nationwide interest such as the Major League Baseball All-Star game.

Promotional Activities

The sports information or public relations staff's involvement in promotional activities will depend on the size of the sport organization. Athletics officials may have to take care of both publicity and promotion for high schools and amateur organizations. Sports information personnel may have to assume some promotional duties at the collegiate level, particularly at the Division II and III levels. At the Division I and professional levels, separate departments generally take care of most promotional responsibilities.

Most of the promotional activities involving SIDs and public relations directors are informational, not marketing oriented. The SID seldom will be involved in advertising and ticket sales, unless the advertising is for the program prepared by the sports information staff. However, sports information personnel may be called on to help with posters, flyers, and other printed materials.

Common Promotional Activities

Social Media entities

posters

prize giveaways

banners

flyers

promotions on back of tickets

event T-shirts

billboards

placemats

bumper stickers

portable signs

grocery stuffers

free merchandise

direct mailings

complimentary tickets

PA announcements at other events

public service announcements

speakers at civic clubs

Major special events generally are an easy sell. Promoting annual events and games is far more challenging, particularly for low-profile sports and losing teams. Obviously, a team in competition for a championship year after year or a team in a city with no other major sports should draw good crowds. The real challenge in marketing is to attract large crowds for less well-known products.

Marketing a losing team takes plenty of work. Promoting a losing professional team is often more difficult than promoting a noncompetitive team at the collegiate level. At the collegiate level, a pool of loyal students and graduates will generally attend regardless of the team's record; however, their interest will also increase dramatically as the victories increase. Game giveaways and other promotions also may fuel interest.

At the Division III collegiate level, the most important "sell" is on campus even if the tickets are free. Although the major purpose of attendance is to generate revenues, the sports information and marketing people can push other attractions, such as school spirit and support.

The following are general suggestions that relate to increasing attendance at games as well as at special events:

1. Establish a budget for promoting attendance, and set realistic goals for the budget. If goals are met, the budget for the next season may be increased.

2. Create and utilize an effective social media plan to enhance the timely dissemination of information and game/event reminders.

3. Make ticket buying easy. Set up a number of ticket outlets with clear information about when, where, and how to secure tickets. This is important not only for professional teams but also for amateur contests.

4. Work with local banks, department stores, gas stations, or other businesses to help in promotion and ticket sales.

5. Keep a mailing/email list of potential ticket buyers. Included on this list should be graduates, new students, area businesses, and past ticket holders.

6. Keep the people on the mailing list informed regarding schedules, ticket prices, season ticket availability, special ticket packages, and special events such as Community Day or Homecoming.

7. Do not overlook less visible or nonrevenue sports on the collegiate level. Any publicity and promotion may bring a few more people into the stands.

8. Utilize students in promotional activities at the collegiate level; the results can be most worthwhile.

9. Design publications that are not only valuable to the media but also act as promotional literature that will help boost attendance in recruitment of athletes.

10. In addition to media guides, flyers and posters should be designed to increase attention and attendance.

11. Contacts with the media should include invitations to promotions and special events. Unexpected positive publicity can result from bonds forged among the media, graduates, and coaches at a golf outing or other activity in connection with a special event.

Media Operations

Considerations in planning for media coverage of a special event are identical to the pregame, game management, and postgame preparations for a press-box/press row operation. The planning process must address credentials, work space, work crews, working materials, and food.

The differences between planning for a game and planning for a special event are a matter of degree—primarily, differences in logistics and in numbers of media to serve. The needs for an annual event, such as an awards banquet, are fewer because most information distributed to the media can be prepared in advance. The setup for a game promotion or postseason playoff match is virtually identical because it is linked closely to the game and the playing field or court. The details and duties for a major event, however, expand a hundredfold, in some cases, because far more members of the media attend. For example, there were 5,800 requests for media credentials for the 2018 Super Bowl. Additionally, some events, such as a golf tournament, may last more than one day.

Summary

Event management encompasses three main categories: game management/game-day operations, press conferences/media days, and special events. They are each unique in their own ways and put the SID's organization in the limelight differently, but each also possess some of the same characteristics.

Game days are the culmination of a week-long effort of hard work, time management, and organization. The days leading up to the game find the SID working closely with the media, overseeing interview sessions, preparing game notes, and being available for any and all needs from media and facility personnel. The day of the game, the SID is at the forefront of the organization's publicity thrust, and game days are arguably the most important opportunity for a team or organization to project a positive image.

Postgame duties for a SID usually are highly stressful because deadlines must be met by both the media and the SID. Postgame duties include everything from facilitating coach and player interviews to writing releases and game notes. Depending on the sport, the entire process is duplicated the very next day in preparation for the next sporting event.

News conferences and media days are a great way to provide the media with a large amount of information at one time and in one location. News conferences usually have a "business-like" atmosphere while media days offer more of a social gathering atmosphere. Both are used as informational gathering tools for the media. News conferences could be called for any number of reasons: the hiring of a new coach, the announcement of a large donation to the sport organization, plans to renovate a facility, or a team's selection and inclusion into postseason play. The planning for the news conference is usually minimal and the entire process can be performed in a day.

Media days usually involve more intricate and advanced planning, sometimes as much as six to nine months in advance, and could involve an entire team or representatives from every team in a conference in a "meet-and-greet" setting with the media. For media days, a wider selection of food is usually provided to attendees.

Special events encompass an entire spectrum of offerings from a one-time hosting of a post-season tournament, to a week-long playoff. They involve special planning, involving a budget and planning committees, and a lot of hard work from the SID focusing on organization, time management, and communication.

Discussion Topics

1. Of the three types of event planning, which one looks the most appealing? Why? Conversely, which one looks the least appealing? Why?

2. What are the main differences between game-management, special event management, and media days/press conferences? What are the similarities?

Suggested Exercises

1. Shadow a local SID or home-game administrator on game-day and report your findings to class.

2. Create a detailed plan for your school's hosting of next year's men's basketball NCAA first and second rounds. What steps will you have to take to ensure that the event goes off without a hitch?

10 | Publicity Campaigns

The dog days of summer are upon you as a college sports information director. Yet, there is no down time as you begin to formulate a plan to promote one of your athletes for All-American honors during the upcoming season. In the now fast-paced world of social media, where news comes and goes in a moment's notice, the task at hand has both its positives and negatives. You are charged with promoting your candidate to the best of your ability, yet must maintain relevance, stay in the voter's forethoughts, and come up with an idea that has staying power and is also fresh.

So, what will you do to promote your candidate? Will you utilize social media, take traditional approaches, come up with a new fresh idea or incorporate a variety of strategies? The choices are abundant and at the fingertips of you, your team, and your athlete. What will you decide to do and what tactics will you implement to create an effective campaign? Those choices could very well be the difference between getting your candidate the appropriate accolades or being just another candidate with a campaign of no substance.

Early Stages of Campaign Development

There are several considerations pertaining to creating a publicity campaign. The early stages of communication within the organization are of the utmost importance and should include the SID, prospective candidate or team, and the coach.

Some coaches are "team" coaches and believe any and all accolades earned by individual players are a direct result of the overall success of the team. Their logic is that the better the team does, the more accolades the individuals will receive. Thus, those coaches are not big fans of publicity campaigns.

Other coaches believe a unique publicity campaign will bring notoriety to the entire team, program, or organization. If an athlete deserves it, and they are granting permission, those coaches are completely in favor of creating a publicity campaign.

Neither opinion is right or wrong. In either regard, both of the opinions represent why it is important that the coach be involved in initial discussions before any further planning or promotion of the athlete or team can begin. If a coach resists a publicity campaign in these preliminary discussions, the SID should strongly consider dropping the campaign.

The campaign is a unique venture outside of the realm of the standard or traditional publicity a SID would normally do. Making the athlete and coach aware that added attention, and thus the added media stressors, will result if the campaign begins is of the utmost importance. The sports information or public relations director should consider both the candidate's athletics performance and his or her personal behavior. If the athlete is unreliable, isn't punctual, and/or is generally just not a good person, then the SID should consider looking for another candidate to promote, or cancel the campaign. An athlete featured in a publicity campaign must fulfill more interview requests and have added media responsibilities that go above and beyond the norm. The campaign may require conducting many more interviews with the media, answering fans' questions in an internet chat, and just generally being more available than usual. Those not willing to put forth the required time and effort, and those that may not be reliable enough to meet the demands, may only hamper the campaign after it has already become irreversible. Again, campaigns are for the benefit of the athletes. If they don't think they can fulfill the added obligations, then the campaigns should not be created.

If the coach and star athlete are in agreement that a publicity campaign is a good idea, the SID should alert the athlete to the dangers of dishonesty, a lack of cooperation with the media, and personal indiscretions. By the end of the conversation, the athlete should be well informed and forewarned of all that may occur once the campaign begins. If the athlete is not fully comfortable and cooperative, the plan should be dropped. Pressing the idea will not serve the athlete or the organization well.

The campaign has a greater chance of succeeding and less chance of backfiring if the athlete's integrity is on the same level as his or her performance. In publicizing an athlete, school officials should never go overboard on a player they know is not worthy. Be sure the player is really as good as the coach, the SID, and others believe the individual to be. Remember, the reputations of all involved are on the line. Making a decision on the worthiness of a candidate is not as easy as it sometimes appears to be.

The publicity campaign also has a greater chance of success if it promotes an athlete or team in a high-profile sport. If the object is to achieve high visibility, the potential gains are minimal if the media pay little attention to the sport anyway. For this reason, football and basketball players most often are the focus of publicity efforts on a college or high school campus. A SID often will focus on an outstanding athlete from one or both of these sports. The SID may achieve success in promoting an athlete in another sport if the campaign identifies and motivates a receptive media audience. For example, a campaign promoting a soccer player should aim at media in cities with all-star voters and consistent soccer coverage as well as at the local media.

In the summer of 2008, West Virginia University opened its campaign for Pat White, not necessarily in order for him to be mentioned among the preseason Heisman Trophy candidates, but rather as a way to further promote one of the school's all-time great football players. Any and all accolades that came as a result of the campaign would be an added bonus. The sports information staff at the school, led by director of football communications Mike Montoro, pitched the campaign ideas to White and then-Coach Bill Stewart, who both agreed it was a good idea to move forward. What resulted was an interactive internet site that included facts, statistics, video clips of White's greatest highlights, and an interactive area where the future NFL quarterback could answer questions posed to him from fans. The campaign was well received and accentuated White's performances on the field.

Coach's Corner with Craig Esherick

Managing egos is often a coach's most delicate responsibility; this is true at every level, not just professional sports. Launching a publicity campaign featuring a single athlete is especially difficult if there is a star athlete on a team sport. So it's important to keep a couple of things in mind: prepare the other members of the team for the added attention focused on the star and counsel the star to appreciate the contributions his or her teammates bring to the team. Experienced media relations professionals understand this dynamic as well as coaches.

Since everyone likes attention, and in an effort to reduce feelings of jealousy, photo shoots and interviews with the featured athlete should, whenever possible, be done away from the other team members. Nothing affects team chemistry more than a diva in the midst! Having said that, don't forget to include the subject of the campaign in the planning of it. Sometimes the most creative ideas for a publicity campaign will come from the featured athlete in the campaign. An experienced communication director who has developed personal relationships with each athlete can use ideas from the athlete to develop a successful publicity campaign. Many college and professional athletes have been using Twitter, Facebook, and Instagram since they were in high school; this experience can help the SID with the publicity campaign. I would add a note of caution here too; many athletes have made mistakes with social media. The direction of the campaign should remain in the control of the communications professional.

When working with college athletes, promoting the _student_ in student-athlete also will pay dividends. Featuring your star studying in the library, sitting in a lecture hall, or walking across campus with a backpack and jeans stresses the importance of your program as part of a larger academic institution—one that is goal oriented, disciplined, and future minded. And never underestimate the power of business attire. Even in this day and age, where dress codes seem quaint, the image of a conservatively dressed student-athlete never fails to impress.

Finally, a well-orchestrated publicity campaign is a great recruiting tool for a college coach. Potential recruits and incoming players look forward to seeing their names and images in print, on TV, or on the web. Media savvy youngsters appreciate a sports information professional who gets their athletes featured in the news. And successful media campaigns featuring an outstanding athlete compiled over the years not only builds and preserves a program's history, but also comes in handy when the coach is selling his or her program to potential athletes, their parents, and their high school coaches. Publicity campaigns focusing on one or two athletes in the world of professional sports can be used in conjunction with season ticket drives, community relations efforts, and sponsorship/marketing plans. A well-orchestrated publicity campaign for an MVP Award or a spot on a league All-Star team might get the attention of a soon to be free agent who could be looking to sign with another team at the conclusion of the season.

If, after discussions with the coach and player, the campaign is to proceed, preparations must begin well before the start of the season for the sport in which the athlete participates. The push must start in late spring for athletes in fall sports such as football, in summer for winter sports, and in fall for spring sports. The SID must organize the campaign and compile and prepare the avalanche of information well before the particular season is underway; consequently, the SID must evaluate candidates well before the season begins. Was the junior who blossomed in postseason play at the end of last year enjoying a short-lived stretch of success or is he/she a superstar in waiting? Is the lone senior on the team, an all-league caliber player, really ready for the added stressors that will be imposed on him/her?

The SID should meet with the coach and player to develop a strategy to increase the star's national visibility. In the case of Joey Harrington, former Oregon Duck standout and a Heisman Trophy candidate, "Joey Heisman" evolved from the campaign, a unique nickname that fit for the Ducks' quarterback, playing to the alliteration of his last name. The nickname created an image of Harrington as a legitimate Heisman Trophy contender and had a catchy ring to it. And it stuck.

More recently, both the Oklahoma Sooners and Mountaineers had quarterbacks worthy of Heisman Trophy consideration. Here are two examples:

NORMAN – The Kyler Murray campaign for the Heisman Trophy has started.

On Thursday night, Oklahoma revealed the website KylerKnows.com which features a homepage picture of the quarterback with shoulder pads and a baseball bat while also unloading facts and statistics.

Murray's football/baseball pose is identical to Bo Jackson at the height of the popular "Bo Knows" campaign by Nike. Jackson played professional football and baseball between 1987–90.

Source: Eric Bailey Tulsa World article 11/16/18

Murray went on to win the 2018 Heisman Trophy.

At West Virginia, the athletic department unveiled "Grier7Heisman.com" to promote its star quarterback Will Grier. The website was comprehensive, chalk full of game highlights, stats, and anecdotes that brought Grier national media attention. Ultimately, it helped him finish fourth in the Heisman Trophy race after a record-breaking season.

In other cases, unique story ideas showing a player's humility, character, or personality; a rare human interest story; or a story detailing an athletic lineage may well be the route to go when kicking off the campaign. If the SID shows a different side of an athlete, that of compassion or of public service, it may do wonders in terms of allowing the media and public to gain new insight on the player.

The SID should conduct an informal but in-depth personal interview with the athlete being featured in the campaign in order to find out as much as possible about the athlete's personal background, likes and dislikes, hobbies and other interests, church and community activities, goals and dreams, and attitudes and beliefs about athletics, education, and other pertinent subjects. The interview will serve two purposes. First, it will give the SID a fuller portrait of the athlete and insight into personal strengths and weaknesses that may affect the campaign. The interview may also forge a strong personal relationship between the athlete and the SID, which is important during those trying times when the pressure becomes unbearable for both the athlete and the SID. Second, the interview may generate a lot of ideas for story angles to develop or to suggest to the media during the publicity campaign.

The next step is for the SID to prepare a budget that will cover the cost of extra printed materials, photography, artwork, videotape, and postage. The budget will dictate the size and scope of the campaign. A small school with a limited budget, for example, would not have the financial means to place a banner in Times Square as the University of Oregon did with its campaign for Harrington.

All photographs used should be of high resolution quality, for use in newspaper and magazine stories as well as the internet. Video footage should show only the best of the athlete's plays, particularly those showing the skills or strengths of the campaign's target so that TV stations may use the clips packages in addition to other video archives of the athlete they may already have.

The SID should complete the bulk of the printed materials prior to the season. Anything that can be done in advance lightens the extra burden the campaign will create when the season commences. The SID should write an introductory news release, prepare a biographical sheet, compile statistical charts and comparisons, and compose hometown and news features for inclusion in the campaign's promotion and for distribution to journalists who request information during the season.

Any area of excellence can be supported with selective use of statistics. How the athlete's ranking, scoring, yardage, and other averages stack up nationally, in the conference, and on the career school charts always provides evidence of excellence. The SID can devise new stats to fit a story idea. Statistics are very good supportive material.

Campaign promotional items for distribution to selected media (and voters for postseason honors and awards) should include photographs (action, informal, and posed), biographical information, feature stories, a statistical history, video highlights provided on a DVD, and other pertinent information regarding the publicity of the individual. If an organization's budget is tight, the material that makes up the media kit could be made available online rather than mailing the entire media kit to what could be hundreds of journalists or voters. It would be a much cheaper venture on a tighter budget and in the end could produce the same results as that from a program with a substantially larger budget that mailed the media kits.

For sports that don't have a large budget or for an Olympic sport that may not get as much attention as football or basketball, but still have a worthy candidate, utilizing social media, email lists, and being creative will help garner national attention for national awards. Simply put, the SID has free reign to garner attention for one of his or her athletes.

The Publicity Campaign Promotional Items

A campaign's promotional items that focus on the athlete at the center of the publicity campaign typically will include a packet of information and artwork that emphasizes the *selling point*, the single element that best illustrates the athlete's excellence. The items could be any as follows:

- **News release**: A story introducing the athlete, built around a news angle.
- **Suggested stories**: A list of story ideas/angles for the journalist who receives the kit. Make it easy for the journalist to pursue a story.
- **Biographical summary**: An information sheet similar to a résumé that includes records set or about to be broken during the upcoming season.
- **Video**: Access to a video link for highlight worthy plays.
- **Reprints**: Copies of newspaper or magazine articles that extol the excellence of the athlete.
- **Quotations**: A list of quotations drawn from what opponents (players and coaches), scouts, and analysts have said about the athlete. These have great value.
- **Fact sheet**: Quick facts on the athlete, team, conference, and school. The fact sheet should include telephone and fax numbers as well as the name of a contact person in the SID office.
- **Statistics**: One or more statistical lists with individual statistics and rankings (career, school, conference, nation).
- **Head shot**: A professional, portrait-style photograph.
- **Action shots**: A couple of posed or candid shots of the athlete in competition.
- **Poster**: A glossy poster of the athlete in action.
- **Other promotional items**: Giveaways the coach, athlete, and SID agree upon such as a notepad containing the athlete's image and campaign slogan.

In addition to a promotional package, there are other ways in which the campaign subject could be prominently featured through various items produced by the school or organization.

Media Guides

The campaign subject should receive special attention in the media guide, as long as the coach approves of the idea. The SID can supplement promotion of the star by using a color photograph of the player on the cover of the media guide and including a more comprehensive biography than the brief sketches of other players inside the guide. In other words, the guide should feature the star in as many ways as possible.

Websites

Arguably the easiest and most cost-effective tool in the publicity campaign is creating a website for the star athlete. The internet is the contemporary one-stop shop used by all. The website is usually created by the sports information staff and is hosted by the school's official athletics webpage, which will include a link to the promotional player page. Using a clever URL, such as "PatWhitePlaysHere.com," or "Grier7Heisman.com," will make it easier for visitors to remember the web address of the page. Once it is created, much of the material contained in the media kit should be incorporated on the website, including statistics, biographical information, and photography and video archives.

Social Media

The fresh and contemporary mode to fulfill an inexpensive and effective way to promote in a publicity campaign is using social media.

Whether it be Twitter, Facebook, Instagram, or a combination of many, social media outlets, when used appropriately, can reach the masses in an instant and have

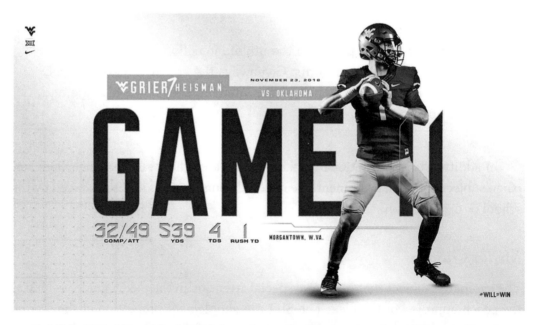

Exhibit 10.1 *West Virginia University webpage promoting Heisman Trophy nominee Will Grier. (Courtesy of West Virginia University.)*

staying power for those that are keen on knowing up-to-the minute information on a candidate's success, whereabouts, and future endeavors.

After all promotional materials have been compiled and products such as media guides and websites have been created, the sports information staff devises a publicity strategy, with news releases timed to coincide with career milestones for the athlete. The SID creates "Countdowns" and "Watches" (with logos) for insertion in game advances and notes columns. Perhaps a newspaper will print an updated chart with each game story, or a TV producer will flash the graphic on the screen with the results of each game. These countdowns and watches can also be utilized effectively on social media or for updates during a campaign with timely videos, photos, or stats of the athlete during a contest.

These types of mentions are invaluable in terms of exposure and what it means for the underlying theme of the campaign. Focusing on small details such as this will result in greater things down the line, especially in the campaign.

Continuing the Campaign

Once the season begins, and a foundation for the campaign has been created, the SID changes modes from planner to facilitator. A good SID will work daily with the star athlete that is at the center of the publicity campaign, fulfilling any media requests as best as possible. The SID could also set the standard for interviews, prearranging the athlete's availability into block times. The SID must remember, especially at the collegiate level, that the athlete at the center of the campaign also has class, strength and conditioning, study hall, practice, and a social life. So it is imperative that interview times and requests be granted with the athlete's best interest at heart. Being organized with a timetable and sticking to the schedule is a must, which now must also include effectively using social media. Once the schedule is set, distribute it to the media so they know when the athlete is available to be interviewed. Should the athlete being promoted have their own personal social media accounts already, and in most cases they will, the athlete should be appropriately coached how to effectively utilize those platforms while under the scrutiny of both fans and additional media. That would include misuse, posting, or sharing inappropriate items, as well as posting positive personal updates for all to see during the campaign. It is also imperative that the SID never give out the athlete's phone number, or the phone number of any athlete, for that matter. Should the athlete be contacted by members of the media, instruct the athlete to request that the reporter arrange the interview through the SID.

Sports information personnel should take care to keep interviews to a minimum close to game day—the further from game day the better, in fact. Disruptions can affect an athlete's mental preparation for the game. Coaches, SIDs, and the media should respect and honor requests for privacy on game day. If a particular writer wants an in-depth interview, the SID should set it up at the convenience of both parties, but well in advance of the next game.

It also may be appropriate for the SID to "coach" the athlete with regard to fulfilling interviews (for more on this see Chapter 5). In addition to being a media manager and time organizer, the SID continues to serve as a publicity mill during the season. The SID can recycle the printed materials, photographs, and artwork that was produced in the early stages of the campaign's development in a variety of ways as the season unfolds. He or she can also put together individual packets for journalists or others who call to inquire about the athlete. The publicity campaign can also include a schedule of timed releases to media on the original mailing list. The SID can send out features on different angles at prearranged intervals. Sports information personnel can also time releases to coincide with achievements during the season. For example, a news release would be timely when the athlete sets a personal, school, or conference record. The savvy sports information director will also effectively utilize social media to coincide with the releases and achievements.

As the season progresses, the SID will continue to update all the factual information regarding the candidate, such as updated statistics, news clippings, photography, and video footage and also use social media effectively, whether it be through a YouTube channel for highlights or Instagram for timely and appropriate photos. Should a request be made from an out-of-town media member, the SID will have all that information readily available.

Ethical Considerations

The SID who undertakes a publicity campaign functions in a foggy area between sports information and *press agentry*. Press agentry is a term applied to publicists in the early days of public relations who promoted a client with all types of gimmicks and tricks. Some of the techniques were intentionally misleading. Others attracted attention because they were so outrageous. The publicists would promote their clients by any means possible. The SID can avoid straying into these areas by measuring every aspect of the publicity campaign and every action in carrying it out by two standards: *honesty* and *information value*.

First, no one associated with the campaign can engage in any deceit or appearance of deceit (such as providing misleading information). The SID cannot hope to hide negative information about the athlete's past or performance, hence why it is important to select a reputable and worthy candidate for the campaign. The SID must not distort any information or statistics. Using statistics selectively to support a point is acceptable; juggling or adjusting statistics to fit the point is not. For example, a statistician yearns to "help" a linebacker set a record for tackles and earn individual honors, so he or she gives the player credit for an assisted tackle any time he's near the football, even though a teammate may have been responsible for the tackle. Judgment call or well-intentioned manipulation? It will be deemed a deception if the totals differ markedly from the statistics kept by the opponent, and word will spread quickly that someone is "cooking the numbers" if it happens in more than one game. Such accusations will undermine the publicity campaign, taint any record the athlete sets, and damage the reputation of the team and the university.

Second, the SID should consider the information value of all materials prepared for the publicity campaign. Certainly, the objective is to "sell" the athlete, but the techniques employed must use legitimate information to do so. The SID may borrow from advertising, using promotional items such as bumper stickers, posters, nickname gimmicks, or giveaways. However, such tools should be clearly identifiable as promotional items and openly distributed as such—that is the honesty in the promotion. Furthermore, all printed materials, photographs, and video should revolve around a core of information consistent with the criteria of news. The media are more likely to use the information if it has news value. The SID should not stage a news conference just to gather a media crowd for the athlete; he or she must have real news information to deliver, or the pseudo event will cross the boundary into misleading manipulation.

Ten Rules for Creating a Publicity Campaign

1. Pick a worthy candidate. Never promote an athlete you do not believe is deserving of recognition (athletically or personally).

2. Seek approval of the coach and the athlete before launching any campaign. Explain the demands and dangers in detail to each when seeking approval. Drop the idea if either has objections.

3. Orient the athlete on what to expect during the campaign. The athlete's athletic and academic standing are at stake.

4. Help the athlete set up a schedule that absorbs the additional time demands as effortlessly as possible. Make an effort to control media contact and to coach the athlete on handling interviews.

5. Remember that you put the athlete in this high-pressure situation, especially in a 24/7 news cycle with multiple forms of social media utilized in the campaign. The SID has a responsibility to help the athlete get through it with as little stress as possible.

6. Borrow techniques from advertising for publicity materials, but do not go overboard. Creative presentation is OK. Exaggeration and flattery are not.

7. Clearly identify promotional elements such as bumper stickers and posters as advertising. Use them as such, not as information.

8. Selective use of statistics is acceptable. Distorting or doctoring statistics is not.

9. Treat the media with courtesy and respect.

10. Never tell a lie. No breach of honesty is acceptable. Always tell the truth in the promotion of your athlete.

Summary

The creation of a publicity plan is a multi-faceted process that involves creativity, cooperation from the athlete and coach, and a resolve to see the process through to its fruition. If done correctly, the attention garnered for the athlete at the center of the publicity campaign will gain instant notoriety. And if the accolades earned on the playing field back up the exposure the campaign provides, then the chances are great that the athlete will receive some sort of national or regional recognition.

Several factors are initially involved in selecting the athlete, informing him/her of the added responsibilities and stressors the campaign may have, and seeking the approval of the coach. If the coach or athlete waiver in the initial discussions of creating a campaign and have reservations about the process, then the campaign should go no further. If the athlete and coach agree to participate in a campaign, further attention is given to the athlete by the SID in the areas of handling, assisting with, and processing the additional daily, weekly, and monthly media stressors that the campaign will bring.

Once the campaign has begun, the SID switches gears from planner to facilitator in assuring that all the plans that were created in the beginning stages are executed while attempting to alleviate, as best as possible, the stressors of the campaign that the player will experience.

Ethical considerations are to be understood and followed in terms of the athlete's statistics and their presentation during the campaign. The SID should simply state the facts and avoid misleading or misrepresenting the athlete's accomplishments.

The campaign is a unique tool and a special presentation for the organization and the athlete at the center of it. It will create added work for the SID and athlete, but if implemented properly, the publicity campaign should prove to be an enjoyable, and hopefully successful, experience.

Discussion Questions

1. What tools used in the publicity of an All-American would you use in running your own campaign? What one tool, in your opinion, would be the most effective?

2. Review the Ten Rules in Creating a Publicity Campaign. Which one do you believe is the most important?

Suggested Exercises

1. Choose a local collegiate athlete and create an All-American campaign for the athlete using the information in this chapter.

2. Research a successful Player of the Year campaign in any of the four major sports in the US. What went right and why did they work? Conversely, in hindsight, what could have been done better in the promotion of that athlete? Discuss with your class.

11

Crisis Management

It's a Monday morning in the middle of the offseason and you just arrived to work in the sports information office at 9 am to start some continued work on your media guide. Not even five minutes after you're comfortably at your desk, a member of the print media comes in with last night's police report that lists your school's star basketball player as having been arrested for DUI. The reporter asks to speak to both the player and the coach. How do you handle the request?

A few minutes later, a broadcast media member from the local CBS affiliate calls to confirm an interview that had been arranged weeks ago with the same player, for later that afternoon, to talk about his upcoming trip with a USA Basketball team that will be competing in the FIBA Americas Tournament. Suspecting that he might still be in jail, what do you do in that situation?

Then, as you begin to gather facts about last night's incident and contact the basketball coach to discuss the situation, you begin to hear rumors from sports information office interns that three athletes on the women's soccer team were involved in a car accident and there was alcohol involved. You have also received several tweets that mention rumors about the members of the soccer team and the basketball player. What do you do now?

All good sports information and public relations directors will tell you that you should have planned well before the problem(s) arose what you would say, what you would do, and how you would deal with a crisis. In today's society, athletes, coaches, and teams perform under a media microscope. The spotlight is constantly on, and it often gets very hot under the lights very quickly. Trouble does arise occasionally, even in the best of sport organizations; many of these problems are predictable. High school and college athletes behave immaturely at times, no matter how hard everyone in the institution tries to guide them properly. Coaches and boosters cross the boundaries of NCAA rules, sometimes intentionally and sometimes inadvertently. Some professional athletes believe they are immune from the law. Others succumb to temptations such as recreational drugs, underage drinking, and gambling. Still other athletes decide they need the edge that performance-enhancing drugs may provide. Occasionally, a crisis emerges that stretches the imagination of all involved (see Chapter 1 regarding Manti Te'o, the former Notre Dame linebacker and his online 'girlfriend'). The equally unpredictable admissions scandal of 2019 tested the media relations skills of sports information directors at schools like Yale, Texas, Wake Forest, Georgetown, and Southern California.

When trouble arises, the spotlight shines brightly on the sport organization as well as on the athlete or coach (and in many cases their families). Revelations about NCAA, Department of Justice, FBI, or NFL investigations; disclosures about athletes' indiscretions, and speculation about business matters (e.g., the firing of a coach or a move to another conference) can evolve into crises that damage the public image of the organization and its relationship with the media, if the matter is not handled quickly and efficiently. The responsibility for effectively filtering the light of media scrutiny and for effecting favorable public reaction rests heavily on the SIDs, director of communication, or the public relations director's shoulders. The media expect assistance, or at least cooperation, in gathering information quickly. Team owners, coaches, school presidents, and athletics administrators demand limits on information released and control of the content; consequently, sports information specialists often find themselves in the middle of a conflict between administrators who do not want to say anything and aggressive journalists who dig out details of the story on their own. In the age of Twitter, Facebook, Instagram, and smartphones, those details are sometimes not too difficult to find. Every smartphone has a camera and every fan thinks he or she is a reporter.

A person who cannot cope with the heat in the middle of a flash fire (or who does not want to deal with it) should not pursue a career in sports information. Crises are challenging, frustrating, and stressful—they are the public arena in which SIDs prove their mettle and earn their salary. If they do not act quickly and decisively, the reputations of athletes, coaches, teams, schools, and owners/administrators may be hurt. If SIDs do not respond tactfully, promptly and aggressively, the relationship between the media and the sport organization may deteriorate. If they do not serve both sides effectively, they may find themselves looking for another job.

A Climate of Cooperation

Sports public relations is challenging, exciting, and rewarding when the work involves interviewing athletes, writing features, creating media guides, managing media days and news conferences, running press-box operations, and directing publicity campaigns. Working with the media, outstanding athletes, and witty coaches during good times and winning seasons is enjoyable. Unfortunately, the business of sports information is not always about distributing positive information and promoting cordial relationships. Sometimes it requires dealing with negative news, losing seasons, and strained relationships.

The relationship between the media and sport organizations is always a push-and-pull association, because their objectives differ. In the case of sports journalism, those who control the media not only select which sports and which events to cover, but they also decide what to emphasize in that coverage. The emphasis may be positive or negative; the newspaper writes the headlines. As much as the sports communications professional would like to control the flow of positive information at all times, the media ultimately will decide what is the best route for their coverage be it positive or not.

The sport organization also presents a selective version of information—a version that promotes the organization's philosophy and goals. The emphasis is always positive, or as positive as circumstances permit. The sport organization attempts to push the selection of events and the emphasis in coverage in the direction it favors. Push comes to shove when the media's selection and coverage emphases are unfavorable or unfair. The last thing the Michigan State men's basketball or football coach wanted to talk about during their 2018 season was the behavior of a doctor who happened to work at the same University. The doctor's past behavior, involving female athletes at Michigan State and USA Gymnastics, was driving the news at Michigan State. Larry Nasser (the Michigan State doctor) is now serving a very long jail sentence. Similarly, during the early days of the Jerry Sandusky sex scandal, Penn State officials and Coach Joe Paterno wanted reporters to focus on the many great teams and fine young men Paterno and the football program had produced during his tenure as head coach. Reporters had other ideas about what they wanted to talk about.

The challenge for the sports information specialist is far broader than simply controlling negative news that reflects unfavorably on the sport organization. The media's coverage selections, particularly as they relate to women's sports and men's low-profile sports, also create a challenging issue for the SID. Shove comes to confrontation most often on issues of commission, rather than those of omission. The primary flashpoints are events or issues that generate information that appears to contradict the image the sport organization presents to the public. However, any threat to the organization's public image represents a potential public relations crisis, and lack of media coverage of men's low-profile sports and women's sports creates an incomplete portrait of the sport organization. Its omission may even suggest the organization is not as committed to those sports as administrators claim.

A crisis for a sport organization is any event, incident, or issue that falls outside the realm of everyday management activities and poses a threat to the reputation of the organization. Crises can strike at any time—crises such as the arrest of an athlete, the dismissal of a coach, the suspension of an athlete for a positive drug test, or a domestic abuse allegation. Crises can also develop slowly over a period of time (e.g., frequent criticism of a coach by a disgruntled reporter). Crises, or at the very least, conflict, can grow out of long-standing issues, such as lack of coverage of men's low-profile sports and women's sports. In college athletics, the decision to become a member of a new conference has tested the skills of many sports information directors at schools like Wichita State, Notre Dame, Brigham Young, Texas A&M, and Maryland.

Each type of crisis may demand a different response from sports information directors, athletics administrators, or team officials. However, three general truths apply to every crisis:

1. The battle for public support during the crisis is usually won or lost in the first 24 hours.

2. The sport organization will probably lose the battle of public perception if representatives of the organization fail to develop specific procedures for early and regular communication with the public during the crisis.

3. The more complex the crisis procedures, the less likely they are to succeed.

The timeframe is critical. First impressions are the most difficult to erase, so the sport organization must develop a course of action and implement it quickly. When possible, providing the media with the maximum amount of information in a minimal amount of time is key. The athletics director, general manager, sports information director, or public relations director will serve as head of the emergency response team that implements the procedures. Even if the SID or public relations director does not lead the team or act as the spokesperson, he/she will be called upon to guide a critical part of the procedure—the part that decides the battle of public opinion.

The SID must balance the objectives of the organization and the needs of the media in implementing crisis-management procedures; in so doing, he/she must serve two bosses, each of whom is operating on a different schedule. The decision-making cycle generally moves slowly in the world of academia; administrators appoint committees to study an issue, to gather data to formulate options, to analyze and test options, to conduct research and to choose a course of action. The process can take months or even longer.

In the realm of the media, the decision-making cycle moves at whirlwind speed and at deadline intervals—for example, 24 hours between daily newspaper editions; 4–5 hours between morning, noon, evening, and late-night newscasts; 30 minutes between radio newscasts; 30 minutes between updates on all-news radio and TV channels; and instantaneously on the internet and in the Twittersphere. Because of the intense competition among the media, reporters, editors, and producers must decide quickly whether a snippet of information is news, how much information they can gather before the next deadline, and what element to emphasize in their presentation of the story. Think about how long it would take a reporter to retweet the report about the basketball player that the SID received in the opening scenario to this chapter.

It is important to remember that the objective of the media is not to analyze the facts and draw conclusions. The role of the media is to present information to the public—to present all the facts that are known at the time of publication or broadcast. Therefore, the media first will churn out facts about the arrest of an athlete on sexual assault charges—whether or not the athlete is guilty. They will attempt to interview people on both sides of the story but if people on one side do not want to talk, the media will report the information they were able to obtain now, report the 'no comment' from the team/school, and continue to try to get the other side for the next news cycle. As a result, the facts of a story may unfold over the course of several news cycles. Reporters usually will not hold a report in order to wait until the story runs its course (judgment on guilt or innocence) unless they have assurances that no competitor will get the information. A reporter might be persuaded to hold a story on an internal investigation by an athletic director or a professional league official, but no amount of cajoling, stonewalling, or withholding comment will stop a story that comes from a police blotter or from any other record open to public inspection.

Sports information personnel, school administrators, and team executives must understand that the decision-making models they typically follow move much too slowly to keep up with fast-breaking stories and even faster-breaking rumors. Whether the crisis is a legitimate story or an unfounded rumor of an investigation into use of performance enhancing drugs by a very popular women's tennis star, news travels swiftly in the community. With the ubiquity of Twitter in the sports world, *swiftly* has an entirely new meaning. The media will report legitimate news, and the private lives of public figures such as athletes, team owners, and coaches fit the media/public criteria of news. The media also will address rumors if they find some factual basis to support them, many of them turning to blogs or Twitter accounts if it's a rumor that at that point in time doesn't warrant an entire story. Sport organization personnel cannot prevent publication or broadcast of a story simply by refusing to talk about it.

Once one accepts the premise that the media dictate the selection and emphasis of news, it is easy to understand why a climate of cooperation is the best response to public relations crises. Sport organization personnel who provide prompt and direct answers to questions stand a far better chance of forestalling rumors than do those who stonewall. Sport organization officials who avoid the media or offer "no comment" run the risk of fueling suspicions and turning a tidbit of fact into a tidal wave of rumor and speculation.

The starting point for effective crisis management is a relationship with the media built on a foundation of cooperation. Charges against a school athletics program or other sports organization, whether they are true or false, should be answered as soon as possible to protect the integrity of the athletics department, one or some of their members, or the institution. When trouble strikes, coaches, athletics directors, college presidents, and members of the board of trustees may find themselves swept into a controversy; those that work at Duke, Michigan State, and Penn State know all too well how an athletic department crisis can impact the entire university community. The arrest and the subsequent trial of Aaron Hernandez, the former tight end for the New England Patriots, was an organization problem—not just a challenge for Hernandez and his legal team.

Expediency in responding to charges is the best course of action. The longer charges go unanswered, the larger the problem of combating negative perceptions.

Three Guiding Principles

An effective climate of cooperation is built on three simple principles: honesty, availability, and fair play. Strict adherence to these principles by all representatives of the sport organization will enhance the relationship with the media and will put the organization in a positive position from a public relations point of view. In the world of sports, the cooperation must come not only from the SID or the public relations staff, but also from all coaches, athletes, athletics directors, administrators, owners, commissioners, and support staff. If all are honest, open, and fair, the media are far more likely to give the organization the benefit of the doubt when facts are in dispute; they are more likely to emphasize the positives, from the institution's perspective. For example, a story about a suspension or fine of a few NFL players for team rules violations might focus more on the forthright manner in which the coach and the team dealt with a disciplinary problem, than on the violations themselves.

How to Create a Climate of Cooperation

1. Deal honestly with the media.
2. Be available.
3. Treat all media members fairly and cordially.

Principle No. 1: Deal Honestly with the Media

Less than complete honesty will return to haunt those who are not straightforward. Mistrust will feed suspicion and give credence to rumors of wrongdoing or deceit.

In a study about crisis communication published in the *Public Relations Journal,* one of the primary conclusions was that the great majority of journalists surveyed would have their suspicions aroused if the organization withheld important information or tried to cover it up (Robertson, 2012). Honesty is especially important when dealing with sensitive or negative situations. Keith (1985) compares a SID to a successful team possessing speed and quickness; such attributes are assets when dealing with the media in a stressful situation.

An honest approach does not require sports information or other representatives of the institution to tell the media everything they know about a given situation. The institution should exercise some control over the release of information; after all, the objective of the sport organization is to influence public opinion favorably through the selective release of information. However, honesty demands that the sport organization avoid deception in the posture it takes when responding to questions or requests for information. If SIDs are forbidden to comment regarding a question or situation because of university, team, or league policy, they should say so. If they cannot comment because of the sensitive nature of the issue, they should say so (see FERPA and HIPAA restrictions in Chapter 13). The SIDs should give a reason for their refusal to comment, in every case. Honest, hard-working members of the media will accept a "no comment" without rancor or suspicion if a SID explains why. Reporters will work around "no comment" responses and search for other sources or documents to complete the factual puzzle.

The SID should establish specific ground rules for release of information in the course of casual conversation or discussion of an issue and should make clear to all reporters the organization's policies on off-the-record comments and anonymous sources. Sometimes a SID or a representative of an organization may need to provide some background information or an explanation to clarify the response to an inquiry. The background or explanation may give the reporter some facts the organization is not ready to announce or disclose. Before discussing the information, the SID must make it clear to the reporter that such information is off the record. *Off-the-record* is a journalistic handshake—an agreement that the reporter who accepts comments off the record will not use the information in the story.

Some organizations attempt to control public reaction by releasing selected information through anonymous sources. Perhaps someone in the organization feels compelled to reveal certain facts but worries about how the public will view the disclosure if the source were revealed. The person may agree to reveal the information provided the journalist attributes it in a manner that shields the name of the source, for instance as "a person with knowledge of the situation." The technique is common practice in Washington political circles, where "an anonymous source" leaks selective information to test public reaction. If the public reacts negatively, no harm is done if the source is anonymous. A member of a sport organization under public assault for firing a coach with a losing record might attempt to douse the negative response by anonymously disclosing private factors (such as a drinking problem) that contributed to the dismissal.

The authors of this book recommend neither off-the-record remarks nor anonymous attributions. Both practices raise ethical questions. Although off-the-record comments are acceptable, representatives of sport organizations must remember that they cannot control information once it has been disclosed. The organization risks revealing information unintentionally or prematurely through off-the-record statements. The sport organization should not stake its integrity and reputation on the honesty of anyone else, including that of journalists. If a journalist violates the agreement, the sport organization should complain about the breach of ethics and trust to the appropriate editor or station executive. Honesty is a two-way street, essential to a positive working relationship on both sides. If the reporter violates the agreement, however, the damage is already done.

Ethics policies for journalistic associations and trade organizations discourage the use of anonymous sources. From the standpoint of the reporter, such sources compromise the credibility of the story somewhat. How can readers or viewers evaluate the accuracy and validity of the information if they do not know the source of the information? The identification of sources helps readers and viewers draw conclusions about conflicting information. As an example, there is a big difference in credibility between charges of team dissension and overwhelming player dissatisfaction from an anonymous player's agent, who has been traded by that team, and those same charges coming from a well-respected team captain who has a history of being straightforward with the press. Journalistic organizations also recommend against the use of unnamed sources because anonymity provides a shield of protection. It is far easier for a source to make wild and exaggerated accusations under the cover of anonymity than to risk the exposure of identity and accountability. Anonymity gives the source an opportunity to distort or lie about the facts and to leave the reporter out there alone to take the fall if the information is incorrect. From the standpoint of the sport organization, a source's attempt to hide behind anonymity raises questions about motives and public posture. From the standpoint of both journalists and representatives of sport organizations, anonymity is, by nature, deceptive—a bruise on the apple of complete honesty.

Principle No. 2: Be Available

The sport organization does not have an opportunity to influence the facts or the focal point of a story if no one talks to the media. Instead of avoiding contact in times of crisis, the designated representatives of the institution or organization should make themselves readily available. The best approach is to remain in the office as much as possible when a crisis arises; give reporters your mobile number, too. If no one can be available to meet with a reporter, speak on the telephone, or return an email, a representative should get back to the reporter as soon as possible. A message should be recorded on voicemail stating the times when someone will be available to answer questions or supply information; providing a cell phone number and email on that voicemail is also a good idea. The representative should be sure to return all telephone calls, text messages, and emails. This admonition applies even if there is no information to release; tell the reporter *that* in the phone call, email, or text message. In addition, he/she should show up for interviews on time and answer all questions as thoroughly as possible without compromising the organization's crisis management objectives.

Administrators, athletics directors, coaches, league commissioners, and sports information specialists should collaborate on a crisis management policy. The plan should outline steps to follow when a crisis occurs and should spell out the responsibilities of all who make contact with the media. In fact, the plan should specify which members of the organization would speak to the media, under what circumstances and any restrictions on what they can say. It should establish a chain of command that details the role of each member in addressing the crisis and should offer guidelines on availability to the media. The plan also should provide direction to everyone in the organization who could possibly be contacted by the media. The phrase "no comment" is not enough as an admonition from the crisis management team. This phrase has come to symbolize that the organization is either guilty or concealing something (Forbes Agency Council, 2017). The crisis management plan should thoroughly explain procedures to follow immediately after the story breaks—press release, news conference, interviews, and so on. Finally, this plan should be dusted off and updated from time to time; at the very least, once a year.

The SID must remember that the decisive battles in the war of public opinion occur in the first 24 hours. The best way to win the battle is to present the positive aspects to the public before the negatives stack up into an insurmountable barrier. Both the public and the media usually look with favor on a prompt response, even if the news is negative; additionally, a prompt response suggests the organization is well organized and accountable, rather than being caught off guard or ducking responsibility. The New England Patriots releasing their All Pro tight end Aaron Hernandez two hours after he was arrested in a homicide investigation is an example of decisive and prompt action by a sport organization. In the team's statement it read, "….we realize law enforcement investigations in this matter are ongoing….we believe this transaction is simply the right thing to do" ("Patriots release," 2013, para. 2).

Officials in the organization must decide quickly whether to answer or to quell rumors. A prompt response may limit speculation and exaggeration. If one journalist runs wild with a story without knowing all the facts, the institution and involved individuals may be hurt even if 99 responsible reporters ignore it. Careers may be ruined and reputations damaged beyond repair if a reporter reveals the name of a player under investigation for gambling on sports events. The SID who makes themselves available can at least say to the reporter, "You are off base on that story, because that player is *not* under any investigation."

Dispelling misinformation is an important reason for sport organizations to respond promptly to accusations of wrongdoing. If a university with an athletics program is under investigation, the SID should urge the administration to report exactly what happened as soon as the inquiry is made public. In the case of an NCAA investigation, the SID should release the facts as soon as they are known rather than sitting on the story and letting competing media dispense partial and piecemeal information. They should be given a full story from the outset. When a crisis erupts, many sport organizations quickly issue a news release spelling out the facts. Whether the athletics program is guilty or innocent, the SID should present the organization's version of the facts to the media and, by extension, to the public. This is one of the advantages of Twitter; the organization can shape their story and send it unfiltered to the press as well as the university community, league, or team's followers. Administrators in the forefront of the investigation should make themselves available to the media. In a situation involving serious charges of wrongdoing, many people in the school or team's hierarchy must be informed before news releases can be written and disseminated to the media. In fact, for a story as potentially damaging as one dealing with NCAA penalties for rules violations, a news conference should be scheduled as soon as possible after the story breaks.

Every member of the media, of course, will want an exclusive interview with everyone involved. Setting up exclusive interviews for a large number of journalists is impossible. A news conference both appeases competing reporters and creates an atmosphere of cooperation that may help to place the stories written and broadcast in a brighter light. If administrators and sports information directors are not available, the opposite is likely to occur. David Stern, the former NBA Commissioner, held a news conference and took questions soon after it was reported that one of the league's referees had been accused of gambling on NBA games. Stern's actions helped to limit the damage to the NBA's reputation and to the rest of the league's referees, who had not been accused of gambling on NBA games (David, 2007).

When an organization is not responsive, the media will begin to ask about accountability and to question the motives behind the secrecy. The silent organization sets itself up for a public flogging in the media. The same rules apply to revelations about individuals, including criminal activity, alcohol or drug abuse, and in-school disciplinary actions. The Family Educational Rights and Privacy Act (FERPA) prohibits disclosure by high schools and colleges of information about students (for more on this see Chapter 13), but institutions can discuss rules and penalties; that gives the SID some control, though not much, over information disclosed. The media can still get the names from police reports or other public documents in some cases, but addressing the issue, even with limited information, is far better than sitting on the story. What the SID should *not* do is hide behind FERPA if the issue is unrelated; actions like these will damage the credibility of the SID and by extension, the institution.

Principle No. 3: Treat all Media Members Fairly and Cordially

Competition within the media is always intense. It is cutthroat when the print media compete against equally aggressive broadcast journalists, all with Twitter accounts. An exclusive or "scoop" on an important story, such as a major trade or free agent acquisition by an NBA team, is the ultimate badge of achievement for a reporter. It is not surprising, then, that an inexperienced, overeager, or unscrupulous reporter occasionally blows a story out of proportion in an attempt to get a scoop.

According to Chamberlin (1990), it is imperative that the SID establish a strong working relationship with the media. Positive attitudes are essential in this communication; the SID must accept the failings of inexperienced and overeager reporters and not shut those reporters out. Sports information personnel must not allow minor mistakes, disagreements about story emphasis, and criticism about athletics programs to damage the working relationship. They also must take care not to end up in the crossfire of competing media, favoring reporters they trust and ignoring journalists most likely to focus on the negative aspects of a story.

Sports information personnel must treat all media fairly in times of crises, when the competition among them is fiercest. First, SIDs must be sure to send news releases to all the media at the same time. Second, they must schedule news conferences at times that are as advantageous, from a deadline standpoint, to as many journalists as possible. Deadline differences necessarily create some inequities, but reporters cannot legitimately complain if the sport organization gives all members of the media the information at the same time. Third, SIDs must not give one reporter any piece of information that they do not give to all the others; favoring a national sports personality over the local beat writer is a big mistake. Any slight—real or imagined—threatens the SID's working relationship with all the media. Despite their competitive nature, the media are a close-knit community. A slight to one is a slight to all. A tidbit of information disclosed to one creates suspicion among all others.

Additionally, the SID must remain impervious to the negative publicity (as long as it is fair) during a crisis and avoid complaining about minor problems. Words look worse in print than they sound when spoken. The temptation is to complain about being misquoted or having comments reported out of context by the media if an administrator criticizes something you said. The temptation is to blame the media if the words do not come out exactly as the SID intended. During contentious public relations crises, the SID is wise not to accuse reporters of misquoting or of taking information out of context unless he/she can verify it. Good reporters write what is actually said, not what they think someone meant or what someone should have said. By whining, the SID suggests he/she really is mad about the content of the story, and his/her complaints are just a way to dismiss the facts in the story. On the other hand, the SID must demand corrections for misquotes or mistakes that can be verified or confirmed.

Negative news does not necessarily reflect poorly on the sports information specialist or organization. Harsh criticism of athletes, coaches, or organization policy is not an indictment of everyone in the organization. The SID must be careful not to overreact to stories with a negative slant, particularly to stories prepared by newspaper columnists, radio and TV announcers/analysts, and talk-show hosts. Part of the job of the columnist, commentator, or talk-show "expert" is to second-guess the institution or organization. These analysts attempt to represent the sentiments of the reading or listening public when providing commentary. When a member of the media levels criticism at an institution, at an event, or at individuals, it usually is intended as honest, constructive criticism. Granted, a few reporters and talk-show hosts are controversial for controversy's sake, but honest journalists abide by an unwritten rule of fair play. When they skewer a team, coach, or players, they give the subjects of their criticism an opportunity to state a position or to take a written or verbal counterpunch. If critics remain aloof from their subjects, professional relationships can deteriorate beyond repair (also see ethics discussion in Chapter 13).

In any event, the SID should never get into a battle with a journalist in the media. A minor story could turn into a major story if public complaints are made about the coverage. Political promoters caution against fighting with someone who buys ink by the barrel; the same goes for online fights on Twitter. In other words, the journalist always has the last word. Furthermore, crisis management and the reputation of the institution may suffer if the working relationship deteriorates into a public squabble in the media.

A Climate of Cooperation

The first line of defense in a crisis is a climate of cooperation. Here are a few guidelines to consider in coping with crises:

1. Do not underestimate the value of daily communication. Foster a positive working relationship through periodic contact with media representatives year-round, not just in times of crisis.

2. Get to know the strengths and weaknesses of reporters. Some are better at digging out information. Some are more likely to favor the organization's side or to tell the story thoroughly. Consequently, some actually may help in a crisis.

3. Getting people to listen after the fact is difficult. You must catch their attention early.

4. Rumors usually are worse than reality. Tackle each issue head on, tracking down the *facts*.

5. The entire organization—not just the public relations department—must be ready for a crisis.

6. All constituencies are equal. Keep all fully informed from the beginning of the crisis.

7. A good lawyer can be the best ally of a public relations operation in a crisis. A lawyer who understands both the legal system (and regulatory system) and the court of public opinion can provide sound advice.

Crisis Management

Crisis management is not easy. Trouble can strike when least expected and twist in unforeseen directions. Each twist may bring a new topic of inquiry, another round of media scrutiny, and renewed public concern—particularly if resolution of the issue comes slowly. It is not uncommon for the media to draw conclusions as incriminating facts become available, even if all the facts are not yet known. Investigations by the NCAA, district attorneys, conferences, professional league offices, or university officials usually drag on for a long time, from several months to a couple of years, such as the many years the University of North Carolina-Chapel Hill and the NCAA spent investigating academic irregularities involving athletes and the African Studies department at UNC-Chapel Hill. During the process, representatives of the sport organization may feel as if they are running from one brushfire to another to stem the spread of negative speculation. If investigators ultimately uncover wrongdoing and a penalty is forthcoming, no magic formula or crisis contingency plan can prevent damage to the institution's reputation.

However, effective institutional response and crisis management may blunt the impact of negative information. If a sport organization allows the media to exercise complete control over the release of the information, the winds of public opinion may fan the brushfires into a firestorm that permanently damages the institution. If the organization openly acknowledges the problem and resolves the problem professionally—in the public's estimation—the damage may be temporary. In fact, effective crisis management and controlled release of information by sports information or public relations directors may restore public confidence. The public ultimately will judge the organization on how well its response matches its philosophy and standards; that is, public opinion will hinge on how well the organization "practices what it preaches." Although negative publicity may be unpleasant, it seldom is fatal if handled effectively.

A real-life example in the world of sports of quick and effective crisis response was the case of the former LA Clippers owner Donald Sterling and the NBA. Sterling was banned permanently from the NBA after a recording of racist statements he had made was released to the public by TMZ. Adam Silver, the NBA Commissioner, announced within a week of the recordings release that NBA owners had removed Sterling from the league. One month after that announcement, the team was sold to former Microsoft CEO Steve Ballmer. Silver received praise from NBA players, from NBA owners and from many members of the press during this stressful time; Silver's crisis management instincts were superb (Stein, 2014).

Of course, crisis prevention is the panacea for public relations dilemmas; that is, SIDs must try to stop problems before they start. For times when there is no doubt that the information will come out, crisis management limits the damage, at best. The best PR plans as it pertains to crisis management are the ones never heard or made public because they were tackled and solved before they saw the light of day.

Crisis prevention can head off dilemmas, and it is the responsibility of everyone in the sport organization. Team owners, league commissioners, school presidents, or school administrators set the standards for the organization and hire people to maintain them. Team or league executives, athletics directors, and coaches implement the standards. They select the players and provide whatever indoctrination is necessary regarding the team or university's philosophy. League executives, general managers, coaches, and players also establish and enforce the rules of decorum, discipline, and punishment that maintain the standards. Sports information directors can offer direction on the most effective ways to communicate the standards to the public through word and action.

The sports information or public relations director also can help by setting up a system to monitor what is happening on campus. The staff should be trained to listen for signs of trouble when they interact with students, faculty, athletes, and other constituencies. Contemporary locales for such a place to listen to the "chatter" would be internet message boards, Twitter feeds, Facebook pages, and chat rooms. If a player mentions a "big hit" on the professional football games over the weekend, perhaps it is a warning signal that someone is gambling on the NFL. The SID also can cultivate internal sources by informing everyone from the university president to physical plant technicians and the local bartender that the sports information staff wants to know what is going on, including rumors, in the interest of crisis prevention. The SID should make it clear that he/she will not disclose the names of people who provide information. Additionally, the SID should put his/her name on every campus mailing list.

No number of internal watchdogs can spot every danger signal; however, sport organization officials can anticipate common problems and be on the alert for warning signs. The staff can study internet message boards for anything that might suggest impending trouble. They also can read trade journals, NCAA literature, and sports magazines/news sites to keep up with the kinds of problems popping up on other campuses, other professional teams, and other leagues and conferences. This type of research can also inform changes to current crisis management protocols that the organization has designed.

Of course, not every danger sign points to an impending crisis. A missed practice and one-game suspension are hardly an impending crisis; if the SID makes too much of it the media will suspect there is more to the story than the sport organization is revealing. Wilcox and Cameron (2009) suggest that in developing a strategic management plan for crises an organization should brainstorm about potential crises, "rating both the 'probability' of a particular crisis and its 'impact' on the organization" (p. 263).

Clues to a Budding Crisis

- The campus and public rumor mills are hyperactive.
- The news media are showing interest in the story, or in the rumors.
- Social media mentions have picked up.
- Customers, business associates, and friends are inquiring about the situation.
- Murphy's Law seems to be at work (if anything can go wrong, it will go wrong).
- The situation requires action on several fronts at the same time.

It is wise to begin a crisis management plan early rather than late. The gestation period is unpredictable. A day? A week? A month? The speed at which the crisis grows depends on the nature of the situation and the enterprise of the media. The safest approach is to implement the organization's crisis management plan when two or more warning signs appear. It is better to start too early than to start too late.

It is imperative that everyone in the organization is also on the same page with the plan and there is an organized, proactive, unified front as it pertains to the message that is presented to the media and the public. Not being on the same page was a hallmark of the Manti Te'o public relations nightmare; the school, the athlete, the athlete's family, and the other parties in this "online relationship" all seemed to be on a different page, which prolonged the bad publicity for all concerned.

That strategy applies to the crisis management plan, as well. Representatives of the team, league, university, or other sport organization should establish or review procedures prior to the start of each season, fiscal year, or school year. The emergency plan should outline a proactive course of action for dealing with the dilemma and the media for specific problem situations (e.g., dismissal of a coach, criminal charges against an athlete or a coach, an investigation by a governing body such as the NCAA, US Anti-Doping Agency, the International Olympic Committee, or Major League Baseball). The document should identify the primary spokesperson for the sport organization for each type of problem. The objective of any plan should be twofold:

1. To quickly and accurately communicate information that will assist in managing the crisis, saving lives, or protecting property.

2. To stabilize the damage to the institution's reputation until the crisis subsides.

Most public relations scholars recommend an open communication policy with the media and all audiences and constituencies in times of crisis. Wilcox, Ault, and Agee (1992) identify three common approaches to crisis management in their book, *Public Relations: Strategies and Tactics*: stonewalling, denying the problem, and refusing to talk to the media; information management, releasing partial and misleading information while concealing damaging facts; and open communication, providing the media with all the facts as well as background information to put the facts in the proper context. Stonewalling may foster an image of arrogance and lack of concern for the public, and information management may smell of "cover-up" when concealed facts appear (Wilcox et al., 1992). They cite Johnson & Johnson's handling of the Tylenol cyanide deaths in 1982 as a case study in effective corporate crisis management. Someone replaced the medication in Tylenol capsules with poison and put the boxes back on store shelves. Following an emergency plan and corporate principles, company public relations officials quickly gathered as much information as possible and set up a phone bank to answer media questions. Company officials cooperated fully with the media, consumers (toll-free number to provide information and to give out capsules in new, tamper-resistant packages), and investigators. The company unveiled the new packaging with a 30-minute videoconference and followed up with an intensive advertising campaign. Tylenol eventually recaptured most of the market share it had lost (Wilcox et al).

Three common approaches to crisis management:

- *Stonewalling*—denying the problem, and refusing to talk to the media;
- *Information management*—releasing partial and misleading information while concealing damaging facts; and
- *Open communication*—providing the media with all the facts as well as background information to put the facts in the proper context.

A sport organization that follows the open communication model will keep the media fully informed at each stage of a criminal case, an NCAA investigation, or the search for a new coach. The organization will not sit on any information unless that information would be detrimental to the investigation or the search.

Creating A Crisis Management Plan

Development of a crisis management plan should begin with interviews of executives and an examination of the organization's philosophy or mission statement. The planning process should include consideration of potential threats, communication channels, notification procedures, and the chain of command. Once the plan has been completed, the principals involved should conduct a dress rehearsal to determine what works and what needs revision.

Research

This should include interviews with the president, the provost, deans, and other appropriate administrators for information on the university's mission, philosophy, and standards. Consulting with other schools and viewing their policy is a good idea as well. If you are the communications director for a professional team, sport organization, or league, investigate how other professional sports organizations handle the development of crisis communication plans. Don't be afraid to think outside the box here too; the military and many corporations compose plans like these all the time (Perlmutter, 2018).

Research should also include review of all documents related to ethical policies and legal regulations—student and staff codes of rights and responsibilities, NCAA regulations, Family Educational Rights and Privacy Act, and so on. A code of conduct typically spells out prohibited conduct on campus, an alcoholic beverage policy, and a sexual harassment policy. It also includes regulations related to disciplinary action and appeals. For a professional team, research entails interviews with the owner (s), president, the chief operating officer, the general manager, key league office executives, and directors of key functional areas. The document examination encompasses league regulations, collective bargaining agreements, as well as team policies and philosophy.

Assessment

This involves brief situational analysis and an evaluation of common crises. The situations may differ among amateur organizations, high school and college athletics departments, national sports federations (e.g., USA Gymnastics), international sport organizations (e.g., FIFA), and professional teams.

Communication Channels

It is important to outline all types of communication channels—news releases, news conferences, phone banks, social media, and so on—to be utilized for each type of potential threat. The outline should specify roles for the president, general manager, athletics director, coaches, athletes, sports information personnel, and anyone else in the organization or institution that will have contact with the media. Professional and college teams have to keep the league office in the loop when a major problem pops up. When collective bargaining agreements are in place, a heads up to the player's union might be appropriate (ex., NFLPA, NBPA).

Notification Procedures

This is the procedure to be followed for notification of each member of the crisis management team when an emergency arises.

Communication Control Center

This is the central location for preparation and release of all information to the media. The location also may serve as the strategy room for meetings of the crisis team as needed.

Crisis Kit

This packet lists all items needed to be set up in a communication center. One list would include telephones, copy machines, materials, and other logistical needs. The packet should also contain a media relations checklist with guidelines for dealing with the media in the first hours of the crisis.

Policies and Procedures

This requires a synopsis of key policies, regulations, and positions on issues, drawn from the document research. Copies of all documents reviewed during the preliminary research should be kept in a designated location listed in the crisis kit.

Appendices

Appendices include lists of addresses, emails, and telephone numbers of executives, managers, employees, media contacts, general counsel's office, and others needed for consultation or for distribution of information. If an athlete, coach, or administrator has hired an attorney that contact information should be on this list.

Rough Draft

A rough draft incorporates the areas mentioned above. One person should prepare the draft; all others on the crisis response team should review it. Include the president, team owner, and board of directors or trustees if they are not assigned duties in the plan.

Final Draft

This is a revision based on input from all who have reviewed the plan. Following approval of the final draft, the SID should send copies to all members of the team and to other appropriate members of the sport organization.

Dress Rehearsal

The dress rehearsal is a test of the plan. The SID should conduct hypothetical exercises or a dress rehearsal to troubleshoot the plan of action, noting the strengths and weaknesses and adapting as needed.

Tough Public Relations Problems

Public relations problems fall into two broad categories: emergencies and ongoing issues. Emergencies are unexpected threats to the image and reputation of individuals or organizations. These generally concern actions or events arising from the behavior of members of the organization, as in the dismissal of a coach. Ongoing issues relate most often to policies and procedures that affect the working relationship between the organization and the media. Common issues range from coverage selections by the media to dressing-room policies of the sport organization.

Emergency Situations

These are situations involving the behavior of members of the organization with the potential to generate negative news. Common stories include the firing of a coach or manager, the release or trade of an athlete, unruly fan behavior, player indiscretions, tragedies (e.g., death of an athlete), internal investigations and disciplinary action against members of the organization, criminal charges against members of the organization, and investigation of individuals or of the organization by regulatory bodies.

Ongoing Issues

These issues involve policies and procedures that damage the working relationship between sport organizations and the media or that distort the image and reputation of either party. Common issues include coverage of men's low-profile collegiate sports, coverage of women's sports, refusal of athletes to speak to the media, and verbal or physical abuse of reporters by players, team executives, or coaches.

A well-designed and well-rehearsed crisis management plan can help an organization take charge of the story in emergencies. With a plan in place, members of the organization can take a proactive approach to dissemination of information. Development of the plan will provide a blueprint for handling the media, training for all institutional officials, and guidelines on how to answer certain questions. The organization and preparation will help members of the sport organization gather facts quickly, recognize and define the problem in their own terms, and come forward with information promptly.

The primary component of the crisis management plan for the sports information or public relations director is the checklist for dealing with the media. The list enables the organization to update the media quickly and to advise them of actions being taken to resolve the issue.

Media Relations Checklist

1. Prepare a one-page guide outlining steps to take in the first few hours of an emergency situation. Remember to use the "max-min" principle giving the maximum amount of information in the most minimal amount of time.

2. Choose an institutional or team spokesperson and a backup. The designated person should release all key information to the media. To ensure a consistent response, no one else should talk to the media without approval and if asked to, should defer to the spokesperson.

3. Think about more than the obvious implications of the problem. Come up with 10 questions the media are most likely to ask and prepare answers for them. Also, consider tangential areas into which the media may probe.

4. Deal with the crisis head-on. Do not hide from the media. Face the media quickly and openly.

5. Gather the facts before the meeting. Assign people to gather information on specific aspects of the situation. They should report to the SID or the designated spokesperson from the scene, from the hospital, from the police station, or from any other point the crisis touches.

6. Respond to every media question. Return every media telephone call, text message, and email within 10 minutes, if possible. There is no established order, but typically, you would want to get back quicker to those media with shorter deadlines, such as internet and television.

7. Never lie—not so much as "a little white lie." Once you lie to one reporter, you leave a permanent crack in your credibility. If you don't know the answer to a question, don't make one up.

8. Do not babble. Review what you want to say in advance and make sure it conforms to the team philosophy or university mission statement. Say exactly what you mean, and mean exactly what you say. Do not leave your comments open to interpretation.

9. Never volunteer negative information.

10. Avoid off-the-record comments. Stick to the facts. Do not speculate in response to hypothetical questions. In short, do not tell the media anything you do not want to see in print or to hear on radio or television. Even off-the-record comments can be repeated. If you do not want to see it in print, do not say it. You can gain the confidence of both organization executives, coaches, athletes, and media by avoiding cat-and-mouse games about what is OK to use and what cannot be repeated.

Most ongoing issues deal with problems that have simmered for years with occasional movement in positive or negative directions. Although such issues may be as critical to the image of the sport organization or to the working relationship with the media in the long term, dealing with them lacks the communication dynamics of an emergency. Because such issues seldom affect sports events per se, they are of less immediate interest to the public as a whole; consequently, a crisis management plan and quick-response procedures are of little value in dealing with them.

Ongoing issues demand a well-organized plan designed to create immediacy in the minds of the public and interest on the part of the media. Of course, immediacy in the mind of the audience will help generate interest on the part of the media. At any rate, a plan of attack on ongoing issues requires a combination of marketing and publicity strategies, much like creating a publicity campaign. Like the publicity campaign, management of ongoing issues is both purposeful and planned. It may include advertising elements, marketing, promotions, publicity releases or community relations activities, and meetings with individual members of the media. Unlike crisis management, in which the SID responds to the media, management of ongoing issues requires the SID to take the institution's message to the public and to the media. The sports information director must prod, sell, and persuade in order to generate movement on ongoing issues such as gender equity in coverage decisions. A great strategy to get your organization's point across is to invite a reporter to lunch or dinner.

The SID bears a responsibility to attack ongoing issues as vigorously as he/she attacks emergencies and should deliberately prepare strategies for resolving the problem, including techniques to be utilized and a timeline for implementation. Sports information personnel can adapt and adjust as circumstances dictate. They also should involve members of the organization at all levels. For example, they can enlist the development office, community relations members or the marketing department in promotional activities. They can stage events on campus that call attention to a particular team, such as a women's soccer clinic. Star players from the local WNBA franchise, with the help of their community relations director, could develop a "read to succeed" program in local elementary schools. The soccer clinic or the reading program may get the attention of a local TV station or newspaper. These options can include other members of the sport organization in the plan, perhaps by setting up a speaker's bureau that sends coaches into the community to sell their sports.

Coverage of women's sports and low-profile men's sports is among the most important ongoing issues at the amateur, high school, and collegiate levels. Some women's professional sports and leagues would also fall into this category. For women's sports, the SID should collaborate with administrators and athletics officials on a plan to "sell" events and teams to the public and the media. Before preparing the plan, organizational officials should analyze the current differences in attendance, coverage policies of various media organizations, and emphasis on women's sports by the institution. Planners can use the information to devise *selling points* and strategies; working with those at the university who have sales experience is a good idea.

The SID should do everything possible to encourage and help the media publicize men's low profile and women's sports. Calling or emailing the media with game reports and statistics is a good strategy; it is hard to turn down a story that has already been prepared. At the very least, it may get a paragraph in a roundup in a newspaper, a mention in a blog post, or a spot on the list of sports scores displayed on the TV screen during a newscast. The SID can pitch features on athletes' standout performances and records to selected reporters and media organizations. The sports information department can also pass along conference standings and individual statistics. The most effective sales techniques are one-on-one. Pitching stories and statistics to selected media members is more effective than blanketing the media at large. It also is less expensive, and it helps the SID identify and cultivate journalists who show some interest; a little research on behalf of the media relations staff can help identify media members who might have an interest in a particular sport. When targeting media, SIDs must remember this old public relations adage: "If you throw enough features on a wall, some of them are sure to stick."

Whereas publicity efforts depend on the media, advertising and promotional activities may take the pitch directly to the public. A SID may plan a schedule of public service announcements for radio to coincide with key games or events. In collegiate women's basketball, the recent trend in promoting key events that draw interest to the sport is the Women's Basketball Coaches' Association "Think Pink" weeklong contests. The initiative is centered on raising breast cancer awareness and some institutions couple it with other promotional events to draw large crowds. The sport of volleyball has an initiative called "Dig Pink," which raises money for breast cancer research and is the brainchild of the Side Out Foundation.

Amateur sports organizations should put public relations strategies right next to fundraising on their lists of responsibilities. Directors or managers should establish communication with the local media, assigning a staff member or volunteer to deliver announcements to the local media about grand openings, facility expansions, special events and tournaments, new equipment, and programs.

Whether the dilemma is an emergency or an ongoing issue, representatives of sport organizations should avoid actions that intentionally or unintentionally strain the working relationship with the media. They should guard against procedures or comments that belittle members of the media, give one member of the media an advantage over another, or impede composition or presentation of a story.

What Not to Do

There are 10 critical errors the SID can make that may have a far-reaching impact:

1. Do not divide the media into groups—that is, opponents and proponents, essential and nonessential, large and small. Pigeonholing suggests unequal treatment.

2. Do not put up roadblocks. Dealing only with selected media members, withholding information, or refusing to discuss an issue makes it more difficult for all concerned to do their jobs.

3. Do not ignore phone calls and emails or wait to return them until the next day. Failure to return a telephone call or email promptly gives the impression you do not think the person is important.

4. Do not scream about negative information in a story. You cannot expect the news media to ignore negative aspects of a story.

5. Do not talk down to reporters. Do not tell reporters, "There is no story here." Do not lecture reporters on their thirst for negative news and tendency to sensationalize stories or to blow them out of proportion. They've heard it already … often.

6. Do not insist that reporters clear all information with the organization before using it. They will ignore you. "No prior restraint" is one of the legal principles in a journalist's creed. (see Chapter 13)

7. Do not promise exclusives to several reporters. Giving information to one reporter that you do not give to all others assuredly will damage your reputation. Giving the same information to all and calling it "exclusive" will have the same effect.

8. Do not torpedo the energetic reporter. Do not badmouth the reporter who breaks a new angle on the story in front of other members of the media. Reporters prize enterprise, even from a competing journalist.

9. Do not threaten to pull advertising. If you threaten to pull advertising over a story, not only do you compromise your integrity, but you also increase the odds the journalist will run the story, too.

10. Do not violate any of these rules. You may gain a temporary ally or two if you favor certain members of the media or criticize competitors, but you ultimately create more enemies.

Lessons Learned: Penn State

Granted, the 2011 sex abuse scandal involving the Penn State football program was of such enormity that it could have overwhelmed even the most media-savvy organization. But Penn State's reaction, and lack of reaction, was almost a textbook case of how not to handle a crisis situation.

Initially, Penn State officials tried to downplay the crisis and redirect media attention back to the football field. Consider this announcement sent out by Jeff Nelson of the sports information department as the scandal broke:

> **From:** *Jeff Nelson*
> **Sent:** *Mon Nov 07 19:20:28 2011*
> **Subject:** *Penn State Football Tuesday teleconference*
>
> ****** MEDIA ADVISORY ******
>
> Media planning to attend Tuesday's Penn State Football weekly teleconference are advised that that primary focus of the teleconference is to answer questions related to Penn State's Senior Day game with Nebraska this Saturday. Head coach Joe Paterno and any Penn State Football student-athletes in attendance will be answering questions about the Nebraska game, Penn State's season thus far and other topics related to the current college football season.

It seems almost incredible that Penn State would hold a news conference and not let reporters talk about the biggest news in the country, but that was the original plan. When the media reacted with predictable outrage, Penn State still would not open up, but decided instead just to cancel the news opportunity. Throughout the scandal the university tried to maintain a veil of silence, which only made reporters angrier and suspicious. In Darren Rovell's CNBC article titled 'Penn State Gets an "F" in Crisis Management 101,' he outlined several missteps that he believed made matters much worse for the University and those involved (Rovell, 2011). Also, as he correctly pointed out, in the age of Twitter and the internet, how quickly you react to a crisis becomes even more important. Another newspaper columnist wrote

> In the darkest days the university has ever seen, it is in desperate need of a leader. But there were none to be found. (President Graham) Spanier, who vowed unconditional support for disgraced athletic director Tim Curley and vice president Gary Schultz, the two administrators accused of perjury and failing to report complaints against Sandusky, was nowhere to be found. Board of Trustees members were

meeting via teleconference deep into the night. Paterno was muzzled. (Collins, 2011, para. 16–18)

Longtime sportswriter Gene Collier, who had covered the Penn State program for years, observed: "The university long has recoiled nearly instinctively at the approach of the media, and that was under optimally sunny circumstances, when the most unflattering 'news' reportable was the perfectly benign and only occasional three-game losing streak... . So do not be surprised that Penn State has no more idea of how to handle a public relations disaster than it does an eyewitness account of a sexual assault on a child in the shower at its football facility" (Collier, 2011, para. 2, 5).

Summary

Working with the media during crises and ongoing public relations problems is the most challenging, stressful, and joyless part of the job of sports information. The sports information specialist's job shifts from publicizing positive news to combating negative information or rumors. The working relationship with the media may change temporarily from that of a partnership to that of a protagonist or antagonist. A misstep or false step may do far more harm; it may hurt an individual, a group of people, or the organization itself. However, the SID's performance in the midst of a public relations dilemma may do more to enhance the image of the organization than a ton of publicity brochures and media days.

Any event, issue, or incident that poses a threat to the reputation of the sport organization represents a potential crisis. A crisis may arise quickly as a result of the behavior or activities of members of the sport organization. A dilemma may develop slowly in connection with an unresolved issue related to coverage decisions, working relationships, or organizational policies.

Regardless of the origin or nature of the crisis, the sport organization should quickly respond to inquiries and implement procedures planned in advance. The quicker the response, the better; the battle for public opinion is usually decided within the first 24 hours. The simpler the emergency plan, the better, because response time is critical. The SID may have to convince superiors of the need for expediency, because the decision-making process moves at a much slower, more measured speed in upper-level management, especially so at a large public institution (e.g., Penn State). In the news media, decision making operates on a deadline cycle, which may be as little as 30 minutes. To deliver its side of a story to the public, a sport organization must be prepared to move at the same speed. Because of deadline demands and competition among the media, a journalist seldom will wait until the sport organization is ready to print or broadcast the story. The increased use of social media, especially Twitter, by many in the sports industry has increased this pressure. A sport organization can use social media to their advantage in these situations.

A SID or public relations director can project a positive image and reinforce the organization's reputation by maintaining a climate of cooperation in all situations. The foundation for a positive atmosphere, even in times of turmoil, rests on three principles: honesty, availability, and fair play. To be effective, representatives of the sport organization must be open and honest, must make themselves available to the media, and must treat all journalists fairly and respectfully. They must attempt to answer all questions honestly, without relying on crutches such as anonymity and off-the-record comments. They must give information to all the media at the same time through news releases and news conferences. They must return telephone calls, texts, and emails promptly, within 10 minutes if possible. They do not complain about the negative elements of stories in the media.

A crisis can arise at any time, and some negative news is inevitable. A crisis seldom is fatal, however, particularly if the sport organization takes control of the story. To put themselves in position to take charge of the situation, members of the sport organization can monitor warning signs of trouble. They can watch internet message boards, campus publications, and trade literature for hints of danger. They also can pay attention to what faculty, staff, students, athletes, and fans are saying. Excessive rumors, heightened media interest, hints on social media, and unusual inquiries from customers, boosters, alumni, and other supporters are among the signals that a crisis is imminent.

To respond quickly in a crisis, members of the sport organization should prepare a crisis management plan. The plan should reflect the philosophy, standards, and ideals of the organization. The two primary objectives should be to accurately communicate information to the media and public that will assist in managing the crisis, and to stabilize damage to the institution's reputation until the crisis subsides.

The sports information expert and school administrators or team officials should work together to develop the plan. The plan should address potential threats, notification procedures (for members of the organization), communication channels (including social media), procedures to follow, and media and institutional contact lists. The procedures should specify the responsibilities of everyone on the crisis management team, particularly those of the individual designated as primary spokesperson. What others are permitted to say to the media, if anything, also should be defined.

A crisis management plan is most effective for dealing with emergency situations that involve behavior or actions detrimental to the image of the organization, as in the firing of a coach, the arrest of an athlete, or an NCAA investigation. Such plans are of little value in handling ongoing issues related to the working relationship with the media, such as coverage choices and access to athletes. The media come to the sport organization in times of crisis. The sport organization must go to the media to address ongoing issues. Such issues lack the obvious expediency and public interest intrinsic to emergency situations. As in crisis management, however, the most effective strategy for dealing with coverage issues is a predesigned plan.

In every type of crisis, honesty and open communication are the best policy. The organization's response to an investigation, player discipline, or contract negotiation may reinforce the image the organization intends to project. The positives may outweigh the negatives in the media and public reaction. The same is true regarding athletes who are in trouble, whether the problem is crime, drugs, alcohol, or discipline. Open communication and early intervention give the SID and the sport organization some control over the flow and focus of information—perhaps not much, but some. Unquestionably, the sport organization stands a better chance of winning the battle of public opinion by employing a proactive plan rather than by sitting on information and conceding control to print, online, and broadcast journalists.

Discussion Questions

1. How does a communications director for an NFL franchise develop a climate of continued cooperation with the local media?

2. Explain in detail how a SID is able to work effectively with his/her two bosses—the institution and the media—in a time of crisis.

3. How can Twitter and other social media be used to help manage a crisis?

Suggested Exercises

1. Students should form groups in a role-playing scenario where an organization is dealing with a potential crisis. One student acts as the sports information director, another as the coach, one student as an athlete, and the rest of the class as reporters. Examples of scenarios might include illegal recruiting, gambling on sports by an athlete, domestic violence accusations, or drug charges against an athlete/coach. Those who are role-playing as reporters should then interrogate the principals in each scenario and write a story.

2. Write news releases announcing that an institution has been accused by the NCAA of cheating in regards to athlete recruitment. Students should use the three principles of crisis management.

3. Explain the differences/similarities in crisis management strategy when the starting quarterback for a college team is arrested for DUI, the starting quarterback for the local professional team is arrested for DUI, and the starting quarterback of the state champion high school football team is arrested for DUI.

4. Select a recent crisis in the sports industry. Analyze the response to the crisis by the sports organization. Read stories written by different news outlets about the crisis. Determine if one news outlet seems particularly tough on the sports organization; are any particularly 'soft' on the sports organization?

12 | Global Sport Media Relations

More than ever, sports journalists, broadcasters, and communications directors across the United States will be assigned to cover sports events, athletes, and coaches outside the borders of the country. Their colleagues in Europe, Asia, Africa, South and Central America, New Zealand, Australia, and the rest of Oceania have seen their working territory expand too. The US is part of an ever-expanding global economy; a big part of that global economy are the sport and media industries. Sport communication professionals who don't have a passport better go apply for one soon.

Author Tom Friedman chronicled in his book *The World is Flat* how advances in technology have made our world smaller (and flatter). Friedman has traveled around the world as a foreign affairs columnist for the *New York Times*. He has also written several best-selling books about international issues, but his work in *The World is Flat* was where he outlined the changing business landscape around the world. In the late 20th century, the two inventions that helped to spur globalization were the jet airplane and the communication satellite. Friedman (2005) noted the next stage of economic development: The creation of a global fiber-optic network along with the refinement of software and new applications has made everyone around the world next-door neighbors. Companies are better able to compete globally and better equipped to collaborate across borders; barriers to enter markets because of geographical distances have been reduced. Friedman points out that the global fiber-optic network also helped to reduce connectivity costs for phone calls, data transmission, and internet connections.

The improvements identified by Friedman in transportation, communication, manufacturing, and technology have opened up new horizons for the sport industry, for athletes, writers, and for sport media businesses. Alexander Wolff, the award-winning writer for *Sports Illustrated* has traveled to China, Iran, Cuba, South Africa, the slums of Rio de Janeiro, and Israel in pursuit of stories and interesting people to write about in the world of sports. The Major League Baseball (MLB) debut of Shohei Ohtani, playing for the LA Angels, has presented a logistical challenge for most of the major media outlets in Japan. They have covered his every move in parallel with the MLB press, who have been mesmerized by this rookie hitting and pitching phenomenon from Japan. CBS *60 Minutes* did a feature on Ohtani while he was still playing for Sopporo in the Japanese professional baseball league. A regular crew of between 50 and 100 reporters from Japanese outlets covered his every move during his rookie campaign. This media frenzy mimicked the early years of South Korean baseball superstar Chan Ho Park. Park was the first Korean baseball player to make a major league team and he enjoyed a long career with the Dodgers, Yankees, and a few other teams from 1994–2010. *Golf Digest* covered the travels of two golfers who decided, on a whim, to hit a golf ball *across* the country of Mongolia. Ron Rutland and Adam Rolston walked 1,250 miles across Mongolia, hitting a golf ball and using social media to update all who were paying attention. Brian Wacker chronicled their modern day version of the Lewis and Clark Expedition in a story titled "Conquering the world's longest golf hole," for *Golf Digest* (Wacker, 2017).

The technological advances in the telephone system in the early 21st century has enabled citizens and communications professionals of the world to be so much more connected to each other; interviews and background research have become much easier. This advance in connectivity has also helped to popularize the use of social media by everyone, not just athletes, coaches, and communications professionals in the world of sports. Sports reporters sitting at their work stations in Chicago or Dallas can call a contact in Moscow or St. Petersburg to find out background information on a story about 2018 World Cup preparations in Russia. In fact, the reporter does not have to be at their desk; he or she can be walking home from work while talking on a mobile phone—and so can their source in Russia. A local Qatari contact can send a picture they just snapped with their cell phone as evidence to that reporter in Chicago or Dallas of the progress—or lack of progress—workers have made in building one of the new soccer venues for the 2022 World Cup. That picture can be posted on Twitter or Instagram for all the followers to see and to comment; with the connectivity of today's internet and phone system, a reporter can develop a following all over the world—and athletes can do the same.

Reporters can use their smartphones to check the Twitter feeds of Ronaldo, Neymar, Messi, or Harry Kane while they participate in the 2018 World Cup, as well as watch the action live via streaming video. The connectivity, the quality of the video, audio, and picture, and the popularity of social media has permitted fans to feel much more of a connection with the stars of the teams they pull for, thus creating customers for TV sports networks, league subscriptions, and merchandise manufacturers and licensors from all over the world.

Global Mega-Events

The World Cup and the Olympics are global mega-events, watched by huge numbers of sports fans around the world and broadcast by major networks from all over the world, who employ communications professionals from all over the world. The cumulative TV audience for the 2010 Vancouver Winter Olympics was estimated to be 1.8 billion viewers, with the dedicated websites (with content written by sports communications professionals) drawing 1.2 billion page views and 275 million video views ("Vancouver 2010," 2010). The 2018 PyeongChang Winter Olympics was the top rated television program in the US for the two weeks the event was covered by NBC, averaging 20 million viewers (Otterson, 2018). The Beijing Olympics in 2008 drew 11 of the top 25 audiences of daily US sports programming in that year (Brown & Morrison, 2008). The 2012 London Olympics was the most watched TV event in US history—219.4 million viewers tuned in to at least one of the events and digital coverage exceeded TV coverage for the first time ("London Olympics," 2012). YouTube had a dedicated channel for the first time in Olympic history, broadcasting individual events from London. During the Rio Olympics, it was estimated that half the world's population watched at least some of the Olympics on either their mobile device, a television, or their computer screens (IOC, 2016). The Beijing Olympics had 61,700 hours of television and digital coverage, and the London Olympics shattered that record with numbers approaching 100,000 hours. The Rio Olympics had close to 350,000 hours of combined TV and digital coverage (IOC, 2016). The London Olympics set social media records on the Olympic Facebook, Twitter, and Google+ sites, and then the Rio Olympics shattered those records in impressive fashion. Again, much of this content from Rio was prepared, written, or edited by sports communications professionals working for the IOC and the local organizing committee in Brazil. It was estimated that 3.2 billion people watched at least some of the 2014 Rio World Cup, from 207 countries and territories, and that 1 billion people watched the final game between Spain and the Netherlands (Media Release, 2015). The estimated audience for the 2018 World Cup topped the Brazil numbers by 200 million viewers (3.4B) (Roxborough, 2018).

The fan interest the aforementioned numbers represent helps to generate excitement for the coverage of these events by news organizations around the world. The 2006 World Cup in Germany saw 18,850 members of the media descend upon the soccer venues in that country. Most of these were employees of the many television networks that covered the Cup; however, there were 4,250 print and internet journalists and editors in Germany accredited by FIFA ("Germany 2006," 2006). The 2010 Winter Olympics saw 10,800 journalists descend on Vancouver, and there were 21,000 accredited journalists in London for the 2012 Summer Olympics. Four hundred and fifty different television channels broadcast the 2010 World Cup (KantarSport, 2010). The estimates for coverage of the Rio Summer Olympics was between 25,000 and 30,000 journalists, including reporters, photographers, and television network employees (Thurston, 2016). There is a process established for press credentials for each of these mega events. Because of the size of the press contingent for the World Cup, journalists had to submit their application through their country's soccer federation more than six months in advance. For example, most journalists working for sports media companies in the United States who wanted to cover the World Cup, had to submit their press credential application to US Soccer by the end of November, 2017. Those journalists also had to register with the FIFA Media Channel before submitting their applications to their country's soccer federation. Any journalist or photographer working for an international news agency (e.g., Reuters, Associated Press) would apply directly through FIFA for their press credentials.

These events have also become big business for the host countries (Shipley, 2009). An Oxford economics study (2012) estimated that the London Olympic Games would generate £16.5 billion for the British economy from 2005 to 2017. A study on the impact of the 2010 World Cup on South Africa concluded that there were major improvements in infrastructure such as roads, telecommunications systems, local transportation, stadiums, and airports (Du Plessis & Venter, 2010). There are estimates that Vladimir Putin's government spent in excess of $55 billion to improve infrastructure in and around the Winter Olympics location of Sochi, as well as to host the event (Orttung & Zhemukhov, 2017). Sochi would also be one of the sites for the 2018 World Cup; hosting several games during the pool stage, and two games during the knockout round, including an exciting game with eventual runner-up Croatia. This type of economic impact thus draws tremendous media attention to the selection process. That media attention is primarily from report-ers based in the countries pursuing the right to host the event, but because of the interest in the Olympics and the World Cup, media companies, and in particular, sports reporters from all over the world cover these decisions. In the year leading up to the selection of Rio de Janeiro to host the 2016 Summer Olympics, there was heightened media interest in Spain, the United States, and Japan, the other three countries that joined Brazil as finalists. This process repeated itself in 2017 when the IOC was slated to make their pick for the 2024 Summer Olympics; in an unusual move, the IOC picked Paris for 2024, but also awarded the right to host the 2028 Summer Olympics to Los Angeles.

The sports media were not the only ones paying close attention to these devel-opments; so, too, did the political and business press. For weeks, newspapers and other media outlets across the world speculated about the impact of the Trump election on the viability of the United States as a host for either the Olympics (2024 and 2028) or the World Cup (2026). The business writers analyzed the amount of new investment, tourism spending, and sponsorship money, but also attempted to put a dollar value on image creation if their respective city was selected as an Olympic host. How much is all that worldwide publicity worth (Cashman & Hughes, 1999)? Representatives from Istanbul, Madrid, and Tokyo were the final-ists for the right to host the 2020 Summer Olympics. The vote for the right to host was taken in Buenos Aires, Argentina, on September 7, 2013 during a meeting of the International Olympic Committee. The three prime ministers from Spain, Turkey, and Japan were all in St. Petersburg, Russia, attending the G20 summit days before the vote. They flew directly to Buenos Aires in order to lobby IOC executives and the IOC members who would be selecting the 2020 host city. All of the leaders gave impassioned speeches, championing their cities, no doubt with support from communications professionals from each of these countries. The Japanese Prime Minister, Shinzo Abe, and his communications professionals were the most persuasive. Tokyo was selected as the host for the 2020 Summer Olympic Games. In the *New York Times* article announcing Tokyo's selection, a total of six writers worked on this story, including those from Buenos Aires, Tokyo, Madrid, and Istanbul (Fackler & Longman, 2013).

Beyond the Borders

The professional sports leagues based in the United States have many teams across the border in Canada. The Toronto Blue Jays, Toronto Maple Leafs, Toronto Raptors, Toronto FC, Montreal Canadiens, Montreal Impact, Vancouver Canucks, Vancouver Whitecaps FC, Edmonton Oilers, Calgary Flames, Winnipeg Jets, and Ottawa Senators are the Canadian professional teams that play in the MLS, MLB, NBA, and NHL. It is very common for journalists and sports information specialists throughout the US to be given assignments, for example, when an NBA team travels to Canada to play the Raptors. All of the aforementioned franchises have team or league media contacts that journalists use to secure a press pass for the game they will cover; some locations have limited seating for the press, but for the most part, recognized journalists will be given access to the event and the press room. Canadian reporters routinely cover all of these leagues. Steven Goff, the soccer expert at the *Washington Post*, will cover a DC United game when they play in Toronto and Vancouver, and he has covered the last few Men's and Women's World Cups, including the 2018 Russian World Cup. NBA beat reporters will draw assignments to travel outside the US for overseas exhibitions and regular season games; the league encourages the media to cover these events and makes credentialing relatively easy for the working press in all of their franchise cities. It is also routine for reporters from the US to travel to Europe, South America, or Africa to write background stories on NBA players from those continents. Ian Begley did a story on Kristaps Porzingis, the former NY Knicks star (now with the Dallas Mavericks) and his byline noted he was in Liepaga, Latvia doing background interviews for the story that was published by ABC News and ESPN in 2016 (Begley). Jack Holmes also traveled to Latvia for a piece he wrote on Porzingis for *Esquire* (2016). Former NBA Commissioner David Stern voiced his intent to have expansion teams in Europe in the next decade (Associated Press, 2010); Mayor Sadiq Khan of London has said that he would like an NFL franchise in his city (Bonesteel,

2018). The NFL introduced the International Series in 2007, in which two NFL teams play a regular-season game at Wembley Stadium. In 2018, for the first time, the NFL played three games in the same month in London; the Seattle Seahawks vs. Oakland Raiders, Tennessee Titans vs. San Diego Chargers and the Super Bowl Champion Philadelphia Eagles vs. Jacksonville Jaguars. There has been talk around the NFL of London being a potential site for the Super Bowl, and Mayor Khan would be all for that development too. The Jacksonville Jaguars owner, Shahid Khan, had placed an offer to buy Wembley Stadium, but that offer was withdrawn in the fall of 2018. Khan already owns a team in the Premier League (Fulham FC). The NFL has also played games in Japan, Mexico, and Germany. All of this cross-border activity is covered regularly by team and league communications professionals, as well as reporters for newspapers, TV networks, magazines, and sports pages around the world.

Many Americans play for professional sports teams overseas, and this can produce a travel assignment and stories for reporters in the United States. Stephon Marbury's career in professional basketball was extended a number of years in China, where he won three China Basketball Association Championships. His exploits on and off the court were followed by many reporters in NY (former home) and around the US.

Every major club in the major basketball leagues in Europe have communications staff who work with the media to facilitate interviews and press passes for games; some of these game pass requests are made on behalf of NBA and WNBA scouts looking for players. Former college basketball stars from men's and women's programs in the United States occupy roster spots for professional clubs all over Europe, South America, Oceania, and Asia. Many of the top American women play in both Europe *and* the WNBA. Beat writers covering professional golf and tennis, and sports information specialists working in these sports may be asked to travel to the Ryder Cup, Davis Cup matches, the British Open, the French Open, the Australian Open, Wimbledon, and other events. Reporters from sports media companies around the world routinely travel to the United States to cover tour events in the LPGA, PGA, ATC, and WTA. The LPGA is replete with golfers from Asia and Europe, and as many as a third of the LPGA events are located outside the US. There are many countries worldwide that have LPGA broadcasting rights; these networks need communications professionals to describe the action for their viewers. Each of these tours (PGA, LPGA, ATC, and LPGA) has a large communications staff to handle media requests. They also set up an office on the site of each tour stop to facilitate further requests, and to help the media cover each day of the tournament. These tennis and golf tours have a very active presence on social media, which can further enhance coverage by the working press. To facilitate the international nature of their audience, the LPGA website has a Chinese, German,

Japanese, Korean, and Thai version, along with the one available to the English speaking audience.

The MLS has been the preferred league for many former soccer stars from top European leagues who have received enticing offers from the American men's top professional soccer league. Zlatan Ibramovic followed in the famous footsteps of David Beckham and joined the LA Galaxy in 2018. Wayne Rooney joined DC United in that same year, just in time to help DC United unveil the brand new $400 million Audi Stadium in downtown Washington, DC. David Villa joined the NYC Football Club and was named the MVP of the MLS in 2016. The MLS franchises are hoping for results on the field and at the ticket window from these European stars, but they also hope to increase the profile of their teams worldwide, with the signing of these world famous players. Media relations professionals working for MLS and the individual teams will play a big part in promoting these players to media outlets worldwide; if they do their jobs well, the profile of the MLS will benefit.

The United States Men's National Team (USMNT) failed to qualify for the 2018 World Cup in Russia. The US team played matches in their Confederation (North America, Central America, Caribbean-CONCACAF) to qualify, and lost a heart-breaking elimination game at Trinidad and Tobago. Some of these CONCACAF matches were played in the US, but the USMNT also had to travel to Honduras, Mexico, Costa Rica, and Panama during the qualifying stage. The soccer reporters for news outlets around the United States assigned to cover all of these games have to develop a comfort level for travel outside of the US, secure the necessary travel documents, as well as develop international soccer expertise to do their jobs well. Many of these players on the CONCACAF teams are members of the top leagues around the world, which many soccer beat writers also cover on a regular basis for their newspapers, magazines, broadcast networks, and websites. US Soccer and their communications staff helps to facilitate travel for the working press, and also recommends hotels for those media covering the qualifying rounds, both for games inside and outside the country. Some of the locations don't have the creature comforts of a US soccer stadium, which is another reason reporters need to do their research before they travel to places like Honduras. WiFi access in the press area, internet access in the stadium, and access to electricity before, during, and after the game are some of the topics that must be discussed with either the US Soccer Federation, or fellow members of the press with more experience working overseas. Even charging a mobile phone or laptop at one of these locations could be problematic.

Traveling abroad to compete isn't just relegated to professionals or teams and individuals competing in mega-events such as the Olympics. More and more college teams, in a variety of sports, are taking overseas trips during vacation periods to such places as Australia, the Caribbean, Europe, and Asia. Others are participating in holiday tournaments in Puerto Rico, the Bahamas, Jamaica, the Cayman Islands, and the Virgin Islands. Texas and Washington played a regular season basketball game in Shanghai in 2015; the first regular season game played in China. This game was a precursor to the Pac 12 signing a deal with Alibaba (Chinese conglomerate) for the rights to televise Pac 12 content in China (Baker, 2017). Notre Dame played the Naval Academy in a college football game in Ireland in 2012; a large contingent of professionals in sport communication made that trip, including the CBS Sports crew that televised the game. Penn State, University of Central Florida, Boston College, and Georgia Tech also played games in Dublin. Other college football teams have traveled to the Bahamas, Bermuda, Australia, Japan, China, and Italy for regular season games. This travel is an opportunity for sports information directors to promote their school to potential foreign students, develop a following for college sports outside of the United States, and promote the coaches and standout athletes on their teams to a new audience. When these teams schedule events like this, it is always a good idea for the sports information directors of these teams to reach out to the media in the countries they visit and try to develop some story angles for the press in the cities where they play.

All-star teams that represent a league or a sport federation like USA Basketball, US Soccer, USA Field Hockey, or USA Softball regularly travel abroad and as Caroline Williams discusses in an interview in this chapter. Williams is a communications professional working for the sports federation and handles all media relations during training and when they compete overseas. The exploits of the players and coaches who travel abroad representing the United States are followed by sports information directors at all of their respective schools, and also interested local reporters; all of these competitions generate content for websites, Facebook pages, Instagram posts, and Twitter feeds.

Each one of the aforementioned professional and collegiate leagues and sports organizations recognize the economic value of the new markets outside the borders of the United States. These are new markets for communications professionals too. The globalization of sports presents new opportunities for leagues, television networks, team owners, advertisers, sporting goods manufacturers, and professional athletes, who now have the opportunity to play in different professional leagues or do business around the world in the sports industry. A great example of this point is John Henry, the owner of the Boston Red Sox of the MLB; the Red Sox feature players from Venezuela and the Dominican Republic. Eight players on the 2018 roster were from outside the US. Henry (and partners in Fenway Sports Group) also own the Liverpool Soccer Club of the English Premier League, Fenway Park (home of the Red Sox), the New England Sports Network, and the *Boston Globe*. There is an international aspect to each one of these businesses that Henry owns. Shahid Khan, the NFL Jacksonville Jaguars owner mentioned previously, also operates across boundaries with his sports industry businesses. It follows that the communication professionals who work for the Red Sox, the Jaguars, the *Boston Globe*, and Liverpool must also develop an appreciation (and expertise) for the international aspects of their sports businesses.

Expanded Media Coverage

Global media companies have emerged to televise teams and leagues all over the world. ESPN, BBC, Star Sports, Brazil Globo, Direct TV, NBA TV, Eurosport, Televisa, China Central TV, Canal France International, Univision, Sport 1 (Hungary), Ten Sports (India), and Fox Sports all bring games from one side of the world to the other. These multinational corporations all hire communications professionals to work as broadcasters, editors, producers, and writers. BeIn Sports, the spinoff of Al Jazeera, now televises a variety of shows about the NBA and the WNBA; they also have rights deals with the English Premier League, and other sporting events from Europe, South America, and Asia. The network has affiliates populated by communications professionals on all continents except Antarctica.

ESPN International reaches every continent, offering television, radio, and online streaming programming; in 2018 they had 26 networks, which could be found in 61 countries around the world (ESPN, 2018). ESPN and Univision televise Mexican Soccer games and have other Liga MX programming in the United States. Another division of ESPN, Star Sports, signed a multi-platform rights deal with Cricket Australia. ESPN provided coverage of these matches on the internet through computers and mobile devices, television, and radio ("ESPN Star Sports," 2007); the network continues to cover sports like cricket, rugby, and soccer for leagues and teams around the world. Several global media companies along with a few Chinese companies submitted bids for the Chinese rights to the most popular professional soccer league in the world, the Premier League of England. Super Sports Media Group secured a six-year deal for the rights and also was able to sell the Chinese internet rights to the Premier League to BesTV (Cushman, 2013; Harris, 2012). A Chinese company, PPTV, which is part of the Suning Companies, took over the broadcast rights in 2019 (Li and Jourdan, 2017). ESPN established a partnership with the Chinese company Tencent and through this partnership, a wide variety of content is provided to hundreds of millions of sports fans in China (ESPN). IMG, the American-based international marketing and management company, has worked with the Premier League on TV rights deals around the world as well as producing studio programming for the league. IMG is also involved in a similar capacity with the Italian first division soccer league (Serie A). The company continues to provide a diverse set of career opportunities for communications professionals at their offices around the world.

With the globalization trend in today's sports industry, new challenges and opportunities are presented to the media companies, journalists, and sports information directors of today. With an increase in digital spectrum for new networks, there are many job opportunities for broadcast journalists, television producers, writers, editors, and former professional athletes interested in TV careers. Each of these sports-related broadcasts usually has a studio host, a play-by-play announcer, and color commentator; many of these television networks also operate websites with sports news that have to be updated regularly by reporters and sports communications professionals. With many of these jobs, the more languages you can speak, the more valuable you become, both as a broadcaster and as a writer for the content on websites. As mentioned above, many of these organizations operate websites in multiple languages.

Job applicants that speak a second (or third) language will find themselves in greater demand, but they will also face stiff competition for those jobs from graduates outside the United States. This growth in sports programming outside the borders of the United States creates opportunities for networks like Fox Sports, Univision, NBC Sports, and ESPN. It is important for students to understand the sports communications landscape that is constantly changing and growing, and also know how to put themselves in the best position to take advantage of these exciting new opportunities. Tom Friedman addressed this point in his book *The World is Flat*; young people today must recognize the changes brought about by globalization and prepare themselves accordingly. Networks and other sports organizations can also "widen the skill base" of their employees and provide lifetime learning opportunities to increase the competitiveness of their businesses and their employees (Friedman, 2005).

National Sports Organizations

Most of the US national sports governing organizations (NCAA, NAIA) or national sports federations (NSOs) hire full-time staff members to provide content to their websites or to prepare their athletes and coaches for media opportunities with members of the press from all over the world. An interview with one member of a national sports organization was presented in Chapter 4 (Cody Norman/AAU), where he discussed his use of social media along with other aspects of his job. Members of the media interact with communications professionals like Cody when they are covering AAU sponsored events or foreign competitions such as the Pan Am Games, Olympics, or World Championships in sports such as basketball, track and field, ice hockey, and swimming. The communications director with these sports federations will also interact directly with the media in arranging interviews for coaches and their athletes, scheduling press conferences at events, and also providing background information for their national teams in the form of bios, press releases, and statistics. International sports federations like FIFA (the governing body of soccer), IAAF (track and field), FINA (swimming and diving), and FIBA (basketball) also have fully developed communications departments. These departments help to manage media relations for the world and regional championships in their respective sports. They will be the organization and the department that provides the media their credentials to cover these events. They also produce newsletters, journals, and rules booklets, and some of these communications departments even produce video content of varying lengths, depth, and quality.

A Communications Director's Perspective

One of the busiest sports federations in the United States, USA Basketball, employs several sport communication professionals that have developed extensive experience working at global sports competitions and with the media that are assigned to cover those events. Caroline Williams is the senior director of communications and she has been with USA Basketball since starting as an intern in 1985. Williams has worked multiple Summer Olympic Games and FIBA World Cups, where she has been the primary media contact for the USA Basketball Women's National Team. She has also worked as a press attaché for two Paralympic Games and the 2006 Winter Olympics. Her work with USA Basketball has led her to more than 35 different countries across five continents.

Exhibit 12.1 *Caroline Williams, Director of Communications, USA Basketball, working an event. (Photo credit: Andrew D. Bernstein/USA Basketball.)*

In order to fully appreciate and understand the job of a communications director of a national sports federation, Williams was interviewed about her role with USA Basketball and was asked to describe some of her experiences during the last 23 years with the organization.

Q: How did you end up at USA Basketball?

Williams: Totally by accident. I was taking a public relations class at George Mason University during my junior year and one of the major assignments was to go out and write about an organization. The professor made us find one so that the assignment was "real." My organization was the sports information office for the athletic department. I had always been interested in sports, was active and followed many teams, but I did not have a desire at the time to make my living in the sport industry. Once I completed this assignment, I worked for two years for the SID at George Mason, Carl Sell. He gave me plenty of responsibility and I had a chance to improve my writing working for him. The end of my senior year, an announcement came into the office from USA Basketball, looking for an intern. Carl told me I should apply for the position. I did, they liked me, and I worked for USA Basketball for six months as their intern. After that, there was a one-year position available leading up to the 1996 Olympics. During that time, I was very involved in starting the USA Basketball website. A job opened up right after the Olympics ended, they liked my work on the website, and I was hired.

Q: How has the job changed since your days as an intern in the mid-1990s?

Williams: Technology has changed everything we do. We make much more use of video and photos now. We were lucky if there was a photographer around at some events so we could post one or two pictures to the website. When I first started, we would type up our releases and game notes, and fax them out to reporters or fax them back to our offices in Colorado Springs. Someone there would then put the finishing touches on the notes and fax them out. We now use email to send out releases and notes. Further, social media was not around when I started in this field. USA Basketball now has more than eight million followers across the USA Basketball social platforms, which include three Twitter accounts, two Instagram accounts, two Facebook pages, and one YouTube and Snapchat account. Keeping up with those accounts takes a lot of time. One of the great things about some of our teams is that they have embraced social media. This makes my job easier in some ways because the athletes are sending out information, too.

Q: USA Basketball selects many different high school, college, and professional basketball coaches for their teams. Does this present a problem relative to your job as the liaison with the press?

Williams: Our coaches have been great to work with and they understand when they sign on as national coaches, they have to work with the media. Each of our teams and coaches has to be available to the press every day during these international events. We also have a rule that practice is open for the last half hour, followed by media availability. For some coaches this is different, but they all have been fully cooperative with USA Basketball's policy. One of our jobs is to help grow the game and coaches understand they can help do so with their time with the media.

Q: *What was a typical day like in Rio in 2016 when the US Olympic team had a game?*

Williams: Because of the traffic in Rio, game days were long days for the USA Basketball communications staff. We would check emails early in the day, start putting the game notes together, and speak with the coaches before shoot around to see if there was anything we needed to know relative to the team and injuries. We traveled with the team to shoot around and then back to the ship (there weren't enough hotel rooms in the city, so we stayed on one of the cruise ships in the harbor like we did in 2004). In between the game day shoot around there may be individual requests from reporters covering the men's or women's team. After a few hours it was time to get back on the bus to the gym for the game.

Similar to past Olympics, the USA Basketball communications staff would walk around to all of the reporters covering the games to pass out game notes or to ask if there was anything that they needed relative to the team or that day's game. Once the game started, we all watched, but also paid attention if we were needed by one of the members of the media during the game. At the end of the game we fanned out and covered the mixed zone, the locker room, and the press conference. We collected quotes to put together later and helped direct players to different media in the mix zone. When we got back to the hotel, we posted stats, quotes, pictures, and video to the USA Basketball website and our social networks. We also wrote a game story for the website, which expanded upon the quick few graphs we posted prior to departing for the ship.

The ship we were on was leased by CISCO, so after each game we were able to utilize CISCO's technology to conduct video interviews stateside.

Our social media plan grew from 2012 on game days as well. Where once we used an organic approach, we began to produce more graphic-styled imagery and videos before, during, and after games. We received a lot of help with these posts from people who were in the office, watching the games from Colorado.

Q: *How does the USA Basketball Communications department staff these international events?*

Williams: For the major events like the World Cup or the Olympics, we will send our entire staff and usually will receive help from some interns. Both our men's and women's teams have done very well in the Summer Olympics over the years, so there is quite a bit of interest from reporters all over the world. There is a large contingent from the United States that also covers these events, particularly the

Olympics. When we send one of our young teams abroad, we usually only send one staff member with that team. For example, I traveled to Belarus in 2018 for the U17 World Cup and was the only USA Basketball member from our communications staff on the trip.

Q: How many different teams does the USA Basketball communications staff have to manage?

Williams: We have the Olympics, World Cups, World Cup qualifiers, Youth Olympic Games, the Pan Am Games, age-based World Cups, and World Cup qualifiers, as well as 3x3 events, which will be in the 2020 Olympics. There is also the annual Nike Hoop Summit, which is a men's game between the US high school players and a World team comprised of athletes 19-and-under. Most of our junior national teams have tryouts that are usually held in Colorado Springs, and we will help manage the trials from the standpoint of the media. We send out regular releases during the trials to members of the media around the country. Once the team is selected, we build a media guide around each team. Additionally, we now host annual USA 3x3 National Championships in the open (no age requirement) and U18 categories.

Q: What are the postgame press conferences like for these international events?

Williams: The governing body for basketball, FIBA, has a few rules governing the press for these events. Postgame, each team must bring one player and their coach to the formal end-of- game press conference. The locker rooms are not open to the press like they usually are in the NBA or at most colleges around the country. The IOC also has very strict rules relative to social media. Our staff has to be very careful with things like posting video, and when and where we tweet. The IOC is attempting to protect the television rights holders as well as the sponsors with this policy.

Since the London Olympics, after each game, the press conferences have been conducted exclusively in English. This was a change from past Olympics and it saves quite a bit of time, and there have been very few complaints. The player usually will go first, before the coach is interviewed and then be excused to head back to the locker room. It is customary to have both teams at the same press conference, which is somewhat different than college or pro basketball, where the teams typically have their own press conferences back to back.

The players that don't go to the formal end-of-game press conference will go into what is called the mixed zone before they board the bus for the ride back to the hotel. This mixed zone is a large room or hallway separated by a barrier of some sort. Players will be on one side and press on the other. At an event like the Olympics, the mixed zone is organized chaos. In Rio the press was three and four deep along the entire length of the mixed zone. In an effort to try to help direct the media to a specific athlete, in Rio we started posting signs that listed each athlete's name every five feet or so and that's where we would direct the athlete to go for interviews. That way, a Phoenix writer would know where to stand in order to wait for Diana Taurasi to stop, or a Cleveland writer would know where to go to wait for Kyrie Irving.

Of course, NBC and other rights-holders are at the front of the line and the first place athletes stop for interviews. Thus, it's possible that an athlete might be requested to stop at three or four positions before he or she gets to their designated print media stop.

While our players are in the mixed zone, the USA Basketball staff records interviews so that we can put together quotes for the post-game press release or to use in the game notes for the next game. We also have one staffer accompany the men's and women's representatives at the press conference to help manage the process and collect quotes.

Q: *Does your staff get involved in advising the players on these teams on how to manage their own media relations?*

Williams: We do spend time with the athletes, especially the younger players, discussing how they can work with the media and also understanding that they have to start thinking about how to "manage their brand." Our players on the younger teams are very involved in social media and we discuss with them the importance of thinking before you post something on social media. We also stress the importance of understanding the impact their posts can have on their teammates. Our staff tells all of the players we are also there if they need advice relative to posting something online. We have put together many examples of athletes making mistakes on social media; they are not hard to find and we discuss them often.

Q: *Talk about how your job differs from that of a journalist working for a newspaper or magazine.*

Williams: One of the aspects of my job I enjoy the most is the opportunity to work with players and coaches. In our jobs we really get to know all of our teams. Some of the players move from the Under-16/17 team to the Under-18/19 team to our Olympic Team or World Cup Team. Some of our coaches, such as our current USA National Team head coaches, Dawn Staley and Gregg Popovich, have a long history with USA Basketball. It is also part of our job to develop story ideas for the working press. This is why you need to get to know all of the players and coaches; the better you know them, the greater opportunity to generate story ideas. Our job is also to educate the media and the sports fan about USA Basketball. Tell folks how these are *not* all-star teams. These young men and women are representing their country in international competition. There is a responsibility on the shoulders of the players and coaches when they understand their role. USA Basketball and our communications office also see our job as promoting the game of basketball. This is something that I enjoy about my job. From my days at George Mason, I have always enjoyed sports and writing. This job has enabled me to see the world and engage in two things that bring me a great deal of job satisfaction.

Q: *What opportunities are out there for students to work in the international sports area?*

Williams: USA Basketball, the United States Olympic Committee, and most of the other national governing bodies have internship opportunities. All of these organizations work with their counterparts in other countries, as well as the International Olympic Committee and their respective international sports federations. The international sports federations also hire interns. The pay is not going to make anybody rich in these internships, but the opportunities are endless.

Also, there are a large group of people from many different countries that work at the Summer and Winter Olympics. They can be hired to work for a few months, for the two or three years leading up to the Olympics, or they may just be hired to work starting a few days before through the end of each Olympics. They can work at a particular venue (like track and field or swimming), in the hospitality area, for the operations staff, or at the press center. People can also volunteer for some of the age group championships that are held around the world. For example, the 2018 FIBA Americas U18 Championship in Canada utilized a number of volunteers in various positions. These are tremendous networking opportunities for future jobs in the sports world.

Q: *If you could offer one or two thoughts to students with regard to a career in sports communication or sports journalism, what would they be?*

Williams: Real world experiences are incredibly valuable to your development. My internship at USA Basketball and my work with the sports information department at George Mason University helped to prepare me for my current job. It also made me realize what I wanted to do for a living after I graduated.

I was very fortunate to work for Carl Sell when I was at GMU. He was proud of the fact that many of his interns went on to work for other colleges and professional teams. Carl had me write features, edit game notes, and other jobs of substance; he gave me real responsibility. My timing was also good. We had just hired Paul Westhead to be our coach and this attracted a tremendous amount of media attention. The experiences gained by internships or simply volunteering at an event are huge in my opinion. They allow prospective employers to find out if you can cut the long hours, whether you work on the weekends without complaint, and if you can get along with others; personality comes into play when you're in close quarters with people for long periods at a time. Even if it's as simple as volunteering for the long Final Four weekend and taking flash quotes, the more experiences gained and the more people with whom an intern/volunteer interacts, the more likely it is that s/he will get an opportunity somewhere down the line. Always strive to make a good first impression (and second and third).

Traveling Abroad

For the beat writer assigned to cover the Philadelphia Flyers, a trip to report on a game in Toronto against the Maple Leafs is a little more complicated than a trip to cover the Washington Capitals. Despite the good relations with our neighbor to the north, US citizens must go through customs when traveling to any city in Canada, and also on the return to the United States. You don't need a visa to travel to Canada, but you will need a valid passport.

However, for those journalists assigned by their editors to cover the 2018 World Cup or the 2014 Winter Olympics in Russia, they would have faced more complications, because a visa is required for US citizens who want to enter Russia. The visa process can be expedited, but it is important to plan ahead. The government of Russia requires the applicant to also have a sponsor. A great majority of the countries where a communications professional may travel have websites with very easy instructions on how to apply for a visa. This process has been made much easier by adding the online application, as well as express delivery. To apply for a visa, you will need a valid US passport. Common questions for most countries when applying for a visa will be the purpose of the visit, the date of entry, local hotel reservation information, and the date of departure. A business visa applicant sometimes will need a letter of invitation from an organization in the country granting the visa, as well as a letter from your employer stating the purpose of the visit. If one doesn't have a passport, it can be obtained from most post offices in the US as long as a birth certificate is supplied when applying for the passport. Passports also have to be updated periodically, so check the expiration date if you do have a US passport.

After reporters have contacted the embassy (or website) of the country they will be visiting to secure a visa, there is a service that the State Department offers those traveling outside the United States. They can register as a traveler in the Smart Traveler Enrollment Program (STEP) and receive current travel advisories relative to the country they are visiting. It is also a good idea to check with their health insurance provider or with the US State Department to determine if they need any inoculations or immunizations prior to the overseas assignment. Matching current medical records with the suggested immunizations of the host country can prevent a visit to the hospital at home or abroad. When checking for immunizations, it is also important to find out what is suggested in the way of food, beverage, and water consumption. Tap water in some countries has caused many reporters days of discomfort; better to be safe with bottled water than be sick and unable to cover the event you were assigned. The State Department has a very helpful website for all of these issues and more. One of the travel advisories from this site is included below, providing useful information to those Americans traveling to Honduras (site of a USMNT FIFA qualifying match in 2009, 2013, and 2017).

Honduras-Level 3: Reconsider Travel

Violent crime, such as homicide and armed robbery, is common. Violent gang activity, such as extortion, violent street crime, rape, narcotics, and human trafficking, is widespread. Local police and emergency services lack the resources to respond effectively to serious crime. Do not travel to Gracias a Dios Department (region) due to the crime. A travel advisory to Honduras has been issued since 2012 due to the high crime rates. The majority of serious crimes, including those against US citizens are never solved. Since 2010 Honduras has had one of the highest murder rates in the world.

If you decide to travel to Honduras:

- Be aware of your surroundings
- Avoid walking or driving at night
- Do not physically resist any robbery attempt
- Be extra vigilant when visiting banks or ATMs
- Do not display signs of wealth, such as wearing expensive watches or jewelry
- Exercise caution using cell phones in public, including inside of cars while stopped in traffic

Source: Travel.state.gov

Assuming the country the communications professionals plans to visit will grant a visa for travel, they must make plane and hotel reservations. Advice from an experienced reporter can come in handy at this point in the planning process. Check with a few people at your organization, the relevant sports federation, or friends in the business that have been to your intended destination. It is also important to understand the nuances of the sports venues where the events will be held. There are several questions to consider. How difficult and expensive is the trip from the hotel to the stadium or arena? Does the city have reliable public transportation? Is there a press bus that can be used to travel to each event? Are taxis reliable and plentiful? How easy will it be to pay with a credit card? Does the country take the credit cards you have? Are ATMs available, safe, and accessible in order to pick up needed cash? Cuba is an example of a potential destination for sports communications professionals. As of 2018, you are not permitted to use American credit cards in Cuba. All transactions must be made in Cuban currency that can be exchanged for American dollars at a bank. A common problem many reporters faced when covering the 2018 World Cup in Russia was a lack of availability of flights or trains between a few of the opening round locations. Many reporters had to pay a driver to take them to their next assignment.

If a reporter is covering an event such as the Olympics or World Cup, will s/he be at one venue the entire time, or expected to cover four or five different events located at different venues? In the past, many Olympic Games have different sports venues located in a neighboring city that is miles away. The 2014 World Cup in Brazil had venues all over the country, including Manaus, Recife, Cuiaba, Salvador, Rio, and Sao Paolo. Reporters covering the World Cup in South Africa could easily move between Johannesburg and Pretoria, a distance of only 33 miles, but if they wanted to cover a game in Cape Town they would have to travel nearly 800 miles. This variety of venues has the potential to cause problems if a reporter hasn't planned ahead. The host country has a local organizing committee that is typically, although not always, helpful to the working press. FIFA is an organization that is very supportive of the working press who cover the World Cup or continental championships sponsored by the international sport federation. Bus service for the working press is usually available for these mega-events, but the ability of reporters to leave and move to another location or return to their hotels for some rest, or to work on a story, may be restricted. Reporters will also be competing with fans for rental cars, hotel rooms, trains, and flights between venues.

The hotel location is important, but equally important is that the hotel has the necessary internet connection to meet one's communication needs. A reporter will usually be able to file stories from the venue, but if it is necessary, s/he should also be able to file stories from the hotel. In the age of social media, a good internet connection wherever you are is vital. When checking for an electric and an internet connection, ask what type of electrical plug is needed for laptops, hair dryers, shavers, chargers, etc. Some hotels have a variety of plugs and adapters for sale or for use for their hotel patrons, but some hotels don't. For the frequent traveler it would make sense to own several different types of adapters.

Another note is that telephone service in many foreign countries is much more expensive than in the United States. Your editor or supervisor would not be happy to receive a receipt for phone calls in the thousands of dollars. It is important for reporters and other communications professionals to communicate ahead of time with their business office. If they have to make calls to their home offices, a suggestion would be to find a cheap internet phone service, several of which offer the ability to make inexpensive phone calls online. A cell phone capable of calling the United States may be a necessary rental, temporary upgrade, or purchase before travel. Additionally, if a reporter is responsible for providing content to a blog or a Twitter account, it is essential to be able to tweet and update the blog from the venues and from your hotel room.

Another important issue for sports communication professionals to consider is the time zone of the event. Sochi (Russia), the host of the 2014 Winter Olympics, was eight hours ahead of New York City (Eastern Standard Time). Time differences impact the filing of stories to make the daily newspaper or a television broadcast of the local news at 6pm or 10/11pm. There are no deadlines for stories posted on a website, but many reporters will be asked to prepare a story for the web as well as file a story in time for the morning edition of the paper delivered to the home of their readers, whatever time zone they may be located. A *New York Times* reporter who covered the 2010 Winter Olympics would know that if a figure skating competition wasn't scheduled to conclude until 11 pm, Vancouver time, there is no way the reporter would be able to submit a story in time for the next day's edition of the newspaper. On the other hand, the soccer beat writer from the *New York Times* who covered the 2018 World Cup had additional time to write a game story and notes for the championship match between Croatia and France that concluded about 9 pm, Moscow time, because of the favorable seven-hour time difference.

When reporters have free time during their assignments abroad many want to take in some of the local sights and experience the culture of a foreign country. US State Department travel advisories may be helpful in providing alerts as to parts of the host country that might be off limits for touring. The USOC, US Soccer Federation, and USA Basketball are American-based NSOs that provide sport communication professionals with guidance when they are working at the Olympics, World Cup, CONCACAF events, or World Basketball Championships. It is important to remember that the respective US sports federation and the international sports federation are very good resources for information when working at international events.

A Journalist's Perspective

Jason Knapp Profile

Jason is a product of Syracuse University, where he graduated with a BS in Broadcast Journalism. He works full time as a play-by-play announcer for CBS, NBC, and several other regional sports networks. He has covered the last four Olympics and, while working for NBC, made the call for the gold medal winning USA Curling final at the PyeongChang Winter Olympics in 2018. During his broadcasting career, Jason has covered 30 different sports, from football, basketball, and baseball, to curling, wrestling, auto racing, rugby, soccer, tennis, boxing, swimming, diving, track and field, beach volleyball, and many more.

Q. *What Olympic sports have you covered?*

Knapp: So far I have worked four Olympics, doing the following sports: 2012 London Summer Olympics (wrestling, archery, plus a little shooting and judo); the 2014

Sochi Winter Olympics (curling); the 2016 Rio de Janeiro Summer Olympics (wrestling and beach volleyball); and the 2018 PyeongChang Winter Olympics (curling).

Q. *What other World Championships have you worked (international events)?*

Knapp: I have called World Championships in wrestling, curling, whitewater kayak/canoeing, speed skating, short track speed skating, plus FINA Jr. Worlds in swimming. I have also called three of the last four Paralympics. I have broadcast over 50 NCAA or NAIA National Championships in events like basketball, lacrosse, softball, volleyball, and soccer.

Q. *What logistical challenges have you had covering the Olympics?*

Knapp: The last Olympics was the farthest I've traveled in my career—going from the East Coast of the United States to South Korea. Since they have been the US Broadcaster for every Olympics going back the last 20 years, NBC understands how to plan for things, especially on this large scale. However, you never know what can happen. Day one, my first flight was cancelled, which means I missed my connection from Chicago to South Korea. Therefore, I had to switch to a later flight, which is fine, but then NBC had to switch my transport from the Seoul Incheon Airport to the Olympic venue area. It all worked out, but made for about a 40-hour travel day from when I left my house in Scranton, PA, to when I arrived at my hotel in South Korea. There is a great rule in TV that is also a great rule in life; expect the unexpected.

Q. *What is the most exciting event you have worked in your career with the Olympics?*

Knapp: I think you can find a great story in any event, if you look hard enough and ask the right questions in your prep work. As far as the Olympics goes, I think my first Olympics had some memorable moments. To me it is the ultimate sporting event to call. The Olympics only happens once every four years (Summer/Winter). The best from around the globe are there with so much history and tradition. The event is a chance for athletes to make their own history. So London 2012, my first day of work, was calling Men's Team Archery. In addition, what do you know; the US Men upset favorite S. Korea in the Semifinals. Suddenly, on day one of my Olympic career, I get to call the US going for it's first gold medal of the London Games. Plans were changed to air the event to a larger audience (i.e., flipped to a different network). And it was so dramatic, the US leading late, it comes down to the last arrow. Team Italy needs a 10, the top score on the target to win the Gold, and they get it. It was really compelling TV, and it was great to be a part of it.

I also think Jordan Burroughs' Olympic Gold in 2012 was special. A young American wrestler had burst onto the international scene after college and wowed everyone, won over 60 matches in a row, including a World Title. Could he do it at the Olympics? He did, in dramatic style, with some key late moves to score and grab Gold. I just felt like he was going to do it, so to build a storyline and set the scene for those joining and watching him come through with an Olympic title, was really neat.

At the same time, calling what's known at the MiraCurl on Ice at the most recent Olympics was truly incredible. The USA Men's Curling Team's gold in PyeongChang was so remarkable for so many reasons. Their skip (John Shuster, think the Team Captain/QB) had failed miserably at his previous to Olympics, and then was basically not invited back into the USA Curling Program for the next four-year Olympic cycle. Then, he and three other curlers, not in the highest level of the USA Curling system at the time, win their way back into that US program, and then finish Top Five at three straight World Championships. Nevertheless, Shuster gets back to the Olympics again (his fourth straight), and it begins like the last two; horribly. He is missing shots, the team gives up some untimely scores, and is saddled with an early losing record in the preliminary rounds. So what happens? Shuster and his team get the first win for a US Curling Team over Canada at the Olympics; they win their final three games to sneak into the playoffs. Then they beat Canada again in the Semifinals and topple a multi-World Champ Niklaus Edin and Sweden in the Final to make USA Curling history. It was one of the funnest/most unlikely rides ever for me in my career. To watch a team transform, from the depth of despair to the pinnacle of their sport—and to do it in less than a week. Amazing.

It also was quite the emotional ride for us. It gave us an adrenaline boost after calling 18 days of curling in a row, with doubleheaders both days and each game roughly two and a half to three hours to play. One of the hardest things my curling partners, Trenni Kusnierek and Kevin Martin, have ever done in our careers. The women's bronze medal curling match started about 40 minutes after we went off the air from the USA men and their win and the gold medal award ceremony. We ran to our compound and commissary to wolf down some food, but we were so tired. We looked at each other and said, "We've got to find some juice, some energy to wake back up and do this next game." We somehow did and had a solid broadcast.

Q. *What was your most memorable Olympic venue?*

Knapp: You would be hard pressed to beat the beach volleyball setup at the 2016 Rio Olympics. About 10–12,000 people in the stadium, right on the sands of Copacabana Beach, filled with fans so passionate about the sport. To call games there was phenomenal. Logistically, it was perfect. Our NBC/Olympic media compound was literally across the street from our hotel. It took me three minutes from my hotel room to my office at work, even with the extra security. That never happens at an Olympics. Sometimes it can take hours in transit.

Q. *Do you make your own travel arrangements when you work the Olympics? How are your flights and hotels arranged?*

Knapp: NBC handles our travel and hotels for the Olympics. With them doing so many Olympics in a row, they have a terrific system in place. For me in Rio, I stayed at one hotel when I broadcast beach volleyball, then switched to another hotel for my second week of work, covering wrestling, which was right near the IOC broadcast center.

Q. *How do you travel from the hotel to the event?*

Knapp: Travel to venues can be challenging. Sometimes you need to take the bus system implemented at all Olympics, for all of the media, including writers, photographers, camera crew, etc. Sometimes it can be confusing, especially in a country where you may not know the language. I got on the wrong bus in South Korea and turned a 30-minute trip into a two hour trip. We also had an issue early on in PyeongChang getting to the curling venue. It would have required a bus change at another Olympic venue that was very inconvenient. NBC juggled its schedule of runners (drivers with vans), and was able to get us rides to and from the venue every day. When you are working 12–16 hour days, every little bit of saved time helps.

Q. *How long are you usually 'at' the Olympic site and away from your family?*

Knapp: I was gone most of February for the 2018 Winter Olympics; about three and a half weeks. NBC likes us to arrive a number of days before our start date, to make certain we have time for prep work, accommodate travel issues, and in the case of a Winter Olympics halfway around the world, get your body used to the time change. In this case, it was a 13-hour difference.

Q. *When and where do you eat?*

Knapp: As far as food, we were able to eat breakfast at our hotel every morning. At most of the venues, either NBC or OBS (Olympic Broadcast System, the crew that provides the world TV for each sport at the venue) has a catering hall set up. Typically, they will have set times for their cafeteria-style meals, usually lunch and dinner at the venue, with coffee, tea, water, and other drinks available at other times. Our NBC compound at the venue also had other snack type items that I could raid to take into the broadcast booth if I needed something to eat during a game, or didn't have time in between assignments.

Q. *How long did it take you to develop a comfort level with sports like curling or speed skating?*

Knapp: For me, it takes a little time to feel fully comfortable with a new sport. I still prep for all of them the same way, intensively. I like to have a lot of prep work about storylines, stats, player bios, and other info done before I get to a venue. Then, when there, with our crew, we can talk to players and coaches, and zero in on other stories that may be fresh or new. Especially when you are working at an event that is two and a half weeks long. I would always ask myself, what is different about this player or team today? What is new? What haven't we talked about? What could we follow up on with a team, coach, or a player? And, as for other topics we have covered in previous broadcasts, how can we advance or expand on those topics or storylines today? In regard to a comfort level factor, when I step into calling a new sport, part of the understanding for me is about the pace of the event, which also leads to the pace of how we do our show. For example, baseball has a different flow than basketball or football. Getting a feel for that pace, to me, allows me to do my job better, understanding when or when not to speak, how to allow events to happen.

Curling gives a great example. All of the players wear wireless mics during big events, which means we can hear their conversations. We often intentionally lay out (not talk), and listen, with the audience, to what they are saying. Oftentimes we may not talk on air for minute plus stretches. It gives viewers a sense of being there, hearing the players and the action. I would rarely lay out in a basketball game for as long as I do at times in curling matches. Understanding the pace of the sport can help allow for this broadcasting strategy.

Q. *Who are the color commentators you have worked with in these sports and what is their background?*

Knapp: I have worked with a variety of analysts in the sports I cover. Most are former coaches or players, who have great insight into their sport. I always tell people, my job as the play by play announcer is the "who, what, and when" of an event. The analyst's job is "how and why," how something happened or why it happened. In curling, I typically work with Canadian Kevin Martin, the Olympic Gold Medalist in Vancouver 2010 and a World Curling Hall of Famer, and American Pete Fenson, 2006 Olympic Bronze Medalist and an eight-time US National Champion. In speed skating it could be an Olympic Gold Medalist like Apolo Anton Ohno or Dan Jansen. In swimming, I get to work with Olympic Gold Medalist Rowdy Gaines at times. All the broadcast partners were great athletes in their sport, with plenty of knowledge and experience, but they all prep and work really hard at their TV jobs. Just being a former great coach or athlete does not guarantee you will be a good analyst. Most of the ones I work with do prep work on par with what I like to do.

Q. *How long is your workday during the Olympics?*

Knapp: Each sport is different. Normally when I do a game or an event, I like to be there two hours before we go on the air. I can get set up, meet with the crew, organize my notes, chase any other interviews or story nuggets needed, with enough time to do any pregame tapings when needed (promos, sponsor reads, taped open, game tease). So for curling in South Korea, it took 20 plus minutes by car to get to the venue, my two hours of prep time, a three-hour game, usually two to three hours between games, then another three-hour game and 20 minute ride home. That is in addition to any other prep time I would do on my own each day before I got to the venue. Also, I worked full eight to ten hour days in my time before the start of each event to finish up notes, because I know it's hard on those long days to get additional work done. You need to find time to get rest, because it is a physical and mental grind during the Olympics.

Q. *Do you ever have time to do any sightseeing while on location?*

Knapp: I was able to do a little sightseeing in Rio and South Korea, but this was before we got busy. Most times, once your events start, there is no extra time. Sugarloaf Mountain and Christ the Redeemer are both absolutely breathtaking in Rio de Janeiro. I also would try to run either before or after work each day, to get in a little exercise and keep mentally fresh. That allowed for a little closer view of neighborhoods near my hotel.

Q. *How do you handle the opening segment of each of these events, when you first go live?*

Knapp: For me, the opening segment of each game or event follows somewhat the same roadmap. It needs to set the scene of the game, event, and venue, give you some sense of "what is at stake" in the upcoming event and give you certain story-lines, players, or coaches to look for during the broadcast. A good opening will pro-vide all the necessary information for our viewers, to give them a reason to watch. Some may be watching for their team or their sport, and the others who are just checking the game out, seem to be more invested when they have the chance to latch on to something interesting about the game. I try and provide that connection at the very beginning of each of the broadcasts.

Q. *How do you research international teams, events, coaches, and athletes?*

Knapp: For the Olympics, most sports federations have good websites to get you information on the event, along with some player bio information. I always try to make contact with media relations members from the nations I am covering, to learn more stories, nuggets for the broadcast, and other background information. I also check on player pronunciations, which is huge at an Olympics. Most notably, working for NBC Olympics, we get the knowledge and research of their amazing Olympic research staff. There are a handful of employees whose job it is to travel in between Olympics, to go to World Championships, and talk to future potential Olympians and get bio information, pronunciations and back stories. This research is amazing and vital to our broadcasts. It is also impressively extensive. The bio books are anywhere from 150–250 pages long, depending on the sport and the number of athletes. It is an amazing tool to help us do our jobs. We have access to live scoring and biographical information in front of us, in our stat computer sys-tem. The IOC sets up this system and is available for every nation's broadcast team; I believe in their own language.

Q. *Describe the media center at the Olympics.*

Knapp: Each venue has a media room set up with seating and a press area for formal interviews. There is also a mix zone, where broadcast crews and radio reporters and others have a chance to talk to players and coaches. They are required to go through there on their way to the locker room. There is also a formal press area. The headline venue for all Olympics is the IOC Broadcast Center. That's where most nations have their broadcast studios that they use to generate most of their studio programming. It would be where Mike Tirico (NBC Sports) did most of his studio hosting for the 2018 Winter Olympics in South Korea. It is a massive facility. It is where the onsite offices and most of the staff for NBC are located during the Olympic Games. It is like moving NBC Headquarters in New York City halfway across the globe.

Q. *How did you get involved in this career?*

Knapp: Out of high school, I had played and had a great love of sports, and had also been involved as a performer in music and theater. I wasn't sure exactly what I wanted to get into, but once I found a passion with sportscasting, it's what I wanted to do. I worked in student radio at WAER (Syracuse University), starting as a sophomore. It was a great place to take the instructional building blocks (classwork) at SU, and learn how to do it firsthand. I also started interning at local TV stations; first in my home market of Philadelphia after my sophomore year and then in Syracuse after my junior year. Eventually that lead to a part-time producing job as a senior, which lead to filling in on-air, which then lead me to my first full-time job after graduating, working as a sportscaster for a small market station in West Virginia. Then I moved to another station in Pennsylvania and eventually got back into announcing live events full-time.

Q. *What international event would you like to do, that you have yet to announce?*

Knapp: I'm fortunate that I have been able to do a lot, and I'm glad NBC and others continue to test me and trust me with new sporting endeavors. I would love to call a golf major, like the US Open or the Masters. I do get to do that in tennis. I have worked for the USTA the last few years, calling the US Open for their World TV feed. An English language broadcast is sent to countries around the world with all of the action from the fourth and final tennis major every year.

Q. *What was the first broadcasting assignment/job you had?*

Knapp: As I mentioned before, I started working for WAER-FM in Syracuse, where professionals oversee the newsroom, but the sports department is all student-run. I started doing sports updates, and then eventually, along with some other top students, studio hosted live events, and did play-by-play of SU football, basketball, and lacrosse. A handful of students each year would split calling the games. As for TV, an internship at a local TV station in Syracuse lead to a part-time producing job while I was still going to school as a senior. Eventually, they let me report and fill-in anchor after graduating, I built up my resume tape, and landed a full-time sports anchor/reporter job in West Virginia. After a little over two years there, I moved to a bigger station in Pennsylvania. In addition, while there, I started doing freelance play-by-play work in my spare time. Eventually I was able to just leave my local TV job and continue doing play by play as a full-time career.

Q. What advice would you give to young professionals interested in this line of work?

Knapp: The industry is constantly changing, so my biggest piece of advice is be flexible. Be open to new ideas and prospects, and test yourself, even if it is uncomfortable. I also think that writing and broadcasting as much as possible is vital. It gets you into the patterns that you need, to get the reps you need, to continue to grow your skills. Much like drills and practice in football, those reps will help. And critique your own work. It's not fun to look back and see what you've done sometimes, but it will make you better. Try to ask someone you respect for his or her thoughts. What they say doesn't mean they are right, but if you value that person's experience and expertise, they may offer some valuable feedback.

Summary

The 21st century is an exciting time for those involved in the sport industry. The Olympics has become a global entertainment event, followed on TV and radio, in newspapers, and online around the world. The World Cup, a celebration of the world's most popular sport, rivals the Olympics in its reach around the world. Fans from all over the globe descend on the host cities and countries of these mega-events. Television, radio, newspaper, and online journalists tell the stories of these events and the great athletes who compete, from countries all over the world. The teams that compete in these events also have their own communications professionals that act as liaisons with the global press, but also tell the stories of their teams and their athletes. These communications professionals must be flexible and willing to learn new skills in order to work in this new international and technological wonderland.

When these mega-events have concluded, it does not lessen the mobility of today's sporting events and today's athletes. European soccer players regularly play in the MLS; NBA players from countries around the world compete in the Olympics and the World Championships, and then head back to their respective teams and adopted cities in the US. The best tennis players and golfers travel the world competing on a tour that is a test of stamina beginning with the travel necessary to make each event. Major League Baseball has websites in English, Japanese, Spanish, Chinese, and Arabic. The professional women's teams in Europe are loaded with former NCAA female college stars; many of the best women's basketball players from around the world play in the WNBA. The world's best professional soccer league, the aptly named Premier League, has developed a regular following all over the world. Fans around the globe follow the games of their favorite teams like Arsenal, Manchester United, and Chelsea. World media companies are now vying for TV rights outside their borders, looking to take advantage of the burgeoning interest in sports programming. Al Jazeera, the Qatari network-established a beachhead in the US with its purchase of Current TV in 2013. The network was rebranded as beIn Sports and has rights to televise sporting events, games and studio programming all over the world. All of these developments offer opportunities for the sports journalists and communications professionals who have prepared themselves for the global marketplace.

Jason Knapp and Caroline Williams, featured in this chapter, have developed a comfort level with the travel each of their jobs require. Both of these communications professionals have been to several Olympic Games. The student who wants to become a sportswriter can experience foreign travel while still in college. There are numerous study-abroad programs at every college and university in the United States. There are volunteer and internship opportunities at all of the major world athletic events. Many of the international sport federations hire interns. Both the Summer and Winter Olympics, along with the Pan Am Games, the World Cup, and Commonwealth Games all rely heavily on volunteers and interns, looking for interesting work experiences in the sports and/or media industries.

Caroline Williams emphasized taking advantage of internship opportunities while still in school. The United States has many national governing bodies, such as USA Basketball that hire interns in the communications field. Because the United States Olympic Committee headquarters is based in Colorado Springs, Colorado, many of these NGOs are also located in that city. All of the professional leagues in the United States continue to make investments overseas, to take advantage of the global economy, so there are opportunities in those organizations to learn some valuable lessons about doing business around the world, marketing to customers outside and traveling outside the United States. Your value also increases when you learn to speak a second language. Taking a minor in Spanish, Arabic, French, or Chinese may set you apart from other job seekers in the sports industry.

With all of these new opportunities and challenges available in the sport communication industry, it is also important to remember that story telling is still fundamental. Expanding your horizons is beneficial, but there is *no substitute* for strong written and oral communication skills.

Discussion Questions

1. What are a few of the differences between the job of a sports reporter for *The New York Times* and a communications director like Caroline Williams (USA Basketball)?

2. Why do sports federations and national Olympic committees around the world hire communications staff? What are some of the essential skills you think are necessary to succeed in that position?

3. What are some of the differences between covering a regular season game in the NBA and the Summer Olympics?

4. China is the host of the 2022 Winter Olympics, and Qatar hosts the 2022 World Cup. What problems will that cause for the TV broadcaster from the United States? The journalist from the United States who has a daily column to file at a newspaper? The online journalist that blogs and also is in charge of keeping the newspaper's website updated during the Olympics and the World Cup? How about the journalist working both of these events who likes to use Twitter?

Suggested Exercises

1. Go to the website of one of the international sports federations, such as FIFA, FINA or FIBA. Who works in their communications department? Critique their website. How do you like the format and appearance? Are the stories well written?

2. Go to the website of one of the United States' national sport organizations. Identify its communications director and others who work in this department. Analyze the content on its website. Determine what types of media it uses to tell its story. Take a look at its media page. How would you contact the organization if you wanted to write a story about one of its coaches or athletes?

3. Research one of the major global media companies that covers the sports industry. What work do they do outside of the borders of the country where they are headquartered? Do they broadcast sporting events? If so, in how many countries? Who is the chief executive in their sports department? What, if any, major sports rights/properties does the company own?

4. Research one of the countries that hosted a recent World Cup or Olympics. Compare the US economy to the country you choose (e.g., GDP, per capita income). What are that country's major newspapers and TV networks? What sports are televised inside that country? Can you watch American pro leagues, college sports, and Premier League soccer if you lived there? What is the cost for sports programming?

5. Go to the websites of the IOC, the South African Olympic Committee and the USOC. Take a look at their communications departments and the rest of the website. How are their websites organized? If you wanted to interview someone from each organization, what are your instructions for contacting them?

13 | Ethics, Law, and Regulations

In the field of sport media relations, the law, ethical codes, and administrative regulations play a big part in governing the behavior of the communication professional, as well as providing the subject matter for countless articles, news segments, and sports broadcasts. NCAA regulations, coaching contracts with buyout clauses, Title IX compliance, collective bargaining agreements, antitrust lawsuits, FIFA corruption, and defamation claims—not to mention drunk driving arrests, handgun charges, and performance enhancing drug suspensions—cry out for at least a cursory understanding of the sports industry's legal and regulatory system for those who cover sports. These legal issues lead to broader discussions of ethics and the role of sportsmanship in athletic contests and behavior outside the lines of competition. In fact, ESPN produces a show called *Outside the Lines,* that discusses many of these very issues. HBO has a program called *Real Sports with Bryant Gumbel,* which covers some of the same ground.

In the first half of this chapter, we will examine the laws and administrative regulations that sport information specialists and journalists should understand in order to successfully perform their duties. Once the legal and regulatory framework has been examined, we will take a look at what the ethical obligations are for the sports journalist and the communication professional. Where can a journalist look for guidance when there is an ethical dilemma? Fortunately for sport communication students and professionals alike, there is plenty of guidance in this area from professional organizations, as well as media companies. Sports information directors (SIDs) can look to the College Sports Information Directors of America (CoSIDA) for suggestions in the form of a code of ethics (see Chapter 5). Sports reporters can consult the Society of Professional Journalists (SPJ) and their Code of Ethics, which they publish in nine different languages; or other professional organizations like the American Society of News Editors (ASNE), and the Associated Press Media Editors (APME). In addition to these sources for guidance, this chapter will also discuss the common components of an ethical code for sports communications professionals.

Law and Media Relations

While you don't need a law degree to work in the sport communication field, it is a good idea to have a basic understanding of some of the specific federal statutes that loom large in the coverage of sports. A reporter may experience some sleepless nights if there has not been some exposure to the relevant prohibitions to publishing personal or private information.

Discussion begins with the cornerstone of the media and communications industries in the United States. The First Amendment of the US Constitution says: "Congress shall make no law… abridging the freedom of speech, or of the press … ." So why did the framers of this amendment include this very explicit protection in the Bill of Rights? James Madison and the other leaders of the fledgling American government recognized that a free press could act as a further check on a powerful, and sometimes oppressive, government. Just as government had been divided into three co-equal branches and further distributed power by granting very broad powers to state governments, it was also necessary to equip the people with the power to criticize their government. The press functions as a source of information for the electorate. True democracy needs information in order to function properly; as *The Washington Post* has been fond of saying after the 2016 Presidential election, "Democracy dies in darkness."

In today's world, if an owner of a Major League Baseball (MLB) or National Football League (NFL) team wants the local taxpayer to shoulder the cost of a new stadium, the press can help inform the taxpayers what the benefit will be to the MLB/NFL team owner and what the benefit and burden will be to the taxpayer. In many of these cases, the sports (MLB or NFL) team owner has the support of local government officials; developers and construction companies that benefit from large projects contribute to those same politicians. The job of the sports reporter, or the reporter who covers local politics is to present the taxpayer with information that may be relevant the next time that taxpayer goes to vote for those politicians who support this stadium subsidy. Is there information that would lead the local populace to believe that this decision is good for most people who live in the area? Will the stadium project create jobs? Are those jobs permanent or temporary? Is there a fan base large enough to support a professional franchise in this location? Or, is this just a handout to a few wealthy political donors?

Madison and those who helped develop our constitution did not know anything about baseball, football, or professional sports for that matter. However, they did understand that if local politicians had the power to license the press, or could censure their publications, the American citizen would lose their ability to receive valuable information about how government is functioning and what interest groups are exerting influence over public officials. Only a truly independent media can provide this service; the press helps to spur public debate about important issues that affect the people.

The rights granted to the press in the First Amendment were the subject of substantial debate before the ratification of the first ten amendments (The Bill of Rights), on December 15, 1791. Many states have included similar "freedom of the press" clauses in their constitutions. The passage of the Fourteenth Amendment, and a subsequent landmark Supreme Court decision established that this freedom and the other freedoms in the First Amendment are checks on state governments, too (*Gitlow v NY*, 1925). The marketplace of ideas coupled with every citizen's power of thought is the best way to keep voters informed; a free press encourages this trade in ideas from a diverse group of people (Brandt, 1965). Courts also must be able to protect the acquisition of information by the press. Citizens need accurate information in order to understand the issues they have been asked to vote upon (Powe, 1991).

Laws and regulations that effect sport communication professionals the most can be broken down into two categories: legal issues and access to information.

Legal Issues in Sport Communication

A basic understanding of some of the more common laws and regulations that members of the sport communication industry will work with on a regular basis is essential. A short review of some of the issues will help to point out the trouble spots.

Defamation

The First Amendment protections are an important foundation to our public discourse, but our system of laws and court decisions protect citizens, both public and private, from over-reaching by the press in the form of state defamation laws. Defamation falls under tort law; a tort is a civil wrong, other than breach of contract, for which the complainant may be compensated by damages or protected by an injunction against a defendant (Garner, 2009). Defamation can take two forms— *slander* or *libel*. Slander is the use of the spoken word to injure reputation. Libel is the written form of defamation. To defame someone, you must diminish their self-esteem, take away from the respect they hold in the community, damage the goodwill they may have acquired, or insert a lack of confidence into their reputation among the members of the community where the statements have been published.

Dissemination of information will be your business. Hopefully, careful review of your work before publication will become a habit. This careful review applies to emails, blogs, Facebook posts, and Twitter posts (tweets) as much as feature-length magazine articles, network documentaries, or news releases. A libelous statement just needs to be "published" to one person to meet one of the requirements of defamation. In a defamation lawsuit brought by MLB players Ryan Zimmerman and Ryan Howard, Al Jazeera and several other parties were accused of publishing false and unsubstantiated claims that Zimmerman and Howard were using performance enhancing drugs in a documentary called, *The Dark Side: The Secrets of Sport Dopers* (Perez, 2016).

Defamation statutes are mostly civil in nature, but in some states you can also commit criminal libel. The most famous of the defamation cases as they relate to the First Amendment and the press, is the US Supreme Court case of *NY Times v Sullivan* (1964). Sullivan was Mr. L.B. Sullivan, the city of Montgomery's (AL) Commissioner in charge of the police and fire department. Sullivan claimed he had been libeled by an ad in *The New York (NY) Times*. He sued for damages and won a large judgment in two state courts in Alabama. *The NY Times* appealed to the US Supreme Court, which decided in favor of *The NY Times* and the press.

This case outlined what a plaintiff must prove in order to secure a defamation judgment against the press. However, the court limits this standard to cases where a public figure was the plaintiff. Was there actual malice involved in the publication of the story? In other words, *should* the newspaper editor or writer have known that the story was false or, *did they know* that the story was false? Was there a reckless disregard for the truth? In analyzing these questions, the court will ask if there were good faith journalistic judgments made in deciding to publish this story (Feinman, 2006).

Debate about public issues should be robust and uninhibited when it comes to the criticism of public officials (Barron & Dienes, 2005). Four years after the *NY Times v Sullivan* case, the Supreme Court also included an athletic director (AD) in the definition of a "public figure." Wally Butts, the AD at the University of Georgia, sued *The Saturday Evening Post* magazine for libel (*Curtis Publishing Co. v Butts*, 1967). Because the AD of a major university like Georgia had inserted himself intentionally into a position that had a great amount of public interest, he would not be given the same protection as a private individual would when seeking redress for defamatory statements. However, the court did rule in Butts' favor. They held that the *Saturday Evening Post* had departed from normal investigative standards of journalism, the magazine had inflicted harm upon Butts in their story, elementary precautions in preparing the story had not been taken, and the reliability of the primary source was called into serious question by trial testimony (*Curtis Publishing Co. v Butts*).

Later Supreme Court decisions have held that a public official or public figure voluntarily enters into the turbulence of criticism that is life in the media's eye. A private individual that has been thrust into a temporary position of public awareness will be given greater protection (*Gertz v Robert Welch*, 1974; *Time, Inc. v Firestone*, 1976). The private individual is more vulnerable to defamation and thus more deserving of relief (*Gertz v Robert Welch*, 1974). The lesson to be learned here for sport communication professionals is to scrutinize your work more closely when publishing information about a private citizen. Most professional athletes, as well as coaches on the college and pro level, are considered public figures.

The basic elements of *defamation* are

- a statement has been made,
- that statement was heard or published by at least one other person, and
- the plaintiff was identified in the statement.

(Carter et al., 2006)

Publication implies that others were intended to hear. A private conversation between two people is not defamation. The defamer also must be the one who publishes the statement. The law does not consider it libel if the plaintiff published the statement. Truth is a defense in a libel action. There is also an absolute privilege of debate in a legislative forum; legislators must be permitted to vigorously debate issues without fear of defamation lawsuits. Those participating in judicial proceedings and members of government involved in executive or administrative session also receive similar protection. If you have been assigned by your editor to cover one of these proceedings, you will be protected by a qualified privilege. If your report is fair and accurate you will fall within the protections of this privilege.

A well-known defamation lawsuit in the sports arena was brought in state court by a member of the Oklahoma football team, who claimed he was defamed by an article in *True Magazine* (*Fawcett Publications, Inc. v Morris*, 1962). The article was titled "The Pill That Can Kill Sports," and the writer alleged that the Oklahoma football team was using amphetamines. The court found that the entire team had been libeled because each individual was subject to public ridicule. The court also found that even though the player was not specifically named in the article, each member was defamed.

This case is important for future sports journalists to consider. Many articles will be written that cover subjects involving behavior off the field. An experienced editor can help in this area, but in the modern era of blogs, tweets, and the constant updates of websites, each journalist better have a clear handle on the words used in a published story. It is very easy to insert the word *alleged* or *allegations* into a story relating to criminal charges, NCAA violations, or performance enhancing drugs. Also, the reach and permanence of the internet can exacerbate the defamation. The useful life of the daily paper is much shorter than a story on the web. An arrest does not mean someone is guilty of a crime. A letter from the NCAA identifying a school, an athlete, or a coach as the target of an investigation does not mean that an NCAA violation was committed.

As has been noted in the two Supreme Court cases just detailed, the reporters will be protected when they have behaved in a reasonable manner, particularly when the story they are covering involves an individual deemed a public figure. However, courts do not like shoddy reporting or assumptions not based on solid facts. The First Amendment and freedom of the press don't grant "the publisher of a newspaper ... special immunity from the application of general laws. He has no special privilege to invade the rights and liberties of others" (*Curtis Publishing Co. v Butts*, 1967, p. 150).

Right to Privacy and Right to Publicity

Consistent with the protections against defamation, we also enjoy a right to privacy that is recognized in common law (from courts/judges), constitutional law, or statutory law in each state in the county. Part of the freedom that we have been promised by Madison, Jefferson, and the Founding Fathers is the right to remain free from unnecessary intrusion into our private lives by the government. The right to publicity was an additional method to protect our right to privacy, as well as a way to establish a property right in our name, picture, and likeness.

Privacy concerns can be found in the First Amendment, the Third Amendment, the Fourth Amendment, and the Fifth Amendment. Former Supreme Court Justice Louis Brandeis and his law partner, Samuel Warren, wrote a pioneering article aptly titled, "Right to Privacy," for a law journal in the early 1900s that was cited by judges for many years thereafter. Brandeis described this right in his dissenting opinion in the *Olmstead* case as the "right of every citizen to be left alone by their government." A string of Supreme Court cases in the 1960s and 70s have outlined a zone of privacy around the individual. The Privacy Protection Act was passed in 1974 and this provides citizens with protection regarding data collected by the government. A citizen has the right to challenge information or correct inaccurate information that governmental agencies collect. Under this act you also have a right to inspect personal records maintained by any governmental agency. Citizens have a zone of privacy surrounding their credit records after the passing of the Fair Credit Reporting Act of 1970.

The right to privacy, and to be shielded from the intrusiveness of the press, merged into the right to publicity and the right to prevent unauthorized business use of your likeness, your name, and your picture. A New York statute provided for a right to privacy in 1903, as well as penalties for unauthorized use of a citizen's name, portrait, picture, or likeness for advertising or any other commercial purposes. A New Jersey judge held that a man's likeness and name were his property, thus it was his decision how to use both. The case involved a pharmaceutical company that had put Thomas Edison's likeness on a medicine bottle without his permission (*Edison v Edison Polyform*, 1907). This *right to publicity* has made many athletes, coaches, and sports reporters like Jim Nance (CBS) and Erin Andrews (Fox and ESPN) quite a bit of endorsement money over the years.

With the invention of radio, television, and sound recordings in the early and middle 1900s, celebrity became a manufactured commercial value. Entertainers and athletes such as Babe Ruth and Ty Cobb were in great demand to lend the celebrity of their name, likeness, picture, or voice for the promotion and marketing of companies and products. Like the right to privacy, this right to publicity is recognized in every state, although how it is defined is different. Many states also recognize the publicity right as descendible to the heirs of the celebrity's estate.

The company CKX paid the estate of Elvis Presley $100 million for an 85% share of the rights to his image and likeness. A year later, the same company paid Muhammad Ali $50 million for an 80% share of his name and likeness. There are many rationales offered for this right. Everyone is entitled to the fruits of his or her labor. You should be able to prevent others from "free-riding" on your reputation and likeness. There is an economic incentive to create, to achieve, and be successful in order to be able to profit from your image.

These arguments all assume that everyone that is a celebrity is "successful." We have many cases today where celebrity is achieved without any measure of accomplishment other than being able to become famous or well-known. In sports, the desire to acquire celebrity-sized endorsements has led to any number of cases of attention-grabbing behavior (Johnny "Football" Manziel and Lavar Ball) that has little to do with performance on the field or the court.

Intellectual Property, Copyright, and Trademarks

This area of the law is designed to protect the creation of fixed forms of expression or inventions by their creators. Copyrights, patents, and trademarks all fall under this definition of intellectual property. A sportswriter like Bill Simmons, who creates a screenplay, writes a book, or produces an investigative piece for a national magazine receives copyright protection for his work. The well-known logo of the NBA, a replica of Jerry West dribbling a basketball, receives trademark protection under the Lanham Trademark Act of 1946. The innovative shoe design of the latest Kevin Durant endorsed Nike basketball shoe receives patent protection by filing the proper paperwork with the United States Patent and Trademark Office. Once the patent is approved, Nike receives protection for a number of years for the exclusive manufacture of this shoe, with this unique design. It is important to note that Nike owns this patent, not the designer who works for Nike.

Subject Matter of Copyright

- Literary works
- Musical works, words
- Dramatic works, music
- Pantomimes, choreographed works
- Pictoral, graphic, and sculptured works
- Motion pictures
- Sound recordings

("Subject matter," 2005)

The foundation for this area of intellectual property is in the US Constitution. Article I, Section 8, Clause 8 states: "Congress shall have the power to … promote the Progress of Science and useful arts, by securing for limited times to authors and inventors the exclusive right to their respective writings and discoveries."

Writers, artists, and musicians were granted the exclusive right to reprint and sell their works for 14 years. Fines were included for those who copied original works without permission. The intent of the legal protection for these works was to motivate the creation of works of art, literature, and music, as well as inventions that have a commercial use. The author, musician, playwright, or inventor would be given a special reward for a limited period of time and after that time lapsed, the public would have access to the use of this work or invention unencumbered by patent or copyright law.

The law was also intended to preserve a publisher's incentive to disseminate copyrighted works, as well as a manufacturer's incentive to contract for an exclusive right to produce an inventor's latest creation (Johnston, 2008). For a work to be copyrighted, it must be an original work and be fixed in a tangible medium of expression ("Subject matter," 2005). The owner of the copyright has the right to produce the work, to distribute copies of the work, to display the work, and to perform the work created. When the FOX network produces a 2018 World Cup game, their production of the game is protected under this body of law; FOX paid FIFA a rights fee for the ownership of these telecasts. The US Copyright Act of 1976 provides copyright protection for the life of the author, plus 70 years after the author's death, 95 years, or 120 years depending on the nature of the copyright ("How long," n.d.) Copyright protection is *not* extended to news reporting, comment, research, or any other educational uses of the copyrighted work; these exceptions are called "fair use" ("Limitations," 2005). This exception gives networks like ABC or CBS the right to show highlights of games on their *news* shows, even if the "copyright" to those games is owned by NBC or FOX.

Trademark protection was a direct result of technological improvements in transportation and communication. Business transactions were no longer face-to-face matters. Individuals and businesses needed a system to identify products and businesses, and consumers needed to be able to have confidence in the products they were purchasing (McManis, 2009). The Lanham Trademark Act was passed in 1946 to help consumers identify a business (e.g., Under Armour) and to identify products produced by that business (stamped with the Under Armour logo or the name). In order for a mark to receive protection, that mark must be in use in the flow of commerce, and the mark must be distinctive. A trademark is a valuable asset of any business and can be a symbol of goodwill to consumers.

In the sports industry there are many examples of trademarks: the MLB team name Tigers and the D with the unique font, for the city of Detroit, that appear on Detroit Tigers baseball hats. The distinctive five colored rings that symbolize the Olympics is a logo owned and protected by the International Olympic Committee (IOC). They also own the rights to the words "Olympic," "Olympiad," and the expression "Citius Altius Fortius;" the IOC zealously protects all of their trademark rights. College or university names, their team nicknames, and their logos all can be trademarked and licensed for sale (Notre Dame, ND, The Fighting Irish). The 'swoosh' is a trademarked symbol of the sporting goods company, Nike.

In 2006, Texas Tech University, a member of the Big 12 Conference, sued a local business that had made and sold unlicensed Texas Tech merchandise. The university had licensed its mark to companies selling pens, book ends, knit caps, coffee mugs, flip flops, and a host of other merchandise. The court found that the marks that the local business was using clearly belonged to the university and that the business was making commercial use of the distinctive nickname, colors, and logos of the university and its athletic teams (*Texas Tech v Spiegelberg*, 2006). The court also protected nicknames and phrases unique to Texas Tech: "Red Raiders," "Wreck'em Tech," and "Raiderland."

Like Texas Tech, many of the owners of these trademarked goods aggressively protect them from counterfeiting. The NFL is one of those owners who aggressively protects team logos and other official marks of the NFL. During the 2018 Super Bowl held in Minneapolis, the league sued a company in order to prevent the unauthorized production and sale of trademarked merchandise owned by the league and the teams (Philadelphia Eagles and New England Patriots) competing in the 2018 NFL game (Kaminsky, 2018). The NFL, NBA, and the Collegiate Licensing Corporation (CLC) have joined a group called the Coalition to Advance the Protection of Sports

Logos (CAPS). CAPS works with law enforcement to enforce the trademark rights of these sports leagues and the universities that form CLC (CAPS, n.d.). Much of the enforcement activity occurs during large sporting events, such as the Final Four, the Stanley Cup, the World Series, and the aforementioned Minnesota Super Bowl.

Several government agencies are involved in the discovery and prosecution of those who traffic in counterfeit goods. These agencies have the power to seize items that have not complied with US trademark law ("Destruction," 2009). At a press conference held in Minneapolis and coinciding with the preparation for Super Bowl 2018, the Immigration and Customs Enforcement Agency (ICE) announced the seizure of $15.59 million worth of sports and entertainment related items from suspected counterfeiters (Operation Team Player, 2018). During this press conference, they also announced that they had made 64 arrests, which resulted in 29 convictions in this year-long enforcement operation. The US Customs and Border Protection (CPB) along with Homeland Security were part of this enforcement effort, dubbed *Operation Team Player.*

A flood of cases like this, involving the importation of "knockoffs" manufactured overseas, spurred the passage of the Trademark Counterfeiting Act in 1984. Congress established criminal penalties, including substantial fines for repeat offenders, as well as large fines for corporations caught in violation ("Recovery," 2009). Injunctive relief can be sought under the statute, and in the most egregious cases, attorney's fees and treble damages can be granted by the court.

The National Intellectual Property Rights Coordination Center is a key weapon in managing the many organizations that protect the creators of intellectual property in the United States ("National Intellectual," 2010). Federal agencies like the FBI, the Department of State, Homeland Security, and the Department of Justice, work with private groups like the International Intellectual Property Institute, and the International Intellectual Property Alliance to devise strategies to combat this problem. The counterfeiting of sports team trademarks and merchandise is a problem facing teams like Real Madrid, Barcelona FC, Arsenal, and Manchester United; this is not an issue particular to the sports industry in the United States.

US Copyright law has evolved over the years thanks to advances made in technology. Motion pictures were granted copyright protection by the Copyright Act Amendment of 1912. Sound recordings were specifically covered in 1971 and broadcasters of television content were protected in 1976 from the unauthorized use of their signal. The 1976 act was a direct result of lobbying from the National Association of Broadcasters, after two different court cases had been decided in favor of cable television operators.

The Digital Performance Right in Sound Recordings Act of 1995 was an attempt to protect the copying of original music. Advances in digital recording technology and peer-to-peer sharing of files had put a huge dent in music CD sales. Record labels, recording artists, songwriters, and music publishers were all lobbying Congress to do something (Lincoff, 2009). The Digital Millennium Copyright Act of 1998 prohibited the removal of locks on copyrighted works, as well as the sale of anti-circumvention devices. Internet service providers were also protected from infringement liability on behalf of third parties. Copyright protection was extended to all parts of a website, including computer programs, HTML code, sounds, designs, video text, and computer programs.

The Sonny Bono Copyright Term Extension Act of 1998 extended copyright protection for creative works 20 more years. The World Trade Organization has become involved with enforcing copyrights and trademark law. They have a dispute resolution mechanism when an infringement complaint has been brought. There have been a series of worldwide conventions attempting to standardize intellectual property law around the globe. Great progress has been made, but significant problems still exist in this area for owners of intellectual property.

The move from analog transmission to digital, the ease with which copies of music and video can now be made, as well as the explosion of the use of the internet around the world has increased the frequency of copyright complaints coming from creators of music, video games, broadcasters, and the motion picture industry. Google has drawn the attention of copyright owners and regulators around the world regarding the aggregation of previously published literary works.

A Chinese author sued Google, Inc., for the unauthorized publishing of her book extracts online (Chao, 2009). A French court sided with a publisher in a suit filed by La Martiniere against Google that was very similar to the Chinese author's suit. Google had also been sued by a group of writers (Author's Guild) and the American Association of Publishers (Kang, 2009). A settlement was reached in this lawsuit and then had to be renegotiated after the original deal drew the attention of the Department of Justice, as well as a few of Google's competitors, most notably Amazon and Microsoft. The American Association of Publishers reached a confidential settlement with Google in 2012 (Albanese, 2012). The class action by the Author's Guild went to trial, was rejected by the US District Court, and on appeal by the US Court of Appeals. Both courts ruled that Google had provided a public service without violating laws governing intellectual property. The Author's Guild appealed this ruling to the US Supreme Court, which declined to review the Appeals Court ruling (Author's Guild, n.d).

The books that were included in the first settlement with Google were from Great Britain, Canada, the United States, and Australia. France and Germany were not happy with the first settlement; their copyright laws are even more protective than those in the United States (Googlemania, 2009). The EU has also publicly funded their own book digitization project called Europeana, which is a website designed as a virtual library for European books, art, history, and culture (Europeana, n.d.).

Google argues that being included in its search engine is good for business for these publishers, newspapers, their writers, other media companies, and book authors. Google also says that it will gladly take down any content if asked to do so by the owner or creator. Sun Jingwei, the lawyer for the aforementioned Chinese author, thinks that Google's position is unreasonable. "You should settle the issue first and then scan and upload the books, not committing infringement first" (Chao, 2009).

Sun has an ally in the Irish rock star Bono, who has called for tougher controls to prevent the unauthorized use of intellectual property over the internet (Bono, 2010). Bono pointed out in an op-ed piece in _The New York Times_ the damage that has been done to the music industry and newspapers around the world due to the ease of file sharing. He also predicted that the movie industry would soon face the same fate as creators of music and literary copyrights, because the technology of file sharing will rapidly improve to the point of allowing quick downloads of entire movies.

Access to Information

Federal and state laws, the rules of regulatory agencies, and institutional policies can both assist and derail attempts by sport journalists to acquire information, and for sports information specialists to control the release of information. The following are some of the most common types of laws, regulations, and policies relating to access of information for sports journalists and communication professionals.

Freedom of Information Act

The Freedom of Information Act (FOIA) was passed in 1966 by Congress and signed into law by President Lyndon B. Johnson. FOIA has since been amended a few times based on historical circumstances and also technological advances in the storage and communication of information online. An amendment in 1974 came in response to some of the abuses that occurred in the Nixon Administration during the Watergate scandal. FOIA was amended in 1996 in response to the recognition that the United States was becoming a nation of computer databases and email, not a nation of paper file cabinets and surface mail. This amendment established that computer databases were records that could be included as the subject of FOIA requests. In 2002, in response to the 9/11 attacks, some protections were implemented to prevent FOIA requests by foreign agents. President Barack Obama released an Open Government Plan in December of 2009 that requires agencies to publish information in a timely manner, and make it easily accessible to the public in the form of an easy-to-use website. The order has guidelines for those agencies with backlogs to reduce them in a timely manner (O'Keefe, 2009). In an executive order effective May 9, 2013, Obama issued new guidelines to ensure that government information was easy to find and was machine readable (PC, smartphone, tablets, etc); the rationale for the order was to promote democracy, efficiency, and economic growth (Exec. Order, 2013). More changes were made in 2016, with the int____tion of lowering costs and providing for the electronic production of more docun_____ _____ __Freedom of Information Act, 2016).

T____ _____ expressed by President Bill Clinton when he signed into l___ _____dments, was to firmly recognize that we are a "country... _____principles of openness and accountability" (Woolley & Pete___ _____ntly all federal agencies must maintain a webpage that out___ _____r that agency. For example, if you log onto the website for _____ations Commission, you will find a short explanation of the Freedom_____tion Act, what files are available at the FCC without an FOIA request, how you can submit an FOIA request, what is available at the FCC under FOIA, what is not available, how much the FOIA request will cost, and many other guidelines to help those seeking information (FCC, n.d.).

Indiana's FOI statute expresses the purpose for this legislation in its opening section:

A fundamental philosophy of the American constitutional form of representative government is that government is the servant of the people and not their master. Accordingly, it is the public policy of the state that all persons are entitled to full and complete information regarding the affairs of government and the official acts of those who represent them ("Public policy," 2006, p. 162).

Arizona's FOI statute states that "[p]ublic records and other matters in the custody of any officer shall be open to inspection by any person at all times during office hours" (Inspection, 2001). Connecticut provides that "[e]xcept as otherwise provided by any federal law or state statute, all records maintained or kept on file by any public agency...shall be public records and every person shall have the right to inspect such records promptly" (Access, 2000).

These freedom of information statutes at the federal and state levels have been invaluable to the reporter looking for information about government actions and public officials; sports information directors working at public institutions will be on the receiving end of these FOIA requests. FOI statutes have helped the sports reporter gather information relative to the actions of athletic department officials at state institutions. Information about NCAA investigations, university trustees meetings relative to a move to a new conference, or coaching salaries have all been the subject of FOI requests around the country by sports reporters. An interesting issue relative to the Jerry Sandusky scandal at Penn State was the fact that the university was not subject to Pennsylvania open records laws, and reporters working to uncover information about Sandusky found this out the hard way (Thompkins, 2012). The University of Louisville, which *is subject* to Kentucky open records laws, was held to have violated the Kentucky Open Records Act on two occasions in 2018, in relation to requests for information relating to the actions of former employees that resulted in NCAA violations, multiple scandals, and substantial penalties against the athletic department (Wolfson, 2018).

Historically, FOI statutes are expensive policies to maintain. There have been tremendous backlogs to comply with these requests, many requests made seem to have no useful purpose, and there is a lack of resources at many federal and state agencies to comply with these requests in a timely manner (McMasters, 2009).

Florida State University was involved in an FOI request in 2009 regarding ongoing NCAA Enforcement proceedings that concerned 61 of their student-athletes and a few athletic department employees. The school had been penalized by the NCAA for academic fraud relative to an online music class and improper help from staff members. A Florida state court judge issued a decision that ordered copies of Florida State documents relative to their appeal of NCAA sanctions turned over to *The Associated Press* and other members of the media. The NCAA challenged this ruling but the Florida appellate court sided with the trial judge ("Florida court," October 1, 2009). The NCAA argument was that secrecy was necessary for its enforcement process, that the documents were created by a private organization (NCAA), and that the fees paid to join the NCAA were actually paid by the Florida State Foundation, a private entity. Both state courts ruled that these documents were public records and needed to be released immediately. They said that if the NCAA rationale were accepted, the "state's public access laws would be emasculated" ("Florida court," October 1, 2009).

Government in Sunshine Act

The Government in Sunshine Act, passed in 1976, mandates that government agencies open up their meetings to the public. The public must be given notice of when and where meetings will be held, as well as what will be covered at these meetings. Except in rare cases, a transcript of the meeting must be made available to the public as well. Exceptions to this open meeting requirement can be made if defense issues are being discussed, personnel matters, criminal matters, conversations of a personal nature regarding members of the agency, or any conversations relative to ongoing legal proceedings ("Public information," 2007). When meetings are closed, these decisions are also subject to judicial review by the federal district courts.

All states have some form of FOIA and Sunshine Laws. The purpose of these state laws is the same as the federal purpose—to allow citizens to know what their elected officials are doing. These statutes permit citizens and the press to attend meetings and to request information from state and local legislatures and state agencies. All states have started to provide information online. In fact, as part of Sunshine Week, a movement sponsored by *The Associated Press* and other media organizations, states were rated as to the ability to find information online about government. The Better Government Association also publishes an Integrity Index ranking states in categories such as their Freedom of Information Laws and Open Meeting Laws (Better Government Association, n.d.).

As an example of specific state legislation in this area, Colorado passed an Open Records Act and an Open Meetings Law. Both of these pieces of legislation would fall under the heading of Sunshine Laws. Their purpose is to ensure that the workings of government are open to view by the public, and that the public is fully informed on the important issues of the day. "It is declared to be the public policy of this state that all public records shall be open for inspection …" ("Legislative declaration," 2001). Any Colorado citizen can ask to inspect and copy those records that fall within this statute. The Open Meetings Law declares that it is a "matter of statewide concern and the policy of this state that the formation of public policy is public business and may not be conducted in secret" ("Declaration," 2001). Notice must be given when and where these meetings of public interest will be conducted.

The issue of notice was raised by a lawsuit in 2000 soon after Indiana University President Myles Brand fired Bobby Knight, the former men's basketball coach. The plaintiff alleged that in accordance with the Indiana Open Door statute, Brand could not meet with trustees to discuss firing Knight unless public notice had been given 48 hours before the meeting. In another example of open meetings statutes and university boards, the University of Maryland's board of regents drew heavy criticism from alumni, fans, and students for its decision to leave the Atlantic Coast Conference and move to the Big Ten. A complaint was also filed by a reporter and a political science teacher that the board of regents did not comply with the state open meetings laws (Anderson, 2013). The state open meetings compliance board agreed with the complainants that the board of regents did violate the law; however, the only penalty for the violation was a public rebuke.

There are exceptions to information requests, as well as exceptions to open meetings in all 50 states. There are some fairly consistent clauses that often will permit state agencies to deny access to information or to meetings; in the aforementioned University of Maryland example, the board of regents cited the Big Ten Conference's need for a timely decision as a rationale for private sessions. They later argued that the press had published multiple stories about the potential move to the Big Ten during this time period, so in effect the public had been informed.

State governments do not like to disclose personal information of their citizens; phone numbers, home addresses, and social security numbers are usually not going to be disclosed. Meetings surrounding criminal prosecutions or investigations, meetings or information housed on databases relative to personnel decisions, or discussions or meetings in preparation for legal proceedings will usually not be given to the public. Confidential records, trade secrets, or financial information that are either personal or can be used to trade in the open market are usually exempt from disclosure requirements under these statutes, as is personal medical history. Many of these states also have penalties to discourage the release of private information to the public.

State Sunshine Laws have been used by many enterprising sports reporters to gather information about state sponsored or funded athletic programs. Private organizations such as professional sports teams and private universities are not subject to many of the aforementioned requirements, by virtue of their status as private entities. But when an NFL or MLB team is asking for the taxpayer to fund the building of a new stadium or improvements to an old one, there are many meetings and related information in which the taxpayer and the well-prepared reporter will be granted access. Knowledge of your state's laws in this area is important. Also, with the continued pressure from First Amendment groups as well as other voters' rights groups that favor open government, information should continue to become more available online.

Regulations

Federal agencies draw up regulations in order to implement legislation; when a new President is elected, changes are typically made to many of these administrative regulations. The federal regulations have the full backing of the federal government. One example is the regulation to implement Title IX. The Department of Education draws up regulations used as guidance by high school and college athletic directors. Sport managers who work for high school and college athletic departments must stay abreast of any changes to these regulations when making decisions related to squad size, funding, facilities, and the addition or elimination of male and female sports teams at their school.

The Federal Communication Commission (FCC) issues regulations governing who can own media companies. If you own a newspaper can you also own a local TV station or a radio station? Many FCC regulations have a significant impact on sports television programming around the country.

The IOC has rules and regulations governing the access to live Olympic events, press conferences, and interviews of Olympic participants. Any reporter from news agencies or sports networks around the world is subject to guidelines covering social media use and other digital publication guidelines relative to pictures, video, or audio content during the Olympic Games.

Governing bodies in college sports such as the NCAA, NJCAA, and the NAIA have rules and regulations for their respective member schools. These relate to recruiting, eligibility, academic performance, squad size, length of sport seasons, and number of teams needed to qualify for each association. These regulations don't have the force of law, but there are enforcement penalties and compliance rules that can cost teams and players eligibility. Also, major violations can be a reason to suspend or fire coaches or athletic department personnel. Sports information specialists working for NCAA Division I schools follow a set of rules governing their behavior, including the release of recruiting information to the media.

FERPA

FERPA stands for Federal Educational Right to Privacy Act and is commonly referred to as the Buckley Amendment. Passed in 1974, its major purpose is to protect students from the disclosure of *statute defined* private records to any individual or group not given permission to view those records. Private information includes grades, standardized test results, disciplinary actions, and records from the school health office. Directory information can be released without the consent of the parents, and this information includes many facts and figures that are of interest to sports reporters. The height and weight of the student can be released. Sports statistics and records of participation in other extracurricular activities can be released. A student's date of birth, place of birth, and major field of study can also be released without permission.

FERPA also permits private information to be released to colleges where that student has applied for admission, to teachers and academicians for legitimate educational reasons, to authorized representatives of the local, state, and federal governments, as well as those conducting legitimate educational studies. If information is released to researchers, biographical information must be deleted. Parents are also given the right to inspect all records that the school keeps on file pertaining to their child under the age of 18. Eighteen-year olds have full access and now become the person to whom the records are released. At universities and colleges, parents don't have the right to inspect or receive a copy of student records unless this permission is specifically given by the student.

A note to those reporters covering high school and college athletics regarding the application of this statute—be careful that the school is not hiding behind FERPA in responding to your questions. FERPA does not prevent the release of *all* information. "Some critics say a number of schools are deliberately misreading the Family Educational Rights and Privacy Act in order to keep scandals and other unflattering news from hitting the media" (Herring, 2009, para. 2). The shielding of grades, test scores, and financial aid records is not disputed, but student conduct issues and enrollment status are areas where reporters can push for the disclosure of information.

HIPAA

HIPAA operates like FERPA, but protects private information held by healthcare providers and insurance companies, so the information relates to the health of the individual, not academics. The Health Insurance Portability and Accountability Act became law in 1996. The Act permits the disclosure of information necessary for a patient's care, but also protects the privacy of the patient in relation to unnecessary disclosure of private health information. The act protects electronic, written, and oral information, as well as permitting the patient a right of inspection and correction. Health records held at elementary and secondary schools are actually considered educational records, and therefore fall under the protection of FERPA.

These laws are required reading for the sports information director who is in the business of providing information to the public about college students. Sports reporters also must be careful how they report on academic and health information when covering high school and college athletes. In the overwhelming number of cases, the disclosure of an injury suffered during the course of a game or practice will not be a violation of these two federal statutes. In many cases, the college athlete has signed a waiver that permits disclosure of this type of injury information to reporters (Conrad, 2006). However, a university sports information director or the director of communication for a sport federation would not post on a website that the star athlete is out for the season because he has HIV-AIDs, or the local sports reporter would not write a newspaper article about a highly recruited basketball player at the local high school is being treated for drug addiction and depression; these disclosures of personal and private health-related information are treated differently than reporting garden variety injury on the football field or basketball court. Where does the health information come from? Who authorized disclosure? Was that authorization made by an adult or a 17-year-old minor? Are we discussing the health of a high school student, college student, or professional athlete? In most cases, sports reporters are not in legal jeopardy, but their sources might be; especially if their sources work at healthcare related facilities.

NCAA Reports and the Student-Athlete Right-to-Know Act

The Student-Athlete Right-to-Know Act was signed into law by President George H.W. Bush in 1990. The bill was the brainchild of two former NBA players who were serving in the US Congress at the time of passage: Sen. Bill Bradley and Rep. Tom McMillen. The bill publishes the graduation rates of college athletes receiving athletic-related financial aid for all NCAA Division I, II, and III institutions, separating out the rates by race, sport, and gender. The NCAA requires that this information is given to all athletes before they sign their commitment letters to the school, as well as being disclosed to the guidance counselors of high schools around the country. The intent of this legislation is to give accurate academic performance information to parents and athletes who are recruited by NCAA schools. Recruited athletes can see what percentage of students at a particular school graduate, and then compare that percentage to scholarship athletes, scholarship athletes in their sport, and scholarship athletes of a particular ethnicity or gender.

The NCAA also releases three different reports on member schools each year. These reports reveal the academic progress rate (APR) for each school, the graduation success rate (GSR) for each Division I school, and the academic success rate (ASR) for each Division II school. The GSR and the ASR are both barometers of how schools have performed in the classroom and bring with them penalties to schools that have not met a benchmark established by the NCAA. These two rates are opportunities for those schools (and their SID office) that have outperformed their rivals to trumpet these results in their media guides, alumni magazines, and websites.

Sports information directors at Division I and Division II programs who work with this report will be aware that the NCAA and the communications professionals working for the NCAA are involved in drafting the report every year. Sports reporters that cover college athletics usually generate a story or two about the performance of a particular team at a local school and its impressive or less than impressive score under this NCAA report. Columnists and reporters that work for national news organizations also generate stories when these reports are published by the NCAA. Trends are discussed and there is usually commentary about reforms that have been recently proposed by coaches, faculty, and concerned groups, like the Knight Commission.

The APR is different from the GSR and ASR in that it actually carries with it penalties for underperformance. For example, in 2012 the University of Connecticut men's basketball team was not permitted to play in its conference tournament or

NCAA tournament because of a failure to meet APR standards ("NCAA hands," 2013). The APR takes into account eligibility of athletes, the school's retention rate of its players, and also the graduation rates of each team. Schools can lose a scholarship in a particular sport, be banned from postseason play, have practice time restricted, or even face department-wide sanctions for continued underperformance. In the NCAA APR report released in May of 2018, nine teams received a postseason ban and the report included a dozen teams that were subject to other, lesser penalties (Hosick, 2018).

Ethics and Media Relations

Every college student has their own unique influences that contribute to the values they carry with them into the field of sport communications and media relations. Influences include parents and family members, religious beliefs, school teachers, and the prevailing cultural values of the student's immediate geographical environment. In addition, once students enter the work force, they will be influenced by the values of their supervisors, colleagues, and professional associations. Editors, journalists, and broadcasters all have very specific published ethical guidelines. There are also ethical guidelines for sports information specialists who work on college campuses.

Is your sports organization for-profit? Are you funded by the state? Are you a nonprofit, like a PBS station, or a sports federation? Do you work for a newspaper? A television network? An online website? A radio station? Were you raised in a household where the press is the enemy of the state? Did you have an elementary school civics teacher who taught you that freedom of the press was God's gift to good governance? Do you have an editor from the school of Machiavelli? Get the story by whatever means necessary? Do you work for a sports organization in China where the laws for dissemination of information are much different than the laws of the United States? Does this present a legal as well as ethical dilemma for you as a journalist?

Are Ethics Important?

Where you work and for whom you work will help you answer whether or not ethics are important. If you don't know the professional values that your company holds dear, you can get yourself fired. On a purely business level, the public does care about ethics. If your newspaper, radio station, or television network is perceived by the public as unethical, it can damage the company's reputation. Low ratings or a drop in subscriptions means budget cuts, which means job cuts, so the very health of the enterprise of sport communication does depend in some way on your organization's behavior and whether your operation is perceived as an ethical actor. "In order for the media to play its role as a watchdog, it relies on public trust;

the people must believe the press in order to take action based upon its reporting" (Bikales, 2018).

Another important consideration is the journalist's role in evaluating and commenting on the ethics of a sport organization, player, coach, or owner. The adage of the glass house and those that throw stones comes to mind. If you have been assigned to cover a story on the use of performance enhancing drugs in baseball, would your story carry less weight in the community if you are perceived as a cheater yourself?

The ethics of journalists and other communication professionals are also important because of the tremendous responsibility the First Amendment places on the press and those who speak and write for a living. Communication professionals are granted wide latitude to publish and broadcast because of the role a free press plays in the United States democracy. The freedom to stimulate robust debate, bring to light wide-ranging opinion from various sources, and the ability to criticize those in power comes with a sense of responsibility. The media should strive to be accurate, truthful, do their research and due diligence, have no conflicts of interest, and reflect on the possible ramifications of what they are about to publish. Language is powerful and words matter. David Von Drehle touched on these issues in an editorial in *The Washington Post*. "The First Amendment...does [not] bestow credibility (on journalists). That must be earned by openness, care, good judgment, transparency, consistency, and fairness" (Von Drehle, 2018).

Lastly, an ethical professional life will carry with it a greater sense of respect for what you do and why you do it (Merrill, 1997). Providing information to the public is a great service. The satisfaction that this service is accomplished with the highest ideals in mind will provide you with a reason to work long hours, typical of those in the sports industry, and you will look forward to arriving on the job each day.

Ethical Codes

Many professional communication and journalism organizations and companies have their own codes of ethics. The American Society of Journalists and Authors, the American Society of Newspaper Editors, and the Society of Professional Journalists all have a code of ethics. The BBC, *The New York Times*, *The Associated Press*, ESPN, and *The Washington Post* to name just a few, have also composed a code of ethics for their respective company's communications professionals. The Sports Information Directors of College and University Athletic Departments in the United States have a professional organization called CoSIDA, which publishes an ethics code.

There are also many policy institutes, or "think tanks," that offer free advice to the media in the form of ethical guidelines. Accuracy in Media, the Center for Media and Public Affairs, the First Amendment Center, the Freedom Forum, and Fairness and Accuracy in Reporting (FAIR) all weigh in from time to time to report how the media rates in terms of their ethical practices. At the Department of Justice, the Office of Information and Privacy deals with the administration of the Freedom of Information Act, as well as the Privacy Act. Federal government employees also have their own Ethics in Government Act, as well as the Public Officials Integrity Act that is designed to provide a check on illegal or unethical impulses.

Communications professionals can also find many journals that publish regular commentary on ethics—*Journal of Mass Media Ethics*, *Public Integrity*, *Journal of Ethics*, *Journal of Moral Philosophy*, and *Online Journal of Ethics* all provide great discussions about real issues journalists and communications professionals must wrestle with in their practice. There have been many recent articles in these journals about the ethical debates that have been created by the use of social media by so many in the world of sports, and in the field of communications more generally.

Ethical Issues in Sport Communication

When examining the various commentaries, codes of conduct, and the codes of ethics mentioned above, a few themes are consistently included. Truth, accuracy, fairness, accountability, and independence are not only relevant for sport communication professionals, but for everyone involved in mass media.

Truth

Don't write, publish, retweet, or broadcast anything that you know is not true. The First Amendment of the US Constitution, coupled with many Supreme Court interpretations, grants the press wide latitude in the performance of their public function to inform citizens. How could the media possibly be executing this function if they are lying to the public in what they are writing, publishing, or broadcasting? It seems hard to believe that media outlets would knowingly sacrifice credibility, but in today's media environment truth often gets sacrificed for speed.

Truth also relates to photos, and seemingly every year there are examples of digital manipulation. *Sports Illustrated* got in some ethical hot water by publishing what appeared to be an innocuous photo of a football game between Baylor and Kansas State. *SI* changed the color of the Baylor uniforms from black to green, which ignited a debate over altering photos. Typically, there are two camps in this debate—those who feel it's "no big deal" to make such an inconsequential change, and those who say you should not change a photo under any circumstances. As a general rule of thumb, if photographers and publishers want to change or alter something, they should choose another photo or clearly label it as an illustration, not a photograph.

Honesty is one of the basic foundations of the modern world. Our laws and values are based on the ability to believe in public institutions, individuals, and private companies. Criminality and unethical conduct is associated with dishonesty. Without honesty, our ability to make contracts, to educate, to inform, and to govern breaks down at every turn. In *The Book of Virtues*, William Bennett says that "to be honest is to be real, genuine, authentic, and bona fide. To be dishonest is to be partly feigned, forged, fake, or fictitious" (Bennett, 1993, p. 599). Can there be a more damning criticism of a media story than it is feigned, forged, fake, or fictitious? Operating today in the age of 'fake news,' the ethical tenet of truth becomes even more important for today's sports reporters and communications professionals. Truth must be a fundamental principal of every communication professional and every media company where their primary job is to inform the public. It must become a habit, exercised every day, and a periodic reminder from managers and supervisors is always a good practice in the business of communication and information.

> **"Don't tell fish stories where the people know you; but particularly, don't tell them where they know the fish."**
>
> *~Mark Twain*

Accuracy

Right behind truth is the ethical requirement to get the story right. This implies a minimal level of attention to detail and hard work. Stories must be proofread for grammar, spelling, fact checking, incorrect quotes, the wrong name associated with a published photo, incorrect statistics, etc. It makes good business sense to be accurate if you are selling news for a living, but it is also the right thing to do. Competition and cost cutting makes this job more difficult, but the fact that a newsroom is understaffed is not an excuse for journalists to not do their due diligence. With all of the blogs and Twitter accounts on the internet, a journalist's mistake will show up quickly. You are not doing your organization or your profession any favors if this becomes a habit. Accuracy also calls for not omitting information that would be helpful to the understanding of a particular story by the reader; an accurate story is also *objective*.

> **"If the writer doesn't sweat, the reader will."**
>
> *~Mark Twain*

If you are going to retweet a story or you are going to send out a picture that you were sent via social media, your name and your organization is now attached to that picture or that story. How confident are you in the accuracy of the story you are retweeting? Former *Washington Post* reporter Mike Wise, who now writes for the CBS affiliate in DC, WUSA9, purposely tweeted a phony story about an NFL player just to see how many other people would retweet it. Wise was suspended by the *Post* and eventually apologized for his breach of ethics, but he also trapped many others in the media who retweeted the story without checking it out. Here are a few questions to ask yourself before you publish:

1. Have you added a sentence or two explaining where the story came from?

2. How confident are you in the accuracy of the picture you are sending out under your name?

3. Have you confirmed that the retweeting of the picture does not present a copyright issue for your organization?

National Public Radio has a social media directive for their reporters and the guiding principle is "what would you put on the air?" ("Social media," n.d.). Its social media guidelines offer two other suggestions—can you confirm the information offline, and have you consulted with NPR's social media team? ESPN guidelines advise that "[i]f you wouldn't say it on the air or write it in a column, don't post it on any social network. This applies to retweets and other social shares" (Skipper, 2017). In an address CBS correspondent Scott Pelley gave at an awards luncheon hosted by Quinnipiac University, he opined that the state of journalism was not in a good place (Blumer, 2013). According to Pelley, there were two primary issues: the pressure to get the story first and an overreliance on social media like Facebook and Twitter. Pelley quoted the revered journalist Fred Friendly, when he offered some advice on this issue to journalism students and some of his fellow reporters: "If you are first, no one will remember. If you are wrong, no one will forget."

In order to be accurate, you also may have to do some quick work in the library, on the phone, or on the internet. What you know is important. In order to inform the public, as the communicator, you have to be informed. The ethic of a *lifetime learner* is a good one for a sports reporter or sports information specialist. You may have to know antitrust law, psychology, contract law, sociology, labor law, geography, history, physiology, chemistry—the list is endless (Neff, 1987). In Tom Wicker's book *On Press*, he talks about the perils of competitive pressures to rush a story to print and the effect that this can have on the media's credibility. Wicker's book was published before Twitter and Facebook, but his concerns apply to all reporting, including today's tweets by sports reporters and his admonitions are very similar to Scott Pelley's, noted above:

> **When faulty stories do get into print, and turn out to be false or misleading or overstated, not only their unfortunate subjects are damaged; so is**

the general credibility of newspapers. Lack of credibility with readers, of course, is a profound limitation on the power of the press; if people don't believe what they read or hear or see, then the supposedly prodigious ability of the press to shape public opinion comes to little. To the extent that the press discredits itself with inaccuracies and wild swings, it ironically limits its own theoretically vast powers—and those inaccuracies and wild swings often are the direct result of competition. (Wicker, 1978)

The British Broadcasting Company (BBC) groups accuracy and truth together in its editorial guidelines. "Accuracy is more important than speed and it is often more than a test of getting the facts right. We will weigh all relevant facts and information to get at the truth" (BBC editorial guidelines, 2010).

Fairness

Another common ethical requirement is that the media respect the dignity of all who they cover or involve in their stories. Children who are the subjects of news stories can't be treated like adults. Their inability to defend themselves changes the dynamic and increases the ethical responsibilities of the press. It is not fair to hold high school athletes to the same standard as professional athletes. Their age and connection with an educational institution call for less exposure to public scrutiny. A 16-year-old athlete's ability to run, jump, and throw *as if an adult* shouldn't obscure the fact that he or she is still a child.

Fairness dictates that the press will not use deception or coercion when covering a story. A reporter should not hide the fact they are covering a story for a news organization. There are rare exceptions to this requirement and the use of those exceptions will inform the public as to the values of that news organization or reporter.

Those who cover the sports landscape must also be aware of the legal presumption of innocence. An arrest is not a conviction. A charge or allegation is not a prison sentence. Competition, a deadline, or sensationalism should not pressure a reporter to forget this very important part of established US common law. Get familiar with the term *allegedly* and use it often when reporting on such stories. The 2006 Duke Lacrosse case is a cautionary example of this point.

Another right to be respected is each citizen's right to privacy. In this age of Kim Kardashian and the rest, it is difficult to believe that there are people who don't want fame, but there are plenty of people out there who have no desire to be featured in the headlines. Respect for an individual's desire to be left alone is important for every communication professional to remember; this is especially true for the families of athletes and coaches.

Accountability

Letters to the editor, opportunities to comment online, and the role of an ombudsman or public editor all speak to the ethical responsibility of the media to allow readers a chance to ask questions, as well as air grievances. Most newspapers publish a corrections section when it becomes necessary to explain mistakes made in previous issues. News magazine television programs use this practice as well, broadcasting letters to the editor and corrections at the end of programs from time to time. These letters are sometimes highly critical of a particular show or an individual broadcaster. A news organization website can be corrected much easier and quicker if a mistake is found. This type of editing happens all the time on the web. In addition, writers or editors are able to provide updates when a new set of facts should be reported to make the story more complete. The public will take note of companies and reporters who don't hide from mistakes—a habit that helps to build trust.

Broadcasters and writers regularly publish an email address where the public can respond to stories. This type of accountability is consistent not only with many codes of ethics, it is also good business. An opportunity to respond can breed a very loyal following. This interactivity has become much easier with online news and the ease of email communication. Many newspapers and other media outlets also offer online chats with readers and their popular commentators. A topic may be introduced for that day's chat but the commentator may also respond to other concerns brought up during the online chat. The public must also feel that they are not being ignored by the media. Do the local media companies cover the entire community? This question will come up regularly in sports coverage decisions by media companies. Why don't you cover more high school games? You never have women's basketball box scores. Why not? How about soccer? The public's source for information must attempt to answer these questions. Shared norms and values will demonstrate trust and accountability, which is an ongoing process (Belmas & Vanacher, 2009).

Another frequently codified ethical mandate under accountability is the right of an individual to respond to a critical story. An athlete, coach, or owner who is the subject of a less than flattering news story should be given the right to know what will be said in the newspaper or on the nightly news. The subject should have an opportunity to rebut the reporter's version of events, or at the very least, present their version to the reporter.

Conflicts of Interest and Independence

The consumers of information expect to be delivered an accurate and truthful version of a story, but there is more to the building of a trusting relationship between the media and the reader or listener. There must be an understanding that the reporter or the broadcaster does not have a personal interest in the story. And if a personal interest is unavoidable, the public deserves to be informed of what that interest is, so as to make an independent assessment as to whether the conflict has upset the credibility or objectivity of the author's version of the facts. A perfect example of this is who employs the color commentator or play-by-play announcer for an NBA or MLB game. Do they work for the Lakers, the Yankees, or the Trailblazers, or for ESPN, TNT, or NBC? The public should be told who pays them, and whether the professional team has the right to approve the announcers who receive their paycheck from a television network.

The New York Times Company policy on ethics in journalism specifically prohibits sports reporters from accepting "tickets, travel expenses, meals, gifts, or other benefits from teams or promoters" (*The New York Times* Company, 2005). There are many other proscriptions under this code that warn against the appearance of a conflict for all reporters that work at *The New York Times*, including accepting speaking fees or meals from a source, or potential source, or also covering stories where a spouse, a family member, or a close personal friend is involved. *The Times* organization places a high value in this code on the goal of protecting the neutrality of its function as a news source.

News judgment, story lines, and the selection of stories by editors can all come into question when readers, bloggers, and media critics analyze the relationship between a writer or media company and a particular story. Advertising considerations, competitive influences, personal relationships, personal financial interests, romantic entanglements, and pressures from ownership are just a few areas of influence that can break down trust in the media. In the Radio Television Digital News Association Code of Ethics, these conflicts are called "unprofessional connection[s]" ("Code of," 2010). Under the Associated Press Statement of News Values and Principles, these influences are discussed in several different sections of this all-encompassing statement. Conflicts in the area of political, social, or financial behavior are discouraged. Free trips, gifts, discounts, and political activities are frowned upon. The behavior or activities of an AP employee should not impact the ability to "report the news fairly and accurately, uninfluenced by any person or action" (Associated Press, 2018). It is important to note that the sport communication professional must steer clear of accepting "freebies" during the performance of their duties from those on whom they must write or talk about. A free meal at a ball game is one thing, and many news organizations explicitly permit this practice. Unlimited alcohol and expensive gifts go too far and should not be accepted.

Another measure of independence is the public's ability to separate the media's news stories from commentary and opinion pieces. These pieces have become a popular staple of the sports media. Can the media consumer easily see the difference? And will the sports media be as accurate in their opinion pieces with the use of facts as they are when writing a pure news story? When the press runs opinion pieces, will those opinion pieces favor those in power? Or will the everyday fan feel their voice is being heard? Is the public being informed or is a sports reporter who wants to write a biography burnishing the image of an athlete who is far less than what s/he seems? The proximity to athletes, coaches, and owners that the press enjoys is understood by the public. That understanding does not make the public blind to the abuses that this proximity can bring to a truthful, accurate, and independent accounting of the day's news.

Summary

The media and sport industries around the world have grown by leaps and bounds in the last 25 years. The size of the newspaper is shrinking and many magazines and daily newspapers have either folded or moved strictly to the internet, but think about how many television stations we have now. How many more websites do we have in just the last few years? How many more blogs? How many more TV networks devoted solely to sports? The posting of stories and pictures to Facebook pages and Twitter feeds has exploded. Twitter is a primary news source for many sports fans (and sports reporters).

This explosion of information comes with a legal responsibility to ensure the integrity of the process of information gathering and publishing. As we discovered in this chapter, the First Amendment grants the reporter and broadcaster freedoms, but also ensures that the disseminators of information take into consideration the individual. Like the checks and balances discussed in our constitutional government, the law of defamation provides a check on an overly aggressive or an irresponsible press.

Our system of copyright, trademark, and patent law provides property rights to the sports biographer, the sportswriter with a talent for creating feature length films, and the sports teams that want to market their names and logos to their fans. It will be interesting to see the evolution of copyright law concerning publication of material on the internet. The pervasiveness of the web and the accessibility of so much information online will provide challenges to writers who want to be paid for their creativity. News organizations also must deal with this issue. Organizations like Google or the Huffington Post that aggregate stories without compensation to newspapers or writers will continue to generate calls for a change to this practice. Do you make sports fans looking for stories online pay for the news? Many newspapers have online pay walls now, and some who don't are experimenting with them.

A basic understanding of the law is important, and so is a grounding in the ethical principles associated with the gathering and dissemination of information. Ethical precepts are the foundation of legal principles like defamation, freedom of the press, and the property protections surrounding intellectual work. The US legal system penalizes dishonesty both in its libel laws and in copyright protections for works like books and screenplays.

I am sure there are many students who look at the newspaper industry in the 21st century and wonder why would we devote any words at all to the topic of ethics when our future livelihood is dying right before our eyes. There is a segment of the industry that feels editors and reporters are too concerned with ethics and not concerned enough with circulation, ratings, job security, and sensational reporting that will draw eyeballs to the TV, the magazine page, the website, or the newspaper. This concern with producing news and stories that draw advertising dollars continues to become more acute.

The increased focus on advertising, profits, and searching for new pay models for newspapers, magazines, and websites does not need to interfere with the bonds of trust that need to be strong between consumers of media and the disseminators of media. Those who consume news must be able to find accurate information to meet their daily needs for news, entertainment, politics, sports, and current events. Trust has an economic value to newspaper companies like *The New York Times* and television networks like NBC. There will always be pressure from the business/ accounting side of media companies, particularly those traded on stock exchanges. Those in the media must also be vigilant that competition between reporters and different media companies does not help to break down trust in the entire industry.

Periodic ethics training can be effective to reinforce the values that have been codified in the various ethical guidelines touched on in this chapter. It is difficult to leave each ethical decision up to the individual. Refresher courses and direction from supervisors, professors, and professional organizations are all valuable methods to encourage communication professionals to engage in an aggressive and *ethical* pursuit of the truth as well as an *accurate* publishing of what was discovered. The rules of conduct relative to the use of social media by reporters and company employees continue to evolve. Reporters and sport communications professionals have been encouraged to communicate with their publics via Twitter and other social media. The direction given to Reuters reporters is a good rule of thumb for all sports communications professionals: "....before you tweet or post, consider how what you are doing will reflect on your professionalism and our [Reuters] collective reputation. When in doubt, talk to your colleagues, your editor, or your supervisor" ("Reporting from," n.d., para. 15).

Discussion Questions

1. Of the federal statutes and other regulations discussed in this chapter, which statutes should college athletic department sports information directors be

aware of and why? How can SIDs make use of this information to promote their school's academic and athletic profile? Why would the local beat reporter want to keep track of this information when covering the college football and basketball programs in their area?

2. We are seeing more and more consolidation in the media industry, with companies becoming bigger and bigger and controlling more and more of the media landscape. Is this good or bad for the consumer of sports information? Is this good for the sports industry as a whole?

3. Outline a few ethical dilemmas you could face as a *Sports Illustrated* reporter, if you were assigned to cover the 2018 World Cup in Russia?

4. You are a producer for ESPN and you have given an assignment to one of your new reporters. The reporter tells you that their religious beliefs prevent them from carrying out this particular assignment. What do you do?

5. ABC and ESPN are owned by Disney. What ethical issues could this raise for journalists at these two television networks?

Suggested Exercises

1. Read the *NY Times v. Sullivan* Supreme Court case. Do you think the case was correctly decided? Should the press be held to a higher standard? What do you think of the dissenting opinion? Is the local college football coach a *public figure* under *The New York Times* standard? How about the local high school basketball star or the family of that player?

2. Read a few stories about how injuries have been reported in the newspaper or on a news/sports website that publishes this type of information. Also read stories about coaches who have taken a leave of absence due to illness. How much information has been revealed? Do you think these federal regulations are much ado about nothing? Have we gone too far in protecting an athlete and coach's privacy?

3. Go to the websites for CoSIDA, ESPN, NPR, and the Association of Professional Journalists. Compare their ethical codes; note the similarities and the differences.

4. Read an article from the *Journal of Mass Media and Ethics*. Write a two-page report on this article.

5. ESPN does not have an ombudsman or public editor; these positions were eliminated. Was this a good idea? Read some of the articles written by these individuals (Robert Lipsyte, Jim Brady, George Solomon, Don Ohlmeyer).

References

Chapter 1

Badenhausen, K. (2011, December 14). The NFL signs TV deals worth $27 billion. *Forbes*. Retrieved from: http://www.forbes.com/sites/kurtbadenhausen/2011/12/14/the-nfl-signs-tv-deals-worth-26-billion/

Bercovici, J. (2012, August 6). Turner Buys Bleacher Report, Next-Gen Sports Site, for $175M-Plus. *Forbes*. Retrieved from: http://www.forbes.com/sites/jeffbercovici/2012/08/06/turner-buys-bleacher-report-next-gen-sports-site-for-175m-plus/

Berg, T. (2015, April 1). The average MLB salary is over $4 million and players still get $100 a day in meal money. *USA Today*. Retrieved from: http://ftw.usatoday.com/2015/04/major-league-baseball-average-salary-meal-money-2015-mlb

Braine, T. (Producer). (1985). *The not-so-great moments in sports.* [Television Program]. United States: Home Box Office.

Chanen, D., & Rayno, A. (2016, March 1). University of Minnesota investigating sex-video on Kevin Dorsey's social media account. *Star Tribune*. Retrieved from: http://www.startribune.com/sex-video-was-posted-on-gophers-basketball-player-s-twitter-account/370574681/

Eisenstock, A. (2001). *Sports talk: A journey inside the world of sports talk radio.* New York: Simon & Schuster.

Enriquez, J. (2002). Coverage of sports. In W. D. Sloan & L. M. Parcell (Eds.), *American journalism: History, principles, practices.* Jefferson, NC: McFarland.

Futterman, M. (2014, May 7). NBC extends Olympic rights through 2032. *Wall Street Journal*. Retrieved from: https://www.wsj.com/articles/nbc-extends-olympic-rights-through-2032-1399480516

Gregory, S. (2009, June 5). Twitter craze is rapidly changing the face of sports. *Sports Illustrated*. Retrieved from: http://sportsillustrated.cnn.com/2009/writers/the_bonus/06/05/twitter.sports/index.html?eref=sihpT1

Guthrie, M. (2013, January 25). Katie Couric's Manti Te'o interview is ratings hit. *Hollywood Reporter*. Retrieved from: http://www.hollywoodreporter.com/live-feed/katie-courics-manti-teo-interview-415338

Haag, P. (1996). The 50,000-watt sports bar: Talk radio and the ethic of the fan. *The South Atlantic Quarterly, 9(2)*, 453–470.

Halberstam, D. (1989). *The summer of '49*. New York: Avon.

Hiestand, M. (2004, August 19). 1984 TV ruling led to widening sweep of the college game. *USA Today*. Retrieved from: http://www.usatoday.com/sports/columnist/hiestand-tv/2004-08-19-hiestand-college-football_x.htm

How much is Bleacher Report worth? (2016). *Worth of the Web*. Retrieved from: http://www.worthofweb.com/website-value/bleacherreport.com/

Hutchins, A. (2013, January 28). Why the Manti Te'o girlfriend hoax story matters. *SB Nation*. Retrieved from: http://www.sbnation.com/college-football/2013/1/28/3915364/manti-teo-hoax-girlfriend-story

Karlinsky, N. (2013, January 18). Lance Armstrong may have lied to Winfrey: Investigators. *ABC News*. Retrieved from: http://abcnews.go.com/US/lance-armstrong-lied-oprah-cover-crimesinvestigators/story?id=18245484#.UY6BLsq6qXg

Kirshner, A. (2018, February 2). The SEC is paying out a record $40.9 million per school, and the Big Ten could pass it soon. *SB Nation*. Retrieved from: https://www.sbnation.com/college-football/2018/2/2/16964186/sec-revenue-distribution-2017

Kloplovitz, K. (2015, September 30). How Muhammed Ali, Joe Frazier and satellites changed tv history. *MediaVillage.com*. Retrieved from: https://www.mediavillage.com/article/how-muhammed-ali-joe-frazier-and-satellites-changed-the-course-of-television-history/

Lacques, G. (2018, July 18). Josh Hader apologizes for racist tweets, claims they 'don't reflect any of my beliefs now.' *USA Today*. Retrieved from: https://www.usatoday.com/story/sports/mlb/allstar/2018/07/18/josh-hader-twitter-all-star-game/794751002/

LaRosa, J. (2009, February 16). No turning back: An interview with Billie Jean King. *Tennis*. Retrieved from: https://www.tennis.com/players/2009/07/no-turning-back-an-interview-with-billie-jean-king/17610/

Love, J. (2015). MAJOR Twitter fails by famous athletes. *Ranker*. Retrieved from: https://www.ranker.com/list/athlete-twitter-fails/jordan-love

Mack, C. (1950). *My 66 years in the big leagues*. Philadelphia: John C. Winston.

McCarthy, M. (2011, June 7). NBC wins right to Olympics through 2020; promises more live coverage. *USA Today*. Retrieved from: http://content.usatoday.com/communities/gameon/post/2011/06/olympic-tv-decision-between-nbc-espn-and-fox-could-come-down-today/1#.UyuxYrXvvTo

McCombs, M. E., & Shaw, D. L. (1972, Summer). The agenda-setting function of mass media. *Public Opinion Quarterly, 36*, 176–187.

Pardon the interruption. (2009, February 17). ESPN.

Patton, P. (1984). *Razzle-dazzle*. New York: Dial Press.

Pickert, K. (2009, January 22). The X games. *Time*. Retrieved from: http://www.time.com/time/nation/article/0,8599,1873166,00.html

Pitts, M. (2013, January 24). What The Manti Te'o Hoax Teaches Marketers About Online Relationships. *Forbes*. Retrieved from: http://www.forbes.com/sites/gyro/2013/01/24/what-the-manti-teo-hoax-teaches-marketers-about-online-relationships/

Schad, T. (2018, February 20) DirecTV raises prices on NFL Sunday ticket package for 2018 season. *USA Today*. Retrieved from https://www.usatoday.com/story/sports/nfl/2018/02/20/directv-raises-prices-nfl-sunday-ticket-package-2018-season/354244002/

Schwindt, O. (2016, April 5). March Madness 2016 championship ratings down 37 percent from 2015. *International Business Times*. Retrieved from http://www.ibtimes.com/march-madness-2016-championship-ratings-down-37-percent-2015-2348827

Smith, C. (1987). *Voices of the game*. South Bend, IN: Diamond.

Smith, R. (2013, August 19). Sirius XM reups major league baseball contract. *The Motley Fool*. Retrieved from: https://www.fool.com/investing/general/2013/08/19/sirius-xm-re-ups-major-league-baseball-contract.aspx

Sowell, M. (2008). The birth of national sports coverage: An examination of the New York Herald's use of the telegraph to report America's first "championship" boxing match in 1849. *Journal of Sports Media, 3(1)*, 51-75.

Staples, A. (2015, May 29). Wild success of SEC Network creating Titanic Two of conference finances. *Sports Illustrated*. Retrieved from: http://www.si.com/college-football/2015/05/29/sec-network-big-ten-revenue-gap

The world's highest-paid athletes. (2018). *Forbes*. Retrieved from: https://www.forbes.com/athletes/#31f4765655ae

Tremblay, S., & Tremblay, W. (2001). Mediated masculinity as the millennium: The Jim Rome show as a male bonding speech community. *Journal of Radio Studies, 8(2)*, 271-291.

Trotter, J. (2010, September 29). OU suspends receiver Jaz Reynolds for Twitter comments about Texas. *Daily Oklahoman*. Retrieved from: http://newsok.com/article/3499714

Williams, D. (2015, January 9). You better check yourselves, players. *The Cauldron*. Retrieved from: https://the-cauldron.com/you-better-check-yourselves-players-f23ad303b072

Zarett, E. Jay. (2018, February 4). How much do Super Bowl commercials cost in 2018? *Sporting News* [website]. Retrieved from: http://www.sportingnews.com/nfl/news/super-bowl-2018-how-much-do-super-bowl-commercials-cost-nbc-coca-cola-hyundai/1qap05f9qd6hd1kn2i9lahwlk3

Zeman, N. (2013, June). The boy who cried dead girlfriend. *Vanity Fair*. Retrieved from: http://www.vanityfair.com/culture/2013/06/manti-teo-girlfriend-nfl-draft

Zurawik, D. (2011, July 12). Baltimore's late newscasts are shifting their focus away from sports. *Baltimore Sun*. Retrieved from: http://www.baltimoresun.com/opinion/columnists/zurawik/bs-ae-local-sports-decline-20110712-story.html

Chapter 2

Ananny, M., & Bighash, L. (2016). Why drop a paywall? Mapping industry accounts of online news decommodification. *International Journal of Communication 10*, 3359–3380.

Arkush, H. (2013, May 31). Pro Football Weekly says goodbye. *Pro Football Weekly*. Retrieved from: https://chicago.cbslocal.com/2013/06/03/pro-football-weekly-says-goodbye/

Bedard, M. (2013, March 3). Les Miles rumor: A lesson to journalists. *The Daily Reveille*. Retrieved from: http://www.lsureveille.com/sports/football/ article_b107bcf6-8480-11e2-bc87-0019bb30f31a.html

Bedore, G. (2013, May 12). Top prospect Andrew Wiggins to announce on Tuesday. *KUsports.com*. Retrieved from: http://www2.kusports.com/news/2013/may/12/top-prospect-andrew-wiggins-decide-tuesday/?mens_basketballButtry, S. (2011, December 19). How a Digital First approach guides a journalist's work. Digital First Media. Retrieved from: http://stevebuttry.wordpress.com/2011/12/19/how-a-digital-first-approach-guides-a-journalists-work/

Conway, T. (2013, April 24). Kobe Bryant shutting down twitter commentary is disappointing but smart move. *Bleacher Report*. Retrieved from: https://bleacherreport.com/articles/1616835-kobe-bryant-shutting-down-twitter-commentary-isif-disappointing-but-smart-move

Davis, J. (2016, May 24). Big data, analytics sales will reach $187 billion by 2019. *Information Week*. Retrieved from: http://www.informationweek.com/big-data/big-data-analytics/big-data-analytics-sales-will-reach-$187-billion-by-2019/d/d-id/1325631

Florio, M. (2013, May 31). 46-year run ends for Pro Football Weekly. *Pro Football Talk*. Retrieved from: http://profootballtalk.nbcsports.com/2013/05/31/46-year-run-ends-for-pro-football-weekly/

For digital journalism, 'there's no such thing as one model.' (2016, August 31). *ASU Now*. Retrieved from: https://asunow.asu.edu/20160831-entrepreneurship-asu-digital-journalism-theres-no-such-thing-one-model

Gallin, P. (2016, July 13). *Pittsburgh Post-Gazette* hikes prices even as circulation plummets. *Newspaper Death Watch*. Retrieved from: http://newspaperdeathwatch.com/pittsburgh-post-gazette-hikes-prices-even-as-circulation-plummets/

Gietschier, S. (1994, April 17). Q & A with Roger Kahn: The Boys of Summer and Others Revisited: Baseball: It was 'The Era,' when the Yankees, the Giants, and the Dodgers ruled the world. *Los Angeles Times*. Retrieved from: http://articles.latimes.com/1994-04-17/sports/sp-47020_1_baseball-writers

Golenbock, P. (1984). *Bums*. New York: Putnam Books. Internet users. (2016). *Internet Live Stats*. Retrieved from http://www.internetlivestats.com/internet-users/

Hebbard, D. B. (2010, May 7) *New Sporting News* publisher, Jeff Price, partners with Zinio on paid daily iPad and web-based news products. *Talking New Media*. Retrieved from: https://www.talkingnewmedia.com/2010/05/07/new-sporting-news-publisher-jeff-price-partners-with-zinio-on-paid-daily-ipad-and-web-based-news-products/Jones, A. (1991, June 13).

The *National Sports Daily* closes with today's issue. *New York Times*. Retrieved from: http://www.nytimes.com/1991/06/13/business/the-media-business-the-national-sports-daily-closes-with-today-s-issue.html

Kafka, P. (2018, September 16). Are there any other billionaires out there to buy *Fortune or Sports Illustrated? Recode*. Retrieved from: https://www.recode.net/2018/9/16/17867814/sports-illustrated-fortune-money-buyers-financials-meredith-marc-benioff-salesforce

Kramer, S. (2008, July 29). '*Sporting News Today*' Publisher: New Digital Daily has 75,000 Subs, Aims for 200,000 Before Ad Push. *paidContent*. Retrieved from: http://paidcontent.org/2008/07/29/419-first-look-sporting-news-today/

Liz Mullen, sports reporter. (2010, June 17). *Quora*. Retrieved from: http://www.quora.com/Liz-Mullen/answers/Sports-Journalism-and-Sports-Writing

MacCambridge, M. (2018, April 11). "Who can explain the athletic heart?" *The Ringer*. Retrieved from: https://www.theringer.com/2018/4/11/17220176/sports-illustrated-future-meredith-sale-history

McLuhan, M. (1964). Understanding media: The extensions of man. New York: McGraw-Hill.

Merron, J. (2012). Olympic social media guidelines muzzle athletes. *Read Write Web*. Retrieved from: https://readwrite.com/2012/06/26/olympic-social-media-guidelines-muzzle-athletes/

Modiano, C. (2016, March 31). Spotlight: Sara Ganim broke the Penn State scandal five years ago—and was ignored for seven months. *New York Daily News*. Retrieved from http://www.nydailynews.com/sports/college/modiano-penn-state-scandal-broke-5-years-article-1.2583942

Mike Wise suspended from *Washington Post* for tweet (2010, August 31). *Huffington Post*. Retrieved from: https://www.huffpost.com/entry/mike-wise-suspended-from-_n_700593

Mirtle, J. (2017, February 27). Letter from the editor" Why *The Athletic* has a paywall. *The Athletic Canada*. Retrieved from https://theathletic.com/40690/2017/02/27/letter-from-the-editor-why-the-athletic-has-a-paywall/

Nardi, B., Schiano, D., & Gumbrecht, M. (2004). Blogging as social activity, or, would you let 900 million people read your diary? *Computer Supported Cooperative Work*, 6(3), 222–231.

Number of internet users worldwide from 2005 to 2018. (2018). *Statista*. Retrieved from: https://www.statista.com/statistics/273018/number-of-internet-users-worldwide/

Peiser, J. C. (2019, February 6). *The New York Times* reports $709 million in digital revenue in 2018. *The New York Times*. Retrieved on from: https://www.nytimes.com/2019/02/06/business/media/new-york-times-earnings-digital-subscriptions.html

PG to offer only e-delivery two days a week. (2018, June 27). *Pittsburgh Post-Gazette*. Retrieved from: https://www.post-gazette.com/business/pittsburgh-companynews/2018/06/27/Post-Gazette-print-edition-drop-two-days-August-digital/stories/201806270227

Plaschke, B. (2000, January–February). The reporter: 'That's twice you get me. I'm gonna hit you right now, right now!' *Columbia Journalism Review*, pp. 42–44.

Price, J., & Howard, G. (2012, December 11). An update on *Sporting News* for 2013. The Sporting News. Retrieved from: https://www.sportingnews.com/us/sport/news/4401027-sporting-news-magazine-ipad-yearbook-2013-ios-android

Schultz, B. (2005). Sports media: Planning, production and reporting. Woburn, MA: Focal Press.

Schultz, B., & Arke, E. (2015). Sports media: Planning, production and reporting. (3rd ed.). New York: Focal Press.

Scorecard. (2000, July 10). *Sports Illustrated*. Retrieved from: https://www.si.com/vault/2000/07/10/8116829/scorecard-rip-sportcarolina-bluesa-williams-samplercams-cameos

Senz, K. (2019, August 1) Why paywalls aren't always the answer for newspapers. *Forbes.* Retrieved from: https://www.forbes.com/sites/hbsworkingknowledge/2019/08/01/why-paywalls-arent-always-the-answer-for-newspapers/#7d2c7ad5429f

Shapiro, M. (2000, January–February). The fan. *Columbia Journalism Review,* pp. 39, 50–51.

Solomon, J. (2016, February 4). Open letter to Ken Starr: Stop stonewalling about Baylor rapes. *CBS.* Retrieved from: http://www.cbssports.com/college-football/news/open-letter-to-ken-starr-stop-stonewalling-about-baylor-rapes/

Sports journalism under microscope industry forum. (2008, January 25). *Holdthefrontpage.com.* Retrieved from: http://www.holdthefrontpage.co.uk/2008/news/sports-journalism-under-microscope-at-media-industry-forum/

Trotter, J. (2016, September 19). Bob Stoops: Austin Kendall's comments on Ohio St. 'ridiculous.' *ESPN.* Retrieved from: http://www.espn.com/collegefootball/story/_/id/17588370/oklahoma-sooners-qb-austin-kendall-comments-ridiculous

Up against the paywall. (2015, November 21). *The Economist.* Retrieved from: http://www.economist.com/news/business/21678799-many-publishers-still-see-little-alternative-continual-cutbacks-up-against-paywall

Wann, D.L. (2006). The causes and consequences of sport team identification. In A. Raney and J. Bryant (Eds.), *Handbook of sports and media.* (pp. 331–352). Mahwah, NJ: Lawrence Erlbaum.

Wanta, W. (2006). Sports coverage in print. in A. Raney & J. Bryant, (Eds.), *Handbook of sports media.* Mahwah, NJ: Lawrence Erlbaum. (pp. 105–116).

Webster, D. (2016, April 3). Roy Williams rips media after final four win over Syracuse. *Bleacher Report.* Retrieved from: http://bleacherreport.com/articles/2629854-roy-williams-rips-media-after-final-four-win-over-syracuse

Wolff, M. (2013, April 1). This tipping-point for paywalls does not fix newspapers' larger crisis. *The Guardian.* Retrieved from: http://www.guardian.co.uk/commentisfree/2013/apr/01 /tipping-point-paywalls-newspapers-crisis

Wolff, M. (2016, February 15). Print's dead—but so is digital. *USA Today.* Retrieved from: http://www.usatoday.com/story/money/columnist/wolff/2016/02/14/wolff-prints-dead-but-so-digital/80284046/

Chapter 3

2014 FIFA World Cup reached 3.2 billion viewers, one billion watched final. (2014). *FIFA.* Retrieved from: https://www.fifa.com/worldcup/news/2014-fifa-world-cuptm-reached-3-2-billion-viewers-one-billion-watched--2745519

Allen, C. (1988). *Parasocial interaction and local TV news: Perceptions of news teams and news personalities in Denver.* Paper presented at the annual meeting of the Association for Education in Journalism and Mass Communication, Portland, OR.

Baig, E. (2016, March 10). Shoot video for the local news, get paid. *USA Today.* Retrieved from: https://www.usatoday.com/story/tech/columnist/baig/2016/03/10/shoot-video-local-news-get-paid/81562956/

Barnes, T. (2016, September 9). Revenue estimates analysis of: Sirius XM holdings Inc. (NASDAQ:SIRI). *News Oracle.* Retrieved from: http://www.newsoracle. com/2016/09/09/revenue-estimates-analysis-of-sirius-xm-holdings-inc-nasdaqsiri/

Benz, K. (2011, March 3). Don't drop sports from local TV news. *Poynter Institute.* Retrieved from: https://www.poynter.org/reporting-editing/2007/dont-drop-sports-from-local-tv-news/

Berkowitz, S. (2016, January 20). Tax return shows SEC made $527.4 million in first year of CFP, SEC Network. *USA Today.* Retrieved from: http://www.usatoday.com/ story/ sports/college/2016/01/19/sec-tax-return-college-football-playoff-sec-network -mike-slive/79006606/

Booton, J. (2018, February 12). 30 percent of fans how stream sports to their phones, tablets. *Sports Techie.* Retrieved from: https://www.sporttechie.com/30-percent -fans-now-stream-sports-phones-tablets/

Bornfeld, S. (2009, January 22). Mediaology: Sportscasters get sent to the penalty box. *Las Vegas Review-Journal.* Retrieved from https://www.reviewjournal.com/ entertainment/sportscasts-get-sent-to-the-penalty-box/

Castillo, M. (2016, September 15). NFL's Thursday Night Football Twitter deal marks social media sports rush. *CNBC.* Retrieved from: https://www.cnbc.com/2016/09/15/nfls- thursday-night-football-twitter-deal-marks-social-media-sports-rush.html

Clement, J. (2019, June). YouTube - Statistics & facts. *Statista.* [website]. Retrieved from: https://www.statista.com/topics/2019/youtube/

Dixon, S. (2015, October 4). Texas player apologizes for halftime tweet in loss to TCU. *Associated Press.* Retrieved from https://www.usatoday.com/story/sports/ncaaf/2015/ 10/04/texas-player-apologizes-for-halftime-tweet-in-loss-to-tcu/73348424/

Ebbets Field. (2001). *Baseball-statistics.com.* Retrieved from: http://www.baseball- statis- tics.com/Ballparks/LA/Ebbetts.htm

ESPN, Inc. fact sheet. (2018). *ESPN.* Retrieved from: https://espnmediazone.com/us/ espn-inc-fact-sheet/

FIFA Media Release. (2018). More than half the world watched record breaking 2018 World Cup. *FIFA.* Retrieved from: https://www.fifa.com/worldcup/news/ more-than-half-the-world-watched-record-breaking-2018-world-cup

Flint, J. (2011, December 15). NFL signs TV rights deals with Fox, NBC and CBS. *Los Angeles Times.* Retrieved from: http://articles.latimes.com/2011/dec/15/business/ la-fi-ct-nfl-deals-20111215

Gaines, C. (2017, March 1). ESPN has lost 12 million subscribers in 6 years, but it's not as bad as it sounds. *Business Insider.* Retrieved from: https://www.businessinsider.com/ espn-subscribers-2017-3

Green-Holloway, M. (2016, May 25). Why TV is becoming #outdated for sports consumption. *Samford University Sports Business Report.* Retrieved from: https://www.samford.edu/ sports-analytics/fans/2016/why-tv-is-becoming-outdated-for-sports-consumption

Greppi, M. (2002, August 19). Time out for sports? Local stations debate how much cov- erage viewers really want. *New Orleans Times-Picayune*, pp. 9.

Griffin, E. (1997). *A first look at communication theory.* New York: McGraw-Hill.

Heine, C. (2016, September 14). ESPN's long-form storytelling could turn sports podcasting on its head. *Adweek*. Retrieved from: http://www.adweek.com/news/technology/espns-long-form-storytelling-could-turn-sports-podcasting-its-head-173478

Hilmes, M. (1997). *Radio voices*. Minneapolis, MN: University of Minnesota Press.

Journalism and ethics integrity project. (1998). *Radio and Television News Directors Foundation*. Retrieved from: https://www.rtdna.org/uploads/files/survey.pdf

King, P., McDonough, W., & Zimmerman, P. (1994). Tint of brown. *In 75 seasons: The complete story of the National Football League, 1920–1995*. Atlanta, GA: Turner Publishing.

Matsa, K. (2016). Local TV news: Fact sheet. *Pew Research Center for Journalism & Media*. Retrieved from: http://www.journalism.org/2016/06/15/local-tv-news-fact-sheet/

McCartney, C. (2009, April 29). Spring's biggest winners and losers. *Sports Illustrated*. Retrieved from: https://www.si.com/more-sports/2009/04/29/spring-winners-losers

New York Yankees. (2016). *Forbes*. Retrieved from: http://www.forbes.com/teams/new-york-yankees/

Ourand, J. (2012, February 13). A strong signal. *Sports Business Daily*. Retrieved from: https://www.sportsbusinessdaily.com/Journal/Issues/2012/02/13/In-Depth/Lead.aspx

Ozanian, M. (2017, September 27). NFL national anthem protests sack DirecTV. *Forbes*. Retrieved from: https://www.forbes.com/sites/mikeozanian/2017/09/27/nfl-national-anthem-protests-sack-directv/

RAB: Radio's digital dollars jump 13% to $700 million. (2018, February 18). Radio Advertising Bureau. Retrieved from: http://www.insideradio.com/rab-radio-s-digital-dollars-jump-to-million/article_3fca3504-0c9e-11e8-8043-9b0be9c408ce.html

Radio's top-billing stations mostly unchanged in 2017. (2018, April 10). Inside Radio. Retrieved from: http://www.insideradio.com/free/radio-s-top-billing-stations-mostly-unchanged-in/article_fb1b1abc-3c3c-11e8-82d9-3fd6bda30203.html

Roxborough, S. (2016, August 8). Rio Olympics worldwide audience to top 3.5 billion, IOC estimates. *The Hollywood Reporter*. Retrieved from: http://www.hollywoodreporter.com/news/rio-olympics-worldwide-audience-top-920526

Sandomir, R. (1997, January 17). As FOX prepares bash, CBS yearns to return to the NFL's fold. *New York Times*. Retrieved from: https://www.nytimes.com/1997/01/17/sports/as-fox-prepares-bash-cbs-yearns-to-return-to-the-nfl-s-fold.html

Schultz, B. (2005). *Sports media: Planning, production and reporting*. Woburn, MA: Focal Press.

Schultz, B., & Sheffer, M. L. (2009, August 8). *The future of news? A study of citizen journalism and journalists*. Paper presented to AEJMC national convention, Boston, MA.

Schultz, B., & Sheffer, M. L. (2010). An exploratory study of how Twitter is impacting sports journalism. *International Journal of Sport Communication* 3, 226-239.

Schultz, B., & Sheffer, M. L. (2011). Factors influencing sports consumption in the era of new media. *Web Journal of Mass Communication Research* 37. Retrieved from: http://wjmcr.info/2019/07/17/factors-influencing-sports-consumption-in-the-era-of-new-media/

Spangler, T. (2017, February 1). CBS buys bankrupt sports video site Scout Media for $9.5 million. *Variety*. Retrieved from https://variety.com/2017/digital/ news/cbs-bankrupt-scout-media-acquisition-1201975820/

Spangler, T. (2018, January) Big media, silicon valley battle for multi-billion-dollar sports tv rights. *Variety*. Retrieved from https://variety.com/2018/digital/ features/ olympics-rights-streaming-nbc-winter-games-1202680323/

Sterling, C. H. (1984). *Electronic media, a guide to trends in broadcasting and newer technologies, 1920–1983*. New York: Praeger.

Stewart, L. (1998, January 13). CBS gets the NFL back. *Los Angeles Times*. Retrieved from: http://articles.latimes.com/1998/jan/13/sports/sp-7916

The global sports media consumption report, 2014. (2014). *Sporting News Media*. Retrieved from: http://sportsvideo.org/main/files/2014/06/2014-Know-the-Fan-Study_US.pdf

Wakefield, J. (2016, June 15). Social media 'outstrips TV' as news source for young people. *BBC*. Retrieved from: http://www.bbc.com/news/uk-36528256

World Series: 7 year rights to MBS, Gillette. (1949, November 7). *Broadcasting*. Retrieved from https://www.americanradiohistory.com/Archive-BC/BC-1949/1949-11-07-BC.pdf

World Series ratings. (2015). *Baseball almanac*. Retrieved from: http://www.baseball-almanac.com/ws/wstv.shtml

Chapter 4

Aguilar, B.P. (2017, June 20). *Disrupt: how twitter changed the rules of sport journalism*. Retrieved from: https://medium.com/bryann-paul/disrupt-how-twitter-changed-the-rules-of-sport-journalism-2474497df967

Aslam, S. (2018, January 1). Pinterest by the numbers. *Omnicore*. Retrieved from: https://www.omnicoreagency.com/pinterest-statistics/

Blumberg, S. J., & Luke, J. V. (2018). Wireless substitution: Early release of estimates from the national health interview survey, July–December 2017. Center for Disease Control. Retrieved from: https://www.cdc.gov/nchs/data/nhis/earlyrelease/wireless201605.pdf

Cohen, David (2018, February 27) Skating and curling dominated 2018 winter Olympic games talk on Twitter, Facebook. *Ad Week*. Retrieved from: https://www.adweek.com/ digital/figure-skating-and-curling-dominated-2018-winter-olympic-games-talk-on-twitter-facebook/

Considine, J. (2018, June 20). Instagram hits 1 billion monthly users. Tech Crunch.com Retrieved from: https://techcrunch.com/2018/06/20/instagram-1-billion-users/

DiFino, N. (2009, August 3). The secret history of WHIP. *The Wall Street Journal*. Retrieved from: https://www.wsj.com/articles/SB10001424052970204619004574318690805089868

Facebook (2018, January 31). Facebook reports fourth quarter and full 2017 earnings results. Retrieved from: https://s21.q4cdn.com/399680738/files/doc_news/Facebook-Reports-Fourth-Quarter-and-Full-Year-2017-Results.pdf

Huddleston, T. (2016, February 3). How ESPN plans to conquer China. *Fortune*. Retrieved from: http://fortune.com/2016/02/03/espn-tencent-china/

Internet World Stats. (2018). Retrieved from: https://www.internetworldstats.com/stats.htm

Johnson, R. (2017, April 17). Which NFL reporters do and do not tweet draft picks ahead of time? *SB Nation*. Retrieved from: https://www.sbnation.com/nfl/2017/4/27/15398990/nfl-draft-tweets-picks-reporters-spoilers-adam-schefter

Kemp, S. (2018). Digital in 2018 global overview. *We Are Social.* Retrieved from: https://wearesocial.com/us/blog/2018/01/global-digital-report-2018

Lunden, I. (2016, December 8). Microsoft officially closes its $26.2 billion acquisition of LinkedIn. *TechCrunch.* Retrieved from: https://techcrunch.com/2016/12/08/microsoft-officially-closes-its-26-2b-acquisition-of-linkedin/

Most followed athletes on instagram as of July 2018. *Statista.* Retrieved from: https://www.statista.com/statistics/647392/most-followers-instagram-athletes

NBA, Weibo partner to entertain China fans. (2017, March 7). *China Daily.* Retrieved from: http://usa.chinadaily.com.cn/sports/2017-03/07/content_28458291.htm

Newsroom (2018). *Facebook.* Retrieved from: https://newsroom.fb.com/company-info/

Number of monthly active twitter users worldwide from 1st quarter 2010 to 2nd quarter 2018 (in millions). *Statista.* Retrieved from: https://www.statista.com/statistics/282087/number-of-monthly-active-twitter-users/

Pew Research Center (2018, February 5) Internet/Broadband fact sheet. Retrieved from: http://www.pewinternet.org/fact-sheet/internet-broadband/

Smith, C. (2018, August 6-12) Lights, camera. ACCtion. *Sports Business Journal.* Charlotte, NC: American City Business Journals

Spangler, T. (2018) Big media, silicon valley battle for multi-billion dollar sports TV rights. *Variety.* Retrieved from: https://variety.com/2018/digital/features/olympics-rights-streaming-nbc-winter-games-1202680323/

Swasy, A. (2017, March 22) I studied how journalists used twitter for two years. Here's what I learned. *Poynter.* Retrieved from: https://www.poynter.org/tech-tools/2017/i-studied-how-journalists-used-twitter-for-two-years-heres-what-i-learned/

Chapter 5

Angst, F. (2018, December 5). Learn about being a sports information director. *The Balanced Careers.* Retrieved from: https://www.thebalancecareers.com/job-profile-sports-information-director-3113309

Our Organization: What is CoSIDA? (n.d.). *CoSIDA.* Retrieved from https://cosida.com/sports/2013/7/25/general.aspx

Shutt, S. (1998, June). *How 2BN SID.* Unpublished manuscript. WVU Athletics Department, West Virginia University, Morgantown, WV.

Chapter 6

Borges, D. (2009, February 21). Conn-frontation. *New Haven Register.* Retrieved from http://emekanadavandcorny.blogspot.com/2009/02/calhoun-erupts.html

Cartwright, G. (1973, November). "Tom Landry: Melting the plastic man," *Texas Monthly.* From: https://www.texasmonthly.com/articles/tom-landry-melting-the-plastic-man/

Dealing with sources. (1993). *The Annenberg/CPB Project.* South Burlington, VT. [Videotape].

Dodd, M. (2004, January 5). Recognizing 'I'm 14 years late,' Rose admits he bet on baseball. *USA Today.* Retrieved from: http://www.usatoday.com/sports/baseball/2004-01-05-rose_x.htm

Hruby, P. (2005, January 19). All kidding a sideline. *Washington Times*. Retrieved from: https://www.washingtontimes.com/news/2005/jan/19/20050119-121313-1306r/

Martzke, R. (2004, January 7). Rose's admission puts Gray's interview in different light. *USA Today*. Retrieved from: http://www.usatoday.com/sports/ columnist/ martzke/2004-01-07-martzke_x.htm

Plaschke, B. (2000, January-February). The reporter: 'that's twice you get me. I'm gonna hit you right now, right now!' *Columbia Journalism Review*, pp. 42–44.

Raissman, B. (2002, December 20). With Burk, Gumbel didn't get 'real.' *New York Daily News*. Retrieved from http://www.nydailynews.com/archives/sports/ 2002/12/20/ 2002-12-20_with_burk__gumbel_didn_t_get.html

Shapiro, M. (2000, January-February). The fan. *Columbia Journalism Review*, pp. 39, 50–51.

Sherman, R. (2002, December 20). "Gumbel fans on Augusta issue." *Chicago Tribune*. From: https://www.chicagotribune.com/news/ct-xpm-2002-12-20-0212200245-story.html

SI.com picks the most embarrassing TV/radio interview moments in sports history. (2004, August 20). *Chicago Tribune*. Retrieved from http://www.chicagotribune.com/news/ ct-xpm-2004-08-20-0408200309-story.html

Chapter 7

Kohler, D. (1994). *Broadcast journalism: A guide for the presentation of radio and television news*. Englewood Cliffs, NJ: Prentice-Hall.

Smith, R. A. (2008). *Becoming a public relations writer: A writing process workbook for the profession* (3rd ed.). New York, NY: Routledge.

Stovall, J. G. (2009). *Writing for the mass media* (7th ed.). Boston, MA: Allyn & Bacon.

Chapter 8

McKindra, L. (2009, August 28). Media-guide proposals affect more than bottom line. *NCAA News*. Retrieved from: https://cosida.com/news/ 2009/8/28/GEN_2252. aspx?path=general

Shutt, S. (1998, June). How 2BN SID.

Chapter 10

Bailey, E. (2018, November 16). OU football: Oklahoma begins Heisman Trophy campaign for Kyler Murray. *Tulsa World*. Retrieved from https://www.tulsaworld.com/ sportsextra/ousportsextra/ou-football-oklahoma-begins-heisman-trophy-campaign-for-kyler-murray/article_6de2b576-07ed-5757-a8b9-e6182c3c43b7.html

Chapter 11

Chamberlin, A. (1990). Sports information. In J. B. Parks & B. R. K. Zanger (Eds.), *Sports and fitness management: Career strategies and professional content*. Champaign: Human Kinetics.

Collier, G. (2011, November 9). PSU handling worst nightmare in worst way. *Pittsburgh Post- Gazette*. Retrieved from https://www.post-gazette.com/sports/psu/2011/11/09/PSU-handling-worst-nightmare-in-worst-way/stories/201111090154

David, D. (2010, February 22). "Miracle" was product of different world. *NFL.com*. Retrieved from http://rangers.nhl.com/club/news.htm?id=518566

Forbes Agency Council (2017, June 20). 13 golden rules of PR crisis management. *Forbes*. Retrieved from: https://www.forbes.com/sites/forbesagencycouncil/2017/06/20/13-golden-rules-of-pr-crisis-management/#2e6dc1231bcfd

Keith, J. (1985). Tough public relations problems. In *NCAA public relations and promotional manual* (NCAA, Ed., p. 69). Mission, KS: The National Collegiate Athletic Association.

Patriots release tight end Aaron Hernandez. (2013, July 26). Retrieved from http://www.patriots.com/news/article-1/Patriots-Release-Tight-End-Aaron-Hernandez/69fbee29-d53e-4f8d-88c6-de 53da754e73

Perlmutter, D. (2018, February 5). A crash course in crisis communication. *The Chronicle of Higher Education*. Retrieved from: https://www.chronicle.com/article/A-Crash-Course-in-Crisis/242443

Robertson, J. (2012) Tell it all?: Challenging crisis communications rules. *Public Relations Journal* Vol. 6, No. 1, 2012. Retrieved from: https://prjournal.instituteforpr.org/wp-content/uploads/2012Robertson.pdf

Rovell, D. (2011, November 8). Penn State gets an "F" in crisis management 101. *CNBC*. Retrieved from: https://www.cnbc.com/id/45206255

Stein, L. (2014, April 30). Eight PR experts on how the NBA's Adam Silver set a crisis management standard. *PRWeek*. Retrieved from: https://www.prweek.com/article/1292512/eight-pr-experts-nbas-adam-silver-set-crisis-management-standard

Wilcox, D. L., Ault, P. H., & Agee, W. K. (1992). *Public relations: Strategies and tactics*. (3rd ed.). New York, NY: Harper Collins.

Wilcox, D. L., & Cameron, G. T. (2009). *Public relations: Strategies and tactics* (9th ed.). Boston, MA: Allyn & Bacon.

Chapter 12

Associated Press. (2010, October 29) David Stern has plan for NBA in Europe. *ESPN*. Retrieved from: https://www.espn.com/nba/news/story?id=5742301

Baker, G. (2017, November 19). Infamous UCLA trip to China was partly a Pac 12 business trip. *Seattle Times*. Retrieved from: https://www.seattletimes.com/sports/college/infamous-ucla-visit-to-china-was-partly-a-business-trip-to-benefit-pac-12/

Begley, I. (2016, June 29). Kristaps Porzingis journey from skinny, sleepy kid to Latvian hero. *ABC News*. Retrieved from: https://abcnews.go.com/Sports/kristaps-porzingis-journey-skinny-sleepy-kid-latvian-hero/story?id=40234604

Bonesteel, M. (2018, March 27). London's mayor wants an NFL team and the super bowl, which seems overly optimistic. *The Washington Post*. Retrieved from: https://www.washingtonpost.com/news/early-lead/wp/2018/03/27/londons-mayor-wants-an-nfl-team-and-the-super-bowl-which-seems-overly-optimistic/?utm_term=.dc9c3c1846ab

Brown, G., & Morrison, M. (2008). *ESPN sports almanac*. New York, NY: Ballantine Books.

Cashman, R., & Hughes, A. (1999). *Staging the Olympics*. Sydney, Australia: University of New South Wales Press.

Cushman, D. (2013, July 2*). BesTV secures online Premier League rights in China*. Retrieved from: http://www.sportspromedia.com/ news/bestv_secures_online_premier_league _rights_in_china/

Du Plessis, S., & Venter, C. (2010, July 16). The home team scores! A first assessment of the economic impact of World Cup 2010. Retrieved from: https://core.ac.uk/down-load/pdf/6248479.pdf

ESPN Media Zone (2018) Retrieved from: https://espnpressroom.com/mexico/ espn-international-fact-sheet-2/

ESPN STAR Sports renews TV Deal with Cricket Australia. (2007, June 9). *SportBusiness*. Retrieved from: http://www.sportbusiness.com/news/1625 18/ espn-star-sports-renews-tv-deal-with-cricket-australia

Fackler, M., & Longman, J. (2013). For 2020 Olympics, IOC picks Tokyo, considered safe choice. *The New York Times*. Retrieved from http://www.nytimes.com/2013/09/08/ sports/olympics/tokyo-wins-bid-for-2020-olympics.html?pagewanted=all&_r=0

Friedman, T. (2005). *The world is flat*. New York, NY: Farrar, Straus and Giroux.

Germany 2006 in numbers. (2006, July 12). *FIFA*. Retrieved from: https://www.fifa.com/ worldcup/news/germany-2006-numbers-29594

Harris, N. (2012, November 24). GBP5.5B: The staggering sum TV companies around the world will pay to screen the Premier League. *Daily Mail*. Retrieved from: http:// www.dailymail.co.uk/sport/football/article-2237955/Nick-Harris--5-5bn-TV-pays-screen-Premier League.html

Holmes, J. (2016, June 23) At home with the future of the NY Knicks. *Esquire Magazine*. Retrieved from: https://www.esquire.com/sports/a46093/kristaps-porzingis-profile -knicks-latvia/

Honduras country specific information. (n.d.). *travel.state.gov*. Retrieved from: https:// travel.state.gov/content/travel/en/international-travel/International-Travel-Country-Information-Pages/Honduras.html

IOC Annual Report 2016. *International Olympic Committee*. Retrieved from: https://stillmed .olympic.org/media/Document%20Library/OlympicOrg/Documents/IOC-Annual-Report/IOC-Annual-Report-2016.pdf#_ga=2.51079273.1529192774.1556758049-1269490304.1556758049

KantarSport. (2010). 2010 FIFA World Cup South Africa: Television audience report. *FIFA*. Retrieved from http://www.fifa.com/mm/document/affederation/tv/01/47/32 /73/2010fifaworldcupsouthafricatvaudiencereport.pdf

Li, P. and Jourdan, A. (2017, July 25). Game on: Suning leads China's $2 billion soccer rights frenzy. *Reuters*. Retrieved from: https://www.reuters.com/article/us-china-sports -broadcast/game-on-suning-leads-chinas-2-billion-soccer-rights-frenzy-idUSK-BN1AA0OC

London Olympics on NBC is most watched television event in US history. (2012, August 14). *NBC*. Retrieved from: http://nbcsportsgrouppressbox.com/2012/08/14/ ondon-olympics-on-nbc-is-most-watched-television-event-in-u-s-history/

Media Release (2015, December 16). *Federacion Internationale de Futbol Association (FIFA)* Retrieved from: https://www.fifa.com/worldcup/news/2014-fifa-world-cuptm-reached-3-2-billion-viewers-one-billion-watched--2745519

Orttung, R.W., & Zhemukhov, S.N. (2017). *Putin's Olympics: The Sochi games and the evolution of twenty-first century Russia.* New York: Routledge.

Otterson, J. (2018, February 26). *Variety.* Retrieved from: https://variety.com/2018/tv/news /2018-winter-olympics-ratings-2-1202710137/

Roxborough, S. (2018, June 14). *The Hollywood Reporter.* Retrieved from: https://www.hollywoodreporter.com/news/soccer-world-cup-2018-global-audience-hit-34-billion-fifa-revenue-reach-6-billion-1120071

Shipley, A. (2009, December 22). Deteriorating USOC-IOC relations threaten both organizations. *Washington Post.* Retrieved from https://www.runnerspace.com/news.php?news_id=8277

Stern lays out vision for NBA expansion in Europe (2008, March 27) *Associated Press.* Retrieved from: http://www.espn.com/nba/news/story?id=3315819

Thurston, S. (2016, August 20). Olympic press center is a journalist's home away from home. *The Boston Globe.* Retrieved from: https://www.bostonglobe.com/sports/olympics2016/2016/08/20/olympic-press-center-journalist-home-away-from-home/eER-ZKApl09O8nH4VQfn9WK/story.html

Vancouver 2010 Olympic Winter Games: Global television and online media overview. (2010). *International Olympic Committee.* Retrieved from: https://stillmed.olympic.org/media/Document%20Library/OlympicOrg/IOC/How_We_Do_It/Broadcasters/EN_Vancouver_2010_Audience_Report.pdf

Wacker, B. (2017, October 23). Conquering the world's longest golf hole. *Golf Digest.* Retrieved from: https://www.golfdigest.com/story/conquering-the-worlds-longest-golf-hole-mongolia

Chapter 13

Access to public records. (2000). Connecticut Freedom of Information Act. Title 1-210. *Connecticut general statutes annotated.* St. Paul, MN: West Group.

Albanese, A. (2012, October 4). Google, publishers settle lawsuit over book scanning. *Publishers Weekly.* Retrieved from: https://www.publishersweekly.com/pw/by-topic/digital/copyright/article/54220-google-publishers-settle-lawsuit-over-book-scanning.html

Albanese, A. (2013, August 27). A year later, opposition briefs filed in Author's Guild v Google. *Publishers Weekly.* Retrieved from: http://www.publishersweekly.com/pw/by-topic/digital/copy right/article/58873-a-year-later-opposition-briefs-filed-in-authors-guild-vs-google.html

American Society of News Editors. (n.d.) [website] https://members.newsleaders.org/

Anderson, N. (2013, February 2). Board finds University of Maryland regents broke open meeting law in big ten talks. *Washington Post.* Retrieved from: https://www.washingtonpost.com/local/education/board-finds-u-md-regents-broke-open-meetings-law-in-big-ten-talks/2013/02/28/4b6f2380-81c3-11e2-a350-49866afab584_story.html

AZ Rev Stat § 39-121 (2015).

Barron, J. A., & Dienes, T. C. (2005). *Constitutional law*. St. Paul, MN: Thomson West.

BBC editorial guidelines. (n.d.). *BBC*. Retrieved from: http://www.bbc.co.uk/guidelines/editorialguidelines/edguide/

Belmas, G., & Vanacher, B. (2009). Trust and the economics of news. *Journal of Mass Media Ethics, 24(2/3)*, 110–126.

Bennett, W. J. (1993). *The book of virtues: A treasure of great moral stories*. New York, NY: Simon & Schuster Adult Publishing Group.

Better Government Association. (n.d.). *BGA-Alper Services Integrity Index*. Retrieved from: https://www.bettergov.org/bga-alper-integrity-index/

Bikales, J. (2018, December 5) American media: The nation's watchdog. *Harvard Political Review*. Retrieved from: https://harvardpolitics.com/united-states/the-nations-watchdog/

Blumer, T. (2013) CBS's Scott Pelley at Quinnipiac luncheon: 'We are getting big stories wrong, over and over again.' *Newsbusters.org*. Retrieved from: https://www.news-busters.org/blogs/nb/tom-blumer/2013/05/12/cbss-scott-pelley-quinnipiac-luncheon-we-are-getting-big-stories

Bono net policing idea draws fire. (2010, January 4). *BBC News*. Retrieved from: http://news.bbc.co.uk/2/hi/technology/8439200.stm

Brandt, I. (1965). *Bill of Rights*. New York, NY: Bobbs Merrill.

CAPS. (n.d.). Retrieved from: http://www.capsinfo.com/

Carter, T. B., Dee, J. L., & Zuckman, H. L. (2006). *Mass communication law*. St. Paul, MN: Thomson West.

Chao, L. (2009, December 31). Chinese author is open to settling with Google. *The Wall Street Journal*, p. 9. Retrieved from: https://www.wsj.com/articles/SB10001424052748704876804574628001516120702

Code of ethics. (n.d.). *The Radio Television Digital News Association*. Retrieved from: https://www.rtdna.org/content/rtdna_code_of_ethics

CO Rev Stat § 24-72-201 (2016).

Conrad, M. (2006). *The business of sports*. Mahwah, NJ: Lawrence Erlbaum Associates.

Curtis Publishing Co. v Butts, 388 US 130 (1967).

CO Rev Stat § 24-6-401 (2012).

Destruction of infringing articles. (2009). Trademarks—The Lanham Act of 1946. 15 USCA 118. *United States code annotated*. St. Paul, MN: Thomson West.

Edison v Edison Polyform Manufacturing Co, 67 A. 392 (NJ Ch. 1907).

Ethical Journalism. (2019)). *The New York Times*. Retrieved from: https://www.nytimes.com/editorial-standards/ethical-journalism.html

Europeana. (n.d.). Retrieved from: http://www.europeana-libraries.eu/

Exec. Order No. 13642, 78 C.F.R. 28111-28113, (2013).

Fawcett Publication, Inc. v. Morris, 377 P. 2d 42. (Ok. Ct. App. 1962).

FCC Freedom of Information Act. (n.d.). *Federal Communications Commission*. Retrieved from http://www.fcc.gov/foia

Feinman, J. M. (2006). *Law 101*. New York, NY: Oxford University Press.

Florida court orders NCAA to hand over records. (2009, October 1). *Reporters Committee for Freedom of the Press*. Retrieved from: https://www.rcfp.org/florida-court-orders-ncaa-hand-over-records/

Garner, B. (2009). *Black's law dictionary.* St. Paul, MN: Thomson West.

Gertz v Robert Welch, 418 US 323 (1974).

Gitlow v NY, 268 US 652 (1925).

Googlemania splits US and EU. (2009, September). *Inter-Media, 37*(3).

Herring, C. (2009, July 16). A privacy law that protects students, and colleges, too. *The Wall Street Journal.* Retrieved from: http://online.wsj.com/article/SB124770187218048509.html

Hosick, M.B. (2018, May 23) Penalties, lost postseason numbers decline. *NCAA.* Retrieved from: http://www.ncaa.org/about/resources/media-center/news/penalties-lost-post-season-numbers-decline

How long does copyright protection last? (n.d.) US Copyright Office. Retrieved from: https://www.copyright.gov/help/faq/faq-duration.html

Johnston, B. D. (2008). Rethinking copyright's treatment of new technology strategic obsolescence as a catalyst for interest groups. *NYU Annual Survey of American Law, 64*(1).

Kaminsky, M. (2018, January 30). Super bowl legal blitz: Inside the NFL's legendary trademark defense. *Forbes.* Retrieved from: https://www.forbes.com/sites/michellefabio/2018/01/30/inside-the-nfls-legendary-trademark-defense/#5be38ad63293

Kang, C. (2009, November 14). Google narrows book rights in revised settlement. *Washington Post.* Retrieved from http://voices.washingtonpost.com/posttech/2009/11/googles_curbed_its_ambitious_d.html

Limitations on exclusive rights; fair use. (2005). Copyrights 17 USCA 107. *United States code annotated.* St. Paul, MN: Thomson West.

Lincoff, B. (2009). Common sense, accommodation and sound policy for the digital music marketplace. *Journal of International Media and Entertainment Law, 2(1),* 1–64.

McManis, C. R. (2009). *Intellectual property and unfair competition* (6th ed.). St. Paul, MN: Thomson West.

McMasters, P. (2009). FOIA: It's always there. *Society of Professional Journalists.* Retrieved from: https://www.spj.org/foiabout.asp

Merrill, J. C. (1997). *Journalism ethics.* New York, NY: St. Martin's Press.

NCAA hands out postseason bans for academics but UCONN is back. (2013, June 11). *The New York Times.* Retrieved from: https://www.nytimes.com/2013/06/12/sports/ncaa-basketball/ncaa-hands-out-postseason-bans-for-academics-but-uconn-is-back.html

Neff, C. (1987). Portrait of the sportswriter as a young man. *Gannett Center Journal, 1*(2), 47–55.

O'Keefe, E. (2009, December 9). Federal agencies must post public data online. *Washington Post.* Retrieved from: http://www.washingtonpost.com/wpdyn/content/article/2009/12/08/AR2009120804121.html

Operation Team Player nets over $15 million in fake sports merchandise. (2018, February 1) *U.S. Immigration and Customs Enforcement.* [website]. Retrieved from: https://www.ice.gov/news/releases/operation-team-player-nets-over-15-million-fake-sports-merchandise

Perez, A.J. (2016, January 5) Ryan Howard, Ryan Zimmerman file defamation suits against Al Jazeera America. *USA Today.* Retrieved from: https://www.usatoday.com/story/sports/mlb/2016/01/05/washington-nationals-ryan-zimmerman-defamation-law-suit-against-al-jazeera-america-the-dark-side-documentary/78328512/

Powe, Jr., L. A. (1991). *The fourth estate and the Constitution.* Berkley, CA: University of California Press.

Public information. (2007). The Freedom of Information Act of 1966 5 USCA 552b. *United States code annotated.* St. Paul, MN: Thomson West.

Public policy. (2006). The Indiana Open Door Law of 1977. Title 5-14-3-1. *Burns Indiana statutes annotated.* Charlottesville, VA: Matthew Bender and Co.

Recovery for violation of rights. (2009). Trademarks — The Lanham Act 15 USCA 117. *United States code annotated.* St. Paul, MN: Thomson West.

Reporting from the Internet and using social media. (n.d.). *Reuters.* Retrieved from: http://handbook.reuters.com/index.php?title=ReportingFrom_the_Internet_And_Using_Social_Media

Skipper, J. (2017, November 2) ESPN's social media guidelines. *ESPN.* Retrieved from: https://www.espnfrontrow.com/2017/11/espns-social-media-guidelines/

Social media. (n.d.). NPR. Retrieved from: http://ethics.npr.org/tag/social-media/

Subject matter of copyright. (2005). Copyrights 17 USCA 102 (a) *United States code annotated.* St. Paul, MN: Thomson West.

Telling the Story (n.d.) Associated Press. [website] Retrieved from: https://www.ap.org/about/news-values-and-principles/telling-the-story/

Texas Tech v Spiegelberg, 461 F. Supp. 2d 510 (2006).

The Freedom of Information Act, 5 U.S.C. § 552 (2016).

Tompkins, A. (2012, July 13). *The Poynter Institute.* Retrieved from: https://www.poynter.org/reporting-editing/2012/would-open-records-have-stopped-abuse-sooner-at-penn-state/

Time, Inc. v Firestone, 424 U.S. 448 (1976).

US Immigration and Customs Enforcement. (2011, May 24) National Intellectual Property Rights Coordination Center Fact Sheet. Retrieved from https://www.ice.gov/es/factsheets/ipr

Von Drehle, D. (2018, June 26) How a reporter's sex life put journalism ethics at stake. *Washington Post.* Retrieved from: https://www.washingtonpost.com/opinions/how-a-reporters-sex-life-put-journalism-ethics-at-stake/2018/06/26/9c2d9754-7964-11e8-93cc-6d3beccdd7a3_story.html

Wicker, T. (1978). *On press.* New York, NY: Berkley Publishing Corporation.

Wolfson, A. (2018, March 16) AGs office: University of Louisville broke open records laws denying courier journal requests. *Louisville Courier-Journal.* Retrieved from: https://www.courier-journal.com/story/news/2018/03/16/university-louisville-open-records-laws-violations-courier-journal-ruling/432129002/

Woolley, J. T., & Peters, G. (1996, October 2). Statement on signing the Electronic Freedom of Information Act Amendments of 1996. *The American Presidency Project.* Retrieved from: http://www.presidency.ucsb.edu/ws/index.php?pid=52035

Index

About the Authors

Craig Esherick is an Associate Professor in the Sport Management Program at George Mason University, where Fall 2019 will be his twelfth year. He is the Associate Director of the Center for Sport Management, the Academic Program Coordinator for the Sport Management program, and also the Internship Coordinator.

Professor Esherick was a scholarship basketball player at Georgetown University while earning an undergraduate degree in finance. He attended the Georgetown University Law Center and was a graduate assistant basketball coach for two of those years. After graduating from law school and passing the DC Bar Exam, Professor Esherick became a full-time assistant coach at Georgetown for the men's basketball team. His tenure as an assistant lasted 17 and a half years and included a stint as the assistant basketball coach for the USA Olympic team that won a bronze medal in the 1988 Seoul Olympics. He became the head basketball coach in 1999 at Georgetown University and held that position long enough to win 103 games. He worked briefly for AOL's new online radio venture from 2004 until 2005, where he commented on-air about college basketball news and wrote articles for the AOL Sports website. Craig took a job with a startup television network in New York in May of 2005; that network, CSTV, has now become CBS College Sports. Esherick came to Mason from NYU, where he taught in their graduate sports management program for two years.

Besides this book, Craig has written or edited several other books, articles, and book reviews on a variety of topics in the sports industry. These works can be found in the *History of Sport Encyclopedia, Sports Management and Marketing Encyclopedia, Case Studies in Sport Diplomacy, Journal of Issues in Intercollegiate Athletics, History and Sport, Leadership in Sport, Cultures of Peace, The Journal of Sport for Development, and the International Journal of Sport Management and Marketing.*

Esherick serves on several Arlington and Fairfax County, Virginia boards and committees. He has worked with the US Department of State on many grants and sport diplomacy projects from 2009 to 2019. Craig provides expert commentary for news outlets, television, and radio during college basketball season, primarily working for the Mid Atlantic Sports Network (MASN) and the Stadium network.

A Martinsburg, W.Va., native and a 24-year resident of Morgantown, **Philip H. Caskey**, MA, MS, gained 11 years of sports information director experience in the West Virginia University Athletic Department from 1999–2010, where he was an award-winning public relations/sports journalist and published author. He served as the primary media relations contact for Mountaineer women's basketball and served as a secondary contact for WVU football. He also assisted with the overall operation of WVU's 15 other varsity sports and supervised a student staff.

A seven-time award-winning College Sports Information Directors of America national and district feature writer, Caskey is also an adjunct instructor in WVU's College of Physical Activity and Sport Sciences graduate sport management program. He served as media coordinator for numerous WVU- and NCAA-hosted sporting events. He earned his first masters in sport management in 2001, and his bachelor's degree in journalism/public relations in 1999, both from WVU.

Caskey earned his second master's in secondary education, with an emphasis in the social studies, from West Virginia University (WVU) in December, 2012. He recently completed his fifth year as a social studies educator at University High School in Morgantown and his fifth overall in secondary education, where he teaches the subjects of American Civil War Studies, Honors Civics, Civics, and AP Research.

He has received numerous awards for excellence in teaching: 2016 Civil War Trust National Teacher of the Year; 2017 West Virginia Daughters of the American Revolution Outstanding Teacher of American History; and 2013 WVU Center for Democracy and Citizenship Model Scholar-Teacher.

His passions and interests are vast, which include the American Civil War, World War II, historical board and miniature war-gaming, reading, traveling the world, seeing his favorite band Pearl Jam live in-concert, and spending time with family and friends.

Brad Schultz, PhD, is a former associate professor in the School of Journalism and New Media at the University of Mississippi. His academic credentials include a bachelor's degree in journalism from the University of Missouri (1984), a master's in telecommunications from Southern Illinois (1999), and a doctorate from Texas Tech in 2002. Schultz's area of research interest is the effect of new technology on sports journalism. He has published nearly two dozen research articles in scholarly journals, including the *International Journal on Media Management*, the *Newspaper Research Journal*, the *Journal of Communication Studies*, the *International Journal of*

| **351**

the History of Sport, and the International Journal of Sport Communication. He has also presented two dozen papers at scholarly research conferences in the US and Canada. In 2006, Schultz launched the Journal of Sports Media, a scholarly journal that publishes twice a year. He continues to serve the journal as editor-in-chief. Schultz has also authored six books. His previous works include The NFL, Year One (2013, Potomac Books), Sports Media: Planning, Production and Reporting (2005, Focal Press), Broadcast News Producing (2004, Sage), and Sports Broadcasting (2001, Focal Press). He wrote a chapter on Sport Communication that appears in Introduction to Sport Management (Kendall-Hunt). Prior to entering academia, Schultz spent 15 years in local television sports and news as an anchor, reporter, news director, producer, editor, videographer, and writer.

Dr. Schultz is now the Pastor at Zion Evangelical Church in Shelbyville, Indiana. He continues to write and contribute on the topics of sports history and sports media, and this is his 12th book. Dr. Schultz invites your comments and can be reached at bschultz27@gmail.com.